Argument
Critical Thinking
Logic and the Fallacies

John Woods
University of Lethbridge

Andrew Irvine
University of British Columbia

Douglas Walton
University of Winnipeg

Prentice
Hall

Toronto

Canadian Cataloguing in Publication Data

Main entry under title:
Woods, John, 1937-
Argument: Critical Thinking, Logic and the Fallacies
Includes index.

ISBN 0-13-085115-9

1. Reasoning. 2. Critical thinking. 3. Logic. 4. Fallacies (Logic). I. Irvine, A.D.
II. Walton, Douglas N. (Douglas Neil). 1942- . III. Title.

BC177.W66 2000 160 C99-932040-8

Prentice-Hall, Inc., Upper Saddle River, New Jersey
Prentice-Hall International (UK) Limited, London
Prentice-Hall of Australia, Pty. Limited, Sydney
Prentice-Hall Hispanoamericana, S.A., Mexico City
Prentice-Hall of India Private Limited, New Delhi
Prentice-Hall of Japan, Inc., Tokyo
Simon & Schuster Southeast Asia Private Limited, Singapore
Editora Prentice-Hall do Brasil, Ltda., Rio de Janeiro

ISBN 0-13-085115-9

Vice President, Editorial Director: Michael Young
Acquisitions Editor: Dawn Lee
Developmental Editor: Lisa Phillips
Production Editor: Alex Moore
Copy Editor: Kelli Howey
Production Coordinator: Peggy Brown
Art Director: Mary Opper
Interior Design: Alex Li
Cover Design: Sarah Battersby
Page Layout: Pixel Graphics / Gerry Dunn

1 2 3 4 5   04 03 02 01 00

Printed and bound in Canada.
Visit the Prentice Hall Canada web site! Send us your comments, browse our catalogues, and more at **www.phcanada.com**. Or reach us through e-mail at **phabinfo_pubcanada@prenhall.com**.

Contents

PART III: Applying Logic to Arguments

Acknowledgments

THIS book is a much revised and expanded edition of John Woods and Douglas Walton's *Argument: The Logic of the Fallacies*, which first appeared in 1982. Some of the original book remains, of course, but much of it, including the last three chapters, is new. In addition, all of the material carried over from the original edition has been revised and rewritten in light of recent research. These updates have been carried out by Woods and Andrew Irvine.

For their assistance in preparing the original edition, Woods and Walton want to thank the following: Patrick Suppes for his conversations on decision theory, Dick Epstein for his discussions and correspondence on relatedness logic, Peter Geach for his correspondence on the fallacies, Charles Hamblin and Nicholas Rescher for their helpful published works, John Barker, Nick Griffin, David Hitchcock, Jim Mackenzie, and David Sanford for their stimulating communications of one sort or another, and Jaakko Hintikka for his contributions to the theory of dialectical reasoning as well as for his interest and support.

For their comments on the first edition, whether in print or as personal communications, which have helped shape the current edition, all three authors want to thank the following: Derek Allen (Trinity College, University of Toronto), Jeremiah Allen (University of Lethbridge), E. M. Barth (University of Groningen), R. W. Binkley (University of Western Ontario), J. Anthony Blair (University of Windsor), Alan P. Brinton (Boise State University), Carl Cohen (University of Michigan), Gary Colman (King's College, Edmonton), Irving M. Copi (University of Hawaii at Manoa), Charles Daniels (University of Victoria), George Englebretsen (Bishop's University), James Ford (Laurentian University), James Freeman (Hunter College, CUNY), Dov M. Gabbay (King's College, University of London), Roderic Girle (University of Auckland), Trudy Govier (Calgary), Rob Grootendorst (University of Amsterdam), Hans V. Hansen (Brock University), Jaakko Hintikka (Boston University), Brent Hudak (Mount Royal College and University of Calgary), Ralph H. Johnson (University of Windsor), Henry W. Johnstone, Jr. (Pennsylvania State University), Charles Kielkopf (Ohio State University), John King-Farlow (University of Alberta), Erik C. W. Krabbe (University of Groningen), Michael Kubara (University of Lethbridge), Jim Mackenzie (University of Sydney), Cheryl Misak (University of Toronto), Julius Moravcsik (Stanford University), Robert Pinto (University of Windsor), Christian Plantin (Université de Lyon Deux, Lumière), the late Richard Routley (formerly of the Australian National University), Timothy Schroeder (University of Manitoba), Harvey Siegel (University of Miami), Patrick Suppes (Stanford University), Frans H. van Eemeren (University of Amsterdam), Paul Viminitz (University of Lethbridge), Mark Weinstein (Montclair State University), Joseph Wenzel (University of Illinois), Charles A. Willard (University of Louisville), and Michael J. Wreen (Marquette University).

For their assistance in preparing the current edition, Woods and Irvine want to thank the following: Doug Walton for his encouragement and support; Tom Irvine, Richard Johns, Murray Mollard, and John Russell for their detailed and helpful criticisms; Jasminn Berteotti, Dawn Collins, Brian Hepburn, Joan Irvine, and Richard Johns for their many editorial suggestions; Dawn Collins, Dawn Ogden, and Randa Stone for their invaluable technical assistance; and Kelli Howey, Dawn Lee, Alex Moore, Lisa Phillips, and Avivah Wargon of Prentice Hall Canada for bringing the book successfully to press.

Finally, all three of us would like to thank our students at the University of Amsterdam, the University of British Columbia, the University of Calgary, the University of Groningen, the University of Lethbridge, the University of Michigan, Simon Fraser University, Stanford University, the University of Sydney, the University of Toronto, the University of Victoria, and the University of Winnipeg. Over the years it has been our students who have continually encouraged and motivated our interest in logic and the fallacies.

John Woods
Department of Philosophy
University of Lethbridge

Andrew Irvine
Department of Philosophy
University of British Columbia

Douglas Walton
Department of Philosophy
University of Winnipeg

Introduction

LEARNING to reason well requires that we learn about arguments. It requires that we learn what makes good arguments good and bad arguments bad. As logicians use the term, an *argument* is a presentation of reasons or evidence in support of some claim. It is an attempt to build a case in favour of a conclusion. An argument in this broad sense is a social exchange, often involving a series of speech acts uttered by two or more parties in a particular context. At the core of every argument in this broad sense is always a sequence of propositions, one of which is the argument's *conclusion*, the rest of which are the argument's *premisses*. Arguments in this more narrow or core sense are abstracted from arguments in the broader sense.

This textbook is designed to introduce readers to both logic and, more generally, the theory of argument, two principal parts of the science of reasoning. *Argument theory* (sometimes called *critical reasoning* or *informal logic*) studies arguments in the broad sense; *logic* (or, more properly, *formal logic*) studies arguments in the narrow sense. Building upon this distinction, many textbooks are content to concentrate on only one or the other of these two areas of inquiry. In contrast, this book studies both. In our view, if cut off from real-life arguments, logic becomes sterile and unanchored; and if cut off from logic, theories of critical reasoning become shallow and uninteresting.

A good part of this book is devoted to discovering how arguments in the broad sense work. We are all more or less adept at offering arguments, but giving a detailed and accurate description of exactly what we do when we construct an argument is another thing altogether. Ultimately, we will want to discover whether an argument is good or bad, and doing this requires that we have a firm understanding of what case-making in the real world actually involves.

At the same time we also need to study arguments in the more narrow sense. Since in David Hume's famous phrase, to reason successfully is to proportion belief to evidence, we need to know what it means for one proposition to support another. This is the business of logic: determining when one proposition—or when a set of propositions—entails, or supports, or makes more probable or plausible a conclusion.

The book itself is divided into three parts. Part I introduces various issues in the theory of real-life argument, including the notion of fallacy, the distinction between logic and rhetoric, and the identification of ambiguities of various kinds. It also looks at various contexts in which real-life arguments are developed.

Part II introduces a number of basic ideas in logic, including the distinction between validity and inductive strength, and the distinction between an argument and its logical form. Although it is the job of observation and the various scientific and other scholarly disciplines to discover evidence for each particular area of human reasoning, it is the job of logic to explain how, and in which cases, evidence justifies conclusions. This part of the book also introduces several elementary systems of formal logic, including classical propositional logic, Aristotle's term logic, relevance logic, three-valued logic, and modal and deontic logic. All of these various logics are introduced as examples of how logicians have tried to characterize the consequence relation in a systematic, scientific way. Natural language applications to ordinary, everyday arguments are stressed throughout.

The final part, part III, applies the materials from parts I and II to several additional real-life contexts, including practical reasoning in law, economics, and artificial intelligence. This final part also discusses some of the most fundamental issues in the philosophy of logic, and relates them to theories of paraconsistent logic and to broader theories more generally.

Although the exposition throughout the book is at the most elementary level, *Argument: Critical Thinking, Logic and the Fallacies* is also distinguished by its attempt to attain a greater depth of analysis of the fallacies. As traditionally explained, a fallacy is an argument that appears to be correct but that in fact is not. In other words, fallacies are errors that arise from our inability to notice the distinction between good arguments and good-looking arguments. Learning to understand this distinction requires that we do more than merely identify examples of poor reasoning. It requires that we analyze such examples carefully and explain where it is that they go wrong. It is for this reason that *Argument: Critical Thinking, Logic and the Fallacies* not only identifies the most significant of the fallacies, it also studies each fallacy within its own theoretical context and offers suggestions about how it can best be avoided.

Instructors will find this book suitable for use in both first-year logic courses and introductory critical thinking courses. For example, a standard introductory logic course could be based primarily upon chapters 1, 4, 5, 6, 7, 8, 9, 10, 11, and 14. A standard critical thinking course could be based primarily upon chapters 1, 2, 3, 4, 10, 11, 12, 13, and 15. Longer or more ambitious courses may involve a wider selection.

When the predecessor to this book first appeared in 1982, it was widely recognized to be the first modern textbook to bring the machinery of formal logic to bear on the study of the fallacies. By integrating the study of arguments in the broad sense with the study of basic formal logic, it was hoped that advances could be made in understanding the fallacies. Keeping this core idea in mind, the present edition has been completely revised and rewritten in light of current research. We hope that it will appeal to both students and instructors alike. Any criticisms, corrections, or suggestions for improvement will be warmly received and may be sent to the authors in care of the publisher.

CHAPTER 1

The Quarrel

REASONING is as natural for human beings as breathing. Like breathing, it is a part of our nature. Even so, there is a common misconception about both that we should try to avoid. This is the mistake of supposing that, since they come to us naturally, they cannot be improved. Yet try telling that to an opera singer or a top-ranked athlete! Just because something comes to us naturally does not mean that it cannot be taught or improved.

Our goal in this book is to learn what it means to reason well. To achieve this goal we will investigate both *logic* and, more generally, the *theory of argument*, two principal parts of the science of reasoning. We will also investigate some of the most famous of the *fallacies*—those common ways in which reason can be misled. Thus, unlike many logic and critical thinking books, our goal will be both to learn why good arguments are good, *and* why bad arguments are bad. Knowing this will help us to think more rationally and critically.

Part I of this book introduces us to various issues in the theory of argument. Part II introduces us to several basic ideas in logic. It is the primary goal of both logic and argument theory to help us determine whether arguments are good or bad. Logic does this by studying the nature of the relation that holds between an argument's premises and its conclusion. Argument theory does so by studying other features of arguments that are relevant to their success or failure, including how they function in specific social or institutional contexts. Both parts I and II include introductory discussions of many of the most important fallacies. The final part, part III, applies what we have learned in parts I and II to a number of contexts, including practical reasoning of various sorts. This final part also discusses a number of fundamental issues in the philosophy of logic, and relates what we have learned to what it means to think carefully and critically.

1. Arguments, Fallacies, Logic, and Argument Theory

One primary goal of both logic and argument theory is to evaluate arguments by dividing them into various groups: the good and the bad, the reliable and the unreliable, the sound and the unsound. As we will see in this book, there are many different kinds of argument. As a result, a necessary preliminary goal will be to identify several types of argument and to determine how best to evaluate them. Even prior to this step of identifying and evaluating types of argument is the step of locating individual arguments themselves. Thus, the first question to ask ourselves is this: What is an argument?

Arguments can be fractious affairs, but they can also be enjoyable events in which participants exchange evidence and ideas in the hope of reaching a consensus on some (often controversial) topic. Sometimes we keep our reasoning to ourselves, while sometimes we make a public display of it. Either way, a common way of giving expression to our thinking is by constructing and exchanging arguments.

Of course, a lot of different things are arguments, including quarrels, legislative debates, diplomatic wrangles, labour negotiations, mathematical proofs, legal arguments, scientific demonstrations, and so on. However, there is an important distinction that helps us classify these different types of argument in a rather useful way. This is the distinction between arguments in the broad sense and arguments in the narrow sense. Arguments in the *broad sense* (or in the *social sense*) are public, multi-person exchanges of comment and counter-comment. Arguments in this sense are exchanges of a sort that illustrate the principle "It takes two to tango," except here we might better have said "tangle"! It is easy to see that quarrels, debates, and the other types of argument listed above are all arguments in this broad sense.

Arguments in the Broad Sense

As logicians use the term, an *argument* is a presentation of reasons or evidence in support of some claim. It is an attempt to build a case in favour of a conclusion. Normally this means that arguments are social exchanges involving a series of speech acts uttered by two or more parties. Familiar examples include quarrels, legislative debates, diplomatic wrangles, labour negotiations, mathematical proofs, legal arguments, scientific demonstrations, and so on. Because they involve a variety of social and psychological, as well as logical, factors, we say that these are arguments in the *broad* (or *social*) *sense*.

On the other hand, arguments in the *narrow sense* are simply sequences of propositions, one of which is the argument's *conclusion*, the rest of which are the argument's *premisses*.[1] Arguments in this sense are obviously a technical concept, since they are abstracted from arguments in the broad sense.

Another way of explaining arguments in the narrow sense is to notice that at the core of every argument in the broad sense is a set of propositions consisting of the argument's premisses and conclusion. The premisses form the basis of the argument. They constitute the evidence offered in support of a further claim, the conclusion.

In order to make this distinction between premisses and conclusion clear, we sometimes place an argument in *standard form*. To do so, we explicitly list the premisses and conclusion, eliminating any unnecessary or redundant words and clarifying any ambiguities. We then separate the conclusion from the rest of the argument by means of a horizontal line.

For example, consider the argument

> Archimedes must be either a hero or a martyr. After all, anyone who dies in battle is one or the other. And, as we know, Archimedes perished during the capture of Syracuse.

We can place this argument in standard form as follows:

> Anyone who dies in battle is either a hero or a martyr
> Archimedes perished during the capture of Syracuse
> _____
>
> Therefore, Archimedes must be either a hero or a martyr.

Once we have identified the premises and the conclusion in this way, we can consider one final aspect of the argument, namely the evidential link that relates the premises to the conclusion. This link, usually referred to as the *consequence relation*, is what determines the logical strength of the argument. To say that this relation is *strong* is to say that the premises, if true, provide *good evidence* in favour of the conclusion. To say that this relation is *weak* is to say that the premises, if true, provide poor evidence in favour of the conclusion. A consequence relation that is neither strong nor weak is said to be *moderate*.

Arguments in the Narrow Sense

At the core of every argument in the broad sense is a set of propositions composed of the argument's *premises* and *conclusion*. We call this an argument in the *narrow sense*. Arguments in the narrow sense are abstractions from arguments in the broad sense.

In order to make clear the structure of an argument in the narrow sense, and to distinguish between its premises and conclusion, we often place the argument in *standard form*. To do this, we identify its premises and conclusion and separate the conclusion from the rest of the argument by means of a horizontal line, as follows:

> 1st premiss
> 2nd premiss
> .
>
> .
>
> .
> *n*th premiss
> _____
> Conclusion.

The premises form the basis of the argument. They constitute the evidence that is being offered in support of the conclusion.

If the premises of the argument are (likely to be) true, and if the consequence relation is (likely to be) a strong one, then the argument will (likely) be a good one.

Much that surrounds these basic elements—such as the method by which an argument's constituent propositions are expressed, the intentions and desires of the participants, the argument's social context, and so on—will also be part of arguments in a broad sense, but if there is no core, no premisses and conclusion joined by a consequence relation, then there is no argument.

Learning to *reason critically* about various issues means being able to create and evaluate arguments. It means being able to use propositions in such a way that they provide good evidence in support of a conclusion and being able to evaluate when this goal has been achieved. In essence, the overall quality of an argument (i.e., whether it is good or bad) depends primarily upon two factors: (1) whether the premisses are (likely to be) true, and (2) whether the consequence relation is (likely to be) strong. Both are necessary. Unless they are true, premisses offered in support of a conclusion will be of very little use. At the same time, unless they are relevant (that is, unless the consequence relation is strong), even true premisses will fail to provide a suitable basis for accepting a conclusion. It follows that there are two main ways to criticize an argument: we can show the premisses to be unacceptable, or we can show the consequence relation to be weak. Other factors may also be important, but these two are absolutely central.

Reasoning Critically and Evaluating Arguments

Reasoning critically about various issues requires that we learn to evaluate arguments. The *quality* of an argument depends primarily upon (1) the *likelihood of the truth of the argument's premisses*, together with (2) the *strength of the consequence relation* that holds between the argument's premisses and conclusion. It follows that there are two main ways to criticize an argument: (1) we can show the premisses to be unacceptable, or (2) we can show the consequence relation to be weak. Other factors may also be important, but these two are absolutely central.

To say that a *consequence relation* is *strong* is to say that the premisses, if true, provide *good evidence* in favour of the conclusion. To say that this relation is *weak* is to say that the premisses, if true, provide poor evidence in favour of the conclusion. A consequence relation that is neither strong nor weak is said to be *moderate*.

It is a primary goal of both logic and the theory of argument to help determine the quality of arguments. *Logic* does this by studying the nature of the consequence relation that holds between the premisses and conclusions of arguments in the narrow sense. In contrast, *argument theory* studies arguments in the broad sense. It studies those features other than the consequence relation that are relevant to an argument's success or failure, including an argument's purpose and social context.

Since at the core of every argument we find a series of propositions, it is worth taking a moment to understand how logicians use this term. In logic, a *proposition* is something that is true or false. For any given proposition we may or may not know which it is, but, if it is a proposition, it must be one or the other. Questions and commands, for example, are not propositions, even though they typically contain or make use of propositions. As the Greek philosopher Aristotle put it, "every sentence is not a proposition; only such are propositions as have in them either truth or falsity. Thus a prayer is a sentence, but is neither true nor false."[2] On this view, a proposition is that which is asserted by a declarative sentence and, although sentences such as "Snow is white" and "*La neige est blanche*" are distinct sentences, they (normally) assert exactly the same thing. Thus we say that they express one and the same proposition.

Identifying Premisses and Conclusions

In an argument, the premisses and conclusion are often indicated by the use of key words or phrases. For example, words and phrases such as "thus," "therefore," "consequently," "so," "it follows that," and "we may conclude that" typically indicate which proposition is functioning as the conclusion. Similar key words or phrases such as "since," "because," "given that," and "on the grounds that" regularly indicate which propositions are functioning as premisses.

Given the set of propositions that make up an argument, how are we to tell which are the premisses and which is the conclusion? The answer is that there is often a key word or phrase (e.g., "thus," "therefore," "consequently," "so," "it follows that," "we may conclude that," etc.) that indicates which proposition is functioning as the conclusion. Similar key words or phrases (e.g., "since," "because," "given that," "on the grounds that," etc.) regularly indicate which propositions are functioning as premisses. Even so, there are many different ways of indicating that a conclusion is being put forward on the basis of argument, and some of these are quite subtle. As a result, we should take care to correctly identify both the premisses and the conclusion of any argument that we want to evaluate.

Because it is sometimes not clear which proposition in an argument is meant to be the conclusion and which propositions are meant to be the premisses, fallacies can occur when conclusions and premisses are confused. A *fallacy* is any argument that deceives us because it appears to be a reliable argument but in fact is not. The unwary, who may not be acquainted with how the fallacies work, are especially vulnerable.

Fallacies
A *fallacy* is a bad argument or a piece of bad reasoning that has a propensity to appear good. It is a common or seductive error in reasoning.

The notion of fallacy was first recognized in the West almost two and a half thousand years ago by Aristotle. Seen the Greek way, fallacies are misuses of reason or rationality (or what the Greeks called *logos*, the methods of rational inquiry that lead to good reasoning). The first fruits of *logos* were developments in physics and astrophysics in the sixth century BCE, but before long these same methods were being applied to other issues as well—for example, to issues in ethics, politics, and the human good. Thus we can see in these early inquiries the stirrings of what would eventually become the humanities, the natural and social sciences, and the main subdisciplines of Western philosophy: metaphysics (the theory of being), epistemology (the theory of knowledge), logic, and value theory. Of these subdisciplines, it was logic that set itself the task of identifying and analyzing the fallacies and of distinguishing good arguments from bad.

At the heart of Aristotle's logic was his theory of the *syllogism*. For Aristotle, a syllogism was a special kind of argument[3] and a fallacy was an argument that *appears* to be a syllogism but is not. In present-day usage it is more common to say that a fallacy is *any* argument whose conclusion appears to be a consequence of its premises but is not.

Flashback on...

Aristotle (384–322 BCE)

ARISTOTLE is generally regarded as the founder of formal logic, or of what he called "analytics." For more than two thousand years he was logic's most influential writer.

Although there were precursors, especially with respect to the study of what is called *dialectic*, Aristotle was the first to recognize the existence of universally valid logical *laws*. He is also responsible for the remarkable accomplishment of developing logic in at least two separate ways, including his almost complete theory of the syllogism and his complex and sophisticated theory of modal logic. In addition, he is noted for his work in axiomatics, and there is some evidence that he also began investigating what is now called propositional logic, although he did not develop these investigations systematically. His claim near the end of *On Sophistical Refutations* that he is the primary creator of the discipline of logic is therefore quite justified.[4]

Aristotle was born in Stagira, in northern Greece, from whence he received his nickname, "the Stagirite." His father, Nicomachus, had been court physician to the Macedonian king Amyntas II, but both his parents died when Aristotle was still a boy. In 367 BCE, Aristotle was sent to Athens to study under the famous philosopher Plato. He remained at Plato's school, the Academy, first as a student and later as an instructor, for almost twenty years. Initially, the students of the Academy made fun of this new foreigner who spoke with a lisp, but Plato himself was impressed with Aristotle and nicknamed him "the intelligence" of the Academy. Upon Plato's death, Aristotle left Athens, perhaps for political reasons, or perhaps because he had not been appointed Plato's successor and was dissatisfied with how the Academy was now being directed. After travelling for awhile he married the (adopted) daughter of a former classmate who had become an Aegean king and in whose court Aristotle for a time served.

In 342 BCE Aristotle was appointed by Philip II of Macedon to tutor his son, the future Alexander the Great. From Aristotle's point of view, the appointment could not have been a pleasant one. He was expected to provide guidance to the young Alexander in a palace noted for its savagery and debaucheries, and at a time when both the father and son were intent upon assassination and conquest. When Alexander finally claimed his father's throne in 336 BCE, Aristotle left the court. Some reports say that Aristotle left well endowed by Alexander; others say that he was lucky to escape with his life. In any event, his influence could not have been too great since Alexander soon ordered Aristotle's nephew, Callisthenes, hanged for refusing to bow to the new king.

When Aristotle finally returned to Athens in ▶

335 BCE, he opened his own school, the Lyceum, in a grove just northeast of the city. Here he planted a botanical garden, began both a library and a natural history museum, and taught philosophy. The school was also known as the Peripatos, or "strolling school," since, at least occasionally, Aristotle lectured to his students while strolling about the school's grounds. It is for this reason that, even today, Aristotle's followers are known as "Peripatetics." In 323 BCE, following the death of Alexander, anti-Macedonian feeling in Athens increased and, because of Aristotle's ties to Alexander's court, the accusation of impiety was raised. Recalling the fate of Socrates, who had been put to death after being found guilty of similar charges, Aristotle returned to Chalcis, his mother's hometown, saying that he did not want Athens to "sin twice against philosophy." He died the following year.

Aristotle's interests were universal. His writings represent an encyclopedic account of the scientific and philosophical knowledge of his time, much of which originated with Aristotle himself and with his school. His extant writings cover logic, rhetoric, linguistics, the physical sciences (including biology, zoology, astronomy, and physics), psychology, natural history, meta-physics, aesthetics, ethics, and politics.

His logical writings, referred to as the Organon, consist of six books: the Categories, De Interpretatione (On Interpretation), the Prior Analytics, the Posterior Analytics, the Topics, and De Sophisticis Elenchis (On Sophistical Refutations).

Transmitted in large part through Arab scholars, Aristotle's writings shaped the intellectual development of medieval Europe. His logical treatises occupied a central place within the medieval curriculum, at which time Aristotle came to be known as the source of all knowledge. Even so, the first modern critical edition of Aristotle's writings did not appear until 1831. The scholarly practice of citing Aristotle's work by a series of numbers and letters still refers to the page, column, and line numbers of this nineteenth-century edition.

While it has often been claimed that Aristotle's dominating authority over such a long period hampered the development of logic (just as it did the development of science), such an observation cannot properly be taken as criticism of Aristotle himself. Instead, it is a telling incrimination of those of less talent and imagination who were to follow his remarkable accomplishments.

Identifying fallacies requires that we become clear about several matters, including the distinction between inference and argument. As we have said, arguments in the broad sense are interpersonal, social phenomena—a kind of public event. Inferences, in contrast, are essentially private affairs. They involve the adjusting of an individual's mental states, or the transition from one belief state to another. Thus, they are something the individual handles solo. Even so, there are similarities. We may say that each public act of argument is an invitation to, or the encouragement of, an inference. As a result, both arguments and inferences may be modelled by what we have called "the core" of an argument, by arguments in the narrow sense of the term.

When two people—say, Sue and Bill—argue, Sue is bidding Bill to update or revise what he believes in light of certain considerations. In other words, through argument she is trying to get Bill to make an inference. Guiding this transaction between Sue and Bill is the following general principle: If Sue's argument is good, Bill's inference, if he draws it, will also be good. By the same token, if Sue's argument is good, then the inference it bids Bill to draw is one that Bill *ought* to draw. It is the *rational* thing for Bill to do.

It is for this reason that arguments and inferences may be said to share a common core. This core is what remains when we abstract from an argument or inference its particular context, suppressing the fact that it was Sue rather than Sally who presented the argument, and that the argument was directed to Bill rather than to Bob. Also suppressed are those institutional, social, cultural, and other background conditions that give shape and emphasis to real-life social exchanges. In those cases in which we believe that these factors are important, we elect to study arguments in the broad sense; in those cases in which we believe that they are unimportant, we elect to study arguments in the narrow sense.

Exercise 1.1

1. Determine whether each of the following sentences expresses a proposition:

   (a) Athens is the capital of Greece.

   (b) Athens was the capital of Greece.

   (c) Athens will be the capital of Greece.

   (d) What is the capital of Greece?

   (e) I believe that Athens is the capital of Greece.

   (f) Either Athens is the capital of Greece or it isn't.

   (g) I wish I knew whether Athens is the capital of Greece!

   (h) Tell me whether Athens is the capital of Greece.

   (i) It is possible that Athens is the capital of Greece.

   (j) If Athens is the capital of Greece, then Athens must be in Greece.

2. Place each of the following arguments in standard form by first writing out the premisses and then separating them from the conclusion by a horizontal line:

   (a) Selling illicit drugs is not only illegal, it is also immoral. No one who brings that degree of misery to anyone can be said to be acting in a morally neutral fashion.

   (b) Although Socrates was thought by many to be a Sophist, in fact he was not. He did not accept money for his teaching, he did not travel with the Sophists, and he did not share their goals or beliefs.

   (c) Pleasure is the only ultimate good. It is the only thing we seek for its own sake. After all, we try to obtain money, health, and education only in order to help us achieve happiness. All these things are instrumental in a way that pleasure or happiness is not.

   (d) It is often claimed that pleasure is the only ultimate good; that pleasure is the only thing we seek for its own sake. But if this is right, why do some people give up pleasure in return for achieving some other end? Why would we ever work hard for our children? Why would we ever put ourselves in danger for another human being?

   (e) The only things that we can ever perceive—even in principle—are sensations, ideas, memories, and impressions. In other words, we can never perceive—even in principle—anything outside our own minds. So it follows that we can never have any evidence for the existence of anything but the mental.

(f) We cannot learn what we do not know. In order to learn, we need to be able to distinguish truth from falsehood and, if we do not already know something to be the case, we will not be able to recognize it as being true. It follows that all learning is impossible, and any knowledge that we will have in the future must already be known to us in the past.

(g) Even though we say we live in a democracy, a universal franchise is not in effect. Prisoners often cannot vote. The mentally ill cannot vote. Non-resident citizens and citizens travelling overseas cannot vote. Until these things change, the franchise is a long way from becoming universal.

(h) Any government that caves in to terrorists must be suffering from a lack of willpower. We know that our government has already implemented a policy of never giving in to terrorists. It follows that our government does not suffer from a lack of willpower.

(i) Assume for the sake of argument that $a = b$. If we multiply both sides by a, we get $a^2 = ab$. Then, subtracting b^2 from both sides we get $a^2 - b^2 = ab - b^2$. Then, factoring both sides, we get $(a + b)(a - b) = b(a - b)$. But this equation has a common term: $(a - b)$. It follows that by cancelling this term we get $(a + b) = b$. Recalling our original assumption, we see by substitution that $(b + b) = b$. So, in other words, $2b = 1b$, or $2 = 1$!

(j) The freedom of all people to speak openly, without fear of government reprisal, is what allows us to raise issues that we as citizens think are important. So free speech, together with freedom of association and peaceful assembly and the freedom to exercise our franchise, is what allows us, as citizens, to exercise our sovereignty over government. In other words, free speech is one of the cornerstones of contemporary democracy.

2. The Quarrel

One common type of argument (in the broad sense) is the *quarrel*. We begin by mentioning two specific examples. Here is the first:

The "Yes, You Did," "No, I Didn't" Quarrel

Sue insists that Bill told her he would spend last Friday in the library. Bill, who was spotted at the beach, contends that he had told Sue he planned to relax there all day. The following conversation results:

Sue: I thought you told me that you were going to be at the library all day.

Bill: No. Don't you remember? I said I would be at the beach.

Sue: No. You said you would be at the library. Otherwise I would have wanted to go with you.

Bill: You are not remembering things correctly—that was the day I said I would be at the beach!

Here, the disagreement is about *what the facts are.* As anyone who has ever had such a disagreement knows, it can be abusive and inconclusive. Sometimes such arguments are great fun; yet more often they are a nuisance, and an impediment to reasoning.

The "You Don't Love Me Anymore" Quarrel

Our second example of a quarrel is quite different. Bill is racked by doubts about Sue's behaviour. When they were first in love, Sue seemed to hang on Bill's every word. She laughed at his jokes, even those that made his other friends groan. She reserved all her free time for him. Recently, however, she hasn't hung on his every word, and last week she even drifted off to sleep while Bill was regaling their friends with a tale about his adventures as a moose hunter. In addition, she remarked that his joke about the farmer's daughter and the astrophysicist was "mindless and sexist." When Bill discovered that Sue had gone to a concert with John, conversations such as the following became typical:

> *Bill:* You don't love me.
>
> *Sue:* But I do! How could I call you a "mindless bore" without caring for you enough to risk giving offence, perhaps even losing you?
>
> *Bill:* Sure, sure. How do I know that this isn't just what you have in mind—losing me, as you call it, or breaking up, as I would say?
>
> *Sue:* Bill, you just don't understand. Be reasonable.

As we can see, in this case Sue and Bill are arguing not so much about what the facts are, but about what the facts mean and how they are to be interpreted. Here, the disagreement is about *what the facts imply.*

Using the terminology of the previous section, we may say that the part of an argument dealing with what the facts *are* constitutes the *premisses* of the argument; the part dealing with what the facts *imply* constitutes the *conclusion* of the argument. A logician would say that in the first argument Sue and Bill disagree about premisses; in the second, they disagree about the conclusion. In the first, we find *premissory instability*; that is, we find that Bill and Sue agree about very few, if any, of the salient facts of the case. They have few or no premisses in common. In the second argument, we find *conclusional instability*; that is, we find that although Bill and Sue agree about (most of) the salient facts, they cannot agree about what these facts imply; thus they cannot agree about what should be *concluded* from their common premisses.

It is not hard to see why premissory and conclusional instability leads to difficulties in the evaluation of an argument. If there is premissory and conclusional instability, then in fact we have *two separate arguments* that do not interact with each other at all. If we try to locate the premisses and the conclusion—the logical core of the argument—we cannot find them. Bill has his premisses and conclusion, Sue has her premisses and conclusion, and we can say nothing about the single argument as a whole. Where there is no common ground, there is no single argument. Instead, we have a multiplicity or plurality of unconnected arguments. Small wonder, then, that the quarrel tends to be neither productive nor enlightening from a logical point of view.

It is now easy to see why quarrels are typically such noisy, inconclusive affairs. If there is premissory insta- bility we cannot even get started on the road to agree- ment, and frustration, accusation, and hurt feelings are bound to follow. References will tend to become per- sonal and disagreeable. Sue might eventually complain that if Bill can't recall what he said last Friday, then he is a simpleton; Bill might retort that Sue is a shrew and, before we know it, things will have taken a nasty turn.

> **The Quarrel**
> An argument is a *quarrel* if (1) it suffers from premissory or conclusional instability (or both), (2) the disputants refuse to agree to disagree, and (3) they lack a shared method for conflict resolution.

Similarly, having got the discussion nicely underway with some basic premis- sory agreement, things may again come to a halt if there is no common conclusion. The same personal disruptions may then be repeated. Bill might contend that Sue shows herself to be a "typical woman" in having no capacity to reason. Sue may earnestly offer to slap Bill's face (and perhaps would be forgiven for doing so).

What's So Special about Logic?

Logic is a principal part of the science of reasoning. It is often distinguished from *rhetoric*, the science of persuasion. The difference is that, while rhetoric is interested in discovering the class of arguments that are *in fact* persuasive, logic is interested in discovering the class of arguments that *ought to be* persuasive, or that would be persuasive to an ideally rational agent. Thus, in contrast to rhetoric, *logic* is often said to be the science of reasoned (or rational) persuasion.

In this context *rationality* (or what the ancient Greeks called *logos*) is said to be the capacity (or ability) to effect the systematic manipulation of a person's beliefs in such a way that they become proportional to his or her available evidence. In other words, we are rational whenever we are able to change our beliefs on the basis of evidence. If we are unable (or unwilling) to alter our beliefs, even though the evidence would appear to demand otherwise, we are not acting rationally. Certain "propositional attitudes" (i.e., attitudes that we have towards propositions, including fear, affec- tion, apprehension, belief, acceptance, denial, etc.) are more difficult to deal with rationally than others. For example, a person who knows that a roller-coaster ride is safe, but who still fears for his or her safety while riding it, may be said to suffer from an irrational (or perhaps a non-rational) fear.

Why do we place such high importance on rationality and logic? There are several reasons, among which are the following:

- First, beliefs based upon reason may be tested and improved in a way that other kinds of beliefs cannot. This is because reasoned arguments are capable of being discussed and evaluated openly according to well-defined standards. Unlike "feelings" or "intuitions"—which also motivate beliefs, but which are essentially private—reasoned arguments provide us with a *well-defined, public mechanism* for the resolution of disagreements.

- Second, reasoned arguments provide us with a safe, non-threatening way of resolving disputes. Unlike physical means of conflict resolution—which range from personal intimidation to warfare—logic gives us a non-harmful mechanism for the resolution of disagreements.

- Third, careful, logical reasoning from acceptable premisses to an acceptable conclusion is the method most likely to lead to accurate beliefs and, hence, to sensible decisions. In turn, these beliefs and decisions are more likely than others to help us live well and improve our lives.

Why, then, do these types of argument get out of hand? With no prospect of getting started and no prospect of reaching a conclusion, the disputants have nothing left to do but fight. Premissory instability and conclusional instability often cause frustration, and frustration often causes aggression. The result is that quarrels tend to be neither pleasant nor enlightening. The moral would seem to be that the best thing to do is to change the subject, or simply to agree to disagree. Of course, a good fight may do wonders for a person's self-image, perk up one's love life, or test a combatant's mettle, but fights only rarely advance the cause of reason. Instead they usually function as impediments to our understanding of things. The logical lessons to be learned from the quarrel are therefore mainly negative:

- Because a quarrel has little or no chance of starting or concluding satisfactorily, there is little chance that it will advance the course of knowledge. *Consequently, a quarrel is a systematically inefficient and inconclusive kind of argument.*

- Premissory and conclusional instability often lead to frustration, and frustration often leads to aggression. Aggression is a well-known trigger of fallacious reasoning. Therefore, *not only is a quarrel likely to be inconclusive; it also risks giving rise to fallacious reasoning.*

- Because premissory and conclusional instability in an argument turn the argument into a quarrel, *it is not reasonable to proceed with such arguments until their instability is eliminated, reduced, or quarantined.*[5] If one's goal is to reason well, and if an argument's instability shows no promise of being reduced, one should stop talking, agree to disagree, or simply change the subject.

The moral is that, whenever possible, quarrels are to be avoided.

Exercise 1.2

1. For each of the following arguments, identify the premisses and the conclusion and place the argument in standard form:

   (a) No computer will ever think. To think, you need to be able to understand the meanings of words, and this is something no computer, whatever its speed or sophistication, will ever be able to do.

(b) The secretary at the mayor's office is not answering her phone. I guess that she has left for the day.

(c) None of Europe's current leaders are real revolutionaries. After all, every one of them was born after the end of the Second World War.

(d) Every right places a corresponding obligation upon someone. If I have a right to life, then you have an obligation not to kill me. If you have a right to free passage, then I have an obligation not to hinder your progress. If we both have a right to be treated equally before the law, then society has an obligation to see that this is so.

(e) International law is bound to be ineffective. The reason is that no law can be effective without appropriate enforcement. But international law, despite its noble origins, can never be strictly enforced.

(f) If we knew what the good life was, we would naturally act in such a way as to achieve it. Thus, any unhappiness we have is a result of our ignorance.

(g) Software engineers are all overpaid. They may work hard, and they may be bright, but until we have safely initiated a human colony on Mars, they don't deserve the salaries they receive.

(h) No woman who has been raped can ever fully recover. After all, her memories will stay with her forever.

(i) No soldier who has seen action can ever fully recover. After all, his memories will stay with him forever.

(j) All languages involve both syntax and semantics and this is something that is characteristic of many complex systems. So all languages are complex.

2. For each of the arguments listed in question 1, determine whether the consequence relation is strong, moderate, or weak.

3. *Ad Baculum* Arguments

One of our primary goals in this book is to learn to avoid fallacious reasoning. As we have said, fallacies are arguments that exhibit a general and recurring tendency to deceive or trick even the careful reasoner. It is because of their capacity to deceive, trick, and obscure that fallacies are the enemy of reason.

In the remainder of this chapter we will discuss two important fallacies often associated with the quarrel: the *ad baculum* and the *ad hominem*. The first of these is the fallacy of inappropriately appealing to force or intimidation; the second is the fallacy of inappropriately appealing to facts (or alleged facts) about one's opponent, rather than addressing his or her argument directly.

In the scenario described a few pages ago, we imagined Sue and Bill in the heat of battle, with Sue threatening to slap Bill's face. This may not be a very impressive example of an *ad baculum* fallacy because it is likely too obvious to fool anyone. However, even the threat of a slap on the face may give Bill pause, making him have doubts about the wisdom of his position. At the same time, it is easy to imagine situations in which disputants resort to more subtle forms of innuendo and to suggestions of unpleasant consequences that are not relevant to the issue at hand. In fact, if the innuendo is not detected, it can create the eerie, even frightening impression that I am doing myself no good in sticking to my side of the argument. The impression is left that somehow I am placing myself in jeopardy.

The *Ad Baculum* Fallacy
An *ad baculum* fallacy occurs whenever a conclusion is drawn, or invited to be drawn, on the basis of an irrelevant appeal to force. (When such an appeal is relevant, the argument is said to be a non-fallacious *ad baculum* argument.)

Like many fallacious strategies of rhetoric, inappropriate appeals to force can be effective because they release strong emotions at the expense of reason. Such appeals often work, not so much as arguments, but as distractions from argument. Aristotle shrewdly points out that the strategy of stimulating anger is often a highly effective, even if undesirable, tactic in argument.[6] If your opponent is winning the argument because of the logic of his position, and you are at a loss to find sufficient evidence in support of your own position, an all-too-effective strategy is to derail the argument by unleashing powerful emotions. Aristotle observes that arguers are often less able to defend themselves when agitated. One way to produce anger is to make it clear to your opponent that you want to use unfair means in the argument; to indicate that you might even resort to violence or force. This tactic is the *ad baculum*. Since *baculum* is the Latin word for "stick," the phrase itself calls to mind former U.S. president Teddy Roosevelt's *ad baculum* about American foreign policy: "speak softly and carry a big stick."

Another not-so-subtle example of an *ad baculum* is furnished by the historian Richard Grunberger. Grunberger reports that, in pre-war Germany, the Nazis used to send this reminder to those who had let their subscription to the Nazi newspaper lapse: "Our paper certainly deserves the support of every German. We shall continue to forward copies of it to you, and hope that you will not want to expose yourself to unfortunate consequences in the case of cancellation."[7]

This example is worth a little reflection. Did the notice give former readers a reason to renew their subscriptions to the Nazi newspaper? In one sense, the answer would seem to be that it did. The party that published the paper had a wholly convincing track record of coercion and mistreatment. Thus, at one level, the argument is a *prudential* argument, an argument about what it is sensible, reasonable, or prudent *to do*. On this analysis, the argument sketches a cost–benefit analysis for the lapsed reader—and none too subtly. "You may not like subscribing to this paper, which involves a cost," the authors imply, "but we shall see to it that not subscribing will exact even higher costs; for example, harm to your property or possible arrest. So, on balance, the prudent thing is to avoid the higher cost."

It is clearly immoral to make threats of this nature, but do we want to say that those who advanced this argument were also incompetent reasoners? Similarly, do we want to say that those readers who were moved by this argument and who resubscribed were tricked by some faulty *logic*? Probably not.

Even so, it is true that faulty logic lurks nearby, ready to invade if we let it. It would be faulty to reason that the premises of this argument imply or justify not the *prudential* claim that readers would do well to resubscribe, but the rather differ-

ent claim that the newspaper's journalistic merits make it a paper worthy of sub-
scriber support. In this latter case, we may indeed say that we have a fallacy. To guide
us in these matters, here is a rule of thumb: Whenever your opponent makes threats,
the most that you can concede to him is the prudence of your doing what his or her
threats bid you, provided that the costs of non-compliance are too high. Drawing
any stronger conclusion will result in an instance of the *ad baculum* fallacy.

Exercise 1.3

1. Determine whether each of the following
contains an *ad baculum* argument:

(a) Sue says to Bill, "You had better stop
smoking, since smoking can kill you."

(b) Bill says to Sue, "If you do me this one
favour, I promise to help you with your
political science assignment."

(c) Bill says to his employer, "I really do
deserve this promotion. After all, an
unhappy worker could really cause problems for the firm, couldn't he?"

(d) A gunman stops Bill in the dead of
night in Stanley Park and after threatening
to kill him demands his wallet.

(e) Sue says to her neighbour, "If you pay
me the going rate, I'll mow the lawn every
week for the rest of the summer."

(f) The latest heavyweight boxing champion
was arrested and found guilty of fraud. So
he's obviously not someone who is especially good with numbers!

(g) An interviewer, wishing to play the role
of the skeptic, asks a fundamentalist
preacher what reasons he can give for
believing in an afterlife. The preacher
replies: "Do you want to go to hell? There
are two possibilities—eternal salvation or
eternal suffering. If you accept the Lord
you will avoid going to hell. You have the

choice of whether to believe or not. But if
you don't believe, that will be the result."

(h) In a session of collective bargaining, the
union spokesman comments, "If that's the
best that management has to offer, we are
left with no choice except to take industrial
action."

(i) A political leader, while defending his
party's dire warnings that racial minorities
will one day become majorities and then
subject whites to harsh treatment, makes
the following claim: "What's wrong with
appealing to fear? Lots of people are
afraid, and justifiably so. Therefore it's a
legitimate political factor to respond to it.
There's nothing immoral about it."

(j) Seeing that Socrates is making a number
of enemies in Athens, a friend gives him
the following advice: "Socrates, I think that
you are too ready to speak evil of men:
and, if you will take my advice, I would recommend you to be careful. Perhaps there is
no city in which it is not easier to do men
harm than to do them good, and this is
certainly the case at Athens, as I believe
that you know."[8]

2. For each of the arguments listed in question 1 that contains an *ad baculum*, determine whether it involves a fallacy.

4. *Ad Hominem* Arguments

Another fallacy often associated with the quarrel is the *ad hominem* fallacy. The term itself is Latin for "to the man," suggesting arguments that are directed primarily to one's *opponent*, as opposed to one's opponent's *arguments*. The most easily identified example of the *ad hominem* fallacy is the *abusive ad hominem*.

In our scenarios involving Bill and Sue, there have been at least two occasions when the contenders have resorted to personal abuse. Bill stands accused of being a "simpleton," and Sue of being a "shrew." Here the abuse is obvious, and so obviously misconceived or irrelevant that it stands little chance of success as a deception. As we have observed, though, if passions run high enough, even a gross and stupid remark can be enraging and can subvert the objectives of good argument.

In a second, more harmful, form, the *ad hominem* is not abusive but, as logicians say, *circumstantial*. A speaker commits a *circumstantial ad hominem* fallacy when he refers not to his rival's argument, but rather to some (non-abusive) fact or alleged fact about his opponent or his circumstances.

The *Ad Hominem* Fallacy

An *ad hominem* fallacy occurs whenever a conclusion is drawn, or invited to be drawn, on the basis of an irrelevant appeal to some fact or alleged fact about one's opponent. (When such an appeal is relevant, the argument is said to be a non-fallacious *ad hominem* argument.) There are two main types of *ad hominem*: the *abusive ad hominem* and the *circumstantial ad hominem*.

The cleverest circumstantial *ad hominem* is one in which the reference to one's opponent is perfectly true, and known to be true, and yet not noticed to be irrelevant. Here is why the strategy often works: If the remark is true, then how could such a reference be contrary to the purposes of responsible reasoning? For is truth not the natural ally of reason?

The following example is instructive: Bill and Sue are again battling. This time the point of contention is whether abortion on demand is morally justifiable. Sue says, in utter exasperation, "Blast you, Bill, you're a man. You just can't see it!"

True, Bill *is* a man. This fact is obvious. Even so, the potential for damage lies not in what Sue is saying, true as it is, but rather in what she leaves unsaid and implied. Her implication is that a man will oppose abortion on demand because, as a man, he cannot ever experience an unwanted pregnancy and, accordingly, cannot help himself in opposing abortion. Because Sue's accusations are not explicitly stated, they are likely to have an *undetected* effect on the argument. This example crops up repeatedly in contemporary discussions about abortion and related issues. Many people commit the "you are a man (so you can't help being opposed)" fallacy. Ironically, they seem not to be aware that women are open to a similar attack. Women, presumably, are in a position to experience an unwanted pregnancy; thus, by parallel reasoning, they will be unable to keep themselves from *favouring* abortion on demand. Yet if neither you nor your opponent is free to choose which side of the argument you are to defend on the basis of evidence (rather than as a result of your own personal circumstances), then what is the use of continuing the argument?

The moral here is that even when the truth is told, if the claim being advanced is *irrelevant* to the point of an argument then what we have is an *ad hominem* fallacy.

Some further examples will help illustrate why this is so.

A circumstantial *ad hominem* arises whenever there is an apparent inconsistency between the thesis that some participant in an argument is putting forward and some circumstance or circumstances pertaining to the participant himself.[9] For example, a person might recommend some policy as a worthwhile principle even though circumstances indicate that he has not followed—or is not following—that policy himself. Any person caught in such an apparent conflict can be highly vulnerable if his opponent attacks *ad hominem*. "You don't even practise what you preach!" his opponent seems to be saying. The policy's advocate then appears to be caught in the most ridiculous kind of inconsistency. He tells us we ought to do something, but he does not even do it himself.

Even so, it is important not to overestimate the force of this form of argument. A person's inability or failure to follow the advice embodied in his own thesis is interesting, significant, and sometimes even comical but, despite this, he may still be able to support his thesis by cogent argument. A speaker from Alcoholics Anonymous may be giving us good advice on how to avoid becoming an alcoholic, even though he himself may remain an alcoholic. True, he once did not practise what he now preaches, but that makes his first-person advice all the more valuable. In such circumstances there is no reason to reject his advice as worthless. The *ad hominem* is tricky, and we should not reject an argument too quickly simply because we detect a circumstantial inconsistency.

On the other hand, some circumstantial inconsistencies are more significant than others. If our speaker from Alcoholics Anonymous shows signs of inebriation while giving his speech, we might have legitimate doubts about his capacity to serve as a spokesman on this particular subject. Another example of a significant circumstantial inconsistency might occur when a government proposes to raise the salaries of politicians even though it has recently encouraged all other sectors in the economy to resist wage escalation.

Another characteristic example of the *ad hominem* occurs in the following sort of dialogue. A parent has just finished citing evidence of links between smoking and lung cancer, and of the other bad effects that smoking has on health:

Parent: So you see, smoking is a bad business to start. Once you start, it is difficult to stop.

Child: Yes, but you smoke. How can you tell me not to smoke if you do it yourself?

Here the child may have a worthwhile point. If the parent is not following the course of action being recommended, this could be evidence of insincerity. Even so, the parent's argument that smoking is bad for one's health may also be based on good evidence, and the fact that smoking is addictive may well figure into both the parent's continuing to smoke and the advice being given to the child. Thus the child should not reject the parent's argument solely on the basis of a circumstantial inconsistency. In such circumstances, two questions need to be addressed: First, is the parent's thesis substantiated by the evidence being cited? Second, does the parent's recommendation conform to his or her own circumstances and, if not, is this inconsistency relevant or irrelevant to the issue at hand?

Circumstantial *ad hominem* arguments have at their core a set of two propositions that are thought to be inconsistent with one another. One proposition is a thesis recommended by the arguer, the other is a proposition that describes some circumstantial fact about the arguer himself. These two propositions may be described as the premisses of the *ad hominem*. Normally, a fallacy occurs when the inconsistency between these two premisses turns out to be irrelevant to the issue at hand, but sometimes a fallacy occurs in an *ad hominem* argument when these very premisses are incorrectly described or confused. This confusion results from a failure to locate and identify the argument correctly in the first place. What can happen is that a third proposition, which resembles one of the original pair, may be illicitly substituted for one of the original premisses in the argument. When this happens, there may appear to be an inconsistency where none really exists. The result is another subtle form of the *ad hominem* fallacy.

An interesting example is the notorious Hunter's Argument reported by the nineteenth-century Irish archbishop Richard Whately.[10] The argument goes roughly as follows:

Critic: How can you derive pleasure from gunning down a helpless animal? Surely the killing of deer or trout for amusement is barbarous.

Sportsman: If you're so concerned, why do you feed on the flesh of animals? Aren't you being inconsistent?

What the sportsman is suggesting is that the critic's actions are inconsistent with his moral pronouncements. The sportsman replies to the critic by arguing *ad hominem*.

Is there, in fact, an inconsistency in the critic's position? According to the sportsman, the critic eats meat while at the same time asserting that hunting is morally repugnant. Is this inconsistent? The answer is (likely) not. It would be inconsistent to hunt while asserting that hunting is morally repugnant, but there is no inconsistency in condemning, as the critic does, the killing of animals *for amusement* while eating a steak dinner. If it can be shown that hunting is (at least in some circumstances) the same as killing for amusement, there is enough of a difference between hunting and meat-eating to invalidate the sportsman's argument.

Related to this example, the nineteenth-century logician Augustus De Morgan describes the *ad hominem* fallacy as an illicit comparison producing what only *appears* to be an inconsistency: "It is not absolutely the same argument which is turned against the proposer," says De Morgan, "but one which is asserted to be like it, or parallel to it. But parallel cases are dangerous things, liable to be parallel in immaterial points, and divergent in material ones."[11] We can see this type of illicit comparison more clearly if we contrast the genuinely inconsistent pair

(1) X asserts that hunting for amusement is wrong
(2) X hunts

with the parallel pair

(1') X asserts that hunting for amusement is wrong
(2') X eats meat.

The sportsman, it seems, has not made a sufficiently strong case against his critic.

To make an accusation *ad hominem* involves a charge of inconsistency. We will learn more about inconsistency as this book proceeds. We will see that a logical inconsistency occurs whenever a proposition is advocated and denied at the same time. To assert that "the cat is on the mat and the cat is not on the mat" is to assert a proposition that is logically inconsistent. In examining the *ad hominem*, we have not been discussing logical inconsistency, strictly speaking; instead, we have been discussing an inconsistency between what *actually happens* and what one *says should happen*. We call this kind of inconsistency a *circumstantial* or *pragmatic inconsistency*. In short, a person's action is *circumstantially* (or *pragmatically*) *inconsistent* with what he proposes or recommends if and only if, were the proposal or recommendation to be an order, the person's action would be an act of self-disobedience.

A speaker can be involved in a circumstance, or even create it himself, that not only makes what he says inconsistent with that circumstance, but also actually *refutes* what he says. A very simple example arises if Bill claims that, "Since I never speak English, what I am now saying is not in English." It is worth noticing that the correct attribution of an *ad hominem* can in fact be conclusion-defeating; not all uses of the *ad hominem* are incorrect or fallacious.

If a pair of propositions is logically inconsistent, one of them must be false.

Flashback on...
the *Ad Hominem*

ARISTOTLE was the first to identify *ad hominem* arguments. Centuries later the Englishman John Locke took up the topic in his 1690 publication *An Essay Concerning Human Understanding*. There he introduced a variety of arguments with the words: "it may be worth our while a little to reflect on *four sorts of arguments*, that men, in their reasonings with others do ordinarily make use of, to prevail on their assent; or at least so to awe them, as to silence."[12]

The third of these four sorts of argument he describes as follows: "a third way is to press a man with consequences drawn from his own principles or concessions. This is already known under the name of *argumentum ad hominem*."[13]

Perhaps the most important thing to say about Locke's *ad hominem* is that, unlike its contemporary namesake, it is *not a fallacy*. To see why this is so, it is instructive to consider a kind of *ad hominem* argument that Aristotle called "refutations." An Aristotelian *refutation* is a deduction (i.e., a conclusive argument) produced in the following way: There are two parties to a discussion, a questioner and a respondent. The respondent gets things started by putting forward a thesis, T (e.g., "All virtue can be taught"). The questioner's role is then to attempt to refute T. He does this by putting questions to the respondent that can be answered either yes or no. Out of the respondent's answers to these questions (say, A_1 and

▶ A_2), the questioner then tries to select propositions that logically imply the opposite of the respondent's thesis. In this way, T's refutation comes from the respondent's own words, since the questioner has presented the respondent with a consequence drawn from the respondent's own concessions. Such a refutation is distinguished from a *sophistical* refutation, an argument that *appears* to be a (successful) refutation but which in fact is not.

It is natural to wonder what a genuine refutation (in Aristotle's sense) establishes. What it does *not* show is that the respondent's thesis, T, is false. In the absence of further information, all a refutation shows is that the respondent has given an inconsistent defence of his thesis. This leads Aristotle to conclude that, "About such matters, there is no proof in the full sense, though there is proof *ad hominem*."[14]

What Aristotle means is that the argument from A_1 and A_2 to the denial of T does not by itself prove T to be false, so it is not a "proof in the full sense." However, it does prove that the respondent cannot consistently continue to affirm T while also accepting A_1 and A_2. In other words, because the respondent has given an inconsistent defence of T, the refutation is a proof *ad hominem*.

Locke shares this understanding of the difference between a proof in the full sense and a proof *ad hominem*. An *ad hominem* refutation of the respondent's thesis shows, Locke says, that the respondent is "in an error" and "in the wrong," but it does not show exactly where the error lies. It could be T, but for all we know it could instead be A_1 or A_2.

Thus, as understood by both Aristotle and Locke, *ad hominem* arguments need not be fallacious. Even so, whenever we make the additional assumption that just because there is a refutation of T (in Aristotle's sense) T must be false, we will have committed a fallacy.

It is interesting that the modern conception of the *ad hominem* has evolved into something quite different from the older concept. It has been quite an evolution: from non-fallacy to fallacy! In discussing the *ad hominem*, care should therefore be taken not to attribute modern views to ancient writers, or to attribute ancient views to modern writers.

However, it is also worth noting that it does not follow that further argument will not remove or explain away a merely apparent inconsistency. In some circumstances the *ad hominem* can be defused. Shortly after the Second World War, the British philosopher and social activist Bertrand Russell advocated attacking the Soviet Union as a way of guaranteeing the non-proliferation of nuclear weapons. Later, in the 1950s, he advocated a "better Red than dead" argument, preferring appeasement to confrontation. Are these two views logically inconsistent? Perhaps. But Russell believed that he was able to explain why he had changed his mind. Before the Soviet Union had acquired nuclear weapons, Russell thought that aggression was a rational policy; later he came to hold the view that such a policy would be irrational in dealing with a country that had a strong, effective nuclear capability. In short, Russell believed he could give a satisfactory account of why a change in his position was warranted. Whether one agrees with his ultimate conclusion or not, Russell should not be faulted for simple inconsistency in his viewpoint. As a result, there is a reasonable basis for defending him against the charge of *ad hominem*.

Exercise 1.4

1. Determine whether each of the following contains an *ad hominem* argument:

(a) At a political rally, Sue says to Bill, "Since Dr. Jones is a twice-convicted embezzler, he's unfit to serve as city treasurer."

(b) While attending their biology class, Bill says to Sue, "Since Dr. Jones is a twice-convicted embezzler, we shouldn't pay much attention to his views about evolutionary biology."

(c) Sue says to Bill, "Since you concede that there are particular circumstances in which abortion is morally permissible, your blanket opposition to abortion is uncalled for."

(d) Bill says to Sue, "I don't think that I should trust your judgment about what software to buy. After all, the last time I used your computer it was always crashing."

(e) Two friends are discussing the current funding of their local elementary school: "It's not surprising that you think the government should be spending more money on education," says one, "you have five children!"

(f) After funding a questionable youth-grant project, the government is accused by the opposition of misusing funds. A member of the government replies that the opposition should be careful in pressing this sort of criticism, given its own notorious record of squandering money on youth grants when it was in power.

(g) Two friends are arguing over which political party has the better foreign policy. One of the two suggests that his friend's party has never been a strong advocate of a high-profile international presence. "Of course not," agrees his friend, "all their political support is to be found at home."

(h) We are told by the Scottish biographer James Boswell that Dr. Johnson, the famous English lexicographer, once asked someone who argued for the equality of all mankind—in the presence of a servant—whether she would allow her footman to sit down beside her.

(i) Another time, after listening to a man who had cleverly argued that the difference between virtue and vice is illusory, Dr. Johnson is said to have remarked: "When he leaves our house let us count our spoons."

(j) In their infamous *Communist Manifesto*, Karl Marx and Friedrich Engels reply to their critics as follows: "But don't wrangle with us so long as you apply, to our intended abolition of bourgeois property, the standard of your bourgeois notions of freedom, culture, law, etc. Your very ideas are but the outgrowth of the conditions of your bourgeois production and bourgeois property ...."[15]

2. For each of the arguments listed in question 1 that contains an *ad hominem*, determine whether it involves a fallacy.

Summary

Our goal in this book is to learn what it means to reason well. As a result, we have begun studying both *logic* and, more broadly, the *theory of argument*. We have also begun studying the *fallacies*—those arguments that often appear to be good but that are not.

An *argument* is a presentation of reasons or evidence in support of some claim. It is an attempt to build a case in favour of a conclusion. Normally this means that arguments are social exchanges involving a series of speech acts uttered by two or more parties. Familiar examples include quarrels, legislative debates, diplomatic wrangles, labour negotiations, mathematical proofs, legal arguments, scientific demonstrations, and so on. Because they involve a variety of social and psychological, as well as logical, factors, we say that these are arguments in the *broad* (or *social*) *sense*.

At the core of every argument in the broad sense is a set of propositions composed of the argument's *premisses* and *conclusion*. We call this an argument in the *narrow sense*. Arguments in the narrow sense are abstractions from arguments in the broad sense.

In order to make clear the structure of an argument in the narrow sense and to distinguish between its premisses and conclusion, we often place the argument in *standard form*. To do this, we identify its premisses and conclusion and separate the conclusion from the rest of the argument by means of a horizontal line. The premisses form the basis of the argument. They constitute the evidence that is being offered in support of the conclusion.

Reasoning critically about various issues requires that we learn to evaluate arguments. The *quality* of an argument depends primarily upon (1) the *likelihood of the truth of the argument's premisses*, together with (2) the *strength of the consequence relation* that holds between its premisses and conclusion. It follows that there are two main ways to criticize an argument: (1) we can show the premisses to be unacceptable, or (2) we can show the consequence relation to be weak.

It is a primary goal of both logic and the theory of argument to help determine the quality of arguments. *Logic* does this by studying the nature of the *consequence relation* that holds between the argument's premisses and conclusion. To say that a consequence relation is *strong* is to say that the premisses, if true, provide *good evidence* in favour of the conclusion. To say that this relation is *weak* is to say that the premisses, if true, provide poor evidence in favour of the conclusion. A consequence relation that is neither strong nor weak is said to be *moderate*.

One type of argument with which we are familiar is the *quarrel*. The quarrel is an argument that suffers from *premissory* or *conclusional instability* (or both) in ways that dispose the disputants to hostility.

In addition, quarrels often involve two well-known types of fallacy: the *ad baculum* and the *ad hominem*. An *ad baculum* argument occurs whenever a conclusion is drawn, or invited to be drawn, as a result of an appeal to force. The argument is *fallacious* whenever the appeal turns out to be *irrelevant* to the conclusion under consideration.

An *ad hominem* argument occurs whenever a conclusion is drawn, or invited to be drawn, as a result of an appeal to some fact (or alleged fact) about one's opponent. Once again, the argument is *fallacious* whenever the appeal turns out to be *irrelevant* to the conclusion under consideration. There are two common types of *ad hominem* fallacy in the modern tradition: the *abusive ad hominem* and the *circumstantial ad hominem*. Both differ from the *ad hominem* as understood by John Locke and Aristotle.

Weblinks

Episteme Links—Logic

www.epistemelinks.com/Topi/LogiTopi.htm

Philosophy in Cyberspace—Logic

www.geocities.com/Athens/Acropolis/4393/logic.htm

Episteme Links—Aristotle

www.epistemelinks.com/Pers/ArisPers.htm

MacTutor History of Mathematics Archive—Aristotle

www-groups.dcs.st-and.ac.uk:80/~history/Mathematicians/Aristotle.html

Notes

1. In this book we adopt the spellings "premiss" and "premisses." The American philosopher C.S. Peirce points out that the spelling appropriate to logic derives from the medieval Latin *praemissa*. In contrast, the spellings "premise" and "premises" (as in "He was removed from the premises for trespassing") come originally from the French *premise*, as in the expression *les choses premises*, used in inventories. We came upon this point in T.A. Goudge, *The Thought of C.S. Peirce* (Toronto: University of Toronto Press, 1950), 5.

2. Aristotle, *On Interpretation*, 4, 17a, 3–4.

3. We will say more about these historical issues as we proceed, especially in ch. 8.

4. See Aristotle, *On Sophistical Refutations*, 34, 183b, 34–6. The claim is also interesting because Aristotle is not normally a braggart.

5. This third alternative occurs as a result of procedures used in debates and criminal trials. These procedures are discussed in ch. 2 and 13, respectively.

6. Aristotle, *On Sophistical Refutations*, 15, 174a, 20.

7. Richard Grunberger, *A Social History of the Third Reich* (London: Weidenfeld and Nicolson, 1971), 398.

8. Plato, *Meno*, 94e.

9. Circumstantial *ad hominem*s of this type are sometimes also called "*tu quoque*" arguments. (*Tu quoque* is Latin for "you too.") For a more detailed analysis, the interested reader may consult John Woods, "Dialectical Blindspots," *Philosophy and Rhetoric* 26 (1993), 251–265.

10. Richard Whately, *Elements of Logic* (New York: William Jackson, 1836), 197.

11. Augustus De Morgan, *Formal Logic* (London: Taylor and Walton, 1847), 265.

12. John Locke, *An Essay Concerning Human Understanding* (1690), bk 4, ch. 17, §19.

13. Ibid., §21.

14. Aristotle, *Metaphysics*, bk. K (11), 5, 1062a, 2–3. See also his *On Sophistical Refutations*, 22, 178b, 17; 33, 183a, 22–24; and *Topics*, bk. 8, 11, 161a, 21–23.

15. Karl Marx and Friedrich Engels, *Manifesto of the Communist Party* (New York: International Publishers, 1948), 26.

CHAPTER 2

The Debate

A SECOND type of argument (in the broad sense) for us to consider is the debate. Since debates have more structure and orderliness than quarrels, they may turn out to be a more useful model of good argument. In a debate, there are winners and losers, and definite rules determine the outcome. As a result, it may be possible to derive some guidelines that will enable us to identify and evaluate arguments in law, science, ethics, and other areas. However, like the quarrel, the debate can sometimes frustrate the rightful role of reason. Like quarrels, debates can become noisy, personal, and fractious affairs. In fact, a failed debate may quickly deteriorate into just another quarrel. At its best, though, a debate can be a noble thing—if not reason's handmaiden, then perhaps reason's court jester—making obvious the ridiculous, challenging the dogmatic, and putting even cherished beliefs and principles to the test.

1. The Debate

Quarrels, it has been said, are arguments reduced to anarchy. In contrast, debates are rule-governed enterprises, presided over by a referee or judge who is committed to fairness and objectivity. In addition, debates are often settled not by the debaters themselves but by a judge, or by a panel of judges. In those cases where the decision is left to the debaters themselves, such as in Parliament or Congress, a simple majority among the voters is usually sufficient to decide the outcome.

This is an important (and fortunate) feature of debates, and is worth emphasizing. Because total agreement among the contending parties is not required, it turns out that debaters can tolerate a high degree of premissory and conclusional instability. Unlike a quarrel, where the goal is to reach agreement between the participants, and where this goal is inevitably frustrated, debates are not subject to the anarchy and chaos that result from premissory or conclusional instability.

Of course, if a debater is to be successful there will need to be a fairly high degree of premissory and conclusional stability between the debater and (at least) a simple majority of the judges. Despite this, debates can tolerate even total premissory or conclusional instability between the contending participants or debaters. We assume that debates are usually businesslike activities, designed to produce bona fide decisions. Sometimes, of course, a debate is arranged merely for fun, and is won or lost on wit or even rudeness; in such a debate, it is not important for the judges or audience to agree with the substance of what is actually said. This kind of debate is a limiting example of argument (though we do not deny that it sometimes occurs in our legislatures!). For the logician, it provides only negative lessons.

In its essentials, the structure of a debate is fairly straightforward. It is a contest that is

- between two or more contending participants, who may be either individuals or groups of individuals;

- presided over by a referee, a chairperson, or a speaker whose function is to maintain order, to apply and interpret the rules and, ultimately, to bring the debate to a vote; and

- decided by a verdict that is (usually) determined by majority vote, either of a judge, or panel of judges or jury, or members of "the house," which may or may not include the debaters themselves—the winning side thus wins "the approval of the house."

One of the virtues of debates is that they are refereed. As a result, they are governed by rules of procedure, rules of conduct, and rules of decision. Debates are exchanges that are meant to be fair, and the main benefit of such a system is that anarchy is averted. Nevertheless, it is also important to recognize that this very "benefit" gives rise to its own special corruptions. A referee or judge is a kind of external authority who inhibits or prevents a debater from having things just his or her own way. Thus, there is the temptation on the part of the debater to evade the weight of authority, not by anarchy, but by *sophistry*, *insincerity*, *flattery*, or *ambiguity*. Let us consider each of these four temptations in turn.

> **The Debate**
> A *debate* is a rule-governed contest presided over by a referee. It is a contest between two or more sides, each of which is attempting to win the approval of the house.

Advantages and Disadvantages of the Debate

Because a debate is resolved by a vote of the house, or by some other similar mechanism, total agreement among the contending parties is not required. Thus, unlike those involved in a quarrel, debaters can tolerate a high degree of premissory and conclusional instability. Even so, there is often a temptation on the part of debaters to score points by the use of less than noble means, including *sophistry*, *insincerity*, *flattery*, and *ambiguity*.

The first temptation of debate is *sophistry*. What is sophistry? A clue is found in the works of Aristotle. In his early writings, a *sophism* is simply the conclusion of what Aristotle calls a "contentious" argument. By a contentious argument, Aristotle means any argument based on beliefs generally accepted but nevertheless untrue, or an argument in which there seems to be correct reasoning, but in which there is not. In some of Aristotle's later writings, "sophism" is used more broadly to refer to any example of a fallacy. Today, "sophistry" thus refers to any use of fallacies to confuse or deceive an opponent. This use need not be deliberate. The use of fallacies can occur inadvertently, as when the arguer himself is tricked by his own sophistry.

A good example of sophistry is found in Plato's *Euthydemus*. In this dialogue, Euthydemus and Dionysodoros are sophists who turn their attention to a young man, Clinias, devastating him with their trickery:

> "But now," said [Dionysodoros], "is Clinias wise or not?"
>
> "He [Clinias] says, not yet ... he's no boaster, you know."
>
> "And you people," said Dionysodoros, "want him to become wise and not to be a dunce?"
>
> We agreed.
>
> "Then you wish him to become one that he is not, and no longer to be one that he is ... Since you want him no longer to be one that he is now, you want him to be destroyed, it seems!"[1]

By trading on different ideas of change, Dionysodoros has tricked his listeners into accepting something that they do not want to accept. Of course, not all fallacies need be as obvious as this one, but in all cases the outcome will be the same—we will have been led inadvertently to error.

The second temptation in a debate is *insincerity*; the third is *flattery*. The following excerpt contains examples of both. The passage is one of Shakespeare's most famous, from Mark Antony's speech in *Julius Caesar*. It should be borne in mind that Brutus, to whom Mark Antony repeatedly refers, has himself just addressed the same throng and openly admitted his part in the murder of Caesar.

> Friends, Romans, Countrymen, lend me your ears;
> I come to bury Caesar, not to praise him.
> The evil that men do lives after them;
> the good is oft interred with their bones;
> so let it be with Caesar. The noble
> Brutus hath told you Caesar was ambitious;
> if it were so, it was a grievous fault;
> and grievously hath Caesar answer'd it.
> Here under leave of Brutus and the rest,—
> for Brutus is an honourable man: so are they all,
> all honourable men,—
> ... come I to speak in Caesar's funeral.
> He was my friend, faithful and just to me:
> but Brutus says that he was ambitious:
> and Brutus is an honourable man.
> He hath brought many captives home to Rome,
> whose ransoms did the general coffers fill:
> did this in Caesar seem ambitious?
> when that the poor have cried Caesar hath wept;

ambition should be made of sterner stuff:
yet Brutus says he was ambitious;
and Brutus is an honourable man.[2]

With his repeated claim that Brutus is an honourable man, Mark Antony is using both flattery and insincerity to try and sway the audience. "Assuming that Brutus has such a virtue," Mark Antony seems to be saying, "would that be enough to justify Caesar's murder?" Of course not, we want to reply and, if so, then it will be even worse if it also turns out that Brutus is not an honourable man.

Here is another example of insincerity. In it we see that the rules of parliamentary debate are openly violated by both participants, and that the wrongdoers merely feign their apologies. This exchange has been attributed to at least four different pairs of English parliamentarians from the time of Henry VIII onwards:

First Parliamentarian: Mr. Speaker, I can only think that the honourable member opposite will die of the pox if not on the gallows!

Second Parliamentarian: I should imagine that the dreadful contingencies to which my friend alludes depend entirely upon whether I embrace his mistress or his principles.

Mr. Speaker: Gentlemen, gentlemen! Order, please.

First Parliamentarian: Abject apologies, sir, I have offended the House.

Second Parliamentarian: And I, sir, have offended truth; I am repentant!

The fourth temptation of the debate is *ambiguity*. The following examples are from Aristotle's early work on logic, *On Sophistical Refutations*. Although they are slightly more convincing in the original Greek, their meaning remains clear enough today:

"There must be sight of what one sees: one sees the pillar: ergo the pillar has sight." ... Also, "speaking of the silent is possible": for "speaking of the silent" also has a double meaning: it may mean that the speaker is silent or that the things of which he speaks are so.[3]

One can easily see that subtler ambiguities can pervade many debates. For example, here is an argument that might at first appear persuasive:

The existence of a law means that there must be a law maker. But we know that the law of gravity and other scientific laws have not been made by any human law maker. So it follows that there must be a non-human law maker, God.

Here there is an ambiguity with respect to the term "law." In the first premiss, the term represents a *prescriptive* claim enacted by a legislature or other government body. In the second premiss it means something quite different, namely a *descriptive* regularity in nature. As a result, an argument that might at first have appeared to be strong turns out, in fact, to be weak.

Other ambiguities trade as much on a sentence's grammatical structure as on the meaning of individual words.[4] For example, in the sentence "Bill needs more suitable companions," it remains ambiguous whether the speaker means that Bill's current companions simply aren't suitable for him, or whether Bill needs a greater number of the kind of suitable companions that he already has. Other examples include the kind of ambiguous recommendations that occasionally end up in letters of reference for less than ideal job candidates; for example, "In my opinion, you will be very fortunate to get this person to work for you," or "I enthusiastically recommend this candidate with no qualifications whatsoever," or "I urge you to waste no time in making this candidate an offer of employment."

2. Mill's Model of Debate

The logical evaluation of a debate is somewhat more complicated than the logical evaluation of a quarrel. As we have observed, the principal object of a debate is to win the approval of the house. This may or may not be compatible with getting at the truth of the issue at hand. If the primary object of the debate is to win at any cost, truth and reason may be sacrificed, or at least temporarily set aside. Thus, in its barest essentials, the debate need not be a friend of truth, and logic can only advise that debating techniques be used with caution.

Even so, one of the major theoreticians of argument in the nineteenth century, and one of the modern world's seminal political thinkers, had a more positive view of the virtues of debate. In his classic book *On Liberty*, John Stuart Mill gives (among other things) his theory of debate, especially when it is used as a tool for political decision-making.

Debates occur in parliaments, congresses, diets, knessets, bundes, and other such government houses. The members of these chambers are individuals; each has his or her own intelligence, experience, opinions, and prejudices. Debates make contending and contradictory claims on these individuals for loyalty and support.

As Mill explains it, in a debate the various sides of the house put each proposition under consideration to the test. Ideally, any member of the chamber can rise to ask questions, or to offer his or her advice or criticisms. As the exchange unfolds, certain alternatives drop from contention; no one will now support these alternatives, for they have not passed the inspection or scrutiny of the house. Sooner or later, a consensus (or something close to it) is reached. The consensus may centre on none of the original propositions in contention; instead, it may support some skillfully made compromise, tempered by the fires of debate. Usually what is endorsed is the proposition most likely to be true and most likely to be worthy of political support, for it alone has survived the furnace of criticism and the onslaught of dogmatism and personal prejudice.

What an interesting and ingenious defence of debate Mill has given us! Admittedly, the objective of any given individual debater may be to get his or her own way, even at the expense of objectivity and truth. In a community, there may

Flashback on...
John Stuart Mill (1806–1873)

JOHN Stuart Mill was born in London, the son of James Mill, an officer in the East India Company. Seeing no need to send his son to school James didn't, and the young Mill was educated at home by his father. After mastering the classics, as well as several languages, John joined his father at the East India Company as a clerk in 1823. Rising to senior levels, he was asked to write a defence of the Company's application for the renewal of its licence in 1857. When the application failed, he left the Company. In 1865 he stood for Parliament and was elected as member for Westminster. Defeated in the election of 1868, he then divided his time between London and Avignon until his death in Avignon five years later.

Mill began his intellectual life as a philosophical radical in the manner of both his father and his father's friend, Jeremy Bentham. Following an emotional crisis at the age of twenty, he came to regard his former radicalism as too skeptical and extreme. There fol-lowed a fertile period of thinking, and Mill's maturing views were given expression in a large number of essays on economics, politics, sociology, and philosophy.

Dismissed by some as a mere pamphleteer incapable of systematic thought, Mill answered his critics in 1843 with the publication of *A System of Logic, Ratiocinative and Inductive: A Connected View of the Principles of Evidence and the Methods of Scientific Investigation*. In this book Mill argued that ethics, politics, and the social sciences are all systematically intelligible once they are developed using the same methods used in the natural sciences. In its day the *Logic* enjoyed a large success and was adopted as a text at both Oxford and Cambridge. Also famous for his political writings, including his two most influential books, *On Liberty* (1859) and *Utilitarianism* (1861), Mill died the most respected British philosopher of his century.

be many such individuals, each having his or her private objectives uppermost in mind. Yet, provided there are procedural rules that enable the contending issues to be freely and openly examined by all concerned, private prejudice will more often than not defer to the general will. Though an individual debater may be no friend of truth, as a community or group activity, the debate is, says Mill, an effective and objective *route* to truth. Our individual prejudices somehow cancel each other out and what is left is something closer to, if not identical with, the truth.

Mill's optimism is refreshing, and no doubt often justified. It is an optimism that reflects two of the modern world's most prominent ideas. The first is that of the *free market*. In a free market, consumers furnish whatever degree of demand there may be for any item offered for sale, and the suppliers and sellers determine the supply. Given these preferences and the limited resources of the consumer, the laws of supply and demand ultimately determine what value is to be accorded each commodity. The worth of a commodity is determined by the degree to which it is accepted or approved by the consumer.

The second idea that we see reflected in Mill's defence of debate is that of *survival of the fittest*. In evolutionary theory, a species is routinely subjected to stresses and afflictions that test its capacity for biological survival. It is generally accepted that a species is eliminated when it cannot adjust to such stresses, and those species that do adjust survive. These survivors are judged by nature to be the fittest.

What Mill is offering us, then, is a kind of free-enterprise, survival-of-the-fittest model—and justification—of debate, one in which truth is understood to be the most important value in the free marketplace of ideas. It is in debate that truth best survives the destructive forces of opposition and criticism.

> ### Mill's Model of Debate
>
> The *goal* of a debate is not explicitly to discover truth but, rather, to win the approval of the house. Even so, because of its structure, Mill holds that the debate remains an effective and objective *route* to truth. In fact, on Mill's view, it is only through open debate—the public offering of conjecture and criticism—that large-scale advances in human knowledge are possible. It is this view that ultimately underlies many of our social institutions and practices, including the jury system, opposition parties in government, a free press, and peer-reviewed scientific and scholarly journals. As Walter Bagehot, the famous constitutional scholar and author of *The English Constitution* (1867) put it, opposition parties in government are crucial for the health of all democracies, since they make "criticism of administration as much a part of the polity as administration itself."[5]

Perhaps the most impressive contemporary example of Mill's conception of free, competitive debate is the judicial system. Here, the most familiar example is that of the criminal courts and, more particularly, the institution of trial by jury. The basic format of trial by jury closely resembles that of legislative debate. The judge presides, interprets procedure, and rules on matters of law. In this way, he is a counterpart to the speaker of the house. The prosecution and defence counsel are counterparts to the debate's contending parties. The jury represents the house itself, or the debate's panel of judges. There are crucial differences, however. For example, in a trial, we have a new kind of participant, the witness, who gives evidence under oath; and this oath commits the witness to tell the objective truth (not just to state his party's, or his side's, position). Sworn testimony is, in the courts, the sole access to matters of fact.

In this context, we can see that the problem of premissory instability takes a new twist. In the quarrel, premissory instability is a serious problem leading to argumentative anarchy; in a debate, premissory instability among the contending participants is no longer a problem. The courts, however, are charged not merely with the responsibility of reaching a decision; their decision must be based upon a scrupulous presentation of objective evidence. Thus, it is a distinctive feature of the criminal trial that it involves procedures for the accumulation of factual evidence about which reasonable observers will tend to agree. The courts respond to this requirement ingeniously, by reserving the evidence-producing aspects of a trial to those who are not contending participants. At the same time, neither the lawyer nor the judge is the arbiter of the facts. This job is reserved for the jury—a fully independent party.

Finally, it is worth noting that correlative with the notion of evidence is the requirement of *proof*. Any contention before a court is settled only by proof. In other words, a trial tries and proves a proposition, and thereby demonstrates that proposition's truth or falsity. The overriding idea is that, in an orderly, open and adversarial competition, freely and impartially judged and fairly presided over, the truth will triumph.

Exercise 2.1

1. Attend at least one political debate, for example, at your local legislature or city council. Alternatively, you might examine the written record of a congressional or parliamentary debate by consulting either the Congressional Record or Hansard. (You can find these documents in most university libraries and at the World Wide Web sites listed at the end of this chapter.) Which features of the debate prove most helpful for deciding an issue? Which features prove most helpful for advancing the truth?

2. Attend at least one examination and cross-examination of a witness at your local criminal or civil court. Which features of a trial prove most helpful for deciding an issue? Which features prove most helpful for advancing the truth? In what ways do trials differ from political debates?

---

3. A Critique of Mill's Model

When considered abstractly, there is no denying that Mill's model looks appealing. Practically speaking, however, there are a number of respects in which it may be less than ideal. One of these is the so-called *bandwagon effect*.

In group-decision-making situations, many people are prepared to go to extreme lengths to avoid being losers. If it appears that the momentum in a committee, say, is going to carry the day for my opponents, then I may switch my allegiance simply to be a part of the winning side. This, in turn, could serve as an incentive for others who may be wavering and who may also hate to lose, especially if I am a person of any standing or reputation on the committee. Then, before you know it, everybody has "jumped on the bandwagon," while ignoring the actual merits of the case at hand.

Other factors impinge as well: the desire to please one's colleagues; the disinclination to prolong a meeting unduly by holding out too long for one's own point of view; an unwillingness to bear up indefinitely under an unyielding and vocal opposition; the self-conscious worry that one is just being pigheaded. None of these feelings is anything to be ashamed of, but all are vulnerable to exploitation; they are all there to be appealed to and hidden behind, even when the real motive for switching sides (or changing one's mind) is that one simply cannot stand being on the losing side.

Another difficulty is that real-life parliaments and congresses are not, by any stretch of the imagination, free markets. Rarely in its contemporary operation is a legislative debate open to all members. Usually a debate has a time limit, and it cannot be guaranteed that the issue at hand will receive sufficient attention to produce a fair and accurate verdict. Many sessions in such bodies—most, in fact—are not well attended. This is not an indication of laziness. Rather, it shows a recognition of the fact that the results of most legislative debates are *faits accomplis*, or foregone conclusions. Why is this so? It is mainly because in parliamentary systems of government, members are bound by party and caucus discipline—they are not free accept new positions, and they are beholden to the party whip; that is, to the member responsible for seeing that all members adhere to the party line.

The courts do not exemplify these same deficiencies, but here, too, there are difficulties. Though eyewitness testimony is intended to give the best possible access to the facts of a case, a number of investigations into the psychology of eyewitness perception show that eyewitness accounts are not always reliable.[6] One problem is the witness's reaction: if the event witnessed first-hand was of a shocking criminal nature, the shock and fear the witness experiences may interfere with the efficiency of his or her perceptual data-processing mechanisms. Even if a witness's memory is in good order, the witness may, without knowing it, be remembering something that was originally misperceived.

There is another difficulty. Sometimes the essential evidence in a trial deals with the barest and dullest of details, which the ordinary observer would not normally see or remember. Surely, it may be suggested, if the witness saw what happened then he must know whether the accused was wearing a bow tie. Experiments indicate that eyewitnesses are extremely receptive to the idea that, if they saw something happen, then they must be acquainted with all or most of the perceptible details of what went on. In fact, no theory of perception supports such a notion, and there is reason to think that eyewitnesses tend to be arbitrarily suggestible about such small details. That is, they invent details that they did not in fact perceive, unwittingly and under pressure of the unwarranted assumption that eyewitnesses record, process, and can retrieve virtually every perceptible aspect of what they have observed.

There is a third difficulty. Since we recognize that direct eyewitness testimony is not the only route to obtaining knowledge of what really occurred, courts often place their confidence in the indirect, implied testimony of experts. Despite this, reliance on the authority of experts can be risky. First, expert witnesses are identified as witnesses for the prosecution or for the defence. This tends to encourage the idea that expert witnesses are, at least to some degree, *partis pris*; that is, prejudiced in favour of one side or the other. Second, arguments that depend on an expert's authority open the door to the possibility of our committing an *ad verecundiam* fallacy. The *ad verecundiam* involves a deficient appeal to, or use of, the expertise of an authority in support of a conclusion.

In broad strokes, fallacious "appeals to authority" may take either of two forms. First, the appeal might cite an authority whose quite genuine expertise offers no legitimate support of the conclusion at hand. For example, Wayne Gretzky is one of the world's finest hockey players, but his television commercials for Coca-Cola products involve an *ad verecundiam*: we are meant to believe that his hockey expertise qualifies him to speak authoritatively for the biochemistry (or aesthetics) of thirst-quenching!

Second, an appeal to authority may involve reference to an expertise that simply does not exist. For example, assume for the moment that Sue is once again absolutely moonstruck over Bill. She just might find herself saying, and believing, "Look, it's as clear as clear can be. The nation-state is outmoded, and will be replaced by the year 2050 with a world federalist structure: my boyfriend, Bill, told me so!"[7] This is not to say that either eyewitness or expert testimony should be ignored, or that it is unhelpful. It is to say that even such testimony can be fallible and that we need to be aware of this when coming to our conclusions.

In summary, despite Mill's optimism, real-life cases of debate can be less than ideal. Specifically, they are subject to the following types of difficulty:

- because the ultimate goal of the debate is to win, factors such as sophistry, insincerity, flattery, and ambiguity may be invoked by the participants even though these same factors may not be conducive to the discovery of truth;

- because of factors such as the bandwagon effect, group decision-making can be notoriously unstable and non-objective;

- many situations in which debates occur are so highly regulated that they cease to be free markets for ideas;

- eyewitness perceptions are often incomplete and are sometimes unreliable; and

- expert testimony can be non-objective and can sometimes involve the fallacy of *ad verecundiam*.

Individually, each of these several shortcomings may normally be overcome. Nevertheless, together they point to some of the weaknesses associated with real-life debate.

4. The *Ad Populum*: Boosterism

Earlier we noticed that in a debate a participant's arguments are directed to a specific person or group of persons—a referee, jury, judge, or other deciding party. For this reason there is yet another danger associated with debate. This is the danger that arguments may be tailored specifically to appeal to the sentiments or prejudices of the person or group that the argument is designed to persuade. The result is (one version of) the *ad populum* fallacy.

The *Ad Populum* Fallacy

An *ad populum* fallacy occurs whenever a conclusion is drawn, or invited to be drawn, on the basis of an irrelevant appeal to popular belief. (When such an appeal is relevant, the argument is said to be a non-fallacious *ad populum* argument.) There are two main types of *ad populum* argument: *boosterism* (in which one's premises are tailored specifically to appeal to the sentiments or prejudices of those that the argument is intended to persuade), and *popularity* (in which one attempts to appeal inappropriately to so-called "common knowledge," which may not be knowledge at all).

Imagine for a minute that Bill and Sue have become political candidates and that they both want to represent their hometown electoral district. At a town hall debate about medicare, the following dialogue ensues:

> *Bill:* If your position is that physicians should not be allowed to opt out of medicare, and must be bound in their practices entirely by standards and rates set by government, how can you defend the declining standard of health care that is resulting from the current emigration of the best-qualified physicians from our community?

> *Sue:* I was born and raised not far from here, and what's clear to me is that the people of this very fine community have a right to medical care when family members are in desperate need. I know that, because people support this fundamental right, they also support medicare, regardless of the travel whims of a lot of fancy, overpaid specialists.

At least one thing that appears to have gone wrong with Sue's reply is that it fails to answer the question of whether the emigration of physicians will, in fact, cause a decline in standards of health care in the region, and whether this is a result of medicare. Instead her strategy is to rely upon a kind of boosterism. It is also a kind of flattery. Rather than examining evidence relevant to the point at issue, she is content merely to point out that she agrees with the popular view that medicare is a good thing.

There is a clear parallel between this version of the *ad populum* fallacy and the modern *ad hominem* fallacy. Of course there is a difference of orientation: the *ad hominem* is negative, given its intent to discredit, whereas the *ad populum* is positive, given its intent to win approval. Despite this, the subjective element governing premiss selection is common to both.

Ad populum arguments of the "booster" sort obviously involve an appeal to bias. Such arguments may include "anti-outsider" arguments, exemplified by local resistance to development plans by powerful players "back east" and by certain types of anti-immigration arguments. Also in this group are "solidarity" arguments of the sort we sometimes see in trade union disagreements with management, in which it is assumed that everyone with the same interests and with the same, or similar, backgrounds will see things the same way.

We say that a person or group, *S*, is *biased* with respect to a proposition, *p*, to the extent that *S* is disposed to accept, or reject, *p* without consulting or revisiting the relevant evidence as to the truth, or falsity, of *p*. It is important to emphasize that, given this definition, human beings are regularly biased in their beliefs and disbeliefs, and that often there need be nothing wrong with this. A person is disposed to believe that he has legs, that $2 + 2 = 4$, that AIDS is a deadly disease, that Paris is the capital of France, and so on. What is more, we are disposed to believe these things even when there is little likelihood that we will consult or revisit the relevant evidence in these matters. Suppose we thought it important to do so with respect, say, to the claim that Paris is the capital of France. In the absence of particular reasons to the contrary, consulting the evidence on this matter would be odd, perhaps even not quite rational. In fact, it is rather obvious that one of the virtues of biased belief is efficiency. If everything we were disposed to believe or disbelieve required the revisiting of evidence, it is doubtful that we would ever survive our caution.

Even so, there are many situations in which the nature of the proposition in question and the circumstances involved make it clearly inappropriate to accept, or reject, the proposition without consulting the relevant evidence. If Bill is charged with an offence, his mother may "just know" that he did not do it, but even if the investigating officers are also disposed to think that he did not do it, it would be irresponsible and inappropriate for them to act on that belief without first weighing the evidence unearthed by their investigation.

Upon reflection, we see that *ad populum* appeals involving bias can therefore go wrong in two ways. First, the disposition a person has to believe or disbelieve *p* can be *evidentially inadequate* given the circumstances of the situation. Most mothers "just know" that their children did not do the terrible acts reported in today's paper, and they do so independently of any evidence about the specifics of these acts. Yet what if evidence presents itself which suggests that Bill was involved? If there is such evidence, and his mother decides to ignore it, this will be an evidentially inadequate response on her part.

Second, a person may be disposed to accept *p* without revisiting the evidence, *p* may be true, and it may be evidentially adequate for that person to accept *p* in present circumstances. However, in these circumstances, invoking *p* may still turn out to be *argumentatively inappropriate* simply because it is not relevant. For example, it may be quite true that Sue's hometown is a wonderful place to live, and a truly splendid community. It may also be evidentially adequate to hold such beliefs without reconsidering the evidence, even in the context of a dispute about whether physicians should be allowed to opt out of medicare. Even so, invoking that belief as a premise in an argument about this question, one way or the other, is simply irrelevant, and it is argumentatively inappropriate to do so. Like many cases of circumstantial *ad hominem*, the fault lies not in the *ad populum* appeal itself, or in the biased nature of the arguer's belief. (After all, Sue's hometown may in fact be the best place on earth!) Rather, the fault lies in the irrelevance of that fact—if it is a fact—to the issue at hand.

5. The *Ad Populum*: Popularity

Aristotle devoted considerable attention in his *Topics* and *On Sophistical Refutations* to a class of arguments involving what he called *endoxa*. *Endoxa*, as he explains it, are beliefs held by everyone, or by the many, or by the wise. We see in this threefold partition the modern distinction between

- common knowledge beliefs, or what "everyone" knows;

- majority opinion beliefs; and

- beliefs based on the opinions and testimony of experts.

Of these three elements, the first two fall under the general heading of "popular beliefs" and thus form a basis for what can be called "the popularity sense" of the *ad populum*. The third is best described in the context of *ad verecundiam* arguments, which will occupy us in chapter 11.

Let us turn, then, to the following form of argument,[8] where *p* stands for any arbitrary proposition:

Everyone believes *p*

———————————————

Therefore, *p* is true.

This form of argument may initially strike us as one that is transparently bad, since it clearly confuses popularity with truth. And clearly, in many cases, we will be correct in thinking it bad. Even so, we should not rush to judgment. After all, as we noted earlier, one and the same argument might be both good and bad in relation to different purposes or standards of evaluation. Thus we must first ask ourselves "What is the appropriate standard against which to evaluate this argument?"

As it stands, the truth of the premiss clearly does not guarantee the truth of the conclusion. For example, in the argument

Everyone believes that water is wet

———————————————

Therefore, water is wet

we see that even though the conclusion is true, its truth is not proved *as a result* of its premiss. Yet if this is so, why would anyone put forward this type of argument? It would be a rare thing to find someone who actually supposes that "Water is wet" is a strict logical consequence of "Everybody believes that water is wet."

Let us consider two possible explanations. Both involve the use of what are termed "enthymemes." An *enthymeme* is any argument in which one or more of its core propositions (a premiss or conclusion) is not stated explicitly, but is merely assumed implicitly to be a part of the argument. For example, in the argument "Sue will make an excellent kindergarten teacher; everyone who loves children always does, you know," we have a case in which one of the premisses is left unstated. Even so, everyone recognizes that what is intended is really the argument

Everyone who loves children will make an excellent kindergarten teacher

[Sue loves children]

Therefore, Sue will make an excellent kindergarten teacher.

Here the unstated or hidden premiss—that Sue loves children—is made explicit, and by placing it in square brackets we indicate that it did not appear explicitly in our original argument. If it turns out that, like this argument, *ad populum* arguments are in fact best understood as enthymemes, it may turn out that they are not as transparently bad as they first appear.

Our first possible explanation begins by assuming that everyone does indeed believe that water is wet. This is perhaps not a surprising consensus but, all the same, it would be good to know *why* it is that everyone believes this to be so. What explains the universality of this belief? One good explanation is that water *is* wet. In other words, it may be that the original argument is an enthymeme which, when more carefully expressed, could be presented as follows:

> **Enthymemes**
> An *enthymeme* is any argument in which one or more of its core propositions (a premiss or conclusion) is not stated explicitly, but is merely assumed implicitly to be a part of the argument.

Everyone believes that water is wet

[Water's being wet is the best explanation of the fact that everyone believes that water is wet]

Therefore, water is wet.

Of course, the ultimate success of this argument will depend on whether water's being wet is in fact the best explanation of our universal belief that water is wet. This in turn will depend upon such things as whether we are all sufficiently exposed to water, and whether, once exposed to it, we are also the kind of creatures who will recognize that water is in fact wet. Even so, the strength of this solution is that it allows that our original argument might be stronger than it first appeared, even though the argument's conclusion still fails to be a strict logical consequence of its premisses. (In other words, even though it is still *possible* that the premisses are true and, at the same time, the conclusion is false, this is not *likely* to be the case.)

If this explanation is correct, then we will have discovered several important facts:

- before deciding whether an argument is fallacious, it is important first to determine whether the argument is in fact an enthymeme;

- any argument that is believed to be an enthymeme will need to be reconstructed in order to exhibit its unstated core propositions; and

- in reconstructing an enthymeme, it is best to honour the principle of charity—that is, we should attempt to give people the benefit of the doubt whenever possible.

> ## Is Water Really Wet?
>
> In order to keep our exposition of the *ad populum* manageable, we have taken some liberties. For example, a critic might reprove us for claiming that water is wet, reminding us that ice is water, and yet it is not wet. This is not an irksome quibble, but rather the stirrings of serious trouble, at least potentially. For suppose we tried to accommodate the critic by amending the claim to read "Water in liquid form is wet." Then the original argument would be reissued as
>
> Everyone believes that water in liquid form is wet
> _____
> Therefore, water in liquid form is wet.
>
> What is wrong with this argument? Why don't we just press on and give it the appropriate reconstruction? The answer is that some people will think that the conclusion of the argument is not only true, but that it is true *by definition*. In other words, they will claim that this new conclusion is *analytic*, or that it is made true by the very meanings of the words "liquid" and "wet." If so, then the objection is a serious one indeed. After all, in such a case, the conclusion will then be necessarily true and if it is the purpose of good arguments to lead us to true conclusions, how could this argument be a bad one? After all, its conclusion will never be false. We are left with the questions, "What more should we ask of good arguments, other than that their conclusions be true?" and "What is it that makes an argument good, if not the likelihood or guarantee that its conclusion is true?"

Let us now turn to our second potential explanation of why someone might reasonably put forward an *ad populum* argument of this type even though we know that "Water is wet" is not a strict logical consequence of "Everybody believes that water is wet." The reason is, in part, that in real-life speech "everybody" rarely means everybody. When we say that everyone knows that *p*, we usually mean that within some tacitly determined class or group (for example, within the present-day research community in plasma physics, or within the citizens of Sue's hometown), everyone knows that *p*. Even then we often mean not everybody, but *nearly* everybody, in the class or group.

Consider a case in which these constraints are taken a little more seriously. Given an argument such as the following,

Everyone believes that the relation of logical consequence is transitive[9]
_____
Therefore, the relation of logical consequence is transitive

we may first conclude that it is best understood as follows:

[Nearly] everyone [in the present-day research community in logic] believes that the relation of logical consequence is transitive
_____
Therefore, the relation of logical consequence is transitive.

Now in this case, although the argument's premiss still does not guarantee the truth of its conclusion, it has the look of being a rather good argument. What gives the argument the appearance of being good is not just that "everyone" believes that the relation of logical consequence is transitive, but that in this case the "everyone" in question is the vast percentage of logicians; that is, those who are experts about logical consequence. Once again, then, we may decide that the argument is in fact an enthymeme and that it is best understood as including two additional premises as follows:

> [Nearly] everyone [in the present-day research community in logic] believes that the relation of logical consequence is transitive
>
> [People in the present-day research community in logic are experts about logical consequence]
>
> [Experts are those people who are most likely to have knowledge of the subjects they investigate]
>
> ---
>
> Therefore, the relation of logical consequence is transitive.

This is interesting. This revised argument not only shows us that an argument we originally dismissed for committing the *ad populum* fallacy may have been dismissed too hastily; it also shows us that what may initially have appeared to be an *ad populum* argument is, after the appropriate reconstruction, in fact an *ad verecundiam* argument, or argument from authority.

Even so, we have not quite got to the heart of this version of the *ad populum*. Is it really appropriate to believe that popular beliefs should always be equated with those of experts or authorities? To answer this point, let us recall what Mill said about the advantages of debate. We noted, of course, that debates are not problem-free, especially in real-life application. Even so, aspects of society can be organized in such a way that propositions are routinely tested for truth or falsity. Human societies are fallible, of course. It is only natural to expect setbacks. But a popular belief is often one that has (so far) survived whatever interest there may have been in discrediting it. By the same token, it is also one that has (so far) survived nature's own habit of disclosing our errors. Thus, with appropriate caution, it seems we can say that *ad populum* arguments may often be plausible, but only to the extent that they are capable of being reinterpreted in such a way that they may be said to have met the kind of tests that Mill envisaged.

In short, we can approach *ad populum* arguments as follows: What accounts for the popularity of, say, the belief that *p*? One possibility is that everybody is an idiot. (Despite its other charms, this hypothesis will not be consistent with the principle of charity introduced above.) Another, more realistic possibility is that *p* is a proposition of a type that will have attracted some rivals. In this case, *p*'s enduring popularity indicates that it has (so far) done better than its rivals in a society of inquirers who are seriously interested in getting things right. Therefore, until we learn better, it is plausible to conjecture tentatively that the reason for *p*'s popularity is that, if not true, it at least has not yet been proven false.

There will remain, however, two situations in which this type of conjecture will *not* be safe to make, even tentatively. First, *p*'s popularity may be short-lived and, as such, it may not yet have come to be tested in any reliable way. Second, *p* may not be the sort of proposition that people are interested in seriously testing.

To sum up, *ad populum* arguments may be, and of course often are, fallacious. However, in some cases, appeals to so-called "common knowledge" do have a role to play in legitimate argument and debate. Just as we saw in the boosterism case that bias alone is not enough to disqualify a belief, in the popularity case, popularity alone is not enough to disqualify a belief either. That a belief is popular is some indication—although certainly a fallible one—that a belief is worthy of the support it has received. The great mistake is not that of being moved by popular belief. Rather, it lies in persisting with a popular belief despite the presence of negative evidence.

Exercise 2.2

1. Place each of the following arguments in standard form. For any that are enthymemes, identify the hidden premises or conclusions using square brackets.

(a) Bill cannot be a capitalist since he doesn't believe that the means of production should be privately owned.

(b) Sue is not answering her phone. I guess she has left for the day.

(c) Bill is bound to be late; he had hockey practice earlier this afternoon.

(d) All natural objects behave strictly according to natural laws. People are natural objects in this sense, so they, too, must always behave strictly according to natural laws. So it follows that our so-called "free will" is an illusion.

(e) The worst tragedy of the current century is that so many people suffer so much. Why? Because there are sufficient resources for everyone to be fed, for everyone to have good medical treatment, and for everyone to receive an education.

(f) Sue didn't study for today's test. I guess she's not going to graduate.

(g) "Number must be either infinite or finite.... Clearly it cannot be infinite; for infinite number is neither odd nor even, and the generation of numbers is always the generation either of an odd or of an even number ...."[10]

(h) "What I have so far accepted as true par excellence, I have got either from the senses or by means of the senses. Now I have sometimes caught the senses deceiving me; and a wise man never entirely trusts those who have once cheated him."[11]

(i) "An opinion that corn dealers are starvers of the poor, or that private property is robbery, ought to be unmolested when simply circulated through the press, but may justly incur punishment when delivered orally to an excited mob assembled before the house of a corn dealer .... Acts, of whatever kind, which without justifiable cause do harm to others may be, and in the more important cases absolutely require to be, controlled by the unfavourable sentiments, and, when needful, by the active interference of mankind."[12]

(j) "Whatever our moralists say, human understanding owes much to the passions, which, by common consent, also owe much to it. It is by the activity of the passions that our reason improves itself; we seek to know only because we desire to enjoy; and it is impossible to conceive a man who had neither desires nor fears giving himself the trouble of reasoning." [13]

2. Evaluate each of the following *ad populum* arguments. If the argument involves a fallacy, which version of the fallacy is involved?

(a) If you want proof that the golden rule is an undeniably sound moral principle, all you need to do is observe that, in one form or another, it is used in every system of ethics ever devised.

(b) We're all working people here. I know what it is to put in a day's work like the rest of you. That's why we must resist any attempts to legislate mandatory wage guidelines. The cost of food and clothing keeps going up. Consequently, fixing wages is a policy that will strangle all our families.

(c) We're all business people here, and we all know the value of a dollar. That's why we must have some form of mandatory wage guidelines before the private sector is strangled by unrealistic wage escalation and the economy comes crashing down. Not fixing wages is a policy that can ruin the financial prospects of all our families.

(d) Our university is the only one in the country not to have adopted a national scholarship program for logic students. It is high time that we caught up with everyone else.

(e) An overwhelming majority of voters decided to support the current government, and to give it a fresh mandate. So this just goes to show you how wrong critics of the government have been in recent years.

3. Consider each of the following:

(a) A person charged with a criminal offence is subject to one of two verdicts: "Guilty" or "Not guilty." (In Scottish jurisprudence a third option exists, "Not proven.") In most jurisdictions the verdict is determined by polling the jury and a unanimous vote is required for conviction. Anything short of this constitutes acquittal. Do these practices involve an *ad populum* fallacy? If so, which sense of the fallacy is involved?

(b) During the early 1950s, U.S. senator Joseph McCarthy instigated the controversial investigation of many suspected communists and communist sympathizers. In a speech he gave to the Senate in 1950 he commented: "Mr. President, it is time to serve notice upon the Communists, fellow travelers, and dupes that they are not going to be able to hide and protect themselves ... The American people realize that we cannot invoke a moratorium on fighting Communists and traitors at home, any more than we can invoke a moratorium on fighting them abroad, without completely disastrous results." [14] Does this speech involve an *ad populum* fallacy? If so, which sense of the fallacy is involved?

(c) In his famous speech in front of the Lincoln Memorial in 1963 on the centennial of the signing of the American Emancipation Proclamation, Martin Luther King, Jr. stated: "When the architects of our republic wrote the magnificent words of the Constitution and the Declaration of Independence, they were signing a promissory note to which every American was to fall heir. This note was the promise that all men, yes, black men as well as white men, would be guaranteed the unalienable rights of life, liberty, and the pursuit of happiness. It is obvious today that America has defaulted on this promissory note in so far as her citizens of color are concerned."[15] Does this speech involve an *ad populum* fallacy? If so, which sense of the fallacy is involved?

(d) In Montreal in July 1997, there was a large rally to commemorate the thirtieth anniversary of Charles de Gaulle's 1967 speech in Quebec City in which he uttered the words *"Vive le Québec libre!"*, a rallying cry for Quebec separatists. At the 1997 rally, an anglophone protester was jostled and derided by an angry crowd. "If you

were one of us," one of the members of the crowd said, "you would know that de Gaulle's remarks were perfectly appropriate!" Does this involve an *ad populum* fallacy? If so, which sense of the fallacy is involved?

(e) In Hollywood, members of the foreign press annually give an award to the "best picture." This is done by a vote of the journalists involved. Does this involve an *ad populum* fallacy? If so, which sense of the fallacy is involved?

6. Appeals to Misery and other Emotive Fallacies

Arguments that appeal to popular sentiment or bias often involve matters of high emotion. In fact, a little reflection reveals that it is difficult to engage in argument in a wholly neutral way, in a way that fails to involve emotion. After all, a beautifully crafted argument is a thing to admire, and admiration is an emotion. Certainly we would not want to counsel against the construction of beautifully crafted arguments, pleading that they let loose emotions of approval!

Even so, in many real-life situations, we know that it is detrimental to mix emotional, non-argumentative appeals together with factual claims. In fact, it has long been recognized that the overall effect of propaganda can be heightened by mixing genuine information with false but emotional claims.[16] Even Joseph Goebbels, the master of Nazi propaganda, often included much genuinely truthful information in otherwise exaggerated and heavily emotional newsreel reports from the battlefront. He realized that the factual elements he included greatly escalated the credibility of his propaganda, propaganda that might otherwise have been difficult to believe.

Fallacies that involve strong (but irrelevant) emotions are grouped together under the name *emotive fallacies* or *fallacies of emotion*. They include, among others, the abusive version of the *ad hominem* and the boosterism version of the *ad populum*. The essence of the emotive fallacy is that emotion can go too far. It can, as we said before, interfere with the ultimate purpose of argument.

Emotive Fallacies
Emotive fallacies occur whenever emotion interferes inappropriately with the ultimate goals of argument. They may involve fallacies of relevance, such as the abusive version of the *ad hominem* and the boosterism version of the *ad populum*, or they may simply involve a degree of emotional intensity among an argument's participants that threatens to divert them from the objective the argument was originally meant to achieve, namely the discovery of truth.

To see this, consider yet another example of a fallacy involving emotion, the *ad misericordiam* fallacy. *Misericordia* is Latin for "mercy." Thus an *ad misericordiam* fallacy is an argument in which mercy (or pity) is either misplaced or misused. The recognition of such arguments goes back at least as far as Richard Whately's *Elements of Logic* (1826).

In the modern treatment, the *ad misericordiam* is either a fallacy of relevance (in which the premiss being offered is simply irrelevant to the issue at hand) or else an attempt to derail the argument by introducing a series of strong emotions. Thus, like the circumstantial version of the *ad hominem*, the *ad misericordiam* can be an argument whose conclusion does not follow from the premises, but which someone might be inclined to accept out of sympathy or pity. This conception is caricatured by the joking argument

The defendant in the trial is an orphan

Therefore, he shouldn't be convicted for the murder of his parents.

(Like all good jokes, this one is grounded in reality. Two thousand years ago, the wily Roman defence attorney Cicero would have his client's wife sit weeping with her ragged, unwashed children in the courtroom in order to appeal to the jury's sympathy.)

In addition, like the abusive version of the *ad hominem*, the *ad misericordiam* can simply consist of an attempt to overload the discussion with emotional disturbance. Here the result is a poisoning or destabilizing of the very conditions that make objective and reflective argument possible. This is not to say that there is no place for emotion in our lives. Rather, it is simply to remind us that emotion cannot be a substitute for good reasoning.

It should be pointed out that the present-day understanding of *ad misericordiam* fallacy tends to overlook what might be thought of as the original version of the *ad misericordiam*. The oversight may be related to the fact that "pity" is not an especially accurate translation of *misericordiam*. As we said, the correct translation is *mercy*. Thus in its original form, an *argumentum ad misericordiam* is an appeal for mercy. An example would be the argument that, although the accused was rightly convicted of a serious crime, and although the sentence proposed by the prosecution would be just, the court is asked to show the accused mercy, owing to his bad health and advanced age. In this sense there is nothing fallacious as such with *ad misericordiam* arguments. Some are stronger than others, and some, of course, are no good at all.

> **The *Ad Misericordiam* Fallacy**
> An *ad misericordiam* fallacy occurs whenever a conclusion is drawn, or invited to be drawn, on the basis of an irrelevant appeal to mercy or pity. (When such an appeal is relevant, the argument is said to be a non-fallacious *ad misericordiam* argument.)

To sum up, many emotional fallacies are not so much fallacies of relevance as they are a poisoning of the atmosphere in which arguments occur. Sometimes emotional assertions also can involve fallacies of relevance but, as emotive fallacies, they are more properly understood as abuses of the process of civil discourse, stirring passions in us that divert us from achieving rational outcomes.

This is not to say that argumentation is competent only when people are being nice to one another, or only when it is transacted dispassionately. Levels of tension can run high in our legislatures, in criminal and civil proceedings, and elsewhere. Even the discourse of diplomacy can be intense and barbed. Emotive fallacies are not just failures of politeness. They are structural faults that take the natural concomitants of passion found in any real-life argumentative discourse to a point where emotional intensity threatens to divert us from the objectives that argument was meant to achieve in the first place.

Exercise 2.3

1. State whether each of the arguments below is an *ad baculum*, *ad hominem*, *ad populum*, or *ad misericordiam* argument.

    (a) I really do deserve a few bonus marks on my last exam, even though I didn't get the answer exactly right. After all, I spent all night studying.

    (b) If you think that investing in foreign corporations is such a great idea, why aren't you investing some of your savings overseas rather than in only local companies?

    (c) Of course this report concludes that more money needs to be devoted to health care. After all, it was funded by the medical profession, wasn't it?

    (d) Cheating on your taxes isn't anything to feel ashamed about. The tax structure in this country is unfair. It taxes regular people so heavily that we can hardly make an honest living. In effect, it cheats us because it leaves us with so little money, and compared to the wealthy we find it hard to make ends meet. For anyone who is short of money, a little cheating here and there is really nothing immoral.

    (e) No thinking person is going to support this legislation. Everyone of any standing in the community who has reviewed it agrees that it cannot be allowed to pass.

    (f) A substantial federal subsidy for our local fruit industry is definitely needed. Growers not only help the local economy, they are our friends and relatives. They are the people who live next door and the people whom we see at church. To say no to them would be to say no to ourselves.

    (g) A substantial federal subsidy for our local fruit industry is definitely needed. Growers have suffered from a late spring, a killing frost, and a serious shortage of field help. The resulting losses have severely depressed the entire industry.

    (h) Bill is obviously the right person to represent our constituency. He won the election by a landslide.

    (i) In reply to the argument offered by the elected member sitting opposite, I need only say that two years ago he vigorously defended the very measure that he now so adamantly opposes.

    (j) There's been some criticism of this government's purchase of our new defence system. It has been alleged that the technology is flawed. Let's study the issue: what we need to recognize is that the defence industry is among the largest providers of jobs in this community and that this purchase will continue to make this so. Imagine what would happen to the local economy should the funds for this project not come through.

2. Determine whether each of the arguments in question 1 above involves a fallacy.

3. Search through newspapers, magazines or other printed material for examples of *ad baculum*, *ad hominem*, *ad populum*, or *ad misericordiam* arguments. Indicate the premisses and conclusions of five such arguments, and determine whether any of these five arguments involve fallacies.

Summary

We have seen that, unlike quarrels, debates are rule-governed enterprises presided over and brought to a vote by a referee or some other type of authority. This gives the debate many advantages over the quarrel. Unlike those involved in quarrels, debaters can tolerate a high degree of premissory and conclusional instability. In addition, because debates are resolved by a vote of the house or by some similar mechanism, total agreement among the contending parties is not required. Even so, there is often a temptation on the part of debaters to appeal to inappropriate means of argument, including *sophistry*, *insincerity*, *flattery*, and *ambiguity*.

Despite this, Mill held that the debate remains an effective and objective *route* to truth. In fact, on Mill's view it is only through open debate—the public offering of conjecture and criticism—that large-scale advances in human knowledge are possible.

Even so, given the temptation debaters have to "score points" by less than noble means, we decided that it was important to try to understand those fallacious types of arguments, such as the *ad populum*, that find their home naturally in the debate. We discovered that *ad populum* fallacies occur whenever a conclusion is drawn, or invited to be drawn, on the basis of an irrelevant appeal to popular belief. Of this fallacy, there were two main types: *boosterism*—in which one's premises are tailored specifically to appeal to the sentiments or prejudices of those that the argument is intended to persuade; and *popularity*—in which one attempts to appeal inappropriately to so-called "common knowledge." Both require careful scrutiny, since it is not always easy to distinguish between legitimate and fallacious appeals to popularity.

In this context we also noticed that some arguments, called *ad misericordiam* arguments, rely upon appeals to pity or mercy. When fallacious, *ad misericordiam* arguments share with some instances of the *ad populum* and the *ad hominem* fallacies a high degree of emotion. As a result, these fallacies are called the *emotive fallacies*.

Weblinks

Episteme Links—John Stuart Mill
www.epistemelinks.com/Pers/JSMiPers.htm

Garth Kemerling's Philosophy Pages—John Stuart Mill
people.delphi.com/gkemerling/ph/mill.htm

Parliament of Canada

www.parl.gc.ca/

Supreme Court of Canada

www.scc-csc.gc.ca/

Government of Alberta

www.gov.ab.ca/

Government of British Columbia

www.gov.bc.ca/

Government of Manitoba

www.gov.mb.ca/

Government of New Brunswick

www.gov.nb.ca/

Government of Newfoundland and Labrador

www.gov.nf.ca/

Government of the Northwest Territories

www.gov.nt.ca/

Government of Nova Scotia

www.gov.ns.ca/

Government of Nunavut

www.gov.nu.ca/

Government of Ontario

www.gov.on.ca/

Government of Prince Edward Island

www.gov.pe.ca/

Government of Quebec

www.gouv.qc.ca/

Government of Saskatchewan

www.gov.sk.ca/

Government of Yukon

www.gov.yk.ca/

Government of the United States—Thomas

thomas.loc.gov/

Notes

1. Plato, *Euthydemus*, 283c–d. Despite the lighthearted nature of this example, there is a serious point behind it: the difficulty of finding identity conditions for things that change over time. For example, why do you remain the same person, despite the fact that you change remarkably over your lifetime? Why does a sporting team remain the same team even when its members or owners change? And why does a car remain the same car even when many of its parts are replaced?

2. Shakespeare, *Julius Caesar*, act 3, scene 2.

3. Aristotle, *On Sophistical Refutations*, 4, 165b, 34 to 4, 166a, 14.

4. We will pursue this distinction further in ch. 5.

5. Walter Bagehot, *The English Constitution* (London: Oxford University Press, 1928), 17.

6. For a disturbing case against the reliability of eyewitness testimony, see E.F. Loftus, *Eyewitness Testimony* (Cambridge: Harvard University Press, 1980).

7. We shall say more about the *ad verecundiam* in ch. 11.

8. What distinguishes an *argument* from an *argument form* is the presence of a lowercase letter, such as *p*, that functions as a variable. Because *p* stands for any arbitrary proposition, it is called a *propositional variable*. We will have more to say about argument forms and their relation to arguments in ch. 5.

9. To say that the relation of logical consequence is *transitive* is to say that, for all propositions, *p*, *q*, and *r*, if *p* is a logical consequence of *q*, and *q* is a logical consequence of *r*, then *p* must be a logical consequence of *r* as well. For further discussion, see ch. 7.

10. Aristotle, *Metaphysics*, bk. M(13), 8, 1084a, 1–4.

11. René Descartes, "Meditations on First Philosophy," *Philosophical Writings* (Don Mills: Ontario: Nelson's University Paperbacks, 1954), 61f.

12. John Stuart Mill, *On Liberty* (London: Penguin Books, 1974), 119.

13. Jean-Jacques Rousseau, *A Discourse on Inequality* (London: Penguin, 1984), 89.

14. Quoted in Allen J. Matusow, *Joseph R. McCarthy* (Englewood Cliffs, N.J.: Prentice Hall, 1970), 47.

15. See Martin Luther King, Jr., "I Have a Dream," in *I Have a Dream* (New York: HarperCollins, 1992), 102.

16. For examples, see Jacques Ellul, *Propaganda* (New York: Knopf, 1972).

CHAPTER 3

Dialectic

IN THE preceding two chapters we have examined two types of real-life argument in some detail. In doing so, we have seen that arguments in the broad sense are dynamic, interactive, social events in which something is said, a challenge or query is then offered, a reply is made, and so on. In the case of the quarrel, we saw that things go awry as a result of premissory or conclusional instability and as a result of the aggression that such instability typically encourages. In the case of the debate, we saw that, because things are more formally regulated, arguments can be drawn to a close but that there is often a temptation on the part of debaters to appeal to inappropriate types of argument. In this chapter we will examine a third type of argument in the broad sense, namely *dialectical arguments*.

In many modern theories, virtually any real-life argument is said to be a dialectical argument. This use of the term is unfortunate since it confuses two overlapping but distinct concepts: arguments involving dialogue between two parties (which we shall call *dialogue arguments* or *dialogical arguments*), and arguments involving questions and answers (a specific type of dialogical argument that we will call *dialectical arguments*). "Dialogical" comes from the Greek words *dia* (for "two") and *logos* (here meaning "discourse," just one of this word's many meanings). A dialogical argument, therefore, is an argument transacted in a particular kind of discourse, namely, a conversation or dialogue. In contrast, "dialectical" comes from the Greek word, *dialektikē*, which refers to the testing of a proposition by question and answer. In modern experience, dialectical arguments most often resemble a type of legal exchange known as an "examination," although in their use in the courtroom, legal examinations are not self-regulated. Even so, in both direct examination and cross-examination lawyers encourage witnesses to answer questions that bear directly on whatever issue is at hand.

In this chapter we examine the concept of dialectical argument. Imagine that two parties disagree about some matter. If, in the ensuing argument, one of the parties cites a fact, perhaps after consulting an encyclopedia rather than eliciting this information from his opponent by means of a question, then the argument at that point is a dialogical argument but not a dialectical one. However, once the parties begin questioning each other, the argument becomes dialectical. It is easy to see that unlike the debate and the trial, but like the quarrel, a dialectical argument is one that is presided over and judged by the participants themselves. Unlike the quarrel, though, dialectical exchanges are governed by rules deliberately designed to help discover the truth of the matter at hand. It is also interesting to note that, like a criminal trial, there is an emphasis on evidence and on what the evidence allows a reasonable person to infer or conclude.

1. Aristotle's Basic Rules of Dialectic

One type of dialectical argument is the *refutation argument*. Here are the basic rules governing refutation arguments, as developed by Aristotle:

- There is one questioner and one respondent, although substitution is permitted.

- The respondent is obliged to defend some thesis on a certain topic, and his defence takes the form of responding to a series of critical, probing questions asked by the questioner. The questions are asked and answered one at a time.

- For his part, the questioner must ask clear and straightforward questions, including what in law are called *leading questions*. Otherwise, the respondent may refuse to respond, and may demand that the question be clarified or re-expressed.

- The respondent must express only his own honest convictions in reply; not merely what he thinks will improve his chances of a successful defence. If, however, his answer contradicts his previous answers, he must amend one or the other until the contradiction is removed.

- If the respondent cannot, because of ignorance, give a reply, it is the questioner's job to formulate new questions that will overcome that ignorance.

- Answers may not be postponed.

- The exchange concludes if the respondent is refuted (i.e., is caught in a contradiction that will not allow him to continue to defend his thesis) or if it is clear to both participants that the questioner's refutation will not succeed.[1]

Of course, refutation arguments are not the only kind of dialectical argument. Also important is the *instruction argument* (sometimes called a *Socratic argument*) in which a teacher attempts, by question and answer, to teach his pupil some fact, p, deducing it from answers the pupil gives to the teacher's questions. Here there is no need for the student to defend the opposite of p, or for the teacher to refute not-p by deducing not-not-p from the pupil's concessions. It is true that this is one way in which the teacher might wish to help his pupil to see that p is true; but, as we mentioned in the flashback on the *ad hominem* in chapter 1, since refutations in this strict sense do not constitute a proof of the falsity of what they refute, care needs to be taken not to overstate the results of a successful refutation. The same is true of the non-refutation form of the instruction argument. In it, the teacher shows that the desired conclusion is a logical consequence of what the pupil has already conceded. In other words, the teacher shows that what the pupil already believes logically implies *p*. However, this alone does not constitute a proof of *p*. It shows only that p should be conditionally accepted, and that it may not be rejected in ways that are logically consistent with the pupil's other beliefs. This remains the case even if the teacher shares those other beliefs—which, if he is a serious teacher, he will certainly be required to do.[2]

A third example of a dialectical argument is the *examination argument*. An examination argument is one in which two parties seek to determine what follows logically from propositions they jointly hold, or from some proposition they are interested in scrutinizing. Questions fulfill the function of determining which propositions the other accepts or concedes; so, in strictness, each party must question the other.

Essential to the effective functioning of dialectic is a willingness of the participants to display objectivity, fairness, and goodwill. The unwary or naive dialectician risks being defeated by an unscrupulous opponent, or by an opponent who is prepared to substitute the style and the objectives of mere debate for those of dialectical inquiry.[3] In any real-life dialectical situation, the dialectician must always be prepared to detect such abuses and to withdraw from the fray. Under such circumstances it is always better to keep one's powder dry and one's procedures intact, and to be ready to contend again another day.

2. Eight Revised Rules of Dialectic

Aristotle's model of dialectic is not graven in stone. It is not the only possible or reasonable conception of dialectic. In fact, it would seem that Aristotle's rules—even when adapted to instruction arguments and examination arguments—are slightly too restrictive to serve as an appropriately general conception of rational inquiry. Accordingly, we will develop an amended and somewhat relaxed version of Aristotle's model, as follows:

How Many Questioners and Respondents Should There Be?

Aristotle determined that there should be just one of each. It would seem that the principles that motivated Aristotle's rule were (1) that the number of participants involved should not overload the discussion, and (2) that the ratio of questioners to respondents should be sufficiently balanced as to allow for a fair discussion.

These are admirable principles that may be accepted without hesitation. However, it is unlikely that Aristotle's "one-on-one" application of these principles will always be ideal. For example, if Bill is highly trained in both medicine and ethics, and Sue is well trained in medicine but has no training in ethics, a one-on-one dialectical exchange about biomedical ethics between Bill and Sue would hardly be fair or fruitful. However, if Sue were joined by Henri, who knows no biology or medicine but whose training in ethics is quite impressive, wouldn't this be a fairer contest with a greater chance of reaching a competent conclusion? If so, we can rewrite our first rule of dialectic as follows:

> The total number of participants, and the relative numbers on each side of the question, should be small enough and sufficiently balanced that the exchange is manageable, fair, and appropriate to the kind of inquiry at hand (i.e., refutation, instruction, examination, etc.).

What Are the Main Tasks of the Participants?

For Aristotle, there is a twofold dynamic involved in any dialectical inquiry. On this view, a thesis is (1) tested by questions designed to refute it, and (2) defended by answering those questions as truthfully as possible.

Some commentators read Aristotle as requiring that questioners test only those theses that are already believed to be false, and that respondents defend only those theses that they already believe to be true. This reading is questionable. In any case, it would seem that dialectic need not be constrained in this fashion. If the dynamic of dialectic is effective, a thesis might be expected to be refuted (or not) regardless of the initial convictions of the participants. There is no particular reason that during a dialectical give-and-take a participant might not surprise himself with an outcome in which a disbeliever becomes a believer, or a believer becomes a disbeliever. Thus the second rule of dialectic is rewritten as follows:

> In a *refutation* respondents must defend a thesis by answering a series of critical queries asked by questioners whose aim it is to refute the thesis. Questioners need not initially disbelieve, nor respondents initially believe, the thesis at hand. In an *instruction argument* a teacher attempts, by question and answer, to teach his pupil some fact, *p*, deducing it from answers that the pupil gives to the teacher's questions. In an *examination argument* two parties seek to determine what follows logically from propositions they jointly hold, or from some proposition they are interested in scrutinizing.

What Kind of Questions Can Be Asked, and How Are They to Be Asked?

Aristotle is quite right to require that questions be intelligible, and quite right to allow the respondent to reject them if they are not. On the other hand, it is not necessary (or desirable) that the dialectician's questions be transparent; they need not clearly indicate the questioner's entire strategy of refutation, instruction, or examination. Clarity is required; naïveté and predictability are not. The third rule, then, is revised as follows:

> The questioner must ask clear and straightforward questions; otherwise the respondent may (and should) refuse to answer them or require that they be clarified.

In What Manner Should the Respondent Make His Responses?

According to Aristotle, the respondent must answer honestly and consistently. That is, he must tell the truth as best he sees it. If the respondent disbelieves the thesis he is defending (as some lawyers do), the honesty of his answers exists in what a *believer* of the thesis would honestly answer. Furthermore, in answering a question, he must not contradict any previous answer. If he does contradict an earlier response, Aristotle requires him to remove the inconsistency before the discussion can continue. He must either change the answer to the current question or he must change an answer previously given.

Here, too, Aristotle is a bit severe. We can think of two quite different ways of handling contradictory answers, either of which may be appropriate in certain circumstances. Perhaps the contradiction concerns an inessential detail and, when confronted with his two conflicting answers, the questioner will not know which reply to stick with. At this point, Aristotle recommends breaking off the dialectical exchange completely. Yet, in these circumstances, it would seem more reasonable that both participants agree to ignore the contradiction. Essentially, the questioner would withdraw both questions. Second, perhaps the contradiction concerns a point of importance, and hence cannot be ignored but, again, perhaps the respondent honestly does not know which of the two conflicting answers to give up. Rather than abandon the discussion, it might be more reasonable to bracket the conflicting answers, to put them "on hold," as it were. The participants may then return to the issue once the discussion has taken on a more substantial shape, and once the participants feel more confident about dealing with the contradiction. When quarantining a contradiction in this way, remember that the dialectic may continue to unfold only if its development does not depend upon a resolution of that contradiction. Thus the fourth rule of dialectic is modified as follows:

> The respondent must reply truthfully and consistently from the point of view of the thesis he is defending or from the point of view of the other propositions he has already admitted. However, if he does contradict an earlier answer, then (1) he must withdraw one of the two answers, or (2) with the consent of the questioner, the contradiction can be ignored as inessential, or (3) again with the consent of the questioner, the contradiction can be quarantined to be returned to later. In this way, the discussion may continue to the extent that it does not depend on a prior resolution of the contradiction.

We may even decide that the present rule could be extended to cover pragmatic inconsistency.[4] If so, dialectical arguments could be used to deal with the circumstantial *ad hominem*, a fallacy that could not be resolved by the quarrel. Given that a participant has been shown, by his opponent's questions, to be caught in a pragmatic inconsistency (i.e., an inconsistency between his present recommendation and some circumstance of his own practice), he might resolve the contradiction by following a variation of (1), namely, by giving up the proposal that "contradicts" his

The Eight Rules of Dialectic

1. *Selecting Participants.* The total number of participants, and the relative numbers on each side of the question, should be small enough and sufficiently balanced that the exchange is manageable and fair, and appropriate to the kind of inquiry at hand (i.e., refutation, instruction, examination, etc.).

2. *Defining a Goal.* In a *refutation* respondents must defend a thesis by answering a series of critical queries asked by questioners whose aim it is to refute the thesis. Questioners need not initially disbelieve, nor respondents initially believe, the thesis at hand. In an *instruction argument* a teacher attempts, by question and answer, to teach his pupil some fact, *p*, deducing it from answers the pupil gives to the teacher's questions. In an *examination argument* two parties seek to determine what follows logically from propositions they jointly hold, or from some proposition they are interested in scrutinizing.

3. *Questioning the Respondent.* The questioner must ask clear and straightforward questions; otherwise the respondent may (and should) refuse to answer them or require that they be clarified.

4. *Responding to the Questioner.* The respondent must reply truthfully and consistently from the point of view of the thesis he is defending or from the point of view of the other propositions he has already admitted. However, if he does contradict an earlier answer, then (1) he must withdraw one of the two answers, or (2) with the consent of the questioner, the contradiction can be ignored as inessential, or (3) again with the consent of the questioner, the contradiction can be quarantined to be returned to later. In this way, the discussion may continue to the extent that it does not depend on a prior resolution of the contradiction.

5. *Dealing with Ignorance.* When his ignorance makes it impossible for a respondent to reply, the questioner should take a leading role in removing that ignorance. He may avail himself of the Socratic technique of question and answer to try to elicit from the respondent a new understanding that will ultimately defeat the respondent's ignorance. If there is reason to think that the questioner would not know the answer to his own question, then it is permissible for the questioner to volunteer to the respondent what he takes to be the correct answer. Then, if the respondent understands what he has been told and genuinely believes that it is a correct answer, he is at liberty to adopt it as his own.

6. *Postponing Answers.* Answers may not be postponed, except for reasonable cause and by mutual consent.

7. *Terminating the Exchange.* In a refutation, the dialectical exchange terminates when the respondent is refuted or when it has become clear to both participants that the questioner will not succeed in his refutation. In an instruction argument, the exchange terminates when the teacher's target proposition has been deduced from the pupil's beliefs and conclusions. In an examination argument, the process terminates on some point of consensus about the issue under examination, or with the parties' agreement to disagree.

8. *Changing Dialectical Roles.* By mutual consent, shifts in dialectical roles between the participants may be allowed.

behaviour, or by following (2) or (3). Thus the participant's recommendation is not necessarily destroyed by a pragmatic contradiction, for the questioner must first give him the option of resolving it.

How Should Dialectic Handle a Respondent's Ignorance?

Sometimes a respondent cannot reply because he simply does not know what answer to give. When this happens Aristotle requires that the questioner take the leading role in overcoming the ignorance that blocks the reply. Aristotle further stipulates that the removal of the respondent's ignorance be restricted to a series of supplementary leading questions, and that these questions be organized into a Socratic form of teaching.

Evidently, Aristotle is trying to avoid (or minimize) the possibility that a respondent will merely accept a questioner's confident assertion concerning the matter about which the respondent is ignorant. Such an assertion, despite the confidence of its advocate, may not be true and, true or not, the respondent's acceptance of it may not be supported by an adequate understanding of the issue. His acceptance may therefore run afoul of the dialectical rule that all answers be given honestly.

Although the Socratic method is one good instrument for replacing ignorance with genuine understanding, it is not the only way of doing so. Aristotle is right to imply that a respondent should not merely take the word of the questioner concerning matters about which he is himself ignorant, but it does not follow that a respondent might not sometimes take a questioner's word at face value. After all, the whole structure of dialectic depends on the integrity and goodwill of the participants.

Aristotle is too skeptical when he assumes that the assertions of a questioner are always to be distrusted—especially when those assertions are designed to help a respondent overcome his ignorance. It is also overskeptical to say that, whenever a respondent accepts the assertion of a questioner in such circumstances, he is always accepting something on blind faith, something he does not understand. We need only consult our own everyday experiences to recognize that this extreme skepticism is out of place in many situations. Accordingly, the fifth rule of dialectic is revised as follows:

> When his ignorance makes it impossible for a respondent to reply, the questioner should take a leading role in removing that ignorance. He may avail himself of the Socratic technique of question and answer to try to elicit from the respondent a new understanding that will ultimately defeat the respondent's ignorance. If there is reason to think that the questioner would not know the answer to his own question, then it is permissible for the questioner to volunteer to the respondent what he takes to be the correct answer. Then, if the respondent understands what he has been told and genuinely believes that it is a correct answer, he is at liberty to adopt it as his own.

May Answers Be Postponed?

Aristotle flatly says no, and we can certainly see why. If an answer can always be postponed, or ducked, then there is no guarantee that the dialectical exchange will ever reach resolution. It becomes possible for the respondent to resort to the simple and dishonest expedient of postponing answers to difficult and probing questions. Even so, it does seem, in certain circumstances and by mutual consent, that answers may be postponed to be dealt with at a later time. Accordingly, the sixth rule of dialectic becomes:

> Answers may not be postponed, except for reasonable cause and by mutual consent.

What Brings Debates to a Close?

On this question, Aristotle would seem to have had the right view of things. Accordingly, the seventh rule of dialectic is this:

> In a refutation, the dialectical exchange terminates when the respondent is refuted or when it has become clear to both participants that the questioner will not succeed in his refutation. In an instruction argument, the exchange terminates when the teacher's target proposition has been deduced from the pupil's beliefs and conclusions. In an examination argument, the process terminates on some point of consensus about the issue under examination, or with the parties' agreement to disagree.

What about other Real-life Complexities?

Even these amended rules of dialectic only partially and somewhat abstractly fit the rich and often complex texture of real-life dialectical inquiry. In many dialectical exchanges, each participant will play the role of both questioner and respondent at various stages of the discussion, and with respect to various points at issue. It is not by any means unusual, say, for Sue to begin as questioner and continue in that capacity for a while, yet for Bill, sooner or later, to say something like, "Now, Sue, let me ask you something. From the tone of your questions up until now, you would seem to believe that so-and-so, but is it not the case that such-and-such?" At this juncture, there has been an exchange of roles. In real-life dialectical situations, a number of difficult questions will no doubt arise. With respect to some of these questions, one participant may feel more confident as questioner. On the face of it, then, there is no good reason that this shifting of confidence should not be reflected in shifts of dialectical initiative and function, at least to a certain extent. However, if such shifts are to be allowed, they should be allowed only by mutual consent. Accordingly, we have an eighth rule of dialectic:

> By mutual consent, shifts in dialectical roles between the participants may be allowed.

We could no doubt offer further rules of dialectical procedure, but the eight rules we have already presented convey a sufficiently developed notion of rational inquiry by cooperative question and answer to serve present purposes. Later we shall expand upon the uses of dialectic and raise still more questions about its logical structure. For the present, though, we can say that the logical description of dialectic is to be found in our eight rules.

Exercise 3.1

1. Select one of the arguments listed in question 1 of exercise 2.3. Then construct an imaginary dialogue between two participants that resolves the point at issue using the rules of dialectic listed above.

3. The Fallacy of Appealing to Ignorance

Dialectic is certainly a benign form of argument and a true friend of reason. Its procedures are designed to promote objectivity and fairness, and its structure allows for a range of outcomes or results that enhance our capacity, however modestly, to get at the truth of things. Here are three sample outcomes:

■ *Refutation in the Strong Sense.* One outcome of a dialectical exchange may be that a given thesis is refuted in what we call the strong sense. To say that a thesis or proposition is refuted *in the strong sense* is to say that it has been shown to be false. In general, if one knows that a given proposition, *p*, is false, one also knows that its opposite, not-*p*, is true. So refutation in the strong sense is one means of discovering truths and advancing knowledge.

■ *Refutation in the Weak Sense.* A thesis is refuted *in the weak sense* when the discussion shows that a respondent has insufficient grounds for holding it. However, it does not follow from the fact that there is not enough evidence to show a thesis to be true that the thesis is false. For all we know, the thesis may still be true; it has simply not been adequately defended. In this kind of situation, we can say that the thesis is refuted only in the sense that its defence has been inadequate. Refutations in the weak sense do not entitle one to claim that the proposition is false or true. Even so, knowing that one's thesis has been refuted in the weak sense is still something worth knowing. One comes to understand that, regardless of whether the thesis is true or false, one's current grounds for holding it are inadequate; therefore, one's claim to know the thesis is incorrect.[5]

■ *Stalemate.* A third possible outcome of a dialectical exchange may be that all participants will concede, sooner or later, that the questioner's critical attack is not going to succeed in refuting the respondent's thesis in either the strong or the weak sense. Given his failure to achieve a refutation, the questioner cannot say that he knows the thesis to be false: nor can he say that he knows the respondent's defence of it is inadequate. At the same time, even though the refutation of this thesis has not succeeded, the respondent is not automatically entitled to assume that his thesis is true, or that his grounds for holding it are entirely adequate. It may be that the thesis is in fact false and that the questioner has simply not been astute enough to penetrate the respondent's defence. Thus it is possible that a false proposition will not be exposed under dialectical examination. Even so, the very fact that a proposition holds up to such examination constitutes some degree of evidence that the proposition has been capably and rationally defended, and that it is likely to be true. Certainly, if a thesis holds up under repeated dialectical examination from all quarters, its truth will appear more and more certain.

We have already made the point that, strictly speaking, all refutations constructed using our eight revised rules are refutations in the *weak* sense. To show that a refuted proposition is also false, it is necessary to construct a supplementary argument, as follows:

There is a refutation of thesis *T*

The premisses of the refutation are not simply conceded by the respondent but are, in addition, true

Therefore, *T* is false.

The *Ad Ignorantiam* Fallacy

An *ad ignorantiam* fallacy occurs whenever a conclusion is drawn, or invited to be drawn, on the basis of an irrelevant appeal to ignorance. (When such an appeal is relevant, the argument is said to be a non-fallacious *ad ignorantiam* argument.) More precisely, the fallacy occurs whenever refutations in the strong sense are confused with refutations in the weak sense. In other words, an *ad ignorantiam* fallacy is an argument of the form, "You are unable to provide a proof of your thesis, *T*; therefore, *T* must be false."

Examples come readily to mind:

A cure for cancer hasn't been found

Therefore, there is no cure for cancer.

The fallacious idea here is that, since a cancer cure is not (yet) known, this alone is sufficient evidence to show that it will never exist. To take another example,

The non-existence of ghosts has not been proved

Therefore, ghosts exist.

As our distinction between refutation in the strong and weak senses shows us, though, ignorance of *p* is, by itself, insufficient for concluding that not-*p*.

Flashback on...
John Locke (1632–1704)

THE SON of a country lawyer, John Locke was born near Bristol, England in the same year as the Dutch philosopher Baruch Spinoza (1632–1671). Locke took his early education at home and later entered Westminster School. After graduating, he entered Oxford in 1652. In 1660 he was appointed lecturer in Greek and subsequently both Reader in Rhetoric and Censor of Moral Philosophy.

While at Oxford, where he was influenced by his friend Robert Boyle, Locke developed a keen interest in the emerging new sciences, especially chemistry and physics. He also studied medicine, taking his degree late (in 1674), owing to the interruption of his academic career nine years earlier when he was appointed secretary to a diplomatic mission at the Elector of Brandenburg. Locke practised medicine sparingly after 1674, having in 1667 caught the eye of the soon-to-be Earl of Shaftesbury. It was thanks to Shaftesbury that he received a series of administrative appointments over many years. Shaftesbury was periodically in the political wilderness, and during these episodes Locke lived in Oxford, France, and Holland. In France he was befriended by the French philosopher Pierre Gassendi, and through Gassendi came to respect the philosophical innovations of Descartes and the Cartesians. With the succession of William of Orange to the English throne

in 1688, Locke returned to his native country and three years later retired. He died in 1704.

Locke's two major works are *An Essay Concerning Human Understanding* and *Two Treatises of Civil Government*. Both were dated 1690, although the *Essay* in fact appeared late in 1689. The *Essay* is an especially important contribution to the empiricist tradition in philosophy. It shares with Francis Bacon and Antoine Arnauld a dissatisfaction with Aristotelian influences on philosophy and anticipates some of John Stuart Mill's later criticisms of Aristotle. Locke's complaints were primarily threefold: that Aristotelian philosophy had become dogmatic and authoritarian; that it could not satisfactorily account for modern science; and that it gave an unrealistic picture of the actual workings of the human intellect.

The *Essay* contains no explicit theory of fallacies, but in three places it deals with issues in ways that encourage plausible conjectures about Locke's thinking on this topic. In chapter 22 of book 4, Locke examines what he calls "wrong assent, or error." Chapter 17 of the same book is given over to a critique of Aristotelian logic, and ends with a brief discussion of *ad hominem*, *ad ignorantiam*, *ad verecundiam*, and *ad judicium* arguments. Finally, chapters 9 to 11 of book 3 deal with the "imperfection and abuse of words." All are worth reading.

Even so, it is sometimes tempting to confuse refutations in the weak sense with refutations in the strong sense. This happens when it seems obvious that the premises of the refutation are, indeed, true and not simply conceded by the respondent.

The modern fallacy of *argumentum ad ignorantiam* bears on this matter. This is the name given to arguments that appeal to (a person's) ignorance. One way of analyzing this fallacy is as a confusion of refutations in the strong sense with refutations in the weak sense. In short, an *ad ignorantiam* argument is one that takes the form

Flashback on…
the *Ad Ignorantiam*

EARLIER we saw that John Locke, in his 1690 book *An Essay Concerning Human Understanding*, spoke of arguments people use "in their reasonings with others … to prevail on their assent; or at least so to awe them, as to silence their opposition."[6] One of these arguments is the *argumentum ad hominem*, which we discussed in the flashback on the *ad hominem* in chapter 1. Another is still known by the name Locke coined for it, the *argumentum ad ignorantiam*. Locke introduces the argument as follows: "Secondly, another way that men ordinarily use to drive others, and force them to submit their judgments, and receive the opinion in debate, is to require the adversary to admit what they allege as a proof, or to assign a better."[7]

We can reconstruct Locke's idea in the following way. Two parties, say Bill and Sue, have been arguing over some proposition, *p*. Bill, let us suppose, is a supporter of *p*, while Sue holds the contrary view. Bill has constructed an argument for *p*; that is to say, he has made a case in support of *p*. It is clear from the circumstances of the case that Sue is still not happy about conceding *p*. Bill now makes an *ad ignorantiam* argument as follows:

> I have made my case for *p*. That is, I have tried to offer some evidence in favour of *p*, but evidently, you are not much moved by my argument. This is fine, as far as it goes, but we are not just fooling around here. I've offered you an argument for *p*, and you still don't concede that *p*. This is not good enough. The "burden of proof," as lawyers call it, has now been shifted to you. This being so, you must "assign a better." That is, you must either demolish my argument or con- struct a more powerful one of your own in support of not-*p*. If you do not discharge this burden, then you have only two rational options: (1) you must yield to my argument and give up your opposition to *p*, or (2) you must be silent on this matter. That is, since you have no answer to make against me, the discussion is over, and we would be well advised to go for a beer.

As with Locke's version of the *ad hominem*, there is no suggestion that he thinks of the *ad ignorantiam* as a fallacy. It is true that, as we have reconstructed it, Bill's *ad ignorantiam* argument is not conclusive. It certainly is not a strict logical consequence of the fact that Bill has made a case for *p* that if Sue does not make a better case (either against Bill's argument for *p* or in favour of not-*p* directly) then she will be required to abandon her opposition to *p* or to be silent on this issue. On the other hand, there is not the slightest reason to think that Locke intended *ad ignorantiam* arguments of this kind to be judged against such very high standards. Rather, the standard he thought appropriate to the *ad ignorantiam* is entirely functional. Does such an argument "prevail on [one's opponents'] assent; or at least so to awe them as to silence their opposition"? It is easy to see that this is often what such arguments succeed in doing, and are right in doing.

In its Lockean form, the *ad ignorantiam* might be summarized as follows: "If you do not know of a better argument, then you have no option but to yield on *p* or, at the very least, to stop speaking against it." It is not the modern and fallacious argument that goes under the same name, "If you do not know a proof against *p*, then *p* must be true."

You, the respondent, are unable to provide a proof of your thesis, *T*

Therefore, your thesis is false.

In other words, because the questioner has found a refutation (in the weak sense) of the respondent's thesis, there is a temptation to assume that the thesis is false.

Even so, there is one type of reasoning for which this analysis is unconvincing. The reasoning in question is sometimes called *autoepistemic reasoning*.[8] A standard form is as follows:

If *p* were the case, I would know that *p*

But I don't know that *p*

Therefore, it is not the case that *p*.

Now suppose we interpret *p* as "I am in the middle of a blizzard." Then our argument becomes

If I am in the middle of a blizzard, then I would know that I am in the middle of a blizzard

But I do not know that I am in the middle of a blizzard

Therefore, it is not the case that I am in the middle of a blizzard.

Now there may be occasions where we will not want to accept this argument; after all, it is possible that I may be in the middle of a blizzard and my physical and mental senses have eroded to such an extent that I am not aware of it. Even so, because these cases are few and far between, the argument remains highly plausible. Thus, as with other arguments such as the *ad baculum*, the *ad hominem*, the *ad populum*, and the *ad misericordiam*, *ad ignorantiam* arguments will sometimes be fallacious and sometimes not.

Exercise 3.2

1. Determine whether each of the following contains an *ad ignorantiam* argument:

    (a) Nobody has ever proved that we have free will. So all our actions have to be determined either by heredity or by the environment.

    (b) Bill can't find the reason his car wouldn't start. So it is likely that the problem has solved itself.

    (c) Bill doesn't know why his car wouldn't

    start. So it is unlikely that he will be able to get to work on time today.

    (d) The conjecture that low-level radiation is linked with cancer and other diseases has never been demonstrated by clear scientific evidence. So low-level radiation must be safe.

    (e) The conjecture that low-level radiation is linked with cancer and other diseases has never been demonstrated by clear scientific evidence. So we just don't know what effects, if any, low-level radiation might have.

(f) The conjecture that low-level radiation is linked with cancer has never been demonstrated by clear scientific evidence. But studies similar to the ones used to look for correlations with cancer have demonstrated clear links to mental illness and birth defects. So we can conclude that low-level radiation doesn't cause cancer.

(g) Despite extensive investigation, no one has been able to come up with a convincing naturalistic explanation of psychic phenomena, including extrasensory perception (ESP). The only alternative left is to conclude that such phenomena have super-natural causes.

(h) "C'mon, spend the night with me."
   "Why should I?"
   "Why shouldn't you?"

(i) To say that punishment does not always cause psychological damage is to evade the issue, for we do not know what reaction the punishment will cause in the individual in later years.

(j) The last time I asked, Sue didn't know what time it was. So I doubt that she knows what time it is now.

2. For each of the arguments listed in question 1 that contains an *ad ignorantiam*, determine whether it involves a fallacy.

4. The Fallacy of Complex Question

Bearing in mind that dialectic is an inquiry generated by a process of question and answer, it should come as no surprise that some of the fallacies to which dialectic falls prey are fallacies dealing with questions. Of these, one of the most interesting is a fallacy known as *complex question*. Simply put, not every question will be appropriate in every set of circumstances. For example, to take a well-known illustration, it is normally unacceptable to ask of an ordinary dog owner whether he has stopped beating his dog. Why? The answer is that the question contains an illicit or unsupported assumption, namely that he has in the past been a dog-beater. The effect of this assumption is that whichever way the respondent replies, yes or no, he appears to have accepted this assumption.

In effect, every question asks the respondent to select from a number of alternative propositions. For example, the question "Is she the ambassador to Australia or is she the ambassador to New Zealand?" invites the respondent to select either the proposition "She is the ambassador to Australia" or the proposition "She is the ambassador to New Zealand." Any such proposition is called a *direct answer*. Any proposition that is implied by all of a question's direct answers is called a *presupposition* of that question.

The Fallacy of Complex Question
The fallacy of *complex question* occurs whenever a question is asked that contains a hidden, illicit, or unsupported assumption. Complex questions, that is, two or more questions rolled into one, are misleading because they can make it difficult for a respondent to counter false or unjustified presuppositions.

In this case, since "She is an ambassador" and "She is the ambassador to Australia or she is the ambassador to New Zealand" are both propositions that are implied by both of this question's direct answers, both of these propositions turn out to be presuppositions of our original question.

Merely asking a question may not at first seem to be harmful, risky, or fallacious. After all, to simply ask a question, we may think, is not to make an assertion. But what if the question has an unjustified presupposition? Such presuppositions can be dangerous. Thus, some questions may not be as innocent as they at first appear; they may provide subtle ways of disguising an aggressive shift in argument, or of shifting the burden of proof.

To sort out the relative riskiness of presuppositions, let us divide propositions into three classes: those that are logically necessary, those that are logically impossible, and those that are logically contingent. *Logically necessary propositions* are those that are necessarily true, or that will be true regardless of how the world might be. (For example, regardless of how the world might be, it will be true that "Either 157 is a prime number or it is not the case that 157 is a prime number.") Similarly, *logically impossible propositions* are those that are necessarily false, or that will be false regardless of how the world might be. (For example, regardless of how the world might be, it will be false that "157 is a prime number and it is not the case that 157 is a prime number.") Finally, *logically contingent propositions* are those that are neither necessarily true nor necessarily false. (For example, "Bob believes that 157 is a prime number" will be true under some circumstances, but not others.)

Logically Necessary, Impossible, and Contingent Propositions

A proposition is *logically necessary* (or a *logical truth*) provided that it is true regardless of how the world might be; it is *logically impossible* (or a *logical falsehood*) provided that it is false regardless of how the world might be; and it is *logically contingent* provided that it is neither logically necessary nor logically impossible.

It turns out that a question will be *safe* only so long as all of its presuppositions are logically necessary; it is called *risky* if it is not safe. In other words, so long as none of a question's presuppositions have the potential to be false, we know that the question itself cannot mislead us. Thus the question "Is she the ambassador to Australia or is she the ambassador to New Zealand?" will be risky since some of its presuppositions (for example, that she is in fact an ambassador) are not necessarily true.

In contrast, the question "Is she the ambassador to Australia or not?" will be safe since the only presuppositions that this question has are logically necessary. To see this, recall that in order to be a presupposition of this question, a proposition must be implied by all of this question's direct answers. Since the only two direct answers to this question are "Yes, she is the ambassador to Australia" and "No, it is not the case that she is the ambassador to Australia," it turns out that all of the presuppositions of this question will be necessary truths, for example, "She is the ambassador to Australia or it is not the case that she is the ambassador to Australia." Should we require it, we can also introduce a category of questions that we might call *moderately safe*. These will be questions all of whose presuppositions are true, rather than necessarily true.

The advantage of safe questions, of course, is that they are guaranteed not to contain any illicit or unjustified assumptions, and the disadvantage of risky questions is that they may contain assumptions that are unjustified, or that disguise the fact that the respondent is being given only a very narrow range of direct answers to consider. In any case where the range of alternatives under consideration is in fact too narrow, we will have found an example of the fallacy of complex question.[9]

Questions that can be answered either yes or no are often safe because their main presupposition typically consists of a disjunction of contradictory alternatives. For example, the only two direct answers to the question "Does God exist?" are "Yes, God exists" and "No, God does not exist." Thus, the only presuppositions of this question will be necessary truths such as "Either God exists or God does not exist."

Even so, not all yes–no questions are safe. The question, "Is God omnipotent?," for example, will have as one of its presuppositions the proposition "God is omnipotent or God is not omnipotent." Yet this presupposition is not accepted by many as being logically necessary. After all, not everyone believes in the existence of God and this is something that is presupposed by both answers. One way of avoiding this conclusion is to understand our original question as asking, "Is God omnipotent or is it not the case that God is omnipotent?," rather than "Is God omnipotent or is God not omnipotent?" If so, then the question will not presuppose the existence of God, since one way that the answer "No, it is not the case that God is omnipotent" will be true is if God does not exist. Thus, this question's only presuppositions will be necessarily true propositions such as "Either God is omnipotent or it is not the case that God is omnipotent." If it turns out that all yes–no questions are best understood in this way, then they will be safe. If not, then although many yes–no questions will be safe, many others will not be.

Let us now return to the example with which we began: "Have you stopped beating your dog?" This question appears in a yes–no form and therefore may fool us into thinking that it should be safe. In fact, it has an important contingent presupposition. The two direct answers, "Yes, I have stopped beating my dog," and "No, I haven't stopped beating my dog" both imply that "In the past I have beaten my dog." Since this is a contingent claim, it turns out that the question is risky. The fallacy arises since what appears to be a genuine choice of alternatives is, in reality, too limited. No matter which alternative the respondent chooses, he is committed to the same unwelcome implication. If the presupposition is false, it will be impossible to give a true direct answer to the question. Thus the only sensible thing to do is to correct the question by pointing out the falsity of this presupposition.

Of course, not all questions that have substantive presuppositions need be fallacious. "Is she the ambassador to Australia or is she the ambassador to New Zealand?" is not likely to be fallacious because its presupposition is not deeply concealed and so is not likely to fool anyone. Even so, asking someone whether he is still a dog-beater or whether he has recovered from his cocaine addiction is less than fair. Even if it might be true that your opponent has a dog that he may have beaten, putting the

A Dissenting Analysis of Complex Question

In this chapter we have been giving what might be called the "standard analysis" of the fallacy of complex question. However, there is reason to think that this analysis is, in some respects, unsatisfactory. To see this, let us return to the dog-beating example. In this example, the respondent must give a yes or no answer to the question, "Have you stopped beating your dog?"

According to the standard analysis, this question contains a false presupposition, namely that the person to whom the question is directed has, in the past, been a dog-beater. On the modern analysis, the effect of this assumption is that, whichever way the respondent replies, he appears to have accepted this assumption.

Is there anything wrong with this analysis? According to some, the analysis goes wrong when it mistakenly assumes that a no answer commits the respondent to accepting the question's presupposition. After all, "Have you stopped beating your dog?" is conceded by all concerned to be a complex question—two (or more) questions rolled into one. But if so, we might conclude, answering no to this one question is in effect to answer no to the entire complex of questions. Thus, if "Have you stopped beating your dog?" is really equivalent to "Do you have a dog you have beaten and, if you have a dog you have beaten, have you stopped beating him?," then answering no is really a way of saying no to both questions. If so, then one natural way to understand a negative answer is that it denies the hidden presupposition, namely that you have a dog you have beaten.

If this analysis is correct, the only fallacy that occurs here is that of a person who defends the standard analysis, for in doing so he fails to see that a "no" answer will do the respondent no dialectical harm whatsoever.

question in such an aggressive way makes him sound defensive; and the more defensive he sounds, the less we will grant him the presumption of moral normalcy.

Dialectic provides a solution to this type of complex question. A participant who is confronted with a question from his opponent is allowed to ask that the question be reformulated if it contains a presupposition that the respondent does not accept or that is unwelcome to him. The respondent may also ask that the question be divided into smaller units, so that he can respond to each separately. Thus, the proper response to the dog-beating question is for the respondent to request that it be broken down into two questions: "Do you have a dog you have beaten?" and "If you have a dog you have beaten, have you stopped beating him?" To say no to the first question is to excuse the respondent from responding to the second, and that puts an end to the inquiry. In contrast, to attempt to hide an illicit or unjustified presumption, or to attempt to force someone to answer a question without being able to respond to each presupposition separately, is to commit the fallacy of complex question.

Exercise 3.3

1. For each of the following questions, list all of its direct answers:

   (a) Are you a pacifist?

   (b) Are you a pacifist or not?

   (c) Are you a pacifist or a loyalist?

   (d) Are you a pacifist or a non-pacifist war-monger?

   (e) Are you a pacifist or, if not, then a war-monger?

2. For each of the following propositions, determine whether it is logically necessary, logically impossible, or logically contingent:

   (a) Socrates died by drinking hemlock.

   (b) Either Socrates died in battle or he died by drinking hemlock.

   (c) It is true both that Socrates died by drinking hemlock and that it is not the case that he died by drinking hemlock.

   (d) Socrates died in Sparta.

   (e) Either Socrates died by drinking hemlock, or it is not the case that he died this way.

   (f) Something exists.

   (g) Something both exists and does not exist.

   (h) Something exists and nothing exists.

   (i) Nothing exists or something exists.

   (j) Socrates exists.

3. Aside from the contingent matter of your existence, determine whether each of the questions listed in question 1 above is safe or risky. If it is risky, list at least one of its contingent (or impossible) presuppositions.

4. What, if anything, is risky about each of the following questions?

   (a) Are you still a heavy drinker?

   (b) What did you use to wipe your fingerprints from the gun?

   (c) Do you feel guilty when you are involved in your criminal activities?

   (d) Don't you feel we should either get out of this foreign entanglement or show some military muscle and smash the guerrilla hideouts with tactical nuclear weapons?

   (e) Do you jog or are you sedentary?

   (f) Where is your car?

   (g) Have you exhibited questionable judgment and unstable behaviour in the past, or are these cognitive shortcomings part of a recent pattern of deterioration?

   (h) If ethics is not a science and is therefore purely subjective, why do you try to defend your guilty behaviour when you know that you are being completely illogical?

   (i) How can you explain the amazing success of astrological predictions in the past?

   (j) Does God exist?

Summary

Rarely will a real-life argument—one in which there is a serious exchange of contending views—conform to just one of the models of argument that we have been studying. If you pay careful attention to the logical structure of a real-life argument you will see that at various stages various models tend to predominate. An argument might begin as a case of dialectic at its best. Yet, after an hour, it may take on more of the flavour of a skilled but polite debate; after another hour, it might degenerate into a loud quarrel. When you are engaged in an argument, you should always be alert to the possibility of an unannounced shift from an argument of one type to an argument of another. Plainly, if I do not detect that you have abandoned the dialectical model for the debating model, I could easily cease to be an effective opponent for you, and I might end up making concessions that would not otherwise be appropriate.

Because dialectic can at times include quite personal elements, some logicians are inclined to think of it as a defective kind of argumentation. We do not entirely share this view. Instead, we assume that dialectic provides a more general and at the same time more practical standard of what constitutes good argument. Because its procedures are designed to be fair and objective, dialectic aims to improve our understanding, eliminate error, and pursue truth.

Even so, like all arguments, dialectical arguments are susceptible to their own fair share of fallacies. Among these are the fallacies of *ad ignorantiam* and complex question. An *ad ignorantiam* fallacy occurs whenever a conclusion is drawn, or invited to be drawn, on the basis of an irrelevant appeal to ignorance. More precisely, it occurs whenever refutations in the strong sense are confused with refutations in the weak sense.

The fallacy of *complex question* occurs whenever a question is asked that contains a hidden, illicit, or unsupported assumption. Complex questions (i.e., two or more questions rolled into one) are misleading because they can make it difficult for a respondent to counter false or unjustified presuppositions.

Despite such fallacies, dialectic is valuable because it provides an extremely practical model of real-life reasoning. Dialectic empowers all parties to press their opponents in ways that require them to defend their theses in unexpected ways. In addition, it has a flexibility that enables participants to stick to what is relevant and to pursue what is likely to be helpful. The result is that dialectical arguments have the capacity to grow and to shape themselves in ways that skillfully put to the test the objects of their investigation.

Weblinks

Episteme Links—Aristotle
   www.epistemelinks.com/Pers/ArisPers.htm
Perseus Project
   www.perseus.tufts.edu/
Episteme Links—John Locke
   www.epistemelinks.com/Pers/LockPers.htm
Garth Kemerling's Philosophy Pages—John Locke
   people.delphi.com/gkemerling/ph/lock.htm

Notes

1. Aristotle, *Topics*, bk. 8; see also C.L. Hamblin, *Fallacies* (London: Methuen Co. Ltd., 1970), 61–62.

2. For a famous example of an instruction argument, see the story of how an uneducated slave boy learns to do geometry simply by answering a series of questions put to him by Socrates in Plato's *Meno*, 81e–85c.

3. Remember poor Clinias in the passage quoted from Plato's *Euthydemus* in ch. 2.

4. Remember, an action, *A*, of a person, *S*, is pragmatically inconsistent with what *S* himself proposes if and only if, were *S*'s proposal a command, his action would be an act of self-disobedience.

5. As we saw in the flashback on the *ad hominem* in ch. 1, Aristotelian refutations are refutations in the weak sense.

6. John Locke, *An Essay Concerning Human Understanding*, bk. 4, ch. 17, §19.

7. Ibid., §20.

8. The word *autoepistemic* derives from the Greek words for "self" and "knowledge."

9. This analysis shows why the fallacy is also sometimes called the *black-and-white fallacy*. For an interesting discussion of the widespread susceptibility of historical writings to this fallacy, see David Hackett Fischer, *Historians' Fallacies* (New York and Evanston: Harper & Row, 1970).

CHAPTER 4

Deductive Logic

WE BEGAN this book by noting that in order to learn what it means to reason well we need to study arguments in both the broad and the narrow sense. Having spent three chapters looking at arguments in the broad sense, it is now time to turn our attention to arguments in the narrow sense, and to logic. In this chapter, we will outline one way of studying arguments in the narrow sense, namely standard—or so-called "classical"—propositional logic.

1. Entailment

As we have already noted, arguments in the broad sense are dynamic, social activities between human beings, activities that take place in a variety of contexts. At the same time, arguments can also be viewed more narrowly as simply premisses and conclusions together with a consequence relation. Once we have good reasons for accepting the premisses of an argument, the only question remaining is whether the relationship between the premisses and conclusion is sufficiently strong. In other words, do the premisses support the conclusion? Do they provide sufficient evidence for what is being claimed? And is the inference from premisses to conclusion rationally warranted or justified?

Taken in this more narrow sense, arguments need not involve any type of exchange between persons; they may simply be written down on a blackboard, or on the back of an envelope, or in a book. In this section we will be occupied primarily with arguments in this more narrow sense. Specifically, we will be looking for the presence or absence of one type of consequence relation, a relation that logicians call *entailment*. When a set of premisses entails a conclusion, this means that the conclusion conclusively follows from the premisses.

Entailment

Entailment is one specific type of consequence relation, defined as follows: A set of premisses is said to *entail* a conclusion if and only if the conclusion *conclusively follows from* the premisses.

What exactly is entailment? What exactly does it mean to say that a conclusion *conclusively follows from* a set of premisses? Among other things, it means that arguments or inferences in which the conclusion is entailed by the premisses will be *truth-preserving*. In other words, if we begin with a set of true premisses, and if a conclusion is entailed by the premisses, it follows that the conclusion will be true as well. This property is so important that it is given the special name *validity*.

What is the relationship between validity and entailment? One suggestion is that they are identical, that validity is all there is to entailment. If this is correct, then an argument's premises will entail its conclusion if and only if the argument is valid. If this is correct, then the idea that a proposition "conclusively follows from" a given set of premises will be explained solely in terms of validity. If so, given two propositions, p and q, and assuming that p is true, p will entail q whenever q must also, of necessity, be true. In such a case, we say that the argument or inference from p to q is valid, or deductively valid, or that q is deducible from p, or that there is a deduction from p to q. *Deductive logic* is the branch of logic that studies validity.

> **Validity**
>
> An argument or inference is *valid* if and only if it is not possible for the premises to be (jointly) true and, at the same time, the conclusion to be false.

For example, let p be the proposition "Bill has three brothers," and q be the proposition "Bill has (at least) three siblings." Here the first proposition, p, entails the second proposition, q, because it is not possible that "Bill has three brothers" could be true while "Bill has (at least) three siblings" is false. It is easy to see that deductive arguments will often be objects of study in disciplines such as mathematics, where the notion of entailment is clearly involved with the notion of exact proof. It is partly in order to test the hypothesis that validity and entailment are identical concepts—and partly because validity is an interesting property in its own right—that we are going to begin investigating the notion of validity in this chapter.

At this point it is worth emphasizing that in order to study the property of validity (or alternatively, the relation of entailment) we need not concern ourselves with whether an argument's premises and conclusion are *in fact* true. Instead the emphasis is entirely on the question of the *relationship* between an argument's premises and conclusion: if we *assume* that the premises are true, is it, or is it not, the case that the conclusion must, as a matter of logical necessity, also be true? If so, then the argument is valid regardless of the actual truth or falsity of the premises and conclusion.

What is the relationship between *valid* arguments and *good* arguments? Obviously they are not identical, since an argument can be valid even if its premises are false, or even preposterous. In other words, an argument can be deductively valid, but nevertheless remain a bad argument. Here is an example:

All dogs are birds
All birds are mammals
_____

Therefore, all dogs are mammals.

Of course, in this argument we have reason to doubt the truth of the premises. So this argument clearly is not a good one. Even so, it remains the case that *if* the premises had been true, the conclusion would have to be true as well. So the argument is good in just this limited sense: it has one feature that is characteristic of good arguments more generally, namely a strong consequence relation. However, this feature alone is not sufficient for characterizing all that is good about good arguments. In order to emphasize this point, we will say that an argument is *sound* if and only if it is valid *and* it has true premisses. Sound arguments thus appear to be one species of good arguments. In a sound argument, not only are the premisses *likely* to be true, they *are* true; and not only is the consequence relation *strong*, it is *fully* truth-preserving.

Put in other words, validity is merely one feature of a sound argument, and it is a conditional feature at that. If an argument is valid, and if the premisses are true, then the conclusion must also be true; but this does not mean that it is necessary for the premisses all to be true (or even for any of them to be true) whenever an argument is valid. When studying validity we are studying only the *relation* between the premisses and the conclusion. Thus, to say that a deduction is valid is not to say that the argument is in all respects acceptable. Rather, it is to say only that the argument is acceptable in just this one, limited respect: if it turns out that the premisses are true, then it follows that the conclusion will be true as well.

To explain this in yet other words, recall that in chapter 3 we defined *logically necessary* propositions to be those propositions that are necessarily true, or that will be true regardless of how the world might be organized. Similarly, *logically impossible* propositions were defined to be those propositions that are necessarily false, or that will be false regardless of how the world might be organized, and *logically contingent* propositions were defined to be those propositions that are neither logically necessary nor logically impossible. To say that an argument from *p* to *q* is valid is thus to say that it is *logically impossible* for *p* to be true and *q* to be false. For example, if "Bill has three brothers" validly implies "Bill has (at least) three siblings," then it is logically impossible for Bill to have three brothers and not to have (at least) three siblings.

One further way to characterize logical impossibility (or inconsistency) is to contrast it with two similar but distinct concepts: *physical impossibility* and mere *improbability*. Again, let's take Bill as an example. We might say that it is improbable that Bill can run a kilometre in eight minutes. If we found out that Bill was a hundred years old and had arthritis, we might even say that it is physically impossible for Bill to run a kilometre this quickly. Despite this, it remains logically possible for Bill to run a kilometre in eight minutes. In other words, it is not self-contradictory or logically inconsistent for Bill to run a kilometre in this time. The proposition, "Bill, who is a hundred years old and has arthritis, just ran an eight-minute kilometre" may be improbable. If it is inconsistent with the laws of nature, it will even turn out to be physically impossible. But unless it is also inconsistent with the laws of logic it is not logically impossible.

In contrast, here is a logically impossible proposition: "Bill is both taller than, and shorter than, Sue." Taken literally, and not as a figurative expression or a joke, this utterance expresses a logically impossible proposition. To say that Bill is simultaneously taller and shorter than Sue is flatly inconsistent. It is in just this sense that we also say that if an argument from *p* to *q* is valid, then it is logically impossible for *p* to be true and, at the same time, for *q* to be false.

Exercise 4.1

1. Which of the following arguments are valid? Assuming that Fido is in fact a dog, which are sound?

   (a) All dogs are mammals and Fido is a dog. So Fido is a mammal.

   (b) All dogs are mammals and Fido is not a dog. So Fido is not a mammal.

   (c) All dogs are birds and all birds are mammals. So, since Fido is a dog, he is a mammal too.

   (d) Either Fido is a bird or a dog. He is definitely not a bird, so he must be a dog.

   (e) All dogs are mammals. So no birds are mammals.

2. Give an example of a valid argument with false premises and a false conclusion, or else explain why this is impossible.

3. Give an example of a valid argument with false premises and a true conclusion, or else explain why this is impossible.

4. Give an example of a sound argument that is not valid, or else explain why this is impossible.

5. Give an example of a sound argument with a false conclusion, or else explain why this is impossible.

6. Which of the following assertions involve logical impossibilities? Which involve physical impossibilities? Which involve mere improbabilities?

   (a) Bill is seven years younger than his own younger (biological) brother.

   (b) Bill is seven hundred years older than his own younger (biological) brother.

   (c) Bill is the same age as his five (biological) brothers.

   (d) Bill believes both that Sue is and is not younger than he is.

   (e) Bill both is and is not younger than Sue.

   (f) Sue drew a square circle.

   (g) Sue calculated pi by hand to the 100,000th decimal place.

   (h) Sue travelled faster than the speed of light.

   (i) Sue is married to a twelve-year-old boy.

   (j) Sue is married to a bachelor.

2. Conjunction, Disjunction, and Negation

In order to help us understand validity more fully, we now turn our attention to elementary, classical deductive logic. "Classical logic" in this sense should not be confused with the main logic of classical antiquity, namely Aristotle's logic of the syllogism. Rather, it is a branch of modern logic that takes its name from the several underlying assumptions it shares with Aristotle's logic. Modern classical logic takes as its basis what is called *propositional* (or *truth-functional*) logic. The structure of propositional logic, in turn, is determined in large measure by a series of logical constants called *propositional connectives.*[1] Propositional connectives, as their name suggests, typically join (or connect) propositions together in order to form larger propositions. A proposition that contains no connectives is said to be *atomic.* A proposition that contains one or more connectives is said to be *molecular* or *compound.* Examples of natural language connectives include English words such as "and" and "or." Given two atomic propositions, say, "Socrates is Greek" and "Socrates lives in Athens," and given the connectives "and" and "or," we can construct new propositions such as "Socrates is Greek and Socrates lives in Athens" and "Socrates is Greek or Socrates lives in Athens."

Connectives

Propositional connectives are words or phrases such as "... and ___," "... or ___," "if ... then ___," and "... because ___" which, together with one or more propositions, can be used to create new propositions. A proposition that contains no connectives is said to be *atomic.* A proposition that contains one or more connectives is said to be *molecular* or *compound.*

In propositional logic, the three most elementary connectives are ∧ (which is used to abbreviate one use of the word "and"), ∨ (which is used to abbreviate one use of the word "or"), and ~ (which is used to abbreviate the phrase "it is not the case that"). Propositional logic also introduces two kinds of letters to stand for propositions. The letters A, B, C, ..., are called *propositional constants* and are used to stand for specific propositions. Hence they are themselves true or false. In contrast, the letters p, q, r, ..., are called *propositional variables* and are used to stand for arbitrary propositions.[2] Because these letters do not have fixed meanings, they are neither true nor false. (This distinction between variables and constants should be a familiar one. In algebra, for example, the distinction is made between the variables $x, y, z, $ ... and the constants 1, 2, 3, ... Thus a statement such as $5 + 7 = 12$ will be true or false; in contrast $x + y = z$ will be neither true nor false.) We should note, however, that once a variable has been used to represent some (arbitrary) proposition in an argument, it cannot be used to represent a different proposition later within that same argument.

Because propositional constants are either true or false, expressions composed of propositional constants together with the connectives (for example, $A ∧ B$, or $A ∨ B$) are themselves propositions and will also be either true or false. In contrast, expressions composed of propositional variables together with connectives (for example, $p ∧ q$, or $p ∨ q$) are known as *propositional forms* and are neither true nor false.[3]

It is important to note that each of the connectives ∧, ∨, and ~ is *truth-functional.* By this we mean that the truth value of any compound proposition using these connectives, no matter how large, is always determined once the truth values of all its component propositions are fixed. In mathematics, a function is something that yields a definite output for any definite input. For example, n^2 is a function because, for any number we substitute for n (say, 3), we obtain a definite number determined by that function (in this case, 9). Much the same will be true for our truth-functional connectives. Once we substitute, say, the true propositions A and B for p and q in the propositional form $p ∨ q$, the resulting new proposition, $A ∨ B$, is also determined to be true. In other words, just as with mathematical functions, given fixed inputs a truth-functional connective will always yield a fixed (or determined) output.

The meanings of our three connectives are now easy to stipulate. The *conjunction* of p with q, written p ∧ q (and read "p and q") is true whenever p and q are both true. If either of its two conjuncts is false, the whole proposition, p ∧ q, is false. The *disjunction* of p with q, written p ∨ q (and read "p or q") is true whenever at least one of p or q is true. It is only false if both p and q are false. Finally, the *negation* of p, written ~p (and read "not-p") is true whenever p is false, and false whenever p is true. That is, ~p always has the opposite truth value to that of p.

> **Truth-functional Connectives**
> A *truth-functional connective* is any connective for which the truth values of its resulting molecular propositions are determined solely by the meaning of the connective together with the truth values of its component propositions.

> ## Conjunction, Disjunction, Negation
>
> - A *conjunction* (∧) is true when, and only when, both of its conjuncts are true.
> - A *disjunction* (∨) is true when, and only when, at least one of its disjuncts is true.
> - A *negation* (~) always has the opposite truth value to that of the proposition negated.

Letting "T" stand for truth and "F" for falsehood, this information can be summed up in the following three truth tables:

Conjunction			Disjunction			Negation	
p	*q*	*p* ∧ *q*	*p*	*q*	*p* ∨ *q*	*p*	~*p*
T	T	T	T	T	T	T	F
T	F	F	T	F	T	F	T
F	T	F	F	T	T		
F	F	F	F	F	F		

To see how truth functions work in practice, it is first helpful to see how these connectives, together with parentheses, can be used to make molecular propositions out of atomic ones. For example, suppose that we want to use disjunction and conjunction to construct a new expression of the form "p and q, or r." As a first attempt, we might construct (p ∧ q ∨ r). However, as it stands, this propositional form is ambiguous: it might mean (p ∧ q) ∨ r, or it might mean p ∧ (q ∨ r). This ambiguity is a problem because these two expressions will have different truth values—and hence different meanings—depending on the truth values of their component atomic propositions.

To see this, we shall construct the truth tables for both (p ∧ q) ∨ r and p ∧ (q ∨ r). Because there are three variables involved, it turns out that there will be exactly 2^3 (or eight) possible assignments of truth values to these propositional forms. (In general, where n is the number of distinct variables, the number of possible truth-value assignments can always be expressed as 2^n.) Wishing to consider each of these possibilities, we list them all in a table as follows:

		p	q	r
(1)		T	T	T
(2)		T	T	F
(3)		T	F	T
(4)		T	F	F
(5)		F	T	T
(6)		F	T	F
(7)		F	F	T
(8)		F	F	F

Here we have alternated truth values under the rightmost of our three variables, *r*. Then we have alternated pairs of truth values, quadruples of truth values, and so on, as necessary, in succeeding columns as we moved left, doubling the number of T's and F's each time. If you check, you will see that the completed table represents all possible combinations of truth values.

Next, we recall the truth-table definition for $\wedge$ and use it to discover the values for $p \wedge q$ in each of our eight rows as follows:

	p	q	r	p ∧ q
(1)	T	T	T	T
(2)	T	T	F	T
(3)	T	F	T	F
(4)	T	F	F	F
(5)	F	T	T	F
(6)	F	T	F	F
(7)	F	F	T	F
(8)	F	F	F	F

It turns out that $p \wedge q$ is true only in rows (1) and (2), because in only those rows are both its component propositions (*p*, *q*) true. Next we recall our truth-table definition for $\vee$ and use it to discover, first, the truth values for ($q \vee r$), and then the truth values for our two propositional forms ($p \wedge q$) $\vee r$ and $p \wedge (q \vee r)$:

	p	q	r	p ∧ q	q ∨ r	(p ∧ q) ∨ r	p ∧ (q ∨ r)
(1)	T	T	T	T	T	T	T
(2)	T	T	F	T	T	T	T
(3)	T	F	T	F	T	T	T
(4)	T	F	F	F	F	F	F
(5)	F	T	T	F	T	T	F
(6)	F	T	F	F	T	F	F
(7)	F	F	T	F	T	T	F
(8)	F	F	F	F	F	F	F

Truth-functional Connectives and Circuit Design

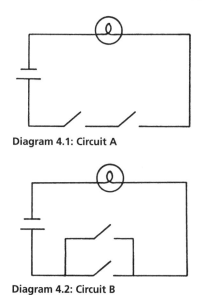

Diagram 4.1: Circuit A

Diagram 4.2: Circuit B

Truth-functional connectives turn out to be useful for representing not only parts of natural language, but other structures as well. For example, consider diagrams 4.1 and 4.2.

In circuit A, the light goes on whenever both switches are closed. That is, just as a conjunction will be false whenever either (or both) of its two conjuncts is false, the light will be off whenever either (or both) of these two switches are open. In circuit B, the light will be off whenever both switches are open. That is, just as a disjunction will be true whenever at least one of its two disjuncts is true, the light will be on whenever at least one of these two switches is closed. In A, both switches must be closed to turn the light on, just as both conjuncts must be true in order to make a conjunction true. In B, only one switch needs to be closed to turn the light on, just as only one disjunct needs to be true in order to make a disjunction true. In other words, circuit A, where the switches are in a row, behaves conjunctively; circuit B, where the switches are in parallel, behaves disjunctively.

The first of our two original expressions turns out to be false only in rows (4), (6), and (8), because—remembering that "or" is false only if both its components are false—only in those rows are both $p \land q$ and r false. By a similar procedure, we see that the second of our two original expressions, $p \land (q \lor r)$, is true in only the first three rows, because in only those rows are p and $q \lor r$ both true.

By inspection, we can now determine that our two initial expressions, $(p \land q) \lor r$ and $p \land (q \lor r)$, have different columns of truth values associated with them. (In rows (5) and (7), we note that $(p \land q) \lor r$ is true while $p \land (q \lor r)$ is false.) As a result, we see that the positioning of the parentheses makes a crucial difference for a proposition's truth or falsity. In other words, it turns out that if we are to formalize our original expression "p and q, or r" in an exact and unambiguous way, we must use parentheses—or some other similar device—to remove ambiguities that could make a difference between the truth and falsity of a proposition, or between the validity or invalidity of an argument.

At this point it is worth noting that, unlike the connectives we have been considering so far, some words that connect propositions are not truth-functional. For example, even though it is a connective, the word "because" is not a truth-functional connective. In other words, the truth value of a compound proposition such as "Bill died because he ate bad sushi" is not determined solely by the truth values of the components "Bill died" and "Bill ate bad sushi." For example, even if we know that both component propositions are true, this is not enough to tell us whether the compound proposition is true. In other words, this is not enough to tell us whether Bill's death was the result of his eating bad sushi.

Are the English expressions "and", "or", and "not" equivalent to the truth-functional connectives "∧", "∨", and "~"? In other words, are they fully truth-functional? The English expression "it is not the case that" certainly appears to be truth-functional. Applying this expression to any English proposition results in a proposition with the opposite truth value. Thus the expression "it is not the case that" (or "not-" for short) and the connective "~" certainly appear to express the same truth function.

It also seems reasonable to expect that "and" and "∧" are equivalent. After all, any proposition formed by joining two true propositions by means of "and" will be true, and if either or both of the original propositions are false, then their conjunction will be false as well. But consider the two true propositions "Bill punched Hank" and "Hank bled profusely." If both of these propositions are true, we may conclude that "Bill punched Hank and Hank bled profusely" will also be true. Alternatively, we may not want to conclude that it is true unless we also know that it was Bill's punching Hank that caused Hank to bleed profusely. In other words, "and" appears sometimes to be used to mean "∧" and sometimes to mean "and then." Thus, in some circumstances, we cannot confidently claim that "and" and "∧" express the same connective. The conclusion we draw is that the natural language term "and" is itself ambiguous, sometimes meaning ∧ and sometimes meaning *and then*.[4]

It is much the same with "or" and "∨". In classical logic, the connective ∨ is such that the disjunction of any two false formulas is false; otherwise it is true. What of its counterpart expression in English? In general, it seems correct to say that whenever you have two propositions, at least one of which is true, then their disjunction by means of "or" will also be true. But consider the following potential counter-example: Assume that it is true, say, that I am going to Tahiti next December. Does it follow that I am going to Tahiti next December or that I am going to Switzerland next October? To the extent that we find this inference doubtful—for example, because it need not follow that there is any connection between a trip to Tahiti and a trip to Switzerland— we may also conclude that there is some reason to doubt that "or" and "∨" express the same connective.[5] Once again, a reasonable conclusion to draw is that the natural language expression "or" is ambiguous, sometimes having the same meaning as "∨", but sometimes not.

This point can be further emphasized by noting that sometimes "or" is not used to mean "either p or q, or both," but rather "either p or q, but not both." For example, if I say, "This number is either even or odd," the "or" here is presumably meant in what is called the *exclusive* sense, the sense of "either p or q but not both." In contrast, if I say, "A sore throat or sneezing is symptomatic of a cold," we may presume that I am using "or" in what is called the *inclusive* sense, the sense of "either p or q or both." The truth table for the exclusive "or" is similar to that for the inclusive "or" defined above, except that the row in which p and q are both true is excluded from being true. Should there be the need, we can define a new connective, $\underline{\vee}$, to represent the exclusive sense of "or" (called *exclusive disjunction*, or *partition*) as follows:

Exclusive Disjunction

p	q	p $\veebar$ q
T	T	F
T	F	T
F	T	T
F	F	F

Even so, it is worth noting that when logicians talk about disjunction, they are almost always referring to the inclusive sense represented by "∨". The reason is that almost all uses of the natural language term "or" are best captured by "∨". In addition, on those rare occasions when we need to express an exclusive "or", we can do so by defining $p \veebar q$ as $(p \vee q) \wedge \sim(p \wedge q)$. These two expressions can be proved to be equivalent by constructing their truth tables and seeing that, for identical inputs, these two functions yield identical outputs.

To sum up, not only do truth-functional connectives such as ∧, ∨, and ~ allow us to express many propositions clearly and unambiguously, they also give us a precise way of calculating the truth values of molecular propositions once the truth values of their atomic components have been determined. For example, given the molecular proposition $\sim(p \vee q) \wedge (\sim p \vee q)$, and given that p is true and q is false, we can easily calculate the resulting truth value. We do so by systematically proceeding from the innermost components to the proposition as a whole. For example, because p is true and q is false, we know that $(p \vee q)$ must be true. Thus $\sim(p \vee q)$ is false; and because we know that p is true, we also know that $\sim p$ is false. Hence $\sim p \vee q$ is also false. We now know that both conjuncts of the original proposition are false; hence the whole proposition itself must be false. In this general way the truth value of any molecular proposition containing these connectives may be calculated.

> **Disjunction Again**
> • An *inclusive disjunction* (∨) is true when, and only when, at least one of its disjuncts is true.
> • An *exclusive disjunction* (∨̲) is true when, and only when, exactly one of its disjuncts is true.

Exercise 4.2

1. Where P is true, Q is false, and R is true, determine the truth values of each of the following propositions:

   (a) $Q \wedge \sim P$

   (b) $P \wedge \sim P$

   (c) $Q \wedge \sim Q$

   (d) $P \vee (Q \vee P)$

   (e) $P \veebar (Q \veebar P)$

   (f) $\sim \sim P \vee (Q \vee R)$

   (g) $\sim \sim P \veebar (Q \veebar R)$

   (h) $(P \vee (Q \vee P)) \vee (R \wedge \sim P)$

   (i) $\sim(P \vee Q) \wedge \sim(\sim Q \vee \sim R)$

   (j) $(Q \wedge \sim P) \vee (P \wedge Q)$

2. Using truth tables, show whether $\sim(p \wedge q)$, which can be read as "not both p and q," and $\sim p \vee \sim q$, which can be read as "not-p or not-q," express the same truth function.

3. Construct a truth function containing only ~ and ∨ that is equivalent to ∧. Use truth tables to prove that the two functions are equivalent.

3. Conditionals and Biconditionals

In addition to the four truth-functional connectives we have considered so far—
negation, conjunction, and inclusive and exclusive disjunction—there are several
others worth considering. Among these are the connectives for both the *material
conditional* and the *material biconditional*.

   A *conditional* is a proposition of the form "If *p*, then *q*," where the part after the
if (the *p*, in this case) is called the *antecedent* (or *assumption*) and the part after the *then*
(the *q*, in this case) is called the *consequent* (or *consequence*). Because both *p* (the
antecedent) and *q* (the consequent) represent propositions, "If … then ___" is clearly
a connective, but is it a truth-functional connective? The answer is yes, but only in a
limited sense.

   Let us see why this is so. Consider the conditional, "If I throw this piece of chalk,
then it will break." If we let *P* stand for "I throw this piece of chalk" and *Q* stand for
"It will break," then we can represent this conditional by the expression "If *P* then
Q." We can then begin to construct a truth table for "If *P* then *Q*" as follows:

	P	*Q*	If *P* then *Q*
(1)	T	T	T
(2)	T	F	F
(3)	F	T	?
(4)	F	F	?

The first two rows are fairly clear. If I throw the chalk and it shatters, then, as row
(1) indicates, our conditional proposition may be said to be true. If I throw the chalk
and it does not shatter, then, as row (2) indicates, the conditional is false. But what if
I do not throw the chalk, as in rows (3) and (4)?

   One answer may be that the truth value remains undetermined, but this may
not be the best answer. After all, given what we know about the fragility of chalk, we
may want to say the conditional would be true even if I never threw it. That is, just as
you do not have to be in Paris for me to know that the proposition "*If* you are in
Paris, *then* you are in France" is true, I also may know that the proposition "If I throw
this piece of chalk, then it will break" is true, regardless of whether I ever throw the
chalk. What can we do?

   First, we can try making rows (3) and (4) both false. This is shown in column (A)
below:

	P	*Q*	(A)	(B)	(C)	(D)
(1)	T	T	T	T	T	T
(2)	T	F	F	F	F	F
(3)	F	T	F	T	F	T
(4)	F	F	F	F	T	T

Here, though, the result is the same as for the truth function $P \wedge Q$, and that can't be right! "If I throw this piece of chalk, then it will break" is surely different from "I throw this piece of chalk and it will break." What about if we try column (B)? Unfortunately, column (B) gives us the same set of truth values as for Q. Yet that can't be right either! "If I throw this piece of chalk, then it will break" is clearly different in meaning from "It will break (whether I throw it or not)." What about column (C)? A little reflection shows that if column (C) is correct, then "If P then Q" would have the same set of truth values as "If Q then P," and surely this, too, is not right. "If I throw this piece of chalk, then it will break" is clearly different from "If it will break, then I throw this piece of chalk." So none of these three possibilities can be correct.

We have now tried our first three columns (A), (B), and (C). What is left? The only alternative is to let both rows (3) and (4) be true, as in column (D). The truth function so defined is called the *material conditional* and is represented by the symbol $\supset$:

Material Conditional

p	q	$p \supset q$
T	T	T
T	F	F
F	T	T
F	F	T

Given this definition, propositions of the form $p \supset q$ will be false only when p is true and q is false. Thus it turns out that this is the same truth function as that expressed by $\sim(p \wedge \sim q)$. This expresses the idea that a conditional can never be true if its antecedent is true and its consequent is false, and this is surely what we want. But this definition also adds the idea that, if you start with a false proposition, your conditional will always be true.

Is there anything wrong with this way of proceeding? Two objections come immediately to mind. First, when the antecedent of an ordinary conditional is false, it appears that the conditional (called a *counterfactual*, as opposed to a *material*, conditional) need not be true. For example, "If I throw this piece of chalk, then it will break" appears likely to be true even if I never throw the chalk, but "If I throw this piece of steel, then it will break" is not likely to be true, whether I throw the steel or not.

Second, like propositions involving $\vee$, the truth value of a proposition involving $\supset$ may be a function of the truth value of just one of that proposition's component propositions, even if the other component proposition is completely unrelated to the first. For example, suppose it is false that Bill loves Sue. It follows from the definition of $\supset$ that the proposition "If Bill loves Sue then $2 + 2 = 4$" will be true even though "Bill loves Sue" seems to be completely unrelated to "$2 + 2 = 4$"!

Of course, both of these objections are weakened significantly once it is recalled that $p \supset q$ just means $\sim(p \wedge \sim q)$ and no more, but it is also reasonable to draw the conclusion that $\supset$ is only one of several possible interpretations of the natural language connective "If ... then ___." That is, just as with "and" and "or", the English phrase "If ... then ___" turns out to be ambiguous. In some contexts we will want to say that "If Bill loves Sue then 2 + 2 equals 4" is true since, after all, 2 + 2 will equal 4 whether Bill loves Sue or not. In other contexts, and with a different meaning of "If ... then ___" in mind, we will not want to agree to this.

Powers' Paradox: A Challenge

Powers' Paradox, named after the American philosopher Lawrence Powers, purports to prove that the material conditional, "... ⊃ ___," is fully equivalent to the natural language phrase "If ... then ___." Here is Powers' argument:

> If, $p \supset q$, then, if p then q
> If, if p then q, then, $p \supset q$

> Therefore, $(p \supset q)$ if and only if (if p then q).

We know that this conclusion must be false since "... ⊃ ___" captures only one of several meanings of the natural language phrase "If ... then ___." So what is the flaw in Powers' argument? Is the argument valid? Is it sound?

In fact, it turns out that although many conditionals are truth-functional, many are not. According to some theories,[6] many conditionals (such as counterfactuals) are best analyzed by invoking so-called *modal logics*, logics that deal explicitly with the notions of possibility, necessity, and contingency. Here, the main idea is that the truth of a conditional does not depend just on whether its antecedent and consequent are, in fact, true or false; rather, its truth depends on whether it is *necessary* for the consequent to be true whenever the antecedent is true.

Other theories suggest that the truth-functional approach to conditionals is too simplistic because it overlooks the question of how the antecedent and consequent are related to each other. These theories suggest that some device is needed to measure the degree of overlap between the subject matter of a conditional's antecedent and its consequent. In this way, conditionals such as "If Bill loves Sue then 2 + 2 = 4," which try to connect propositions that are completely unrelated to each other, will clearly turn out to be false.[7]

Each of these two observations suggests ways in which truth-functional logic might be enriched in order to enable us to deal more successfully with conditional claims. However, for current purposes, ⊃ will suffice. Provided that we recognize the limitations of ⊃, and are clear that $p \supset q$ really means nothing more than $\sim(p \land \sim q)$, we will not get into trouble.

We began this section by noting that both conditionals and biconditionals were important enough to deserve special study. Having looked at the idea of a conditional, let us now turn to that of a biconditional. The conditional is a one-way relation. In other words, "If p then q" is not the same conditional as "If q then p." "If you run, you will tire" is not the same proposition as "If you tire, you will run." In contrast, a conditional that goes in both directions is called a *biconditional*.

In natural language, biconditionals are normally expressed using phrases such as "if and only if" or "just in case." Thus, when we say "Wood floats just in case it is lighter than water," we mean that if wood floats then it is lighter than water *and* if wood is lighter than water then it floats. Being lighter than water is thus both a necessary and a sufficient condition for floating. In other words, letting ≡ stand for "if and only if," $p \equiv q$ can be defined in terms of ⊃ and ∧ and will mean the same as $(p \supset q) \land (q \supset p)$.

> **The Material Conditional and the Material Biconditional**
> • A *material conditional* (⊃) is false when its antecedent is true and its consequent is false; otherwise it is true.
> • A *material biconditional* (≡) is true when, and only when, its two component propositions share the same truth value.

What is the truth table for $p \equiv q$? Knowing that $p \equiv q$ is the same as $(p \supset q) \land (q \supset p)$, all we need to do to answer this question is construct the truth table for $(p \supset q) \land (q \supset p)$. We do this as follows:

	p	**q**	**p ⊃ q**	**q ⊃ p**	**(p ⊃ q) ∧ (q ⊃ p)**
(1)	T	T	T	T	T
(2)	T	F	F	T	F
(3)	F	T	T	F	F
(4)	F	F	T	T	T

In other words, using the definition of ⊃, we construct the column for $p \supset q$. Then, using the same definition, we construct the column for $q \supset p$, and using the definition of ∧ we construct the column for $(p \supset q) \land (q \supset p)$. Doing so gives us the following definition for ≡:

Material Biconditional

p	**q**	**p ≡ q**
T	T	T
T	F	F
F	T	F
F	F	T

From this truth table we can see that a biconditional will be true whenever p and q have the same truth value; otherwise it is false. Of course, just as there were weaknesses in defining "If … then ___" to mean ⊃, there will also be weaknesses in defining "… if and only if ___" to mean ≡. Natural language connectives are simply too rich in meaning and too flexible to be captured fully by a single, purely truth-functional connective. Even so, just as ⊃ is useful because it captures one important use of "If … then ___," ≡ will be useful for much the same reason.

Finally, it is worth noting that several other natural language connectives can be analyzed using truth-functional logic. Among these are the connectives "neither …

Necessary and Sufficient Conditions

What is the difference between "if" and "only if"? In other words, what is the difference between "Sue will become prime minister *if* she is elected" and "Sue will become prime minister *only if* she is elected"?

The first of these two propositions states that Sue's election is a *sufficient* condition for her becoming prime minister. In other words, if she is elected, then it follows that she will become prime minister. Here, no claim is made about whether being elected is the only way that she may become prime minister.

In contrast, the second of these two propositions states that Sue's election is a *necessary* (as opposed to a sufficient) condition for her becoming prime minister. If she is to become prime minister she must first be elected. Here, no claim is made about whether, if she is elected, this will be sufficient for her becoming prime minister.

In order to keep this distinction between necessary and sufficient conditions clear, it is helpful to note three additional points. First, even though they are quite different, these two conditions may be *interdefined*. In other words, sentences of the form "If *p* then *q*" are equivalent to sentences of the form "*p* only if *q*." In other words, if Sue's being elected is a sufficient condition for her becoming prime minister, then her becoming prime minister is a necessary consequence of her being elected.

The second is that even though they may be interdefined, necessary and sufficient conditions remain *independent* of each other. In other words, given two propositions of the form "If *p* then *q*" and "Only if *p*, then *q*," neither proposition need entail the other.

Third, it is possible to express *necessary and sufficient conditions* together by the use of phrases such as "if and only if." If we want to express the claim that Sue's election is both a necessary and a sufficient condition for being prime minister, we can say "Sue will become prime minister if and only if she is elected."

In summary, we have the following several equivalences:

p is sufficient for *q*
≡ if *p* then *q*
≡ *q* if *p*
≡ *q* is necessary for *p*
≡ *p* only if *q*
≡ only if *q*, then *p*

p is necessary for *q*
≡ if *q* then *p*
≡ *p* if *q*
≡ *q* is sufficient for *p*
≡ *q* only if *p*
≡ only if *p*, then *q*

p is (both) necessary and sufficient for *q*
≡ if *p* then *q* and only if *p* then *q*
≡ if *p* then *q* and if *q* then *p*
≡ *p* if and only if *q*
≡ *q* if and only if *p*
≡ *p* iff *q*
≡ *q* iff *p*

nor ___" (symbolized by ↓, and named *nor*), and "not both … and ___" (symbolized by ↑, and named *nand*). We give their definitions as follows:

	Nor				Nand	
p	*q*	*p* ↓ *q*	*p*	*q*	*p* ↑ *q*	
T	T	F	T	T	F	
T	F	F	T	F	T	
F	T	F	F	T	T	
F	F	T	F	F	T	

Together with our previously defined connectives, these connectives allow us to represent all truth-functional connectives in propositional logic.

> **Nor, Nand**
> • A *nor proposition* (↓) is true when its two component propositions are false; otherwise it is false.
> • A *nand proposition* (↑) is false when its two component propositions are true; otherwise it is true.

Alternative Notations

As logic developed around the world, different logicians invented different notations. Thus, if you are reading other books about logic, you may notice that not all authors use the same logical notation. A sampling of the most common notations for the logical connectives is as follows:

Negation: it is not the case that *p*
~*p*   ¬ *p*   –*p*   *p*′   *p̄*   N*p*

Conjunction: *p* and *q*
p ∧ *q*   *p* · *q*   *p* & *q*   *pq*   K*pq*

(Inclusive) Disjunction: *p* or *q*
p ∨ *q*   *p* + *q*   *pq*   A*pq*

(Exclusive) Disjunction: *p* or *q* but not both (*p* or else *q*)
p ⊻ *q*   *p* ⊕ *q*   *p* ≢ *q*   J*pq*

(Material) Conditional: if *p* then *q*
p ⊃ *q*   *p* → *q*   C*pq*

(Material) Biconditional: *p* if and only if *q*
p ≡ *q*   *p* ↔ *q*   *p* ~ *q*   *p* iff *q*   E*pq*

Nor: neither *p* nor *q*
p ↓ *q*   *p* ⊽ *q*   X*pq*

Nand: not both *p* and *q*
p ↑ *q*   *p* | *q*   D*pq*

Upon encountering alternative notations, readers are well advised to check each author's conventions carefully since some symbols, such as ~ and →, are used in a variety of ways by different authors.

Exercise 4.3

1. Where *P* is true, *Q* is false, and *R* is true, determine the truth values of each of the following propositions:

    (a) $P \supset (Q \supset \sim R)$

    (b) $(P \supset R) \supset (\sim P \supset \sim R)$

    (c) $(Q \supset P) \supset (\sim Q \supset \sim P)$

    (d) $((P \wedge R) \supset Q) \supset (P \supset (R \supset Q))$

    (e) $((P \supset R) \supset P) \supset Q$

    (f) $(R \supset P) \supset (R \supset Q)$

    (g) $(P \supset Q) \equiv (R \supset Q)$

    (h) $(P \equiv R) \equiv (P \wedge \sim Q)$

    (i) $((P \wedge Q) \supset R) \equiv (P \supset (Q \supset R))$

    (j) $(R \uparrow P) \vee (R \downarrow Q)$

2. Using truth tables, prove that $(p \wedge q) \vee (\sim p \wedge \sim q)$ and $p \equiv q$ express the same truth function.

3. Using truth tables, determine whether $\sim(p \equiv q)$, which can be read as "*p* is not equivalent to *q*," and $p \veebar q$, which can be read "*p* or *q* but not both," express the same truth function.

4. We have seen that $\supset$ is a one-way relation. That is, $p \supset q$ is not the same truth function as $q \supset p$. In other words, $\supset$ cannot be reversed or, as logicians say, it is not commutative. We saw, however, that $p \equiv q$ is the same truth function as $q \equiv p$. That is, $\equiv$ is commutative. Use truth tables to determine whether $\wedge$ and $\vee$ are commutative.

4. Testing Arguments for Validity

One important feature of truth-functional connectives is that they can be used to test for various interesting logical properties. Specifically, they can be used to test for a certain type of validity called *truth-functional validity*. A valid argument, we recall, is one where it is logically impossible for the premises to be true and the conclusion false. If this property comes about as a result of the argument's propositional form we say that the argument is truth-functionally valid.

To test a natural language argument for validity in this way, we must first formalize the argument using truth-functional logic. We do this by replacing all of the argument's atomic propositions with propositional constants (*P*, *Q*, *R*, etc.) and by replacing all of the argument's connectives, "and," "or," and so on, with their symbolic counterparts ($\wedge$, $\vee$, $\supset$, etc.). Once an argument has been formalized in this way, a truth-table test for validity can be applied to determine whether its form is valid.

For example, consider the following deduction:

If 12 is an even number, then 12 is divisible by 2
12 is an even number

Therefore, 12 is divisible by 2.

In order to reconstruct this argument using the language of propositional logic, we let *P* stand for "12 is an even number" and let *Q* stand for "12 is divisible by 2." We then label the conclusion "(C)", and number each of the premises "(P1)", "(P2)", and so on, as follows:

(P1) $P \supset Q$
(P2) P

_____

(C) Q.

The argument form corresponding to this argument can now be obtained by replacing each propositional constant with its corresponding variable, as follows:

(P1) $p \supset q$
(P2) p

_____

(C) q.

This argument form is very common and is called *Modus Ponens*. We can verify the validity of this argument form by the following truth table:

	(P2)	(C)	(P1)
	p	q	$p \supset q$
(1)	T	T	T
(2)	T	F	F
(3)	F	T	T
(4)	F	F	T

Recall that an argument is valid if and only if it is impossible for the premises to be true when the conclusion is false. As a result, we look at the above truth table to see if there is ever a case where both premises have the value T and yet the conclusion has the value F. In row (1), both premises, $p \supset q$ and p, are true, and the conclusion, q, is also true. In rows (2), (3), and (4), at least one premiss is always false. Thus no row exists where the premises are both true and the conclusion is false. We therefore conclude that this form of argument, *Modus Ponens*, is valid. Because no valid argument form can have an invalid argument as one of its substitution instances, we also conclude that the argument with which we began will be valid too.

Here is another example:

If Bill throws the fight, Sue will reject him
If Bill doesn't throw the fight, the mob will take him for a ride
Either Bill will throw the fight or he will not

_____

Therefore, either Sue will reject Bill or the mob will take him for a ride.

This deduction takes the form of a dilemma. Here we let P = "Bill throws the fight," Q = "Sue will reject Bill," and R = "The mob will take Bill for a ride." Then we have

(P1) $P \supset Q$
(P2) $\sim P \supset R$
(P3) $P \lor \sim P$

_____

(C) $Q \lor R$.

In this argument there are three distinct propositional constants—P, Q, and R—so there will be 2^3, or eight, possible combinations of truth values to be assigned to these constants. The argument form corresponding to this argument can again be tested for validity. We do so as follows:

					(P1)	**(P2)**	**(P3)**	**(C)**
	p	q	r	$\sim p$	$p \supset q$	$\sim p \supset r$	$p \lor \sim p$	$q \lor r$
(1)	T	T	T	F	T	T	T	T
(2)	T	T	F	F	T	T	T	T
(3)	T	F	T	F	F	T	T	T
(4)	T	F	F	F	F	T	T	F
(5)	F	T	T	T	T	T	T	T
(6)	F	T	F	T	T	F	T	T
(7)	F	F	T	T	T	T	T	T
(8)	F	F	F	T	T	F	T	F

Having completed the first three of these columns as before, we next used the definitions of $\sim$, $\supset$, and $\lor$ to complete the columns for the premisses and the conclusion. Having done so, we can now check for validity. In this case, rows (1), (2), (5), and (7) are the only ones in which all the premisses, $p \supset q$, $\sim p \supset r$, and $p \lor \sim p$, are true; but in each of these rows the conclusion is also true. Thus there is no case where the premisses are all true and the conclusion is false. As a result, we conclude that this argument form is valid and, once again, because no valid argument form can have an invalid argument as one of its substitution instances, we conclude that the argument with which we began will be valid as well.

We now consider one final example:

If Sue is busy, then she is doing well financially
She is doing well financially

_____

Therefore, Sue is busy.

Letting P = "Sue is busy" and Q = "Sue is doing well financially," we now place the argument in standard form as follows:

(P1) $P \supset Q$
(P2) Q

———————

(C) P

The truth table for the argument form corresponding to this argument is then constructed as follows:

		(C)	(P2)	(P1)
		p	*q*	*p* ⊃ *q*
	(1)	T	T	T
	(2)	T	F	F
X	(3)	F	T	T
	(4)	F	F	T

Note that, unlike our previous two examples, this truth table contains a row in which both the premisses, $p \supset q$ and q, are true and yet the conclusion, p, is false. This row, marked with an X, demonstrates that the argument form is not valid. Thus we cannot conclude that the original argument is valid. Since the underlying form is a common one, it is given a name: the *fallacy of affirming the consequent*.

As we can see from these examples, once an argument has been formalized using the language of propositional logic, checking for truth-functional validity or invalidity becomes a purely mechanical procedure. (Similar tests can also be introduced for other logical properties such as consistency and inconsistency.) However, it can be tricky moving from English into a "formal language" such as the one we have begun to develop here. Since natural language is a many-splendoured thing, and because natural-language sentences are sometimes vague or ambiguous, we will not have an exact set of rules for English the way we do for our truth-functional connectives. Formalization is thus as much an art as it is a science. Unless we know exactly what a speaker intends, arguments that occur in natural language, even mathematical or scientific arguments, might not be translated easily into propositional logic. Since we cannot expect sentences of a natural language to be as exact as those of a formal language, formalization itself can never be a completely mechanical procedure. Indeed, one of the most useful functions of formal logic is to help make natural language arguments more precise. Thus, formality has its limitations, but also its advantages.

Exercise 4.4

1. Formalize each of the following propositions, showing as much logical structure as possible.

    (a) Is Bill dishonest? No! Of course not!

    (b) Not only is Sue encouraged by the result, she is also pleased with the process.

    (c) Bill went to the movies but Sue did not.

    (d) Despite his being late, Bill gave an excellent speech.

(e) Bill was late but pleased with himself.

(f) Although she was busy, Sue made time to finish her correspondence.

(g) Bill and Sue went to the movies together.

(h) Sue or Bill will be able to work at today's charity event.

(i) If this is Sue's pen, she will want it back.

(j) If this is Sue's pen, not only will she want it back, she will be annoyed with Bill for losing it.

(k) Bill will be at the meeting provided that Sue reminded him.

(l) Sue will be at the meeting only if Bill will be there.

(m) Being a graduate is a necessary condition for Bill's being elected to the alumni council.

(n) Being a graduate is a sufficient condition for Bill's being able to vote in this election.

(o) Being a graduate is both a necessary and a sufficient condition for Sue's being able to vote in this election.

(p) Bill will come unless the weather is bad.

(q) Neither Bill nor Sue lives in Montreal.

(r) At least two of Bill, Sue, and Carol live in Amsterdam.

(s) At most two of Bill, Sue, and Carol live in Miami.

(t) Exactly two of Bill, Sue, and Carol live in Sydney, unless I am mistaken.

2. Construct truth tables for each of the following argument forms. Identify which are truth-functionally valid and which are not.

(a) $p \supset q$
    $\sim p \lor \sim q$
    _____
    $\sim p$

(b) $p \supset q$
    $\sim q$
    _____
    $\sim p$

(c) $p \supset q$
    $q \supset r$
    _____
    r

(d) $p \equiv q$
    $\sim q$
    _____
    $\sim p$

(e) $p \supset q$
    $q \supset p$
    _____
    $p \equiv q$

(f) p
    $p \supset q$
    _____
    $p \lor q$

(g) p
    $p \supset q$
    _____
    $p \land q$

(h) $p \equiv q$
    _____
    p

(i) p
    $p \equiv q$
    _____
    q

(j) p
    $p \supset \sim p$
    _____
    q

5. The Truth-table Test for Validity

At this point it will be worth reviewing the method we have developed to test arguments for truth-functional validity. The method consists of seven steps, as follows:

Step 1–Identify the Premisses and Conclusion

Write down the premisses of the argument. Then draw a line and write down the conclusion. In doing so, try to make each proposition as unambiguous as possible. This will involve replacing any ambiguous words (including "he," "she," "they," or "it") with less ambiguous terms. It will also require making all truth-functional connectives as explicit as possible. As an example, consider the following argument:

> If the Blue Jays or the Mets win their next game, the Red Sox will be out of the series. But the Blue Jays win their next game only if the Mets don't. So, whatever happens, they will be out.

This argument becomes:

> If the Blue Jays win their next game or the Mets win their next game, then the Red Sox will be out of the series
>
> The Blue Jays win their next game only if it is not the case that the Mets win their next game
> _____
> The Red Sox will be out of the series.

Step 2–Identify all Atomic Propositions

In order to translate an argument from a natural language such as English into the language of propositional logic, we will need to identify all the atomic propositions that appear in the argument and replace them with propositional constants. For example, in the above argument there are exactly three atomic propositions. As a result, we let

> P = "The Blue Jays win their next game,"
> Q = "The Mets win their next game,"

and

> R = "The Red Sox will be out of the series."

Step 3–Identify all Truth-functional Connectives

After identifying all of an argument's atomic propositions, it is usually relatively easy to identify the argument's truth-functional connectives. For example, in the above argument we see that the first premiss contains both a disjunction (∨) and a conditional (⊃); the sec-

Steps for Testing for Validity Using Truth Tables
1. Identify the premisses and conclusion
2. Identify all atomic propositions
3. Identify all truth-functional connectives
4. Formalize the argument
5. Design a truth table
6. Complete the truth table
7. Test for truth-functional validity

ond premiss contains both a conditional ($\supset$) and a negation ($\sim$); and the conclusion contains no connectives at all.

Step 4–Formalize the Argument

Having identified all of an argument's atomic propositions and truth-functional connectives, it is now a straightforward matter to formalize it. We do so by replacing each atomic proposition with its corresponding propositional constant, by replacing each truth-functional connective with its appropriate symbol, and by labelling each premiss "(P1)", "(P2)", and so on, and the conclusion "(C)". For example, the above argument can now be formalized as follows:

(P1) $(P \lor Q) \supset R$
(P2) $P \supset {\sim}Q$

———————

(C) R

Step 5–Design a Truth Table

We now want to determine whether the form of this argument is valid or invalid. To do so, we will need to construct a truth table representing all logically possible combinations of truth-value assignments that may be made to the argument's atomic propositions, its premisses, and conclusion. To do this, we first list variables (in this case p, q, and r) representing all of the argument's propositional constants, followed by the propositional forms of the argument's premisses and conclusion. We also list the propositional forms of any other molecular propositions whose truth values will be needed in order to complete the truth table. In this case, we will need to determine the truth values of $p \lor q$ before we will be able to determine the truth values associated with the form of our first premiss, $(p \lor q) \supset r$. We will also need to determine the truth values of $\sim q$ before we will be able to determine the truth values associated with the form of our second premiss, $p \supset {\sim}q$. In order to distinguish such expressions from those that represent the form of the argument's premisses or conclusion, we label the appropriate propositional forms (C), (P1), (P2), and so on, as follows:

		(C)		**(P1)**		**(P2)**
p	q	r	$p \lor q$	$(p \lor q) \supset r$	${\sim}q$	$p \supset {\sim}q$

Next, we recall that, if our argument contains n atomic propositions, the truth table will require 2^n rows. Thus if there are three atomic propositions, as in the current example, we will require 2^3, or eight, rows. We then fill in the columns beneath the single variables. In the rightmost column we alternate between T's and F's. Moving one column to the left, we then alternate between pairs of T's and pairs of F's. We continue doing this, doubling the number of T's and F's each time we move one column to the left, until we have exhausted our supply of variables. In the current example, we now will have three completed columns and eight rows.

	p	q	r	**(C)** p ∨ q	**(P1)** (p ∨ q) ⊃ r	~q	**(P2)** p ⊃ ~q
(1)	T	T	T				
(2)	T	T	F				
(3)	T	F	T				
(4)	T	F	F				
(5)	F	T	T				
(6)	F	T	F				
(7)	F	F	T				
(8)	F	F	F				

Step 6–Complete the Truth Table

Using the definitions of each of our connectives, we are now able to complete the truth table. We first complete the column for p ∨ q. The next column, containing (p ∨ q) ⊃ r, can then be completed using the definition of ⊃ together with the columns under p ∨ q and r. In row (1), for example, p ∨ q has the value T and r has the value T; thus (p ∨ q) ⊃ r will also have the value T. When complete, the truth table will appear as follows:

	p	q	r	**(C)** p ∨ q	**(P1)** (p ∨ q) ⊃ r	~q	**(P2)** p ⊃ ~q
(1)	T	T	T	T	T	F	F
(2)	T	T	F	T	F	F	F
(3)	T	F	T	T	T	T	T
(4)	T	F	F	T	F	T	T
(5)	F	T	T	T	T	F	T
(6)	F	T	F	T	F	F	T
(7)	F	F	T	F	T	T	T
(8)	F	F	F	F	T	T	T

Step 7–Test for Truth-functional Validity

Having completed our truth table, we can now test for formal validity. If there is no case where the premisses are all true and the conclusion is false, then the argument form is a valid one. Alternatively, if there is any row—one or more—where all the premisses are true and the conclusion is false, then the argument form is invalid. In our example, there is exactly one row, row (8), in which the premisses are both true and yet the conclusion is false. Thus the argument form is not valid. We indicate this by placing an X to the left of this row and conclude that we have been unable to prove that the argument we began with is valid.

		p	**q**	**r**	**(C)** $p \lor q$	**(P1)** $(p \lor q) \supset r$	$\sim q$	**(P2)** $p \supset \sim q$
	(1)	T	T	T	T	T	F	F
	(2)	T	T	F	T	F	F	F
	(3)	T	F	T	T	T	T	T
	(4)	T	F	F	T	F	T	T
	(5)	F	T	T	T	T	F	T
	(6)	F	T	F	T	F	F	T
	(7)	F	F	T	F	T	T	T
X	(8)	F	F	F	F	T	T	T

Exercise 4.5

1. Let P = "The Blue Jays win their next game," let Q = "The Mets win their next game," and let R = "The Red Sox win their next game." Formalize each of the following propositions using the language of propositional logic:

(a) If the Blue Jays win their next game, then both the Red Sox and the Mets win their next game.

(b) If the Blue Jays win their next game, then both the Red Sox and Mets do not win theirs.

(c) If the Blue Jays win their next game, then the Red Sox do not win their next game. But if the Red Sox do not win their next game, then the Mets win theirs.

(d) If either the Blue Jays or the Red Sox win their next game, then the Mets will not win their next game.

(e) Neither the Blue Jays nor the Mets will win their next game unless the Red Sox win their next game.

(f) The Blue Jays will win their next game just in case both the Red Sox and the Mets do not win their next game.

(g) The Blue Jays will win their next game only if the Red Sox do not win their next game.

(h) The Blue Jays will win their next game only if either the Red Sox or the Mets do not win their next game.

(i) The Blue Jays will win their next game only if both the Red Sox and the Mets do not win their next game.

(j) If the Mets win their next game then the Red Sox, the Mets, and the Blue Jays all win their next game.

2. Formalize each of the following arguments using the language of propositional logic:

(a) Superman will die if and only if he is exposed to kryptonite. It follows that he will die and that it will be because he is exposed to kryptonite.

(b) Geometry is a part of either mathematics or physics. But it is not a part of mathematics. Therefore it is a part of physics.

(c) If China invades Taiwan, the United States will start a nuclear war. But the United States will never start a nuclear war. Therefore, China will not invade Taiwan.

(d) Athens is the capital of Greece and Paris is the capital of France. But if the Second

World War had lasted into the 1950s, then Athens would not be the capital of Greece. So the Second World War could not have lasted into the 1950s.

(e) Athens is the capital of Greece and Paris is the capital of France. But if the encyclopedia is right, then Athens is not the capital of Greece. So the encyclopedia must be wrong.

3. Formalize each of the following arguments using the language of propositional logic; then use truth tables to determine whether they are formally valid:

(a) If Bill moves his knight, Sue will move her queen. But Bill failed to move his knight. So Sue did not move her queen.

(b) If Bill moves his knight, Sue will move her queen. But if Bill moves his bishop, she will not. So Sue may or may not move her queen.

(c) If Bill moves his knight, Sue will move her queen. So, since she didn't move her queen, it follows that Bill didn't move his knight.

(d) Either Bill will move his rook or his pawn. If he moves his pawn, Sue will counter with a capture and Bill will lose. If he moves his rook, she will again counter with a capture, and Bill will again lose. So either way, Bill will lose.

(e) Either Bill will move his rook or his pawn. In either case he will lose. So I hope he moves his bishop.

(f) If Bill moves his knight, Sue will move her queen. If Sue moves her queen, the game will be a stalemate. Therefore, if Bill moves his knight, the game will be a stalemate.

(g) If Bill moves his knight, Sue will move her queen. So if the game is a stalemate, Bill moves his knight.

(h) If Bill moves his pawn, his queen will be

in jeopardy. If he moves his rook, he will lose it. But if he doesn't move his pawn, he must move his rook. Clearly, therefore, it cannot be true both that his queen will not be in jeopardy and that he won't lose his rook.

(i) Bill will move his pawn only if Sue moves her queen. But if Sue moves her rook, Bill will knock over the board. It is not true that Sue will move her queen and not move her rook. Therefore, if Sue moves her queen, Bill will move his pawn and knock over the board.

(j) Bill will move his pawn only if Sue moves her queen. But if Sue moves her rook, Bill will move his knight. It is not true that Sue will move her queen. So Bill will move his knight.

4. An explorer has reached a river that is one of the boundaries of an exotic country he wishes to study. In this country there are only red-haired people and brown-haired people. It is impossible for people with red hair to tell anything but the truth; it is impossible for people with brown hair to tell anything but lies. It is now sunset, and our explorer sees, across the river, the figures of three men who are members of this strange tribe silhouetted against the sinking sun. He cannot make out the colour of their hair. The explorer and the men have the following conversation.

Explorer: Hello! Will you please tell me which you are, red-haired or brown-haired?

First Man: … [Because the first man spoke so softly, the explorer did not hear his reply.]

Second Man: He says he is red-haired and he is red-haired.

Third Man: Don't be silly, he is brown-haired.

What is the hair colour of each of the three men?

6. Fallacies of Relevance

In previous chapters we saw that *ad hominem* and *ad baculum* fallacies introduce irrelevant emotional or circumstantial appeals of one sort or another. This type of move is fallacious because it attempts to avoid a particular argument simply by changing the subject. The *ad hominem* and *ad baculum* are thus fallacies of irrelevance, fallacies that illicitly attempt to change the subject matter of whatever it is that is under discussion. Aristotle called this kind of fallacy *ignoratio elenchi*, which means literally "misconception of refutation." He recognized that, when confronted by an argument one is unable to refute, a clever strategy is to mount another argument—any other argument that seems plausible—even if in doing so one does not directly respond to the first argument. Often the audience will not notice the shift of territory, especially if the irrelevant counter-argument seems somehow related to the original one, or if it is colourful enough to make us forget about the first argument altogether. In the modern period, this type of fallacy has often been called a *red herring*. The name comes from the sport of fox hunting, where a dried herring (which is red) is drawn across the trail. This distraction makes it difficult for the dogs to pick up the scent of the fox and therefore adds a degree of difficulty to the sport that it would not otherwise have.

For example, consider the claim that hunting should not be considered cruel because it brings enjoyment to many people, or the claim that a university's land development project should not be thought harmful to the environment because of the employment that will accompany it. Both claims remain unjustified since the purported justifications are really examples of *ignoratio elenchi*, cases in which irrelevant information is offered by way of justification. After all, unless the evidence being offered in favour of a conclusion is directly relevant to the issue at hand, and unless it concerns the same subject matter, it can hardly be logically appropriate.

In this context it is worth noting that because classical propositional logic is concerned only with relations between truth values, it cannot tell us whether two or more propositions share a common subject matter. Thus classical propositional logic cannot tell us whether an *ignoratio elenchi* has occurred. For example, in propositional logic, arguments of the form "p, therefore $p \lor q$" are valid; so are arguments of the form "$\sim p$, therefore $p \supset q$," even if p and q are completely unrelated. As we saw before, in some contexts we will want to say that "If Bill loves Sue then $2 + 2$ equals 4" is true since, after all, $2 + 2$ will equal 4 whether Bill loves Sue or not. In other contexts, and with a different meaning of "If ... then ___" in mind, we will not want to say this. Thus, at least in some contexts, the fact that classical logic fails to take into account subject matter will be a serious limitation. Classical logic yields an account of validity that is unable to identify some of the worst fallacies of irrelevance imaginable.

We conclude that, because it is open to fallacies of this kind, classical logic cannot serve as a complete model of argument. Whether, or to what extent, it can be extended to cope with this limitation is a question that we will address in future chapters.

Flashback on...
Ignoratio Elenchi

WE HAVE seen that the modern *ignoratio elenchi* is often equated with the *red herring fallacy*. This fallacy, in turn, is similar to what is known as the *straw man fallacy*, the fallacy of misrepresenting an opponent's position so that it is easier to criticize it. In both cases, the fallacy-maker draws consequences from, or develops an argument in support of, some proposition or set of propositions different from the proposition about which the argument began, and under the tacit assumption that this proposition is still the locus of the argument.

Aristotle had a rather different view. For him the *ignoratio elenchi* fallacy is a mistake made by a questioner in the course of attempting a refutation of a respondent's thesis. Hence it is literally the mistake of "ignorance of what makes for a refutation."

In contrast, the modern conception of *igno-ratio elenchi* dates from the *Port Royal Logic* of 1662. There it is the fallacy of "proving something other than what is in question." There are, say the authors of the *Logic*, two common ways of committing this fallacy: first, by challenging an adversary's opinion with consequences he does not accept; and second, by imputing to an adversary an opinion he does not hold and then refuting it. This second way has a decidedly modern ring to it, with clear connections to the straw man fallacy. In Whately's *Elements of Logic* (1826), *ignoratio elenchi* is much the same thing. It is a "non-logical or material" fallacy, by which Whately means a logically valid argument whose defect is other than one of logic. It is the mistake of validly deriving an "irrelevant conclusion," a mistake that has more than a passing resemblance to the modern red herring fallacy.

Summary

A set of premises is said to *entail* a conclusion if and only if the conclusion *conclusively follows from* the premises. Entailment is thus the strongest form of consequence relation and is one desirable feature of good arguments.

Classical propositional logic begins the study of entailment by considering those arguments that are valid as a result of their *propositional form*. An argument (or inference) is said to be *valid* (or truth-preserving) whenever it is not possible for its premises to be true and, at the same time, its conclusion to be false. It is said to be *valid as a result of its propositional form*, or *truth-functionally valid*, if its being valid results from those formal relations that are characterized by *truth-functional connectives* such as ~, ∧, ∨, ⊃, and ≡. Since no valid argument form has an invalid argument as one of its substitution instances, *truth tables* provide an effective, mechanical way of testing for truth-functional validity.

Even so, classical propositional logic has at least two significant limitations. First, given the complexity of natural language it would be surprising if the logic of truth functions were rich enough to exhibit all relations of validity or entailment. For example, because the material conditional does not tell us anything about non-actual—but possible—situations, classical logic is not capable of handling counter-factual conditionals in any significant way.

Second, because it limits itself solely to the study of truth values, classical propositional logic fails to take into account any connections between propositions other than those between the truth values of their constituent propositions. Thus, classical propositional logic cannot tell us whether propositions share a common subject matter and so cannot identify instances of the fallacy of *ignoratio elenchi*.

However, within these limitations, classical propositional logic does help us study some of the most important features of formal argument. In subsequent chapters, we will try to discover whether it can be extended to provide a fuller theory of both formal argument and the fallacies.

Weblinks

Episteme Links–Logic
www.epistemelinks.com/Topi/LogiTopi.htm
Philosophy in Cyberspace–Logic
www.geocities.com/Athens/Acropolis/4393/logic.htm

Notes

1. Propositional logic is also sometimes referred to as *sentence logic* or *sentential logic*, and the propositional connectives as *sentence connectives* or *sentential connectives*.

2. Some authors choose to call propositional constants *sentence constants*, and propositional variables *sentence variables*.

3. Some authors choose to call propositional forms *sentence forms*.

4. For a more detailed discussion, see John Woods, "Is There a Relation of Intensional Conjunction?," *Mind*, 76 (1967), 357–368, and R.E. Gahringer, "Intensional Conjunction," *Mind*, 79 (1970), 259–260.

5. Again, a more detailed discussion may be found in R.E. Jennings, "Or," *Analysis*, 26 (1966), 181–184, and in *The Genealogy of Disjunction* (Oxford: Oxford University Press, 1994) by the same author.

6. For examples, see David Lewis, *Counterfactuals* (Oxford: Blackwell, 1973) and W.L. Harper *et al.*, *Ifs*, (Dordrecht: Reidel, 1981).

7. For example, see Richard L. Epstein, "Relatedness and Implication," *Philosophical Studies*, 36 (1979), 137–173, and Stephen Read, *Relevant Logic* (New York: Blackwell, 1988).

CHAPTER 5

Formal and Informal Logic

AT THIS point in our discussion, we need to ask the following question: Is logic primarily a *formal*, or primarily an *informal*, discipline? In other words, as we begin to develop precise theories of good and bad arguments, should we be looking primarily at the form or structure of arguments, or should we be looking primarily at some other feature of arguments, such as their content or subject matter?

Many philosophers resist introducing concepts from formal logic when studying critical thinking and the fallacies; instead they adhere to a tradition that studies the fallacies only informally. In contrast, we believe that insights from formal logic can help us understand what makes good arguments good and bad arguments bad.

In what follows, we will explain in more detail what formal logic is and what is meant by an argument's "logical form." In doing so, we will see that formality admits of degrees. We will also see that any analysis of good and bad reasoning should be formal to some extent, but that the degree of formality required will vary from context to context. Formality cannot be adhered to as strictly as some philosophers might like, but it cannot be ignored either.

1. Logical Form

As with other sciences, logic has a general, rather than a particular, orientation. Physics, for example, tells us about mass and energy in general, and not just about this or that chunk of metal, or this or that beam of sunlight. Similarly, logic attempts to reveal the most general or universal truths about rational inference. It does this by studying *argument forms*. By learning about the formal properties of arguments, formal logicians hope that they will be able to learn everything there is to know about what makes good arguments good and bad arguments bad.

Let us begin again with propositional logic and the following very simple deduction:

Bill has $5 in his pocket

Therefore, Bill has $5 in his pocket.

Here is another, similar argument:

Sue has visited California

_____

Therefore, Sue has visited California.

Both are good deductions, to be sure,[1] but they are also trivial. However, this triviality is of an important kind. Not only are these very easy and obvious deductions, and not only do their conclusions merely repeat their premises, they also both share a common pattern or *form*, namely

(P1) *p*

_____

(C) *p*.

What's more, it is this common pattern or form, called *repetition*, that accounts for the validity of both of these deductions. In other words, in both cases it is because of the argument's form (rather than the argument's content or subject matter) that the argument is valid. Because no argument of this form could have, at the same time, a true premiss and a false conclusion, every argument obtained from this argument form by uniformly substituting a propositional constant for the propositional variable *p* will be valid.

Grammatical versus Logical Form

The distinction between grammatical and logical form is important, and worth getting straight. The *grammatical form* of a proposition (or of an argument) is the structure of the proposition (or argument) as indicated by the surface grammar of its natural language. In contrast, the *logical form* of a proposition (or of an argument) is the logically effective structure of the proposition (or argument) as indicated by the meanings of the logical terms it contains.

As an example, consider the following exchange between Alice and the King in Lewis Carroll's *Through the Looking Glass:*[2]

"I see nobody on the road," said Alice.

"I only wish *I* had such eyes," the King remarked in a fretful tone. "To be able to see Nobody! And at that distance too! Why, it's as much as *I* can do to see real people, by this light!"

Here the King has been misled by the grammatical form of Alice's statement when he should have been concentrating on its logical form. The statements "I see nobody on the road" and "I see somebody on the road" have the same grammatical form. Both have a subject ("I"), a verb ("see"), and an object (either "nobody" or "somebody") together with a prepositional phrase ("on the road") that is used to modify the object. Despite this, these two propositions have quite different logical forms: "I see nobody on the road" is an abbreviated way of saying "It is not the case that I see somebody on the road." In other words, "I see nobody on the road" is really the negation, or denial, of "I see somebody on the road." The humour of the King's remark arises from his ignoring this fact.

> Being aware of a proposition's logical form not only helps us discover the proposition's logical properties, it also helps us remove ambiguities. For a more mundane example, consider the proposition "Tom, Dick, and Harry lifted the box." Until we know the proposition's logical form, we do not know whether the speaker means to indicate that the team of Tom, Dick, and Harry together lifted the box, or whether Tom, Dick, and Harry each, individually, lifted the box. The former has (in part) the logical form "(Tom, Dick, Harry) lifted the box." The latter has (in part) the logical form "(Tom lifted the box) and (Dick lifted the box) and (Harry lifted the box)."

Here are two more deductively valid arguments to consider:

Bill is in New York or Bill is in London
It is not the case that Bill is in New York

———————————————————————

Therefore, Bill is in London

Sue went to the movies or Sue left town
It is not the case that Sue went to the movies

———————————————————————

Therefore, Sue left town.

Here, too, both deductions are valid solely in virtue of their logical form, namely

(P1) $p \lor q$
(P2) $\sim p$

—————

(C) q.

Again, this form is common enough that it has been given a name, *disjunctive syllogism*. And again, because no argument of this form could have true premisses and a false conclusion, all arguments that are instances of this form must be valid.

Now consider an additional argument that is an instance of this same form:

Tay-Sachs disease is infectious or spina bifida is congenital
It is not the case that Tay-Sachs disease is infectious

———————————————————————

Therefore, spina bifida is congenital.

Many of us do not know what Tay-Sachs disease or spina bifida are. Still, even if we do not know what these sentences mean, we will have no difficulty in seeing that the argument is valid. Even if we do not understand the medical terms involved, we can still see that the argument is an instance of a valid argument form, a form in which it is impossible for the premisses to be true and the conclusion false.

In contrast, consider the following "argument":

Bill is in New York glarg Bill is in London
Ooglah Bill is in New York

_____

Therefore, Bill is in London.

This is an "argument" that no one will understand because it contains the invented words "glarg" and "ooglah." As a result, no one will be able to determine whether or not it is valid, or whether or not its constituent propositions are even meaningful.

What these last two arguments show is that although logical properties such as validity need not depend on the meanings of all of an argument's constituent words or expressions, they do depend on the meanings of some of them.[3] Those topic-neutral terms (such as "and" and "or") that logical properties (such as validity) do depend on are called the argument's _logical terms_. The remaining ones are called its _non-logical terms_, and it is by replacing all of an argument's non-logical terms with variables that we are able to discover its main logical form.

Material Content versus Logical Form

Two factors appear to be relevant in determining an argument's validity. The first is _material content_; the second is _logical form_. To see this, compare the following two arguments:

Socrates is a father

_____

Therefore, Socrates is male.

All men are mortal
Socrates is a man

_____

Therefore, Socrates is mortal.

In the first of these two arguments it is the material content (or meaning) of the non-logical terms "father" and "male" that makes the argument valid. It is because fathers are always male that we can reliably infer the conclusion from the premiss.

In the second of these two arguments it is the logical form (or logical structure) of the argument that makes the argument valid. The meanings of the (non-logical) terms ("men," "mortal," and "Socrates") turn out not to be relevant, since any other (non-logical) terms may be (uniformly) substituted for them without affecting the argument's validity.

Noticing this distinction between material content and logical form prompts us to ask two types of question. The first concerns the nature of logical form. How is an argument's logical form to be identified? Is it discovered or created? And when do two or more arguments share the same logical form?

The second type of question concerns the relationship between logical form and logical properties such as validity. Is validity always a function of an argument's logical form? And despite the seemingly important role of material content, can all logical rela-

> tions (including validity, inductive strength, consistency, inconsistency, etc.), be
> explained in terms of logical form?
>
> In answer to the first of these two types of question, it is often emphasized that
> logical form can itself be seen to be a function of so-called topic-neutral logical oper-
> ators (i.e., logical terms and connectives such as "not," "and," "or," "all," and
> "some"). Identifying a proposition's logical form then becomes a matter of identify-
> ing its logical and non-logical terms.
>
> In answer to the second of these two types of question, logicians typically fall
> into two camps. *Formalists* claim that, despite our initial intuition, logical properties
> of arguments such as our first one may always be explained via logical form. In the
> case of this argument, for example, it may be that the argument is valid only once we
> recognize our implicit acceptance of a hidden premiss such as "All fathers are male."
> The resulting argument
>
> Socrates is a father
> [All fathers are male]
> _____
>
> Therefore, Socrates is male
>
> is then valid as a result of its logical form.
>
> In contrast to the formalists, *anti-formalists* claim that our first intuitions remain
> correct and that our first argument was valid not because of its logical form, but
> because of the material content of the non-logical terms involved.
>
> Whether it is the formalists or the anti-formalists who are in fact correct remains
> an open question.

Once we have discovered an argument's logical form, it is relatively easy to construct new arguments having the same form. For example, given the preceding argument we can obtain the new argument

Bill is in the library or Bill is visiting his father
It is not the case that Bill is in the library
_____

Therefore, Bill is visiting his father.

We do so by a very simple operation, namely, substituting the propositions "Bill is in
the library" and "Bill is visiting his father" for the propositions "Tay-Sachs disease is
infectious" and "Spina bifida is congenital."

There are two points about this operation of substitution to which we need to pay
special attention. First, only non-logical terms are affected; logical terms such as "or,"
"and," and "it is not the case that" are not replaced. Second, the replacement must be
uniform. In other words, any replacement of a given non-logical term by another
will result in the replacement of every other occurrence of that same non-logical
term as well.

We can now see that any number of arguments may be constructed from any
given argument by the uniform substitution of one set of non-logical terms for

another. Similarly, we can also see that any number of arguments may be obtained from a given argument form by the uniform substitution of propositions for propositional variables. Such arguments are called *uniform substitution instances* of their respective argument forms.

Exercise 5.1

1. Determine whether the following argument is a uniform substitution instance of each of the argument forms (a) to (e) below.

   If Bill has gone, Sue will leave
   Sue will not leave
   _____

   Therefore, Bill has not gone.

   (a) (P1) $p \supset q$
   (P2) q
   _____
   (C) p

   (b) (P1) p
   (P2) q
   _____
   (P2) r

   (c) (P1) $p \vee q$
   (P2) $\sim p$
   _____
   (C) q

   (d) (P1) $p \vee q$
   (P2) r
   _____
   (C) s

   (e) (P1) $p \supset q$
   (P2) $\sim q$
   _____
   (C) $\sim p$

2. Determine whether the following argument is a uniform substitution instance of each of the argument forms (a) to (e) in question 1 above.

   Either Bill has gone or Sue will leave
   Bill has not gone
   _____

   Therefore, Sue will leave.

3. For each of the following propositions, determine all of the propositional forms for which it is a uniform substitution instance:

   (a) A

   (b) $\sim A$

   (c) $\sim \sim A$

   (d) $A \supset \sim B$

   (e) $A \supset (\sim B \supset A)$

   (f) $\sim A \supset (\sim B \supset \sim A)$

   (g) $(A \vee B) \supset (C \vee D)$

   (h) $(A \vee B) \supset (A \vee D)$

   (i) $(\sim A \vee B) \supset (\sim A \vee D)$

   (j) $A \equiv \sim B$

2. Formal Logic

It is the goal of *formal logic* to discover those formal attributes of propositions and arguments that affect validity and other interesting logical properties. As we have seen, in at least some cases it is because of an argument's form—and not because of its content or subject matter—that the argument is valid. In other words, because some argument forms are such that no argument having that form could have true premises and a false conclusion, it follows that every argument obtained from that form by uniformly substituting propositional constants for propositional variables will be valid. The importance of formal logic is therefore clear.

However, this still leaves open the question of whether *all* valid arguments are valid as a result of their form, and whether logic should be viewed as a completely formal discipline. Will formal logic in principle be able to provide us with a complete theory of what makes good arguments good and bad arguments bad?

Before trying to answer this question, it is worth reminding ourselves that one way of thinking about logical form is as follows: an argument can be studied from a formal point of view only to the extent that it can be checked for logically interesting properties without attending to the meaning of its constituent elements. Yet if this is correct, formality will be a matter of degree. Only arguments of the form

> **Formal Logic**
> *Formal logic* studies those formal or structural features of arguments that affect validity and other interesting logical properties. Topic-neutral terms (such as "and" and "or") that affect logical properties (such as validity) are called *logical terms*; all remaining terms are called *non-logical terms*. An argument's logical form is obtained by replacing the argument's non-logical terms with variables. Because some argument forms are such that no argument having that form could have true premises and a false conclusion, it follows that every argument obtained from that form by uniformly substituting propositional constants for propositional variables will be valid. We call such forms *logically valid argument forms*.

(P1) p

———

(C) p

will be completely formal. Other groups of arguments will be able to be studied formally, but in differing degrees.

Let us now look at an argument that is clearly a good deduction but that does not appear to be valid as a result of its form. The argument is as follows:

Bill's shirt is red

———————————————

Therefore, Bill's shirt is coloured.

As we said, this is clearly a good deduction. The argument is valid, and if the premiss is true, it will be sound as well. Even so, this argument's validity appears to be a function not of the argument's form, but, rather, of the meanings of the terms "red" and "coloured." In fact, the only constituent elements whose meanings need not be taken into account are the two occurrences of the phrase "Bill's shirt," for anything that is red is also coloured. Does this mean that terms such as "red" and "coloured" should be counted as logical terms? Or does it mean that the validity of some arguments is a function primarily of the argument's material content and not of its formal structure?

It turns out that, even today, this remains an open question. Over the centuries, logicians have been able to discover more and more formal laws, but whether *all* logical properties will ever be capable of being characterized formally is still being debated today.

What we can say is this:

- There is a precise respect in which logic can be said to be formal: logic is formal exactly to the extent that it studies or deals with logical form.

- The *logical form* of a proposition or of an argument is the logically effective structure of that proposition or argument.

- An argument admits of formal treatment (or, more briefly, it is a "formal argument") to the degree that its logical properties (such as validity) depend upon its formal structure rather than upon the meanings of its constituent non-logical terms. General, topic-neutral terms such as "and" and "or," which logical properties (such as validity) depend on, are called *logical terms*; the remaining ones are called *non-logical terms*.

- To discover that a given argument form is valid in propositional logic is to discover that all arguments obtained from that form by the uniform substitution of propositional constants for propositional variables are valid; thus formal logic makes possible the discovery of very general truths, or laws, just as in any other science.

- To discover the validity of a given argument, it is therefore sufficient to discover that it is an instance of a valid argument form.

- Even so, the question remains: Are all logical properties, including validity, capable of being explained as a result of logical form?

At this point it may be helpful to return to the study of the fallacies. Fallacies occur more regularly in natural languages, such as English, than in the languages of formal logic. Thus it is natural to ask whether formal logic can help us identify and eliminate fallacious reasoning. We thus turn to two fallacies that depend expressly on the ambiguities of natural language: the fallacies of equivocation and amphiboly.

3. Equivocation and Amphiboly

The fallacy of *equivocation* occurs whenever a word that can be interpreted or defined in more than one way plays an important but changing role in an argument. To take a simple example, a word like "bank" is ambiguous—it may mean either "river bank" or "savings bank," depending on the intention of the speaker and the context of its use. Ambiguities such as this are called *semantic ambiguities*. In most contexts they remain harmless enough, provided that the speaker makes it clear what is meant, or provided that the ambiguity does not matter. Sometimes, however, ambiguities do mat-

Flashback on...
Bertrand Russell (1872–1970)

ALTHOUGH known to many primarily as a philosopher and social critic, Bertrand Russell was most influential as a result of his work in early-twentieth-century mathematical logic. His most significant contributions were his work in developing the idea of logical form, his discovery of Russell's paradox, his introduction of the theory of types (Russell's way of avoiding paradoxes), his refining and popularizing of predicate logic, and his defence of logicism, the view that mathematics is in some important sense reducible to logic. As much as any other logician, Russell is responsible for attempting to show how the notion of logical form helps to clarify puzzles in philosophy.

Russell was born the grandson of Lord John Russell, who had twice served as prime minister to Queen Victoria. Following the death of his mother (in 1874) and of his father (in 1876), Russell and his brother went to live with their grandparents. (Although Russell's father had granted custody of Russell and his brother to two atheists, Russell's grandparents had little difficulty in getting his will overturned.) Following the death of his grandfather (in 1878), Russell was raised by his grandmother, Lady Russell. Educated at first privately, and later at Trinity College, Cambridge, Russell obtained first-class degrees both in mathematics and in the moral sciences in 1893 and 1894.

While at Cambridge, and like other later-to-be-famous intellectuals such as John Maynard Keynes, G.E. Moore, Henry Sidgwick, Alfred Tennyson, A.N. Whitehead, and Ludwig Wittgenstein, Russell was a member of the secret Cambridge undergraduate society, the Society of the Apostles. As Henry Sidgwick described it, "The essential value of the Society is a belief that we *can* learn, and a determination that we *will* learn, from people of the most opposite opinions."[4]

Although elected to the Royal Society in 1908, Russell's career at Trinity appeared to come to an end in 1916 when he was convicted and fined for anti-war activities. He was dismissed from the College as a result of the conviction.[5] Two years later Russell was convicted a second time. This time he spent six months in prison. It was while in prison that he wrote his well-received *Introduction to Mathematical Philosophy* (1919). He did not return to Trinity until 1944. Married four times and notorious for his many affairs, Russell also ran unsuccessfully for Parliament in 1907, 1922, and 1923. Together with his second wife, he opened and ran an experimental school during the late 1920s and early 1930s. He became the third Earl Russell upon the death of his brother in 1931.

While teaching in the United States in the late 1930s, Russell was offered a teaching appointment at City College, New York. The appointment was revoked following a large number of public protests and a judicial decision, in 1940, which stated that he was morally unfit to teach at the College. Nine years later he was awarded the Order of Merit. He received the Nobel Prize for Literature in 1950.

During the 1950s and 1960s, Russell became something of an inspiration to large numbers of idealistic youth as a result of his continued anti-war and anti-nuclear protests. Together with Albert Einstein, he released the Russell-Einstein Manifesto in 1955, calling for the curtailment of nuclear weapons. He became the founding president of the Campaign for Nuclear Disarmament in 1958 and was once again imprisoned, this time in connection with anti-nuclear protests, in 1961. Upon appeal, his two-month prison sentence was reduced to one week in the prison hospital. He remained a prominent public figure until his death nine years later at the age of 97.

ter. For example, if we agree to meet at the bank, we may be disappointed to learn that we have gone to different locations.

A more challenging example is contained in the following argument:

The end of a thing is its perfection
Death is the end of life

_____

Therefore, death is the perfection of life.

Something seems badly wrong here. It would appear that the argument is deductively valid, and the premises are true enough, yet the conclusion is clearly false. We know, though, that no sound argument can have a false conclusion. What has gone wrong? The error is not hard to spot. In the first premise the word "end" means goal or purpose, while in the second premise the same word means termination or end point. This ambiguity is not harmless at all. Rather it leads to a pernicious confusion. What may seem to be a plausible argument in reality contains a rather tricky deception.

But what is really wrong with the argument? The answer is that it is not really an argument at all! More specifically, it is not just one argument, but four. This multiplicity arises from the ambiguity of the word "end," which allows us to find four interpretations of what originally seemed to be a single argument. Here are the four versions of the original argument:

> **The Fallacy of Equivocation**
> The fallacy of *equivocation* occurs whenever an argument inappropriately depends on a semantic ambiguity. In other words, it occurs whenever a word that can be interpreted or defined in more than one way plays an important but changing role in an argument.

(1) The goal of a thing is its perfection
     Death is the goal of life

     _____

     Therefore, death is the perfection of life

(2) The termination of a thing is its perfection
     Death is the termination of life

     _____

     Therefore, death is the perfection of life

(3) The goal of a thing is its perfection
     Death is the termination of life

     _____

     Therefore, death is the perfection of life

(4) The termination of a thing is its perfection
     Death is the goal of life

     _____

     Therefore, death is the perfection of life.

Taken individually, none of these arguments is any good. Argument (1) has an implausible premiss, namely "Death is the goal of life." Argument (2) also has an implausible premiss, namely "The termination of a thing is its perfection." Argument (4) shares this implausible premiss in addition to containing the implausible premiss "Death is the goal of life." Only argument (3) has two quite plausible premisses, but it, like argument (4), is not valid. Despite our original intuition, not one of these arguments is sound.

The nineteenth-century logician Augustus De Morgan points out a similar, and rather delightful, equivocation that turns on the ambiguous use of the word "cross." Says De Morgan, "A person undertakes to cross a bridge in an incredibly short time: and redeems his pledge by crossing the bridge as one would cross a street, that is, by traversing the breadth."[6] Here the word "cross" has a second, special meaning that could not easily be inferred from its dictionary definition. The context in which the sentence occurs plausibly leads us to think that the speaker will cross the bridge in the sense of going from one end of the bridge to the other. Instead, the person is successful in meeting his objective by interpreting the word in a quite different sense, namely in the sense of going from one side of the bridge to the other.

Sometimes it is not one word but the whole sentence that is ambiguous, and it is this difference that underlies the distinction between *equivocation* and *amphiboly*. Specifically, logicians distinguish between the fallacy of equivocation and the fallacy of amphiboly by pointing out that the fallacy of amphiboly occurs whenever an argument depends on a grammatical, rather than a purely semantic, ambiguity. For example, the slogan "Save old cardboard boxes and waste paper" is grammatically ambiguous since it can be interpreted in different ways, depending on whether "waste" is understood as a verb or as an adjective.

Of course, ambiguities of this kind can arise in any number of different contexts without being fallacious. For example, the sign in the laundromat that states "Customers are required to remove their clothes when the machine stops" is simply an (ambiguous) statement of fact, not an argument. The same is true of the road-house sign that reads "Clean and decent dancing every night except Sunday" and the service station sign that reads "Eat here and get gas." Strictly speaking, these statements are not fallacies because they are not arguments. They are simply grammatically ambiguous sentences.

> **The Fallacy of Amphiboly**
> The fallacy of *amphiboly* occurs whenever an argument depends inappropriately on a grammatical, rather than a purely semantic, ambiguity.

Even so, it is also easy to imagine cases in which this type of ambiguity gives rise to fallacies. For example, the argument

Thrifty people save old cardboard boxes and waste paper

Therefore, thrifty people waste paper

will mislead us if we mistakenly believe that it has the valid form

$p \wedge q$

$q.$

However, once we recognize that the argument really has the form

$$p \land q$$
$$\overline{}$$
$$r$$

we are less likely to be misled.

The case of amphiboly is therefore quite similar to that of equivocation. Once we recognize the ambiguity, we see that there really is more than one argument under consideration. Mistakes will arise whenever we lump together two or more of these arguments, none of which is good in all respects.

A more challenging example concerns the following argument:

Everything has a cause

Therefore, there is something that causes everything.

Here the premiss may appear plausible enough, either as a principle of scientific explanation or perhaps as an article of scientific faith. It says that any phenomenon, if you examine it carefully enough, will turn out to have some causal antecedent that helps to explain how it came to be. However, even if this proposition is true, the conclusion—namely, that there is some one thing that causes everything—need not be. The reason is that the premiss says only that for every event, E_i, there is some cause, C_i (see diagram 5.1).

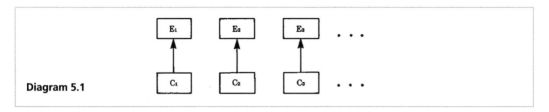

Diagram 5.1

In contrast, the conclusion says that every event, E_i, has the *same* cause, C_1 (see diagram 5.2).

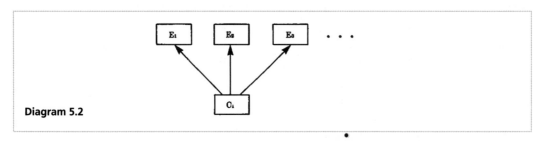

Diagram 5.2

If the argument were valid, it could be used to prove the existence of God. Unfortunately for natural theology,[7] the argument involves an ambiguity. Since this ambiguity is one that rests on the structure of the entire proposition, and not just on the equivocation of a single term, we say that this is again an instance of *amphiboly*.

Both equivocation and amphiboly turn out to be of interest to the moral philosopher as well as to the logician since they represent ways of not quite telling the truth, yet they fall just short of lying. Two interesting medieval examples are worth recalling in this regard. In the first, knowing that the answer to a given question is yes, one nevertheless answers by saying: "I *say* no," which is of course misleading but literally true. In the second, a monk is hiding a fugitive. To the query of whether the fugitive is with him, he replies "*Non est hic.*" The straightforward meaning of this Latin phrase is "He is not here," but the monk consoles himself with the thought that his words could be taken to mean "He is not eating here." Most of us would probably say that the monk had lied but, like the first case, it depends on what one means by *lying.*[8] Cases such as these leave the equivocator (or amphibolator) a handy excuse— he or she can always say, "Oh, I'm sorry you misunderstood, but I meant you to take it the other way."

Here is one final example: When King Croesus of Lydia in Asia Minor asked the Delphic Oracle whether to wage war against the Persians, the clever Oracle gave him the following advice: "If you should wage war against the Persians, you will destroy a mighty empire." When it turned out that Croesus waged war and lost, the Oracle was able to claim that the "mighty empire" referred to was that of Croesus himself.

To sum up, when they occur as fallacies, equivocation and amphiboly do not really occur in a single argument, but in many arguments masquerading as one. Both are fallacies that arise through ambiguity or multiple meaning. Thus, as always, before evaluating any argument it is always good advice to locate and identify the precise set of premises and conclusion in question.

Exercise 5.2

1. Identify and explain any ambiguities contained in the following examples. Are these ambiguities instances of amphiboly or equivocation?

    (a) The press should print all news that is in the public interest to be discussed. The public interest in this murder case is intense. Therefore, the press should print news about this case.

    (b) Saints and heroes who have sacrificed everything for others did so because they freely wanted to do so. In other words, they were really acting selfishly. Consequently, no free human action is unselfish. Altruism and human decency simply do not exist.

    (c) Jones showed great discrimination while hiring his department's sales reps. But discrimination is both illegal and immoral. So, at the very least, he deserves to be fired.

    (d) My uncle told me that my hunting is terrible. So I guess he must be against the killing of wildlife.

    (e) For sale: Newfoundland dog; will eat anything; very fond of children.

    (f) That dog is a mother and she is yours, so she must be your mother.

    (g) Bill loves chocolate more than Sue.

    (h) Sue told her mother that she had a stain on her jacket.

    (i) Nothing is too good for my friends.

    (j) Nothing is better than being in love, and a dollar is better than nothing; so a dollar is better than being in love.

4. The Paradox of the Liar

One final topic relating to the limits of formal logic concerns the famous paradox of the liar. Although an early version of this paradox can be found in one of St. Paul's epistles,[9] a more famous report comes from the Roman writer Cicero. Says Cicero, "A man says that he is lying. Is what he says true or false?"[10] Obviously, if what the man says is true, then it is true that he is lying, and so what he says must be false. Similarly, if what the man says is false, then it is false that he is lying, and so what he says must be true. In either case, it appears that what he says is both true and false, something that is clearly impossible.

In case we think that the paradox might somehow be avoided because lying involves the intention to deceive, the paradox can easily be recast using the simple proposition "This proposition is false." Once again, if this proposition is true, then it is true that it is false, and so it must be false. Similarly, if the proposition is false, then it is false that it is false, and so it must be true. In either case, it appears that the proposition is both true and false, something that again is clearly impossible.

The Paradox of the Liar

Consider the following proposition:
  This proposition is false.

Is this proposition true or false? If it is true, then it is true that it is false, and so it must be false. Similarly, if it is false, then it is false that it is false, and so it must be true. In either case, it appears that the proposition is both true and false, something that is clearly impossible.

In trying to resolve this paradox, many logicians have suggested that it is important to understand the distinction between object language and metalanguage. A *metalanguage* is any language used to talk about a (usually separate) language. The language being talked about, and which is used to talk about other (usually non-linguistic) objects, is called the *object language*. Within the current context it is important to note that any of the object languages we might wish to discuss will contain those arguments that we ultimately wish to evaluate. In contrast, the language in which our evaluations take place will be our metalanguage. In many contexts, of course, a person's object language and metalanguage are one and the same (e.g., English), but this need not be so.

Object Language versus Metalanguage
A *metalanguage* is any language used to talk about a (usually separate) language. The language being talked about, and which is used to talk about other (usually non-linguistic) objects, is called the *object language*.

In fact, the logician Alfred Tarski has argued that if we want to avoid inconsistencies such as those of the liar paradox then we will need to distinguish more carefully than we usually do between expressions in our object language and expressions in our metalanguage.[11] According to Tarski, any language suitable for argument should not be *semantically closed*. By a semantically closed language, Tarski means one in which the conventions that govern meaning and truth are formulated in that very language itself. To put the point another way, a language is semantically closed whenever it serves as its own metalanguage.[12] According to Tarski, if we want to investigate the logically interesting properties of any given language, and if we use that language itself as our vehicle of investigation, we will be caught in a kind of vicious circle. Paradoxes will then inevitably ensue. If Tarski is right, the moral is that semantic closure must not be allowed.

Exercise 5.3

1. Many people think that the problem with the paradox of the liar is that it involves both self-reference and a truth predicate. Which of the following paradoxes involve self-reference? Which involve a truth predicate?

(a) *The Postcard Paradox*: Consider the paradox that arises when, on one side of a postcard are the words: "The proposition written on the other side of this postcard is true," while on the other side of the postcard are the words: "The proposition written on the other side of this postcard is false." If the first proposition is true then it must be false, since the second proposition will truthfully say that it is false. Alternatively, if the first proposition is false then it must be true, since the second proposition falsely says that it is false. So, since it must be either true or false, it follows that it must be both true and false.

(b) *The Heterological Paradox*: Some adjectives, but not all, have meanings that describe themselves. For example, the word "short" is short, but the word "long" is not long. Similarly, the word "English" is itself English, but the word "French" is not itself French. Let us call adjectives, like "short" and "English," whose meanings can be predicated of themselves, autological; all others are said to be heterological. Now, is "heterological" heterological? If it is, its meaning does not apply to itself, and so it is not heterological. But if it is not, then its meaning does apply to itself, and so it is heterological. So since it must be one or the

other, it seems to follow that it must be both.

(c) *The Barber Paradox*: Consider the case of the barber who shaves all, and only, the men in his village who do not shave themselves. Who shaves the barber? If he shaves himself, then he must not shave himself since he shaves only those who do not shave themselves; but if he does not shave himself, then he must shave himself since he also shaves all those who do not shave themselves. Yet since the barber either shaves or does not shave himself, it follows that he must both shave himself and not shave himself.

(d) *The Protagoras Paradox*: The story is told that Protagoras agreed to teach Euathlus rhetoric on the condition that Euathlus would pay him a fee when he won his first case in court. But after completing his training, Euathlus failed to take on any clients. Growing impatient, Protagoras sued Euathlus for his fee. Once in court he argued as follows: "If I win this case, Euathlus will be required to pay me, since the court will have found in my favour. If I lose, Euathlus will still be required to pay me as a result of our agreement, since he then will have won his first case. So whatever happens, Euathlus will be required to pay me and the court should therefore find in my favour." But Euathlus, having learned his lessons well, replied: "If Protagoras wins this case, then I shall not be required to pay him, for I need not pay him until I win my first case; alternatively, if Protagoras loses, this court will have decided that I need not pay him, and so I need not do so. In either case I will not be required to pay and the court should therefore find in my favour." Since both arguments appear to be sound, it follows that the court should find both in favour of and against Euathlus.

(e) *Russell's Paradox*: Some sets, such as the set of teacups, are not members of themselves. Other sets, such as the set of all non-teacups, are members of themselves. Call the set of all sets that are not members of themselves "*S*". If *S* is a member of itself, then by definition it must not be a member of itself. Similarly, if *S* is not a member of itself, then by definition it must be a member of itself. Yet it must be one or the other. So *S* must both be, and not be, a member of itself.

Summary

We began this chapter by introducing the notion of *logical form*. We also saw that it is the goal of *formal logic* to discover those formal attributes of arguments that affect validity and other interesting logical properties. Because some argument forms are such that no argument having that form could have true premises and a false conclusion, it follows that every argument obtained from those forms by uniformly substituting propositional constants for propositional variables will be valid. The importance of formal logic for discovering valid arguments is therefore clear.

Despite the seemingly important role of an argument's subject matter (or material content), it even seems plausible to hypothesize that all logical relations (including validity, consistency, inconsistency, and so on), might be explainable in terms of logical form. Unfortunately, fallacies such as *equivocation* and *amphiboly* and paradoxes such as the *paradox of the liar* mean that, on this question, the jury is still out.

Weblinks

Stanford Encyclopedia of Philosophy—Informal Logic
plato.stanford.edu/entries/logic-informal/
Episteme Links—Bertrand Russell
www.epistemelinks.com/Pers/RussPers.htm
Stanford Encyclopedia of Philosophy—Bertrand Russell
plato.stanford.edu/entries/russell/
Bertrand Russell Archives
www.mcmaster.ca/russdocs/russell1.htm

Notes

1. They are good deductions but not good arguments. Both are circular. This point will be discussed further in ch. 10.

2. Lewis Carroll, *The Complete Works of Lewis Carroll* (New York: Vintage, 1976), 223.

3. There is exactly one exception to this rule; that is, one form of argument that can be known to be valid without knowing the meaning of any of its constituent terms. Can you identify it?

4. Richard Deacon, *The Cambridge Apostles* (London: Robert Royce Ltd., 1985), 43, 200ff.

5. The details of the dismissal are recounted in *Bertrand Russell and Trinity* (Cambridge: Cambridge University Press, 1942) by G.H. Hardy and in "Russell's Dismissal from Trinity: A Study in High Table Politics" by Paul Delany in A.D. Irvine, *Bertrand Russell: Critical Assessments*, 4 vols., (London: Routledge, 1999), vol. 1, 124–142.

6. Augustus De Morgan, *Formal Logic* (London: Taylor and Walton, 1847), 246.

7. Natural theology is that branch of theology that seeks to discuss the properties of divinity by inference from various facts within the natural world.

8. These examples are from Josef L. Altholz, "Truth and Equivocation: Liquoi's Moral Theology and Newman's Apologia," *Church History* 64 (1975), 73–84. See also two interesting articles that deal with how to define "lying," Frederick A. Siegler, "Lying," *American Philosophical Quarterly* 3 (1966), 128–136, and Roderick Chisholm and Thomas D. Feehan, "The Intent to Deceive," *Journal of Philosophy* 74 (1977), 143–159.

9. See *Titus* 1: 12–13.

10. See Cicero's *Prior Academics*, 2, 96.

11. See Alfred Tarski, "The Semantic Conception of Truth," *Philosophy and Phenomenological Research* 4 (1944), 341–75, and "The Concept of Truth in Formalized Languages," in *Logic, Semantics, Metamathematics* (New York: Clarendon Press, 1956), 152–278.

12. Yet another way of saying this is that a language is semantically closed whenever the following two conditions are met: (i) the language is sufficiently powerful to be able to refer to its own expressions, and (ii) the language contains a (universally applicable) truth predicate. For example, see A.D. Irvine, "Gaps, Gluts and Paradox," in Bruce Hunter and Philip Hanson (eds) "Return of the *A priori*," *Canadian Journal of Philosophy*, Supplementary vol. 18 (1993), 273–299.

CHAPTER 6

Formal Deductive Systems

UNTIL NOW we have been relying on a somewhat intuitive understanding of many logical concepts. In this chapter we want to rectify this by showing how logic can be organized into formal systems. To do so, we will develop the rudiments of an elementary formal system called "system *P*."

1. Formal Systems

A *formal system* (or *logistic system*) allows for the systematic study of the consequence relation and of other logical properties and relations. Each formal system is defined by a *primitive basis* consisting of an *object language* and a *logic*.

Each formal system's object language includes

- a *vocabulary* of primitive linguistic elements, and

- a *grammar* (sometimes referred to as a set of *formation rules*).

Together, the vocabulary and grammar allow us to construct a set of grammatically acceptable propositions or sentences, often called the *well-formed formulas* (or *wffs*) of the language.

Each formal system's logic includes

- a (possibly empty) set of *axioms*, and

- a set of *rules of inference* (sometimes called *transformation rules*).

Together, the axioms and rules of inference allow us to derive a set of propositions called *theorems*, all of which share some desirable property that we wish to study.

To be of use, a formal system must also satisfy the following two requirements:

- *The construction requirement*, which requires that the system provide an effective, reliable mechanism for constructing and identifying grammatically well-formed formulas of the object language; and

- *The decision requirement*, which requires that the system provide an effective, reliable mechanism for detecting the presence or absence of the logically interesting properties that we wish to study.

Formal Systems

A *formal system* (or *logistic system*) provides a systematic way of studying the consequence relation and other logical properties and relations. Each formal system is defined by its *primitive basis*. A primitive basis consists of four parts:

- a *vocabulary*,

- a *grammar*, sometimes called the language's formation rules,

- a (possibly empty) set of *axioms*, and

- a set of *rules of inference*, sometimes called *transformation rules*.

The vocabulary and grammar together constitute the *object language* of the formal system. The axioms and rules of inference together constitute the *logic* of the formal system. Those propositions that can be derived from the axioms by means of the rules of inference are called the *theorems* of the formal system.

A formal system that includes axioms is called an *axiomatic system*; a formal system that does not is called a *natural deduction system*. A formal system in which meanings are assigned to the various vocabulary items is said to be *interpreted*; otherwise it is said to be *uninterpreted*. By an *elementary system* we mean a formal system that studies the simplest parts of deductive logic, namely the truth-functional connectives. The formal system we introduce in this chapter is an elementary natural deduction system that is capable of being interpreted. The language used to describe and study a formal system is known as the system's *metalanguage*. We shall use English, supplemented with a variety of special symbols, as our metalanguage.

2. System *P*

Here is the primitive basis for the formal system *P*:

Vocabulary

The vocabulary for system *P* consists of three parts: propositional constants, propositional connectives, and grouping indicators. For our *propositional constants* we will use

$A, B, C, D, E, A_1, A_2, \ldots A_n, \ldots B_1, B_2, \ldots B_n, \ldots$

It is worth noticing that we have given ourselves quite a lot of propositional constants—in fact, infinitely many of them. By doing so, we are able to guarantee that there will be no argument, however complex, that we cannot analyze simply because we might run out of propositional constants.

The *propositional connectives* for system *P* are as follows:

- the tilde, ~, read "not ..."

- the vel, ∨, read "... or ____"

- the cap, ∧, read "... and ____"

- the hook (or horseshoe), ⊃, read "if ... then ____"

- the triple bar, ≡, read "... if and only if ____"

We appreciate that in this formal system the meaning of some of the constants will not be exactly the same as that of the corresponding words or phrases in English, if only because natural language connectives are ambiguous in a way that these connectives are not. The most pronounced deviation, as we saw in chapter 4, will be with the hook: ⊃.

Finally, we introduce the *grouping indicators*, or parentheses, "(" and ")".

Grammar

The grammar (or formation rules) of a formal system allows us to construct grammatically well-formed formulas in our object language using the items from our vocabulary. The formation rules for system *P* are as follows:

1. Any propositional constant standing alone is a well-formed formula (or wff) of system *P*.

2. For any two well-formed formulas of *P*, say, *p* and *q*, the following will also be well-formed formulas of *P*:

    $(\sim p)$

    $(p \lor q)$

    $(p \land q)$

    $(p \supset q)$

    $(p \equiv q)$.

3. Nothing else is a well-formed formula of *P*.

Suppose we want to construct the proposition $((A \lor B) \supset (\sim C))$. We can do so as follows: knowing (from rule 1) that *A*, *B*, and *C* are all wffs, we can construct $(A \lor B)$ and $(\sim C)$ by rule 2; then, using the two new wffs $(A \lor B)$ and $(\sim C)$, we can construct $((A \lor B) \supset (\sim C))$, again by rule 2. Informally, we may add the convention that the outermost parentheses of a formula may be dropped whenever this does not lead to ambiguity. For example, no ambiguity results from writing the formula $(A \lor B)$ as $A \lor B$. In contrast, the formula $(A \lor B) \land C$ may not be rewritten as $A \lor B \land C$, since the parentheses are needed to distinguish between the two formulas $(A \lor B) \land C$ and $A \lor (B \land C)$. We will also add the convention that the grouping indicators "[...]" and

"{...}" may be understood to be just sloppily written instances of "(...)", and so they may be used in order to avoid multiple nestings of parentheses, which can sometimes be difficult to read.

As before, any well-formed formula that contains no connectives is said to be *atomic*, while any well-formed formula that is not atomic is said to be *molecular* or *compound*. Any formula (i.e., any string of symbols from our vocabulary) that is not well-formed is said to be *ill-formed*.

The Primitive Basis for System *P*

The primitive basis for system *P* consists of the following:

- a *vocabulary*, composed of an infinite number of propositional constants (A, B, C, D, E, A_1, A_2, ... A_n ... B_1, B_2, ... B_n, ...), five propositional connectives ($\sim$, $\vee$, $\wedge$, $\supset$, $\equiv$, and two grouping indicators (the left and right parentheses),

- a *grammar*, composed of three formation rules that allow us to construct and identify all well-formed formulas (or wffs) of the system, and

- twenty-two *rules of inference*, based upon ten conditional argument forms, ten biconditional argument forms, and two hypothetical argument forms, together with the truth-table method introduced in chapter 4.

Axioms

In this treatment of propositional logic, the set of axioms is empty. (In other words, *P* is a natural deduction system rather than an axiomatic system.)

Rules of Inference

The rules of inference (or transformation rules) of *P* allow us to construct proofs (i.e., valid arguments) in which a conclusion can be seen to follow from a (possibly empty) set of premises. We have already introduced one set of rules for proving validity in system *P*; this was the *truth-table method*, introduced in chapter 4. In addition to this first method, it is possible to introduce another method for identifying these logical properties. In this second method, every proof will consist of a series of lines. Each line is numbered and contains a single well-formed formula (or proposition) together with its justification. Each such formula is justified by appeal to

- its existence as a premiss, or

- the fact that it follows from one or more previous lines through the application of a rule of inference.

No other justification for a line may be used. Because all uniform substitution instances of valid argument forms are valid, any valid argument form can serve as a rule of inference, provided that we specify that only uniform substitution instances of these forms will count as proofs or components of proofs.

The twenty-two rules of inference of system *P* fall into three groups: those based on *conditional argument forms*, those based on *biconditional argument forms*, and those based on *hypothetical argument forms*.

The ten rules of inference based on conditional argument forms are (1) *Modus Ponens* (also called Affirming the Antecedent), (2) *Modus Tollens* (also called Denying the Consequent), (3) Conjunction, (4) Simplification, (5) Addition, (6) Repetition, (7) Disjunctive Syllogism, (8) Hypothetical Syllogism, (9) Constructive Dilemma, and (10) Destructive Dilemma. Each rule allows us to derive a new line in a proof on

---

Conditional Rules of Inference

Modus Ponens (MP)
(Affirming the Antecedent)

$p \supset q$

p

_____

$\therefore q$

Modus Tollens (MT)
(Denying the Consequent)

$p \supset q$

$\sim q$

_____

$\therefore \sim p$

Conjunction (Conj)

p p

q q

_____   _____

$\therefore p \wedge q$ $\therefore q \wedge p$

Simplification (Simp)

$p \wedge q$ $p \wedge q$

_____   _____

$\therefore p$ $\therefore q$

Addition (Add)

p

_____

$\therefore p \vee q$

Repetition (R)

p

_____

$\therefore p$

Disjunctive Syllogism (DS)

$p \vee q$ $p \vee q$

$\sim p$ $\sim q$

_____   _____

$\therefore q$ $\therefore p$

Hypothetical Syllogism (HS)

$p \supset q$

$q \supset r$

_____

$\therefore p \supset r$

Constructive Dilemma (CD)

$p \supset r$

$q \supset s$

$p \vee q$

_____

$\therefore r \vee s$

Destructive Dilemma (DD)

$p \supset r$

$q \supset s$

$\sim r \vee \sim s$

_____

$\therefore \sim p \vee \sim q$

the basis of one or more previous lines. We justify the new line by citing the previous line or lines together with the rule being used. For example, given the rule *Modus Ponens*,

$$p \supset q$$
$$p$$

$$\therefore q$$

we are able to introduce a new line, q, provided that there exist previous lines $p \supset q$ and p.

For example, consider the argument

(P1) A
(P2) $(A \lor B) \supset {\sim}C$
(P3) ${\sim}C \supset D$

(P4) D.

In order to show that this argument is valid we can construct a proof using two of the preceding rules as follows:

1. A	Premiss
2. $(A \lor B) \supset {\sim}C$	Premiss
3. ${\sim}C \supset D$	Premiss
4. $A \lor B$	1 Add
5. ${\sim}C$	2, 4 MP
6. D	3, 5 MP.

In this proof, every line is justified, either because it is a premiss or because it follows from one or more previous lines as a result of our rules of inference. In this example, lines 1 and 4 constitute a uniform substitution instance of the argument form Addition; lines 2, 4, and 5 and lines 3, 5, and 6 constitute uniform substitution instances of the argument form *Modus Ponens*.

The ten rules of inference based on biconditional argument forms are (1) Double Negation, (2) Implication, (3) Commutation, (4) Association, (5) Distribution, (6) De Morgan's Rules, (7) Contraposition (also called Transposition), (8) Exportation, (9) Tautology, and (10) Equivalence. Each rule allows us to derive a new line in a proof on the basis of a single previous line. We justify the new line by citing the previous line together with the rule being used. For example, given the rule Double Negation,

$$p :: {\sim}{\sim}p,$$

and reading "::" as "is equivalent to," we are able to do any of the following four things:

- introduce a new line, ${\sim}{\sim}p$, provided that there exists a previous line, p;

- introduce a new line, p, provided that there exists a previous line, ${\sim}{\sim}p$;

- introduce a new line that contains a molecular proposition with $\sim \sim p$ as one of its constituent parts, provided that there exists a previous line that is identical to the new line except that, where the new line contains the proposition $\sim \sim p$, the previous line contains the proposition p; and

- introduce a new line that contains a molecular proposition with p as one of its constituent parts, provided that there exists a previous line that is identical to the new line except that, where the new line contains the proposition p, the previous line contains the proposition $\sim \sim p$.

For example, consider the argument

(P1) $A \supset (B \vee C)$
(P2) $\sim A \supset \sim D$

(C) $D \supset (C \vee B)$.

In order to show that this argument is valid we can construct a proof using three of the preceding rules as follows:

Biconditional Rules of Inference

Double Negation (DN)

$p :: \sim \sim p$

Implication (Impl)

$p \supset q :: \sim p \vee q$

Commutation (Comm)

$p \vee q :: q \vee p$
$p \wedge q :: q \wedge p$

Association (Assoc)

$p \vee (q \vee r) :: (p \vee q) \vee r$
$p \wedge (q \wedge r) :: (p \wedge q) \wedge r$

Distribution (Dist)

$p \wedge (q \vee r) :: (p \wedge q) \vee (p \wedge r)$
$p \vee (q \wedge r) :: (p \vee q) \wedge (p \vee r)$

De Morgan's Rules (DeM)

$\sim(p \wedge q) :: \sim p \vee \sim q$
$\sim(p \vee q) :: \sim p \wedge \sim q$

Contraposition (Contra)
(Transposition)

$p \supset q :: \sim q \supset \sim p$

Exportation (Exp)

$(p \wedge q) \supset r :: p \supset (q \supset r)$

Tautology (Taut)

$p :: p \wedge p$
$p :: p \vee p$

Equivalence (Equiv)

$p \equiv q :: (p \supset q) \wedge (q \supset p)$
$p \equiv q :: (p \wedge q) \vee (\sim p \wedge \sim q)$

1. $\sim A \supset \sim D$ Premiss
2. $D \supset A$ 1 Contra
3. $A \supset (B \vee C)$ Premiss
4. $D \supset (B \vee C)$ 2, 3 HS
5. $D \supset (C \vee B)$ 4 Comm.

Once again, every line is justified, either because it is a premiss, or because it follows from one or more previous lines as a result of our rules of inference. In this example, lines 1 and 2 constitute a uniform substitution instance of the argument form Contraposition; lines 2, 3, and 4 constitute a uniform substitution instance of the argument form Hypothetical Syllogism; and the consequents of the conditionals in lines 4 and 5 constitute a uniform substitution instance of the argument form Commutation.

It is important to note that our rules involving biconditional argument forms are more versatile than our rules involving only implicational argument forms. This occurs for two reasons. First, each such rule works "in two directions." For example, using Double Negation we can not only derive propositions of the form $\sim \sim p$ from propositions of the form p, we can also derive propositions of the form p from propositions of the form $\sim \sim p$. Second, each such rule can operate both on complete lines and on well-formed formulas that are themselves contained within complete lines. For example, in the preceding proof, the rule of Commutation was applied only to the consequent of the conditional in line 4, and not to the entire line.

Finally, we introduce two rules of inference based on hypothetical argument forms, namely (1) Conditional Proof and (2) Indirect Proof (also called *Reductio ad Absurdum*). Each rule allows us to derive a new line in a proof on the basis of a series of previous lines. We justify the new line by citing the relevant series of previous lines together with the rule being used. Both rules differ from previous rules in that they allow the use of *hypothetical* (or *provisional*, or *temporary*) *assumptions*. In the case of Conditional Proof, a conditional proposition of the form $p \supset q$ is proved by showing that the consequence of the proposition, q, follows from the temporary assumption of the antecedent, p. In the case of Indirect Proof, a proposition, p (or $\sim p$), is proved by showing that the temporary assumption of its denial, $\sim p$ (or p), leads to a contradiction, $q \wedge \sim q$. In both cases we draw a *vertical line* to the left of the proof

---

Hypothetical Rules of Inference

Conditional Proof (CP)	**Indirect Proof (IP)**	
	(*Reductio Ad Absurdum*) (RAA)	

p Assump (CP) p Assump (IP) $\sim p$ Assump (IP)
$\vdots$ $\vdots$ $\vdots$
q $q \wedge \sim q$ $q \wedge \sim q$

$\therefore p \supset q$ $\therefore \sim p$ $\therefore p$

to remind us that a temporary assumption is in place. The assumption is said to be *discharged* once either of our two hypothetical rules is invoked. No proof can be complete until all of its temporary assumptions have been discharged.

For example, consider the argument

(P1) B ∨ C
(P2) A ⊃ ~C

———————

(C) A ⊃ B.

In order to show this argument to be valid we construct a proof using Conditional Proof, as follows:

1. $B \lor C$	Premiss
2. $A \supset {\sim}C$	Premiss
3. A	Assump (CP)
4. ~C	2, 3 MP
5. B	1, 4 DS
6. $A \supset B$	3–5 CP.

In this example, lines 2, 3, and 4 constitute a uniform substitution instance of the argument form *Modus Ponens*; and lines 1, 4, and 5 constitute a uniform substitution instance of the argument form Disjunctive Syllogism. The only other lines that are not premisses are lines 3 and 6, both of which are justified through the rule of Conditional Proof.

For an example involving Indirect Proof, consider the argument

(P1) $A \land {\sim}C$
(P2) $B \supset C$

———————

(C) $\sim B$.

In order to show this argument to be valid we can construct a proof using Indirect Proof as follows:

1. $A \land {\sim}C$	Premiss
2. $B \supset C$	Premiss
3. B	Assump (IP)
4. C	2, 3 MP
5. ~C	1 Simp
6. $C \land {\sim}C$	4, 5 Conj
7. $\sim B$	3–6 IP.

In this example, lines 2, 3, and 4 constitute a uniform substitution instance of the argument form *Modus Ponens*; lines 1 and 5 constitute a uniform substitution instance of Simplification; lines 4, 5, and 6 constitute a uniform substitution instance of Conjunction. The only other lines that are not premisses are lines 3 and 7, both of which are justified through the rule of Indirect Proof.

This completes the primitive basis for system *P*.

Exercise 6.1

1. Using the formation rules for system *P*, determine whether each of the following formulas is, or is not, a well-formed formula:

   (a) $(p \supset q) \vee (r \supset (p \vee p))$

   (b) $(A \supset B) \vee (B \supset C) \supset (A \supset C)$

   (c) $((A \supset {\sim}B) \wedge (B \supset {\sim}C)) \vee D$

   (d) $(A \wedge B \vee C)$

   (e) ${\sim}(({\sim}A \supset {\sim}B) \supset ({\sim}B \supset {\sim}A))$

2. Using truth tables, prove that the argument form corresponding to each of the following conditional rules of inference is valid:

   (a) *Modus Ponens*

   (b) Addition

   (c) Disjunctive Syllogism

   (d) Hypothetical Syllogism

   (e) Destructive Dilemma

3. Using truth tables, prove that the argument form corresponding to each of the following biconditional rules of inference is valid:

   (a) Double Negation

   (b) Contraposition

   (c) Implication

   (d) De Morgan's Rules

   (e) Exportation

4. Name the rule that justifies each of the following inferences:

   (a) $A \wedge (C \supset D)$
   _____
   $C \supset D$

   (b) $A \supset (C \supset D)$
   $(C \supset D) \supset B$
   _____
   $A \supset B$

   (c) $A \supset (C \supset D)$
   ${\sim}(C \supset D)$
   _____
   ${\sim}A$

   (d) $A \supset (C \supset D)$
   A
   _____
   $(C \supset D)$

   (e) $A \supset (C \supset D)$
   $B \supset (E \vee F)$
   $A \vee B$
   _____
   $(C \supset D) \vee (E \vee F)$

   (f) $A \wedge (C \supset D)$
   _____
   $(C \supset D) \wedge A$

   (g) $A \supset (C \supset D)$
   _____
   ${\sim}(C \supset D) \supset {\sim}A$

   (h) ${\sim}A \vee {\sim}(C \supset D)$
   _____
   ${\sim}(A \wedge (C \supset D))$

   (i) $A \supset (C \supset D)$
   _____
   $A \supset ({\sim}{\sim}C \supset D)$

   (j) $(A \supset (C \supset D)) \wedge ((C \supset D) \supset A)$
   _____
   $A \equiv (C \supset D)$

3. Working in System *P*

In chapter 4 we introduced our first method for identifying valid arguments, the method of truth tables. Because of its mechanical nature, that method was not only effective, it was also easy to learn and easy to apply. In contrast, discovering natural deduction proofs is as much an art as it is a science. This is partly because the rules of inference used in systems such as *P* typically allow each result to be proved in more than one way. (In fact, in system *P* there are an infinite number of ways to prove each result!) Partly, too, it is because it is not always easy to decide which rules are best applied in any particular circumstances. For example, consider the following argument:

(P1) [(*A* ∧ *B*) ⊃ ~*C*] ∧ [~*D* ⊃ ~(*A* ∧ *B*)]
(P2) *A* ∧ *B*
(P3) [*C* ∨ (*D* ∧ *B*)] ∧ *E*

(C) *D* ∧ *E*.

This argument can be proved valid as follows:

1. [(*A* ∧ *B*) ⊃ ~*C*] ∧ [~*D* ⊃ ~(*A* ∧ *B*)]	Premiss
2. *A* ∧ *B*	Premiss
3. [*C* ∨ (*D* ∧ *B*)] ∧ *E*	Premiss
4. (*A* ∧ *B*) ⊃ ~*C*	1 Simp
5. ~*C*	4, 2 MP
6. *C* ∨ (*D* ∧ *B*)	3 Simp
7. *D* ∧ *B*	6, 5 DS
8. *D*	7 Simp
9. *E*	3 Simp
10. *D* ∧ *E*	8, 9 Conj.

It can also be proved valid as follows:

1. [(*A* ∧ *B*) ⊃ ~*C*] ∧ [~*D* ⊃ ~(*A* ∧ *B*)]	Premiss
2. *A* ∧ *B*	Premiss
3. [*C* ∨ (*D* ∧ *B*)] ∧ *E*	Premiss
4. ~*D*	Assump (IP)
5. ~*D* ⊃ ~(*A* ∧ *B*)	1 Simp
6. ~(*A* ∧ *B*)	5, 4 MP
7. (*A* ∧ *B*) ∧ ~(*A* ∧ *B*)	2, 6 Conj
8. *D*	4–7 IP
9. *E*	3 Simp
10. *D* ∧ *E*	8, 9 Conj.

Similarly, if our goal is to prove ~A ∨ A (from no premisses), we can do so using the rule of Conditional Proof as follows:

1. A	Assump (CP)
2. A	1 Rep
3. $A \supset A$	1–2 CP
4. $\sim A \vee A$	3 Imp.

We can prove the same result using the rule of Indirect Proof instead:

1. $\sim(\sim A \vee A)$	Assump (IP)
2. $\sim \sim A \wedge \sim A$	1 DeM
3. $A \wedge \sim A$	2 DN
4. $\sim A \vee A$	1–3 IP.

What is the most efficient way to discover such proofs? Here are seven helpful strategies:

Strategy 1 – Identify Argument Forms that Correspond to Valid Rules of Inference

For example, consider the following two arguments:

(P1) $A \supset (C \wedge D)$

_____

(C) $\sim(C \wedge D) \supset \sim A$

and

(P1) $[(D \supset B) \wedge A] \supset [A \supset (B \supset C)]$

_____

(C) $\sim[A \supset (B \supset C)] \supset \sim[(D \supset B) \wedge A]$.

Even though they appear to be quite different, and even though the second may appear to be much more complex than the first, once we notice that both arguments are instances of the argument form for Contraposition we see immediately that both conclusions can be proved using a single rule of inference.

Strategy 2 – Break Long Proofs into a Series of Shorter Subproofs

For example, consider the following argument:

(P1) $[\sim(B \wedge \sim A) \supset \sim B] \wedge \sim C$
(P2) $B \supset (\sim A \supset C)$

_____

(C) $\sim B$.

In this case, we know that our ultimate goal is to prove $\sim B$, and that $[\sim(B \wedge \sim A) \supset \sim B]$ comes from (P1) immediately by Simplification. So our intermediate goal should be to try to prove $\sim(B \wedge \sim A)$. Once we have $\sim(B \wedge \sim A)$ we will be able to prove $\sim B$ by *Modus Ponens*. Looking at what we have to work with, it seems reasonable to believe that we might be able to prove ~(B ∧ ~A) using (P2) together with ~C (from (P1)), for example, by using Exportation and *Modus Tollens*. Keeping the intermediate goal of proving ~(B ∧ ~A) in mind, the proof then can be constructed as follows:

1. [~(B ∧ ~A) ⊃ ~B] ⊃ ~C	Premiss
2. B ⊃ (~A ⊃ C)	Premiss
3. (B ∧ ~A) ⊃ ~B	1 Simp
4. (B ∧ ~A) ⊃ C	2 Exp
5. ~C	1 Simp
6. ~(B ∧ ~A)	4, 5 MT
7. ~B	3, 6 MP.

Proof Strategies

1. Identify argument forms that correspond to valid rules of inference.

2. Break long proofs into a series of shorter subproofs.

3. Try to use atomic propositions early and often.

4. Look for propositions that are repeated (including propositions that are themselves constituents in other propositions).

5. Work both from the top down and from the bottom up, especially in long proofs.

6. Recall that some rules introduce connectives while others eliminate them.

7. When stuck, or when a result needs to be proved in the absence of premisses, use CP or IP.

Strategy 3 – Try to Use Atomic Propositions Early and Often

For example, consider the following argument:

(P1) (B ∧ C) ⊃ ~A
(P2) ~D ∨ (B ∧ C)
(P3) A

_____

(C) ~D.

Seeing that (P3) is atomic, and seeing that A appears in only one other proposition, we immediately try to use A in combination with that other proposition. The result is as follows:

1. (B ∧ C) ⊃ ~A	Premiss
2. ~D ∨ (B ∧ C)	Premiss
3. A	Premiss
4. ~ ~A	3 DN
5. ~(B ∧ C)	1, 4 MT
6. ~D	2, 5 DS.

Strategy 4 – Look for Propositions that Are Repeated

This includes propositions that are themselves constituents in other propositions. Use them with rules such as DS, HS, MP, and MT.

For example, consider the following argument:

(P1) [A ∨ (~B ⊃ C)] ⊃ [~D ∨ (C ∧ E)]
(P2) ~[~D ∨ (C ∧ E)]

(C)　~[A ∨ (~B ⊃ C)].

Here, even though this looks like a very complex argument, in fact only a single step is required. Once we notice that both [A ∨ (~B ⊃ C)] and [~D ∨ (C ∧ E)] are repeated, it is easy to see that the entire argument is simply a single instance of the argument form *Modus Tollens*. The entire proof is thus only three steps long—two lines for the premisses and one for the conclusion!

1. [A ∨ (~B ⊃ C)] ⊃ [~D ∨ (C ∧ E)]	Premiss
2. ~[~D ∨ (C ∧ E)]	Premiss
3. ~[A ∨ (~B ⊃ C)]	1, 2 MT.

Strategy 5 – Work from the Top Down and from the Bottom Up

Work both from the top down and from the bottom up, especially in long proofs. For example, consider the following argument:

(P1) ~(~A ∧ ~B)
(P2) B ⊃ C
(P3) ~A
(P4) ~(C ∧ ~D)

(C)　D.

In this case, knowing that we want to finish our proof by asserting D, we begin with (P4) since this is the only premiss that mentions D. Recognizing that De Morgan's Rules will apply to it, we now have the following incomplete proof:

1. ~(~A ∧ ~B)	Premiss
2. B ⊃ C	Premiss
3. ~A	Premiss
4. ~(C ∧ ~D)	Premiss
5. ~C ∨ ~ ~D	4 DeM
.	.
.	.
.	.
n. D	…. .

We then look for ways to reach our goal. For example, recognizing that $\sim\sim D$ is equivalent to D, we might look for a way to obtain the denial of $\sim C$ (that is, $\sim\sim C$) in the line immediately prior to our last line, n. Then, using that line together with line 5, we could justify line n via DS. The completed proof is as follows:

1. $\sim(\sim A \wedge \sim B)$	Premiss
2. $B \supset C$	Premiss
3. $\sim A$	Premiss
4. $\sim(C \wedge \sim D)$	Premiss
5. $\sim C \vee \sim \sim D$	4 DeM
6. $\sim C \vee D$	5 DN
7. $\sim \sim A \vee \sim \sim B$	1 DeM
8. $A \vee \sim \sim B$	7 DN
9. $A \vee B$	8 DN
10. B	9, 3 DS
11. C	2, 10 MP
12. $\sim \sim C$	11 DN
13. D	6, 12 DS.

Strategy 6 – Recall that Some Rules Introduce Connectives while others Eliminate Them

For example, the $\vee$ may be introduced to a new line in a proof using Addition or Tautology, and it may be eliminated from previous lines using Disjunctive Syllogism or Tautology. Similarly, $\wedge$ may be introduced using Conjunction or Tautology and it may be eliminated using Simplification or Tautology; $\sim$ may be introduced using Double Negation and it may be eliminated using this same rule; $\supset$ may be introduced using Conditional Proof and it may be eliminated using *Modus Ponens*, *Modus Tollens*, Constructive Dilemma, or Destructive Dilemma; and, finally, $\equiv$ may be introduced using Equivalence and it may be eliminated using this same rule. In addition, Indirect Proof may be used to introduce or eliminate all five connectives. For example, if we need to prove $\sim(B \vee \sim B) \supset A$, we may do so using Conditional Proof in the standard way, or we may do so as follows:

1. $\sim[\sim(B \vee \sim B) \supset A]$	Assump (IP)
2. $\sim[\sim \sim(B \vee \sim B) \vee A]$	1 Impl
3. $\sim[(B \vee \sim B) \vee A]$	2 DN
4. $\sim(B \vee \sim B) \wedge \sim A$	3 DeM
5. $(\sim B \wedge \sim \sim B) \wedge \sim A$	4 DeM
6. $\sim B \wedge \sim \sim B$	5 Simp
7. $\sim(B \vee \sim B) \supset A$	1–6 IP.

Strategy 7 – When Stuck, Use CP or IP

When stuck, or when a result needs to be proved in the absence of premisses, use CP or IP.

For example, consider the following argument:

(P1) ~[~A ∧ (A ∧ C)] ⊃ B

_____

(C) B.

In this case, providing that we could prove ~[~A ∧ (A ∧ C)], we see that B would then follow immediately by *Modus Ponens*. But how can we prove ~[~A ∧ (A ∧ C)]? Realizing that there are no additional premisses to rely on, we turn to our hypothetical argument forms, CP and IP. Since ~[~A ∧ (A ∧ C)] is not a conditional proposition, we rightly guess that IP will be more efficient than CP. The result is as follows:

1. ~[~A ∧ (A ∧ C)] ⊃ B	Premiss
2. ~A ∧ (A ∧ C)	Assump (IP)
3. (~A ∧ A) ∧ C	2 Assoc
4. ~A ∧ A	3 Simp
5. A ∧ ~A	4 Comm
6. ~[~A ∧ (A ∧ C)]	2–5 IP
7. B	6, 1 MP.

Sample Proofs

I. (P1) [A ⊃ ~B] ∧ ~C
(P2) B ⊃ (~A ⊃ C)

_____

(C) ~B

1. [A ⊃ ~B] ∧ ~C	Premiss
2. B ⊃ (~A ⊃ C)	Premiss
3. A ⊃ ~B	1 Simp
4. ~C	1 Simp
5. (B ∧ ~A) ⊃ C	2 Exp
6. ~(B ∧ ~A)	5, 4 MT
7. ~B ∨ ~ ~A	6 DeM
8. ~B ∨ A	7 DN
9. B ⊃ A	8 Impl
10. B ⊃ ~B	9, 3 HS
11. ~B ∨ ~B	10 Impl
12. ~B	11 Taut

II. (P1) $A \equiv B$
     (P2) $\sim A \lor \sim B$
     (P3) $\sim C \lor (B \land D)$
     _____

     (C) $\sim C$

1. $A \equiv B$	Premiss
2. $\sim A \lor \sim B$	Premiss
3. $\sim C \lor (B \land D)$	Premiss
4. $(B \land D) \lor \sim C$	3 Comm
5. $\sim \sim (B \land D) \lor \sim C$	4 DN
6. $\sim (B \land D) \supset \sim C$	5 Impl
7. $(\sim B \lor \sim D) \supset \sim C$	6 DeM
8. $\sim (A \land B)$	2 DeM
9. $(A \land B) \lor (\sim A \land \sim B)$	1 Equiv
10. $\sim A \land \sim B$	9, 8 DS
11. $\sim B$	10 Simp
12. $\sim B \lor \sim D$	11 Add
13. $\sim C$	7, 12 MP

Or ...

1. $A \equiv B$	Premiss
2. $\sim A \lor \sim B$	Premiss
3. $\sim C \lor (B \land D)$	Premiss
4. $(A \land B) \lor (\sim A \land \sim B)$	1 Equiv
5. $\sim (A \land B)$	2 DeM
6. $\sim A \land \sim B$	5, 4 DS
7. $\sim B$	6 Simp
8. $\sim B \lor \sim D$	7 Add
9. $\sim (B \land D)$	8 DeM
10. $\sim C$	3, 9 DS

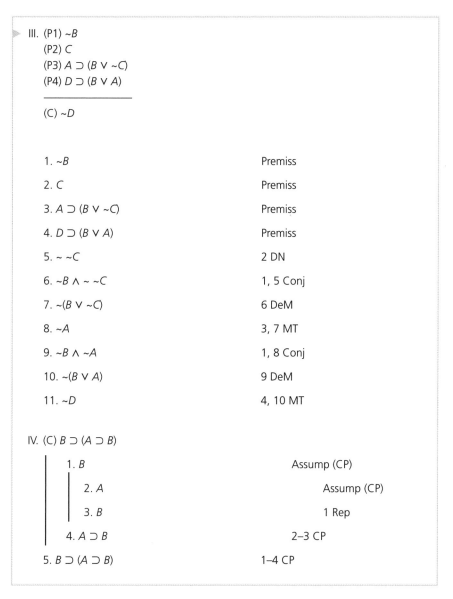

III. (P1) ~B
(P2) C
(P3) A ⊃ (B ∨ ~C)
(P4) D ⊃ (B ∨ A)
_____

(C) ~D

1. ~B   Premiss

2. C   Premiss

3. A ⊃ (B ∨ ~C)   Premiss

4. D ⊃ (B ∨ A)   Premiss

5. ~ ~C   2 DN

6. ~B ∧ ~ ~C   1, 5 Conj

7. ~(B ∨ ~C)   6 DeM

8. ~A   3, 7 MT

9. ~B ∧ ~A   1, 8 Conj

10. ~(B ∨ A)   9 DeM

11. ~D   4, 10 MT

IV. (C) B ⊃ (A ⊃ B)

   │   1. B   Assump (CP)
   │   │   2. A   Assump (CP)
   │   │   3. B   1 Rep
   │   4. A ⊃ B   2–3 CP
   5. B ⊃ (A ⊃ B)   1–4 CP

Natural deduction proofs in system *P* are thus a helpful supplement to the equally effective, but often more cumbersome, truth-table method introduced in chapter 4. In addition, just as with truth tables, this new system of proofs can be used to help clarify natural-language arguments. For example, consider the following argument:

Sue will enroll in either Philosophy 220 or Philosophy 230. If it conflicts with her computer science lectures, she won't enroll in Philosophy 230. So assuming that there is a conflict, it not only follows that she won't enroll in Philosophy 230, it also follows that she will enroll in Philosophy 220. So if there is a conflict between Philosophy 230 and Sue's computer science lectures, Sue will enroll in Philosophy 220.

If we let

A = Sue will enroll in Philosophy 220
B = Sue will enroll in Philosophy 230
C = Philosophy 230 conflicts with Sue's computer science lectures

then we can formalize this argument as follows:

1. *A* ∨ *B*	Premiss
2. *C* ⊃ ~*B*	Premiss
3. *C*	Assump (CP)
4. ~*B*	2, 3 MP
5. *A*	1, 4 DS
6. *C* ⊃ *A*	3–5 CP.

Unlike truth tables, this way of formalizing the argument lays bare its "natural" structure.

Exercise 6.2

1. Using the rules of inference of system *P*, prove each of the following arguments to be valid:

(a) *A* ⊃ *B*
   A ∨ (*B* ∧ *C*)
   ———————
   B

(b) *B*
   A ⊃ ~*B*
   C ∧ *D*
   ———————
   ~*A* ∧ *D*

(c) *A* ⊃ ~*B*
   ~*C* ⊃ *D*
   ~*D* ∨ *B*
   ———————
   ~*A* ∨ *C*

(d) *A* ⊃ ~*B*
   ———————————
   (~ ~*B* ⊃ ~*A*) ∨ ~ ~*C*

(e) *A* ⊃ (~*C* ⊃ [*B* ⊃ ~*D*])
   A ∧ ~*C*
   ———————
   D ⊃ ~*B*

(f) ~*C*
   D ⊃ *C*
   (~*D* ∨ *E*) ⊃ (*A* ⊃ *B*)
   ———————
   ~*B* ⊃ ~*A*

(g) *A* ⊃ (*B* ∧ *C*)
   D
   ~*C*
   ———————
   D ∧ ~*A*

(h) *A* ⊃ (*B* ∧ *C*)
   A ⊃ (*D* ∧ *E*)
   E ⊃ ~*C*
   ———————
   ~*A*

(i) *A* ⊃ ~*B*
   ———————
   B ⊃ ~*A*

(j) *C*
   ———————
   C ∧ (*B* ∨ ~*B*)

2. Prove that from contradictory premisses, anything follows.

3. Formalize the following natural-language arguments and then prove them to be valid using the rules of inference for system *P*:

(a) If unemployment continues to rise, taxes will increase. If taxes increase, then money will become scarce. This, of course, will be sufficient to cause Bill to be unhappy. So, if unemployment continues to rise, Bill is bound to be unhappy.

(b) Sue has an interest in philosophy if she has read Plato's *Apology* or Russell's *In Praise of Idleness*. She's told us that she has never read Russell's *In Praise of Idleness*, but that she has read the *Apology,* and so she must be interested in philosophy.

(c) Being interested in philosophy is a sufficient reason for Bill to read the works of Bertrand Russell. But Bill isn't acquainted with Russell's writings if he isn't a history buff. So, since Bill isn't a history buff, it follows that he isn't interested in philosophy.

(d) Bill parked his car in either the Blue lot or the Red lot. If he parked it in the Blue lot then it would still be there. But it's not. So he must have parked it in the Red lot.

(e) Exactly two of Bill, Sue, and Carol attended the lecture. We know that Sue was there and that if Sue was there then Bill would have been there too. So Carol must not have been there.

4. Evaluating System *P*

Let us now consider whether system *P* satisfies our two requirements for any good formal system, namely the construction requirement and the decision requirement.

The Construction Requirement for System *P*

This is the requirement that there must be an effective, reliable mechanism for constructing and identifying grammatically well-formed formulas (wffs) of the object language. Clearly the vocabulary and formation rules of *P*'s primitive basis allow for the construction of well-formed formulas. By means of these same rules we can also determine whether an arbitrary formula is, or is not, well formed. For example, consider the formula $\sim(A \lor B) \supset ((\sim A \land \sim B) \equiv A)$.

We can prove that this formula is a wff of *P* by applying our formation rules, starting from the innermost formulas and working outwards. First, we know that all occurrences of A and B are wffs. Second, we know, by the formation rule for $\sim$, that placing the symbol $\sim$ in front of any wff produces a new wff. So we know that $\sim A$ and $\sim B$ are wffs. Next, we know that putting a $\lor$ or a $\land$ between any two wffs yields a new wff, so we know that both $(A \lor B)$ and $(\sim A \land \sim B)$ are wffs. Proceeding in this way, we next see that $\sim(A \lor B)$ and $((\sim A \land \sim B) \equiv A)$ are wffs, and finally, that the entire formula $\sim(A \lor B) \supset ((\sim A \land \sim B) \equiv A)$ is well formed.

In much the same way we can also prove that the formula $\sim A \lor B \lor \sim C$ is ill formed. As before, we recognize that A, B, and C are all wffs, and that $\sim A$ and $\sim C$ are wffs as well. Then, although we can show that both $\sim A \lor B$ and $B \lor \sim C$ are wffs, and that $(\sim A \vee B) \vee \sim C$ and $\sim A \vee (B \vee \sim C)$ are wffs, there is no rule or combination of rules that allows us to form $\sim A \vee B \vee \sim C$. We conclude that the formula is not well formed.

The Decision Requirement for System *P*

This is the requirement that there must be an effective, reliable mechanism for detecting the presence or absence of the various interesting properties we wish to study. Among the several interesting logical properties that we may be interested in studying are the following:

- the (logical) necessity, (logical) impossibility, and (logical) contingency of propositions;

- the (deductive) validity and (deductive) invalidity of arguments;

- the (logical) consistency and (logical) inconsistency of sets of propositions; and

- the (logical) equivalence and (logical) non-equivalence of pairs of propositions.

We define these properties as follows: A proposition is *(logically) necessary* (or a *logical truth*) if and only if it is true regardless of how the world might be; it is *(logically) impossible* (or a *logical falsehood*) if and only if it is false regardless of how the world might be; and it is *(logically) contingent* if and only if it is neither (logically) necessary nor (logically) impossible. An argument is *(deductively) valid* if and only if it is (logically) impossible for the premises to be true and the conclusion to be false; it is *(deductively) invalid* if and only if it is not (deductively) valid. A set of propositions is *(logically) inconsistent* if and only if it is (logically) impossible for all of the propositions in the set to be true together; it is *(logically) consistent* if and only if it is not (logically) inconsistent. Finally, a pair of propositions is *(logically) equivalent* if and only if it is (logically) impossible for the two propositions to have different truth values; they are *(logically) non-equivalent* if and only if they are not (logically) equivalent.

System *P* helps us study these properties. In what follows it is assumed that all propositional constants represent atomic propositions and that distinct propositional constants represent distinct propositions.

- *Necessity, Impossibility, and Contingency.* A proposition that is necessarily true as a result of its truth-functional connectives is said to be a *tautology*, or a *truth-functional necessity*. The tautologies form a proper subset of the logical necessities and constitute the theorems of system *P*. Any proposition whose corresponding truth table shows that it cannot be false is a tautology. Similarly, any proposition for which there is a corresponding proof from no premises that has been constructed using the rules of inference of system *P* is a tautology. Any proposition that is the negation of a tautology is a *contradiction*, or a *truth-functional impossibility*. Any proposition that is neither a tautology nor a contradiction is a *truth-functional contingency*. Examples of tautologies include

$A \vee {\sim}A, A \supset A$, and $(A \supset B) \equiv ({\sim}B \supset {\sim}A)$. Examples of contradictions include $A \wedge {\sim}A, {\sim}(A \vee {\sim}A)$, and ${\sim}(A \equiv A)$. Examples of truth-functional contingencies include $A \supset B, A \vee B$, and ${\sim}A \equiv B$.

■ *Validity and Invalidity.* An argument that is (deductively) valid as a result of its truth-functional connectives is said to be *truth-functionally valid*, or valid *in P*. The truth-functionally valid arguments form a proper subset of the valid arguments. Any argument whose corresponding truth table shows that it cannot have, at the same time, true premises and a false conclusion is truth-functionally valid. Similarly, any argument for which there is a corresponding proof that goes from the argument's premisses to its conclusion and that has been constructed using the rules of inference of system *P* is truth-functionally valid. Those arguments that are not capable of being proved truth-functionally valid using these methods are *truth-functionally invalid*. Examples of truth-functionally valid arguments include

> **Testing for Truth-functional Necessity**
> A proposition that is necessarily true as a result of its truth-functional connectives is said to be a *tautology*, a *truth-functional necessity*, or a *theorem* of system *P*. Any proposition whose corresponding truth table shows that it cannot be false is a *tautology*. Similarly, any proposition for which there is a corresponding natural deduction proof from no premises is a tautology. Any proposition that is the negation of a tautology is a *truth-functional impossibility*, or *contradiction*. Any proposition that is neither a tautology nor a truth-functional impossibility is a *truth-functional contingency*.

$A \supset B$

A

―――――

$\therefore B$

and

${\sim}A \supset B$

$B \supset C$

―――――

$\therefore {\sim}A \supset C.$

Examples of truth-functionally invalid arguments include

A

―――――

$\therefore B$

and

$$A \supset B$$

$$\sim A$$

$$\therefore \sim B.$$

Testing for Truth-functional Validity

An argument that is valid as a result of its truth-functional connectives is said to be *truth-functionally valid*. Any argument whose corresponding truth table shows that it cannot have true premises together with a false conclusion is truth-functionally valid. Similarly, any argument for which there is a corresponding natural deduction proof that goes from the argument's premises to its conclusion is truth-functionally valid. Those arguments that are not truth-functionally valid are *truth-functionally invalid*.

■ *Consistency and Inconsistency.* If, as a result of their truth-functional connectives, the members of a set of propositions cannot be jointly true, the set is said to be *truth-functionally inconsistent*. The truth-functionally inconsistent sets form a proper subset of the logically inconsistent sets. Any set of propositions whose corresponding truth table shows that its members cannot be jointly true is truth-functionally inconsistent. Similarly, any set of propositions for which there is a corresponding proof that uses the members of that set as premises, that results in a proposition of the form $p \wedge \sim p$, and that has been constructed using the rules of inference of system P is truth-functionally inconsistent. Any set of propositions that is not truth-functionally inconsistent is *truth-functionally consistent*. Examples of truth-functionally inconsistent sets of propositions include $\{A, \sim A\}$, $\{A, A \supset B, B \supset \sim A\}$, and $\{A \equiv \sim A\}$. Examples of truth-functionally consistent sets of propositions include $\{A, \sim B\}$, $\{A \supset B, B \supset \sim A\}$, and $\{A \supset \sim A\}$. (Note that here a symbol such as "$\{A, B\}$" is not itself a proposition. Rather, it is the name for the set, or collection, containing the two propositions A and B.)

Testing for Truth-functional Inconsistency

If, as a result of their truth-functional connectives, the members of a set of propositions cannot be jointly true, the set is said to be *truth-functionally inconsistent*. Any set of propositions whose corresponding truth table shows that its members cannot be jointly true is truth-functionally inconsistent. Similarly, any set of propositions for which there is a corresponding natural deduction proof that uses the members of that set as premises and that results in a proposition of the form $p \wedge \sim p$ is truth-functionally inconsistent. Any set of propositions that is not truth-functionally inconsistent is *truth-functionally consistent*.

■ *Equivalence and Non-equivalence.* If, as a result of their truth-functional connectives, a pair of propositions must always have the same truth value, the propositions are said to be *materially* or *truth-functionally equivalent*. Propositions that are truth-functionally equivalent form a proper subset of the propositions that are logically equivalent. Any two propositions whose corresponding truth table shows that they cannot have opposite truth values are truth-functionally equivalent. Similarly, any two propositions for which there are corresponding proofs that have been constructed using the rules of inference of system P and that show that each proposition is derivable from the other are materially or truth-functionally equivalent. Any two propositions that are not truth-functionally equivalent are *materially* or *truth-functionally non-equivalent*. Examples of pairs of propositions that are truth-functionally equivalent include $\{A, A \vee A\}$, $\{A \supset B, \sim B \supset \sim A\}$, and $\{A \vee \sim B, \sim(\sim A \wedge B)\}$. Examples of pairs of propositions that are truth-functionally non-equivalent include $\{A, B\}$, $\{A \supset B, B \supset A\}$, and $\{A \vee B, \sim B \vee A\}$.

It is easy to see that these properties will be of special interest to logicians. Logic is intended to help us get at the truth of things. If we are able to determine that a given formula is a tautology, we will have learned at least a small part of the truth of things. Similarly, if we discover that a given formula is truth-functionally inconsistent, we will know that that formula cannot under any circumstances be true. In the case of a formula that is truth-functionally contingent, we discover that the formula may be true under some circumstances and false under others; moreover, we also discover what those circumstances are.

> **Testing for Truth-functional Equivalency**
>
> If, as a result of their truth-functional connectives, a pair of propositions must always have the same truth value, the propositions are said to be *materially* or *truth-functionally equivalent*. Any two propositions whose corresponding truth tables show that they cannot have opposite truth values are truth-functionally equivalent. Similarly, any two propositions for which there are corresponding natural deduction proofs that show that each proposition is derivable from the other are truth-functionally equivalent. Any two propositions that are not truth-functionally equivalent are *materially* or *truth-functionally non-equivalent*.

Just as importantly, propositional logic gives us perfectly reliable procedures for discovering these properties. Procedures such as those stated earlier, which successfully detect the presence and abscnce of these logically interesting properties, are said to be *effective*. Properties for which effective procedures exist are called *decidable* properties. Since there exist many decidable properties that are expressible in system P and that are of interest, the decision requirement for P is clearly satisfied.

At this point, it is also worth making explicit the relationship between a justified (or warranted) inference and logical entailment. In several places, we have spoken of these concepts, as well as of validity and truth-functional validity. Do these various notions interrelate? Indeed they do.

First, if a conditional proposition of the form $p \supset q$ is a tautology, then any argument from the single premiss p to conclusion q will be valid. In addition, any argument, all of whose premises can be conjoined to form p and whose conclusion is q, will be valid as well. Second, if the argument from p to q is valid, then p has been shown to entail q, and the inference from p to q will be a warranted one.

Thus, the logical properties studied in system P are incredibly important. Not only are the notions of warranted inference, entailment, and truth-functional validity closely related to one another, system P shows that there is important overlap among all three.

Despite this, we have known all along that system P achieves its theoretical simplicity at the expense of what it ignores—namely, any question of the connections between atomic propositions. The resulting vulnerability to the fallacy of *ignoratio elenchi* appeared, for example, as a result of our acceptance of formulas such as $p \supset (p \vee q)$. The fact that this formula is a tautology means, of course, that from p we are warranted to infer $p \vee q$, for any p and q, even if these two propositions are completely unrelated. From the statement "Socrates lived in Athens," for example, we can validly infer "Either Socrates lived in Athens or Tuesday is Bill's birthday." Thus it

Truth-functional Validity and Warranted Inference

If this propositional form is tautologous ...	then this argument is valid ...	and this inference is warranted ...
$((p \supset q) \wedge p) \supset q$	$A \supset B$ A ——— $\therefore B$	From $A \supset B$ and A, it is warranted to infer B
$((p \supset q) \wedge \sim q) \supset \sim p$	$A \supset B$ $\sim B$ ——— $\therefore \sim A$	From $A \supset B$ and $\sim B$, it is warranted to infer $\sim A$
$p \supset (p \vee q)$	A ——— $\therefore A \vee B$	From A, it is warranted to infer $A \vee B$
$((p \vee q) \wedge \sim p) \supset q$	$A \vee B$ $\sim A$ ——— $\therefore B$	From $A \vee B$ and $\sim A$, it is warranted to infer B
$(p \wedge q) \supset p$	$A \wedge B$ ——— $\therefore A$	From $A \wedge B$, it is warranted to infer A
$((p \supset q) \wedge (q \supset r)) \supset (p \supset r)$	$A \supset B$ $B \supset C$ ——— $\therefore A \supset C$	From $A \supset B$ and $B \supset C$, it is warranted to infer $A \supset C$

occurs to us to ask how we might try to extend or modify *P* in order to cope with this limitation. The answer is to construct a new system, which we will call *RP*.

Exercise 6.3

1. Using the rules of inference for system *P*, prove the following arguments to be truth-functionally valid:

   (a) (P1) $(A \land B) \supset (\sim C \lor \sim D)$
       (P2) $\sim(\sim C \lor \sim D)$
       _____
       (C) $\sim A \lor \sim B$

   (b) (P1) $(E \supset B) \supset C$
       (P2) $\sim D \lor A$
       (P3) $\sim D \supset (\sim E \lor B)$
       (P4) $\sim A$
       _____
       (C) C

   (c) (P1) $(A \supset \sim B) \land \sim C$
       (P2) $B \supset (\sim A \supset C)$
       _____
       (C) $\sim B$

   (d) (P1) $A \land B$
       (P2) $\sim D$
       _____
       (C) $C \supset [\sim(A \land D) \land B]$

   (e) (P1) $B \supset [(A \lor C) \supset D]$
       (P2) $(D \lor E) \supset A$
       _____
       (C) $B \supset (C \supset A)$

2. Using the rules of inference for system *P*, prove the following propositions to be tautologies:

   (a) $C \supset [(A \lor \sim D) \lor \sim A]$

   (b) $\{A \land ([(A \lor B) \land C] \supset D)\} \supset (C \supset D)$

   (c) $\sim(A \land [B \lor C]) \lor A$

   (d) $\{[(A \land B) \supset C] \land [\sim D \supset (B \land A)]\} \supset (\sim D \supset C)$

   (e) $\sim[C \supset C] \supset [C \supset C]$

3. Using the rules of inference for system *P*, prove the following propositions to be contradictions:

   (a) $(A \land D) \land (\sim A \lor \sim D)$

   (b) $[(A \supset (B \lor C)) \land \sim(\sim A \lor C)] \land \sim B$

   (c) $\sim\{(A \lor C) \supset (\sim A \supset C)\}$

   (d) $(A \equiv \sim C) \land \sim(A \supset \sim C)$

   (e) $\sim(A \supset A)$

4. Using truth tables, prove the following sets of propositions to be truth-functionally inconsistent:

   (a) $\{A , A \supset B, B \supset \sim A\}$

   (b) $\{A , A \supset (B \land C), \sim(B \land C)\}$

   (c) $\{A \lor \sim B, \sim A \land B\}$

   (d) $\{A \lor \sim B, \sim(\sim A \supset \sim B)\}$

   (e) $\{A \equiv \sim A\}$

5. Using truth tables, prove the following sets of propositions to be truth-functionally consistent:

   (a) $\{A \lor C, A \supset \sim C\}$

   (b) $\{A \lor C, A \supset \sim C, C\}$

   (c) $\{A \lor D, D \supset \sim D\}$

   (d) $\{A \lor C, A \lor D, \sim A \supset [D \land \sim C]\}$

   (e) $\{A \land B, A \supset \sim C, C \supset \sim B\}$

6. Using the rules of inference for system *P*, prove the following pairs of propositions to be truth-functionally equivalent:

   (a) $(B \land A), (A \land \sim\sim B)$

   (b) $(A \lor B), (A \lor B) \land \sim(A \land \sim A)$

   (c) $(A \lor B), (A \lor B) \lor (A \lor B)$

   (d) $(\sim B \supset A), (A \lor B)$

   (e) $[(A \supset B) \land (B \supset A)], (B \equiv A)$

Summary

In this chapter we have introduced the idea of a *formal system* and seen how classical propositional logic can be developed in such a system. After introducing the *primitive basis* (vocabulary, grammar, and rules of inference) for system *P*, we saw how this system could be used to study a variety of logical properties. Specifically, we were able to satisfy the system's *construction requirement* by using the formation rules for system *P* to identify all well-formed and ill-formed formulas of this system. In addition, we were able to satisfy the system's *decision requirement* by using truth tables and the system's rules of inference to identify each of the following properties: truth-functional necessity, impossibility and contingency; truth-functional validity and invalidity; truth-functional consistency and inconsistency; and truth-functional equivalence and non-equivalence.

Any proposition whose corresponding truth table shows that it cannot be false, or for which there is a corresponding proof from no premises, is a *truth-functional necessity* or *tautology*. Similarly, any proposition that is the negation of a tautology is a *truth-functional impossibility*, or *contradiction*, and any proposition that is neither a tautology nor a truth-functional impossibility is a *truth-functional contingency*.

Any argument whose corresponding truth table shows that it cannot have true premises and a false conclusion, or for which there is a corresponding proof, is *truth-functionally valid*. Those arguments that are not capable of being proved truth-functionally valid using these methods are *truth-functionally invalid*.

Any set of propositions whose corresponding truth table shows that its members cannot be jointly true, or for which there is a corresponding proof that uses the members of that set as premises and that results in a conclusion of the form $p \land \sim p$, is *truth-functionally inconsistent*. Any set of propositions that is not truth-functionally inconsistent is *truth-functionally consistent*.

Finally, any two propositions whose corresponding truth tables show that they cannot have opposite truth values, or for which there are corresponding proofs that show that each proposition is derivable from the other, are *materially* or *truth-functionally equivalent*. Any two propositions that are not materially or truth-functionally equivalent are *materially* or *truth-functionally non-equivalent*.

Weblinks

CHAPTER 7

Extending Deductive Logic: I

IS THERE a way to extend or modify system *P* in order to make it less vulnerable to the fallacy of *ignoratio elenchi*? In this chapter we will consider one way of doing so. Using a new formal system, *RP*, we will introduce the idea of a common subject matter between propositions. We will then use this idea to modify our original notion of valid inference. We will also consider a number of other proposed modifications to classical propositional logic. These modifications are designed to describe, in a systematic way, several types of reliable, truth-preserving inference not captured in ordinary propositional logic.

1. System *RP*

In many respects, system *RP* is similar to system *P*. It has the same propositional constants and grouping indicators, but the propositional connectives of *RP* are defined slightly differently. Instead of ⊃ (the hook), we will introduce a new conditional, → (the arrow), and the other connectives will be changed slightly as well. Additionally, in *RP* we will introduce a relation between propositions, $R(p, q)$, read "*p* is related to *q*." This relation holds if *p* is related to *q* in a particular way, but fails to hold if *p* and *q* are not so related. It is hoped that *RP* will help us avoid the fallacy of *ignoratio elenchi* in a way that *P* does not.

We explain relation *R* as follows: Associated with every argument will be a set of *topics*. Call this set *T*. *T* can be any set of topics clearly agreed upon. Roughly, we can think of it as describing the subject matter of the argument under consideration. Any proposition, *p*, in the argument will then mention a number of different topics that are listed in *T*. For example, suppose *T* contains "Socrates" and "Athens," as well as other topics. The proposition "Socrates lived in Athens" will then mention two topics from *T*, namely "Socrates" and "Athens."

We will say that *p* is related to *q*, written $R(p, q)$, if and only if there is at least one topic in common between *p* and *q*. For example, if *p* is "Socrates lived in Athens" and *q* is "Athens is in Greece," then *p* and *q* are related: both have in common the subject matter "Athens."

We can further understand what is meant by relation R if we see that it has three characteristic properties: first, R is reflexive; second, R is symmetric; and third, R is non-transitive. We define these properties as follows:

- *Reflexivity*: Relation R is reflexive if and only if, for all propositions, p, $R(p, p)$. In other words, R is reflexive if and only if, for all p, p is related to itself. It is reasonable to assume that R is reflexive since any proposition will clearly have identical subject matter to that of itself.

- *Symmetry*: Relation R is symmetric if and only if, for all propositions, p and q, $R(p, q)$ if and only if $R(q, p)$. In other words, R is symmetric if and only if, for any p and q, p is related to q if and only if q is related to p. Once again, it is reasonable to assume that R is symmetric, since if p shares one or more topics with q, then q will share those same topics with p. Sharing subject matter works both ways.

- *Non-transitivity*: Relation R is non-transitive if and only if, for all propositions, p, q, and r, if $R(p, q)$ and $R(q, r)$, it need not follow that $R(p, r)$. In other words, R is non-transitive if and only if, even though p and q might be related, and even though q and r might be related, it need not follow that p and r are related. For example, "Socrates lived in Athens" shares a topic with "Athens is in Greece," and "Athens is in Greece" shares a topic with "Greece is the birthplace of democracy," but "Socrates lived in Athens" does not share any subject matter with "Greece is the birthplace of democracy."

Reflexivity, Symmetry, and Transitivity

For any relation that holds between two (possibly distinct) objects, we say that the relation is

- *Reflexive* if and only if, for all objects x, x is related to itself;

- *Symmetric* if and only if, for all objects x and y, if x is related to y, then y is also related to x;

- *Transitive* if and only if, for all objects x, y, and z, if x is related to y and y is related to z, then x is also related to z.

A relation that is reflexive, symmetric, and transitive is said to be an *equivalence relation*. A relation that is not reflexive is *non-reflexive*; a relation that is not symmetric is *non-symmetric*; and a relation that is not transitive is *non-transitive*. Relation R, which holds between propositions that share a common subject matter, is reflexive, symmetric, and non-transitive.

Now that we have some idea of what R means, we can define the conditional, $\rightarrow$, in RP. If p is related to q, then the truth-table definition for $\rightarrow$ in RP will be the same as the truth-table definition for $\supset$ in P. Alternatively, if p and q are unrelated, we will say that $p \rightarrow q$ is false. We define $\rightarrow$ this way because we want "If p then q" to be false whenever p and q are unrelated. In other words, if p and q are unrelated and an *igno-*

ratio elenchi has occurred during the inference from *p* to *q*, then the conditional must fail to hold. Accordingly, the truth table for → is defined as follows:

R-Conditional

p	*q*	*R(p, q)*	*p → q*
T	T	T	T
T	F	T	F
F	T	T	T
F	F	T	T
T	T	F	F
T	F	F	F
F	T	F	F
F	F	F	F

The idea here is simple. If *p* and *q* are related, the truth table for → is the same as the truth table for ⊃. If *p* and *q* are not related, *p → q* is always false.

R Connectives

- An *R-negation* (¬) always has the opposite truth value to that of the proposition negated.

- An *R-conjunction* (∧) is true when and only when both of its conjuncts are true.

- An *R-disjunction* (∨) is true when and only when its two disjuncts are related and at least one of its disjuncts is true.

- An *R-conditional* (→) is false when and only when its antecedent is true and its consequent is false, or its antecedent and consequent are unrelated to each other.

- An *R-biconditional* (↔) is true when and only when its two component propositions are related and they share the same truth value.

Definitions for the other connectives are equally straightforward. In *RP*, ¬ (negation) is defined just as ~ is in *P*. The reason is that negation does not appear to be influenced by subject matter. In *RP*, ¬ *p* always has the opposite truth value of *p*, regardless of what *p* is about. Thus, the truth table for ¬ is defined as follows:

R-Negation

p	*R(p, p)*	*¬ p*
T	T	F
F	T	T

Conjunction and disjunction might also be defined with or without regard to relatedness, but it seems natural to think that "and" does not usually require relatedness, while "or" most often does. "Either Socrates lived in Athens or 2 + 2 = 4" does not sound natural. In contrast, in natural language we often construct propositions such as "Socrates lived in Athens and 2 + 2 = 4," where the conjuncts of these propositions may not share any subject matter at all.

For current purposes, therefore, we will define $\wedge$ just as $\wedge$ is defined in P, but we define $\vee$ as follows: $p \vee q$ is true if p is related to q, and p is true or q is true: otherwise it is false. Alternatively, $p \vee q$ is false if both p and q are false, or if they are unrelated. The truth tables are thus constructed as follows:

R-Conjunction and R-Disjunction

p	q	$R(p, q)$	$p \wedge q$	$p \vee q$
T	T	T	T	T
T	F	T	F	T
F	T	T	F	T
F	F	T	F	F
T	T	F	T	F
T	F	F	F	F
F	T	F	F	F
F	F	F	F	F

Finally, the biconditional, $p \leftrightarrow q$, is defined as $(p \rightarrow q) \wedge (q \rightarrow p)$. So the truth table for $\leftrightarrow$ will also require mention of relation R:

R-Biconditional

p	q	$R(p, q)$	$R(q, p)$	$p \leftrightarrow q$
T	T	T	T	T
T	F	T	T	F
F	T	T	T	F
F	F	T	T	T
T	T	F	F	F
T	F	F	F	F
F	T	F	F	F
F	F	F	F	F

In order for system RP to be of use, we also need to indicate when molecular formulas containing the connectives $\neg$, $\vee$, $\wedge$, $\rightarrow$, and $\leftrightarrow$ are related to each other. Given a formula p and a formula q, no matter how complex they might be, we need to be able to decide whether they are related. For example, if p is the proposition A, and if q is the proposition $B \rightarrow C$, we do not yet have any way of automatically determining whether A is related to $B \rightarrow C$. It could be that A is related to B, say, but not to C. If so, would A be related to $B \rightarrow C$? We might want to say that A is not related to $B \rightarrow C$ unless A is related to both B and C, or we might want to claim that A is related to $B \rightarrow C$ provided that A is related to at least one of B or C.

We will say that any two formulas of the form p and $q \rightarrow r$ are related if and only if p is related to q or p is related to r. This assumption seems reasonable. Say we have a conditional such as "If Socrates lived in Athens, then Einstein discovered relativity." As a conditional in RP it is false, since its antecedent is unrelated to its consequent, but should we say that "Einstein was absentminded" is related to it? Yes, it would seem to be so, since the latter proposition is related to one of the conditional's two component propositions.

The relatedness rules for $\lor$, $\land$, and $\leftrightarrow$ are the same as for $\rightarrow$. In other words, p is related to $q \lor r$, and to $q \land r$, and to $q \leftrightarrow r$, if and only if p is related to q or p is related to r. For negation, p is related to $\neg q$ if and only if p is related to q.

As in system P, it will be the case in RP that the truth value of any well-formed formula depends on two things: (1) the truth values of its constituent formulas, and (2) the meanings of its constituent propositional connectives. The only significant difference between P and RP is that in RP some of the connectives are defined in a way that requires knowledge of R. Despite this, using procedures very similar to those associated with the formation rules for P, we can always determine whether a formula is well formed in RP. A property similar to the truth-functionality of P also holds in RP: given the truth values of the constituent propositions of any formula of RP, and given the relatedness relations that hold between these constituent propositions, we can always determine the truth value of that formula. In RP, just as in P, the truth-table method will always tell us—reliably and mechanically and using a finite number of steps—the truth value a proposition will have, given the truth values and relations of its constituent formulas.

Exercise 7.1

1. Are the following relations reflexive? Are they symmetric? Are they transitive?

   (a) x is north of y (for all locations x and y)

   (b) x is a brother of y (for all persons x and y)

   (c) x is a sibling of y (for all persons x and y)

   (d) x loves y (for all persons x and y)

   (e) x is taller than y (for all persons x and y)

   (f) x is the same height as y (for all persons x and y)

   (g) x is not the same height as y (for all persons x and y)

   (h) p implies q (for all propositions p and q)

   (i) p is implied by q (for all propositions p and q)

   (j) p is equivalent to q (for all propositions p and q)

2. If $R(A, B)$, but $\sim R(B, C)$ and $\sim R(A, C)$, determine which of the following pairs of formulas are related to each other in RP:

   (a) $A \lor C, B$

   (b) $B \rightarrow C, A \rightarrow A$

   (c) $A \rightarrow (B \rightarrow A), C$

   (d) $\neg A \lor B, A \rightarrow C$

(e) $A \lor \sim A, B \to B$

3.   Suppose R(A, B), but ~R(B, C) and ~R(A, C).
     Also, suppose that A and B are true but
     that C is false. Determine the truth values
     of each of the following formulas of *RP*:

(a) $A \to B$

(b) $A \to (B \to \neg C)$

(c) $A \lor \neg B$

(d) $A \lor \neg C$

(e) $A \land (B \lor C)$

(f) $A \land (B \lor \neg B)$

(g) $(A \to B) \lor (B \to C)$

(h) $(A \lor \neg C) \to C$

(i) $B \to \neg C$

(j) $\neg (B \leftrightarrow A) \leftrightarrow C$

2. Evaluating System *RP*

Just as in system *P*, certain formulas will be true in *RP* no matter what truth values
their constituent propositions have. For example, consider the truth table for
$A \lor \neg A$:

	A	R(A, ¬ A)	¬ A	A ∨ ¬ A
(1)	T	T	F	T
(2)	F	T	T	T

We know that $R(A, \neg A)$ is always true, because a formula, p, is related to a negated
formula, say, $\neg q$, if and only if p is related to q, and because A is always related to
itself. Thus, A is always related to $\neg A$, regardless of the truth value of A. Completing
the truth table, it follows that $A \lor \neg A$ will always be true. We shall call any formula like this, which is universally true in *RP*, a *relatedness tautology*.

  Similarly, if a formula of *RP* is sometimes true and sometimes false, we will call
it a *relatedness contingency*, and a formula that is always false will be called a *relatedness contradiction*. For example, $A \land \neg A$ is always false in *RP*, just as $A \land \sim A$ is
always false in *P*.

Tautologies, Contradictions, and Contingencies in *RP*

- A *relatedness tautology* (or a *relatedness necessity*) is a well-formed formula
  that is necessarily true as a result of its connectives in system *RP*.

- A *relatedness contradiction* (or a *relatedness impossibility*) is a well-formed formula that is necessarily false as a result of its connectives in system *RP*.

- A *relatedness contingency* is a well-formed formula that is neither a relatedness
  tautology nor a relatedness contradiction.

Do systems *P* and *RP* differ in which formulas they classify as tautologies? In fact, they do. Some formulas that are tautologies in *P* are not tautologies when expressed as formulas of *RP*. For example, consider the truth table for A ⊃ (B ⊃ A):

	A	*B*	*B ⊃ A*	*A ⊃ (B ⊃ A)*
(1)	T	T	T	T
(2)	T	F	T	T
(3)	F	T	F	T
(4)	F	F	T	T

In the above truth table, every row of the last column is true; thus the formula *A ⊃ (B ⊃ A)* is a tautology in *P*. In contrast, consider the truth table for the parallel formula of *RP*, *A → (B → A)*:

	A	*B*	*R(A, B)*	*B → A*	*R(A, B → A)*	*A → (B → A)*
(1)	T	T	T	T	T	T
(2)	T	F	T	T	T	T
(3)	F	T	T	F	T	T
(4)	F	F	T	T	T	T
(5)	T	T	F	F	T	F
(6)	T	F	F	F	T	F
(7)	F	T	F	F	T	T
(8)	F	F	F	F	T	T

In this truth table there are two rows in which *A → (B → A)* is not true: rows 5 and 6. So, clearly *A → (B → A)* is not a relatedness tautology. As the truth table shows, it is a relatedness contingency.

It is interesting to try to discover how many argument forms from system *P* remain valid in *RP*. Such a comparison should give us some idea how *P* and *RP* are related. In fact, it turns out that *P* is an extension of *RP*. That is, all valid forms of *RP* are also valid in *P* (once they are suitably recast using the connectives of *RP*), but there are some forms that are valid in *P* that are not valid in *RP* (again, once they are suitably recast).

Consider the argument form *Modus Ponens*:

> *p ⊃ q*
> *p*
> ─────────
> ∴ *q*.

We know that this argument form is valid in *P*, but is the corresponding argument form in *RP*,

$$p \rightarrow q$$
$$p$$
_____
$$\therefore q$$

also valid? Doing the truth table, we obtain the following:

	p	*q*	*R(p, q)*	*p → q*
(1)	T	T	T	T
(2)	T	F	T	F
(3)	F	T	T	T
(4)	F	F	T	T
(5)	T	T	F	F
(6)	T	F	F	F
(7)	F	T	F	F
(8)	F	F	F	F

To test for validity, we look to see if there are any rows in which both the premisses p and $p \rightarrow q$ are true, but the conclusion, q, is false. Since there is no such row, we conclude that *Modus Ponens* is deductively valid in *RP*.

However, if we consider another argument form that we know to be valid in *P*, namely Addition,

$$p$$
_____
$$\therefore p \vee q,$$

it turns out that the corresponding argument in *RP*,

$$p$$
_____
$$\therefore p \vee q,$$

is not valid. To prove this, we once again construct the corresponding truth table:

		p	*q*	*R(p, q)*	*p ∨ q*
	(1)	T	T	T	T
	(2)	T	F	T	T
	(3)	F	T	T	T
	(4)	F	F	T	F
X	(5)	T	T	F	F
X	(6)	T	F	F	F
	(7)	F	T	F	F
	(8)	F	F	F	F

Then, once again, we look to see whether it is possible for the premiss to be true and, at the same time, the conclusion to be false. Since there are two rows, 5 and 6, in which p is true but $p \lor q$ is false, we conclude that this argument form is not valid in RP. It is clear why this is so. The relatedness disjunction, $p \lor q$, requires that p and q be related in order that $p \lor q$ follows from p. Since they are not always so related, we cannot infer $p \lor q$ for any arbitrary q. In RP, the argument "Socrates lived in Athens, therefore Socrates lived in Athens or Einstein discovered relativity" is not valid.

In summary, we see that RP is as systematic and orderly as P, but that there are important differences between the two systems. In particular, many argument forms that are valid in P are not valid in RP.

Why should there be these differences? The answer is partly that system RP is designed to do a different job from P. In P, only truth values affect the way the connectives are defined. In RP, however, relatedness (or lack of relatedness) between subject matters is also a factor. So, many arguments that are valid in P fail to be valid in RP, simply because they lack common subject matter.

We know that system P is open to the fallacy of *ignoratio elenchi* because it ignores the issue of subject matter. In contrast, RP takes subject matter into account and therefore represents a different understanding of what it means for an argument to be a good one. Put another way, both of the formal systems P and RP attempt to capture the notion of entailment, but they do so in quite different ways. Although the two systems agree about the validity of many argument forms, they differ about others.

For example, if we look at those arguments that are judged to be valid in P, we can see that P does indeed embody the view that relatedness does not matter. Consider these arguments, all of which are valid in P:

(1) p
———
$\therefore p \lor q$

(2) p
———
$\therefore q \supset p$

(3) $\sim p$
———
$\therefore p \supset q.$

As substitution instances of each form, we might obtain the following arguments:

(1) Socrates lived in Athens
———————————————————————
Therefore, Socrates lived in Athens or Einstein discovered relativity

(2) Socrates lived in Athens
———————————————————————
Therefore, if Einstein discovered relativity, then Socrates lived in Athens

(3) It is not the case that Socrates lived in Athens
_____

Therefore, if Socrates lived in Athens, then Einstein discovered relativity.

None of these arguments appear to entail their conclusions in anything but the very weakest sense of this term, so it is not surprising that none of these arguments is valid in RP

Another way of looking at this issue is to notice that, far from ignoring the issue of relatedness, P embodies a view of argument that presupposes that all propositions are related to each other. In other words, if we confine an argument to propositions that we know to be related to each other, then we will not need to worry about relatedness at all, and we can use system P; but if we have concerns about whether the propositions being used in an argument are related to each other, then we should use RP.[1]

Exercise 7.2

1. Determine whether the following formulas are tautologies, contingencies, or contradictions in P.

    (a) $A \lor (B \lor \sim B)$

    (b) $\sim A \supset (A \supset B)$

    (c) $(A \land B) \supset \sim A$

    (d) $[(A \supset B) \supset B] \supset (\sim A \supset B)$

    (e) $A \equiv \sim A$

2. Determine whether the following formulas are relatedness tautologies, relatedness contingencies, or relatedness contradictions in RP.

    (a) $A \lor (B \lor \neg B)$

    (b) $\neg A \to (A \to B)$

    (c) $(A \land B) \to \neg A$

    (d) $[(A \to B) \to B] \to (\neg A \to B)$

    (e) $A \leftrightarrow \neg A$

3. Determine whether the following arguments are valid in RP:

    (a) $A \land B$
        _____
        $\therefore A$

    (b) A
        $\neg B$
        _____
        $\therefore \neg (A \to B)$

    (c) $A \to B$
        _____
        $\therefore \neg (A \land \neg B)$

    (d) $A \to B$
        $A \to C$
        _____
        $\therefore A \to (B \land C)$

    (e) $A \to B$
        $A \to \neg B$
        _____
        $\therefore \neg A$

    (f) $B \to A$
        $\neg B \to A$
        _____
        $\therefore A$

(g) $\neg\ (A \rightarrow B)$
_____

$\therefore B \rightarrow A$

(h) $A \lor B$
$A \rightarrow C$
$B \rightarrow D$
_____

$\therefore C \lor D$

(i) $A \land (B \lor C)$
_____

$\therefore (A \land B) \lor (A \land C)$

(j) $A \lor (B \land C)$
_____

$\therefore (A \lor B) \land (A \lor C)$

3. Modal Logics

System *RP* provides a way of modifying classical propositional logic that attempts to capture more accurately the relation of entailment. As we saw, *RP* restricts its consequence relation in an attempt to make the system less vulnerable to the fallacy of *ignoratio elenchi*. In contrast, other modifications to classical logic that logicians have introduced involve extending, rather than restricting, the consequence relation. These extensions to classical logic typically have as their goal the construction of a broader, more inclusive type of consequence relation than that found in systems *P* and *RP*.

Among the most important extensions to classical logic is a family of logics known as *modal logics*. These are logics that emphasize inferential relations based upon the so-called *alethic modalities*[2]—*necessity, possibility, impossibility,* and *contingency*. Such logics are obtained from classical logic by the addition of axioms and rules of inference governing the following two connectives: $\Diamond$ (which is read "It is possible that ..." or "Possibly ...") and $\Box$ (which is read "It is necessary that ..." or "Necessarily ..."). Like negation, both $\Diamond$ and $\Box$ are *unary connectives*. That is, they are applied to a single proposition in order to create a new proposition. For example, if *p* is the proposition "Nitrous oxide is more dense than methane," then $\Diamond p$ is the proposition "It is possible that nitrous oxide is more dense than methane" and $\Box p$ is the proposition "It is necessary that nitrous oxide is more dense than methane."

Just as some deductions are valid by virtue of their truth-functional form, others will be valid by virtue of their modal form. For example, the deduction

Bill is in Banff
_____

Therefore, it is possible that Bill is in Banff

exhibits this perfectly general (and valid) modal form

p
_____

$\therefore \Diamond p.$

Similarly, the argument

Possibility and Necessity
The two main propositional connectives
of *modal logic* are ◇ (which is read "It is
possible that" or "Possibly") and □
(which is read "It is necessary that" or
"Necessarily"). For example, if *p* is the
proposition "The square root of
1,136,356 is 1,066," then ◇*p* is the
proposition "It is possible that the square
root of 1,136,356 is 1,066" and □*p* is
the proposition "It is necessary that the
square root of 1,136,356 is 1,066." Also
called *alethic modal operators*, both connectives are only *partially truth-functional*.

It is not possible that Bill is in Banff

Therefore, it is necessary that Bill is not in Banff

is also valid as a result of the form

~◇*p*

∴ □~*p*.

The goal of modal logic is to systematically describe these and other valid modal inferences.

One way to think about these two new modal connectives is to recall how we first characterized the idea of a truth-functional connective in chapter 4. Connectives such as ~, ∧, ∨, ⊃, and ≡ were said to be *truth-functional* because the truth values of their resulting molecular propositions are a function of (that is, they are completely determined by) the meanings of the connectives together with the truth values of their constituent propositions. For example, for any proposition, *p*, if *p* is true then ~*p* is false, and if *p* is false then ~*p* is true. This is true regardless of the meaning (or material content) of *p*.

At the same time, we also noticed that many natural language connectives are ambiguous. For example, the "and" in "Bill and Sue are intelligent" functions quite differently than the "and" in "Bill and Sue are lovers," and both of these function differently from "Bill drove off the road and hit a moose." In the first of these three propositions the "and" is functioning as the truth-functional connective ∧. In other words, "Bill and Sue are intelligent" is equivalent to "Bill is intelligent and Sue is intelligent," but this is not the case with either the second or third of these three propositions. In the case of "Bill and Sue are lovers" the "and" is functioning *non–truth-functionally*. "Bill and Sue are lovers" simply means something different than "Bill is a lover and Sue is a lover." The same is true of "Bill drove off the road and hit a moose," where the "and" is being used in yet a third sense. Here, once we recognize that "Bill drove off the road and hit a moose" means something different from "Bill hit a moose and drove off the road" we see that in this context "and" really means "and then."

Another example of a non–truth-functional connective is the connective "It is believed that." Like negation, this connective operates on a single proposition. For example, given the proposition "Sue will arrive on time," we can create a new proposition, "It is believed that Sue will arrive on time." To see that it is not truth-functional, let "B" stand for "It is believed that." Then try to complete the following truth table:

It is believed that ...

p	B*p*
T	?
F	?

Here the fact that *p* is true (or false) does not tell us anything about the truth value of B*p*. In other words, just because a proposition such as "511,732,423 is a prime number" is true (or false), this alone does not tell us anything about the truth value of the proposition "It is believed that 511,732,423 is a prime number." After all, it may turn out that no one has even considered this proposition, let alone formed a belief about its truth or falsehood.

Some connectives also turn out to be *partially truth-functional*. For example, let "K" abbreviate the phrase "It is known that" and then try to complete the following truth table:

It is known that ...

p	K*p*
T	?
F	F

Here, if *p* is true, this does not tell us anything about the truth value of K*p*. In other words, just because a proposition such as "There is an infinite number of twin primes" is true, this alone is not sufficient to also make it true that "It is known that there is an infinite number of twin primes."[3] Once again, even though this proposition is true, it may turn out that no one has ever formed a belief about its truth or false-hood, let alone been justified in believing this proposition in a way that constitutes knowledge. In contrast, if *p* is false it follows immediately that K*p* must be false as well. Since knowledge is a kind of true belief, it is impossible for anyone to know a false proposition. (Of course, *believing* that we know something that is in fact false is quite a different matter!)

Two other partially truth-functional connectives are ◇ and □. For example, given the truth table for ◇,

It is possible that ...

p	◇*p*
T	T
F	?

it is easy to complete the first line. If *p* is in fact true, then it must be possible for *p* to be true. However, the second line is more difficult. Just because *p* is in fact false does not tell us anything about whether *p* is possible. For example, if *p* is the proposition "Bill is in two (distinct) places at one time" then "It is possible that Bill is in two (distinct) places at one time" will be false. However, if *p* is the proposition "Bill is in Melbourne," then "It is possible that Bill is in Melbourne" will be true, and this will be true even if "Bill is in Melbourne" is false.[4] Thus, in order to complete this second line of the truth table, we need to know more than just the truth value of *p*.

Similarly, given the truth table for □,

It is necessary that ...

p	$\Box p$
T	?
F	F

it is easy to complete the second line. If p is in fact false, then p cannot be necessarily true. However, this time it is the first line that is more difficult. Just because we know that p is in fact true, this is not enough for us to determine whether p is necessarily true. For example, if p is the proposition "Bill is in Sydney or it is not the case that Bill is in Sydney" then "It is necessary that (Bill is in Sydney or it is not the case that Bill is in Sydney)" will be true. However, if p is the proposition "Bill is in Sydney," then "It is necessary that Bill is in Sydney" will be false even if "Bill is in Sydney" is in fact true. Thus, in order to complete this line of the truth table, we will once again need to know more than just the truth value of p.

Given that they are not truth-functional, what exactly are the properties of $\Diamond$ and $\Box$? Perhaps surprisingly, there is no single answer to this question. Rather, several quite different systems of modal logic have been developed. In a sense, each can be thought of as a hypothesis about how best to characterize the ideas of possibility and necessity. Among the most influential of these logics are the systems $S1$ to $S5$, introduced by the American logician C.I. Lewis. Each system can be introduced as an extension to our formal system P. To do so, we supplement the primitive basis of system P as follows:

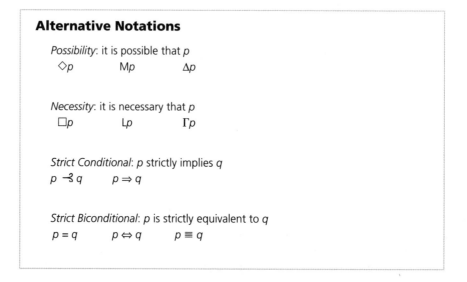

Alternative Notations

Possibility: it is possible that p

$\Diamond p$ Mp Δp

Necessity: it is necessary that p

$\Box p$ Lp Γp

Strict Conditional: p strictly implies q

$p \prec q$ $p \Rightarrow q$

Strict Biconditional: p is strictly equivalent to q

$p = q$ $p \Leftrightarrow q$ $p \equiv q$

Vocabulary

To the vocabulary of system P we add the single unary propositional connective, "$\Diamond$." This connective is named *diamond* and is read "It is possible that ...." For ease of discussion, we also add the following definitions:

D1. $\Box p =df \sim\!\Diamond\!\sim\!p$

D2. $(p \Rightarrow q) =df \Box (p \supset q)$

D3. $(p \Leftrightarrow q) =df [(p \Rightarrow q) \wedge (q \Rightarrow p)]$.

The unary connective, $\Box$, is named *box* and is read "It is necessary that ...." The binary connective, $\Rightarrow$, is named *broad arrow* and is read "... strictly implies ___." Finally, the binary connective, $\Leftrightarrow$, is named *broad double arrow* and is read "... is strictly equivalent to ___." Each of these connectives may be thought of simply as notational shorthand for the more complex formulas involving only $\Diamond$.

Given the first of these definitions, it turns out that to say that $\sim\!p$ is impossible is to say that p is necessary, and to say that $\sim\!p$ is not necessary is to say that p is possible. Given the second and third of these definitions, it turns out that a formula, p, strictly implies another formula, q, if and only if it is not possible that both p and $\sim\!q$, and a formula, p, is strictly equivalent to another formula, q, if and only if it is not possible for p and q to have different truth values.

Grammar

To the grammar of system P we add the formation rule: Given any well-formed formulas, p and q, the formulas $(\Diamond p)$, $(\Box p)$, $(p \Rightarrow q)$, and $(p \Leftrightarrow q)$, will also be well formed.

Axioms

To the empty axiom set of P we add the following axioms:

For system *S1* we add

A1. $(p \wedge q) \Rightarrow (q \wedge p)$
A2. $(p \wedge q) \Rightarrow p$
A3. $p \Rightarrow (p \wedge p)$
A4. $[(p \wedge q) \wedge r] \Rightarrow [p \wedge (q \wedge r)]$
A5. $[(p \Rightarrow q) \wedge (q \Rightarrow r)] \Rightarrow (p \Rightarrow r)$
A6. $[p \wedge (p \Rightarrow q)] \Rightarrow q$.

For system *S2* we add axioms A1 to A6 plus

A7. $\Diamond (p \wedge q) \Rightarrow \Diamond p$.

For system *S3* we add axioms A1 to A6 plus

A8. $(p \Rightarrow q) \Rightarrow (\sim\!\Diamond q \Rightarrow \sim\!\Diamond p)$.

For system *S4* we add axioms A1 to A6 plus

A9. $\Box p \Rightarrow \Box\Box p$.

For system *S5* we add axioms A1 to A6 plus

A10. $\Diamond p \Rightarrow \Box\Diamond p$.

Many of these axioms represent modal versions of rules of inference in system *P*. For example, axiom A1 is a strengthened version of Commutation; axiom A2 is a strengthened version of Simplification; axiom A3 is a strengthened version of Tautology; axiom A4 is a strengthened version of Association; axiom A5 is a strengthened version of Hypothetical Syllogism; and axiom A6 is a strengthened version of *Modus Ponens*.

Rules of Inference

To the rules of inference of system *P* (recast to include all the wffs and connectives of this new logic) we add the Rule of Uniform Substitution (Sub): Given any axiom, the result of uniformly replacing variables by wffs yields a theorem. This rule reflects a principle we discussed in chapter 5, namely that every uniform substitution instance of a valid wff is itself a valid wff.

Having supplemented the primitive basis for system *P* in this way, the resulting formal systems can be used to prove many new results. For example, to prove that the proposition $A \Rightarrow \sim \sim A$ is a theorem, we construct a proof in *S1* as follows:

1. $A \Rightarrow (A \wedge A)$ A3 Sub

2. $(A \wedge A) \Rightarrow A$ A2 Sub

3. $A \Rightarrow A$ 1, 2 HS

4. $A \Rightarrow \sim \sim A$ 3 DN.

Similarly, in order to prove $\sim(\sim\Diamond B \wedge \Diamond [A \wedge (A \Rightarrow B)])$, we construct a proof in *S3* as follows:

1. $[A \wedge (A \Rightarrow B)] \Rightarrow B$ A6 Sub

2. $([A \wedge (A \Rightarrow B)] \Rightarrow B) \Rightarrow (\sim\Diamond B \Rightarrow \sim\Diamond [A \wedge (A \Rightarrow B)])$ A8 Sub

3. $\sim\Diamond B \Rightarrow \sim\Diamond [A \wedge (A \Rightarrow B)]$ 2, 1 MP

4. $\sim \sim\Diamond B \vee \sim\Diamond [A \wedge (A \Rightarrow B)]$ 3 Imp

5. $\sim(\sim\Diamond B \wedge \Diamond [A \wedge (A \Rightarrow B)])$ 4 DeM.

Among the other theorems that can be proved in these formal systems are the following:

S1: $(A \Rightarrow B) \Rightarrow (A \supset B)$

      $[A \wedge (A \supset B)] \Rightarrow B$

S2: $\Diamond A \Rightarrow \Diamond (A \vee B)$

      $\Box (A \wedge B) \Rightarrow \Box A$

S3: $A \Rightarrow (A \wedge A)$

      $(A \Rightarrow B) \Rightarrow (\Box A \Rightarrow \Box B)$

S4: $(A \Rightarrow B) \Rightarrow \Box (A \Rightarrow B)$

$(A \Rightarrow B) \Rightarrow (\sim\Diamond B \Rightarrow \sim\Diamond A)$

S5: $\Diamond A \Rightarrow \Box\Diamond A$

$\Box A \Rightarrow \Box\Box A.$

It turns out that each of Lewis's systems is stronger than its predecessor. That is, every theorem in *S1* is a theorem in *S2*, every theorem in *S2* is a theorem in *S3*, every theorem in *S3* is a theorem in *S4*, and every theorem in *S4* is a theorem in *S5*, but not vice versa. Of course, many of the axioms and theorems of these systems are non-controversial; however, others are not. For example, axiom A7 states (in effect) that if a conjunction is possible, then so are its conjuncts. Yet just because two propositions, *p* and *q*, are possible together, should this be sufficient to guarantee that *p* (or *q*) is possible by itself? Many people's modal intuitions say yes, but others disagree. Similarly, axioms A9 and A10 state that modal propositions are always necessary. Yet this idea is also not universally accepted. For example, why should it be the case that modal propositions necessarily have the modal properties they do? Is it not possible that modal properties, like other properties, will hold contingently?

It is also interesting to note that fallacies can occur when an arguer gets the scope of a modal operator wrong. For example, consider the difference between the two formulas $\Box (p \supset q)$ and $p \supset \Box q$. As both the American philosopher Robert Sleigh and the Australian philosopher David Stove have pointed out, $\Box (p \supset q)$ means that the whole hypothetical "If *p* then *q*" is a necessary truth, or that *p* necessarily implies *q*. In contrast, $p \supset \Box q$ means that if *p* is true then *q* is a necessary truth, which is something quite different. For example, consider the proposition "Bill is in Palo Alto and Sue is in San Francisco." This proposition clearly entails that "Bill is in Palo Alto." So necessarily, if the first proposition is true, so is the second. Here $\Box (p \supset q)$ is appropriate. At the same time, even if the proposition "Bill is in Palo Alto and Sue is in San Francisco" is true, this does not warrant the conclusion that "Bill is in Palo Alto" is necessarily true. Quite the contrary. There is nothing necessary about Bill's being in Palo Alto. He could have decided, for example, to spend the day in San Francisco with Sue instead. So $p \supset \Box q$ is not true. To think that it is true is to commit what has become known as *Sleigh's Fallacy* or, as David Stove puts it, the *fallacy of misconditionalization*.

This point may seem to be a simple one, but the ambiguity of the common idiom "If *p* then it must be that *q*" often makes it difficult to understand exactly what a speaker means. For example, since we know that $p \Rightarrow p$, we might make the claim that "If Bill is intelligent, then it must be that Bill is intelligent," and from here slide to the conclusion that "Necessarily, Bill is intelligent," or that being intelligent is an essential or defining characteristic of Bill. Yet this is simply not justified, and to think that it is amounts to another example of Sleigh's Fallacy.

Exercise 7.3

1. Prove each of the following to be a theorem of system *S1*:

   (a) $(A \wedge B) \Leftrightarrow (B \wedge A)$

   (b) $A \Leftrightarrow A$

   (c) $(\sim A \Rightarrow B) \Rightarrow (\sim B \Rightarrow A)$

   (d) $[A \wedge (B \wedge C)] \Leftrightarrow [(A \wedge B) \wedge C]$

   (e) $\sim \sim A \Rightarrow A$

2. The argument form "$\square (p \vee \sim p)$; therefore, $\square p \vee \sim p$" is not valid in modal logic. Find an example of an argument in English that fallaciously trades on a scope confusion of this sort.

3. Is this argument valid? Why or why not?

   It is possible that I walk

   It is possible that I sit

   ───────────────────────────

   Therefore, it is possible that I walk and sit.

4. Epistemic and Deontic Logics

As we saw in the previous section, modal logics are motivated in part by the observation that, even though they are not captured in classic propositional logic, arguments such as

   Bill is in Palo Alto

   ───────────────────────────

   Therefore, it is possible that Bill is in Palo Alto

are not just valid, they are valid as a result of their logical form. Much the same can be said of arguments such as

   It is known that Bill is in Palo Alto

   ───────────────────────────

   Therefore, it is believed that Bill is in Palo Alto

and

   It is obligatory that Bill is in Palo Alto

   ───────────────────────────

   Therefore, it is permissible that Bill is in Palo Alto.

Arguments such as the second of these three, which deal with properties relating to knowledge and belief, are said to be *epistemic arguments*; arguments such as the third, which deal with properties relating to obligation and permission, are said to be *deontic arguments*. Both types of arguments give rise to their own logics and, like modal logics, epistemic and deontic logics may be viewed as extensions of classical logic.

   The two main propositional connectives of *epistemic logic* are "It is believed that ..." and "It is known that ...." Given the proposition "There is an inactive volcano on the dark side of the moon," we can create two new propositions, "It is believed that there is an inactive volcano on the dark side of the moon" and "It is known that there is an inactive volcano on the dark side of the moon." The first of these two connectives is usually represented by the letter **B**; the second by the letter **K**. Like the connectives in modal logic, neither of these connectives is fully *truth-functional*.

Similarly, the two main propositional connectives of *deontic logic* are "It may be the case that ..." (or "It is permissible that ...") and "It ought to be the case that ..." (or "It is obligatory that ..."). Given the proposition "Sue is in Whistler," we can then create two new propositions, "It is permissible that Sue is in Whistler" and "It is obligatory that Sue is in Whistler." The first of these two connectives is usually represented by the letter **P**; the second by the letter **O**. Again, neither of these connectives is fully truth-functional.

Among the valid argument forms of epistemic logic are the following:

> **K**p
> _____
> ∴ p

> **K**p
> _____
> ∴ **B**p.

The first of these argument forms is based upon the fact that knowledge implies truth; that is, it is based upon the fact that you cannot know what is not true. (As we mentioned earlier, this is something different from *believing* that you know what is in fact not true.) The second of these forms tells us that knowledge implies belief; that is, it tells us that if you do not believe something, then you can hardly be said to know it.[5]

However, in epistemic logic, just as in modal logic, there are also a number of more controversial argument forms. Here are some examples:

> **K**p
> _____
> ∴ **KK**p

> **K**p
> $p \supset q$
> _____
> ∴ **K**q

Belief and Knowledge
The two main propositional connectives of *epistemic logic* are "It is believed that ..." and "It is known that ...." For example, given the proposition "There is an inactive volcano on the dark side of the moon," we can create two new propositions, "It is believed that there is an inactive volcano on the dark side of the moon" and "It is known that there is an inactive volcano on the dark side of the moon." Like the connectives in modal logic, neither of these connectives is fully *truth-functional*.

Permission and Obligation
The two main propositional connectives of *deontic logic* are "It may be the case that ..." (or "It is permissible that ...") and "It ought to be the case that ..." (or "It is obligatory that ..."). For example, given the proposition "Sue is in Whistler," we can create two new propositions, "It is permissible that Sue is in Whistler" and "It is obligatory that Sue is in Whistler." Neither of these connectives is fully *truth-functional*.

Bp

———————

∴ **BB**p

Bp

$p \supset q$

———————

∴ **B**q.

The first of these argument forms says that if there is something that we know, then we also know that we know it. The second says that if there is something that we know, then we also know the consequences of that knowledge. The third and fourth of these argument forms express parallel claims with respect to belief.

Now, these may at first strike us as reasonable conjectures. Upon closer examination, though, we may not want to accept them. For example, upon more careful reflection, we may decide that having knowledge of knowledge is likely to depend upon how aware we are of our own mental states. It may also depend upon what we mean by knowledge. For example, one highly respected definition of knowledge comes from Aristotle's teacher, Plato. According to Plato, an agent, A, knows that p if and only if the following three conditions hold: (1) p is true; (2) A believes that p; and (3) A has sufficient reason for believing that p.

If this is the correct definition of knowledge, then it is entirely possible that one could know without knowing that one knows. For example, suppose that I believe some true proposition, p, and suppose that I believe it as a result of evidence, e. Must it be the case that I am aware of this, and of the process by which I came to have my belief in p as a result of e? Young children, for example, often have beliefs which we, as adult observers, would say they are justified in holding, even though the children themselves are unaware of why it is, exactly, they have the beliefs they do. Alternatively, is it not possible that I may doubt that e sufficiently justifies my believing p, but be wrong about this? What if, unknown to me, e provides a perfectly sound justification for believing p? Then it would be the case that p is true, that I believe that p is true, and that I have adequate reasons for believing that p is true, even though I do not know that I have adequate reasons for believing p. Similar concerns may also be raised for the other argument forms listed above.

In the case of deontic logic, examples of non-controversial valid argument forms include the following:

Op

———————

∴ **P**p

Pp

———————

∴ ~**O**~p.

Op
_____
∴ ~**P**~p.

The first of these argument forms says that obligation implies permission, that any-thing that is obligatory must also be permissible. The second gives effect to the claim that permission is the same as the non-obligation of a denial, and the third to the claim that obligation is the same as the non-permissibility of a denial.

In contrast, neither of the following argument forms is valid:

Op
_____
∴ p

p
_____
∴ **P**p

Sadly, in our world at least, obligation fails to imply actuality and actuality fails to implies permission.

Exercise 7.4

1.   Are these arguments valid?

(a) It is known that Neil Armstrong first stepped on the surface of the moon on July 20, 1969.

_____

Therefore, Neil Armstrong first stepped on the surface of the moon on July 20, 1969.

(b) It is believed that Neil Armstrong first stepped on the surface of the moon on July 20, 1969.

_____

Therefore, Neil Armstrong first stepped on the surface of the moon on July 20, 1969.

(c) It is known that Neil Armstrong first stepped on the surface of the moon on July 20, 1969.

_____

Therefore, it is believed that Neil Armstrong first stepped on the surface of the moon on July 20, 1969.

(d) It is obligatory that Bill studies his math-ematics or his philosophy.

_____

Therefore, it is obligatory that Bill studies his mathematics or it is obligatory that Bill studies his philosophy.

(e) It is permissible that Bill studies his mathematics or his philosophy.

_____

Therefore, it is permissible that Bill studies his mathematics or it is permissible that Bill studies his philosophy.

5. Multi-valued Logics

One important feature of classical logic is its commitment to exactly two truth values: truth and falsehood. In classical logic, any proposition that is not true is false and any proposition that is not false is true. In contrast to this traditional view, there are several arguments in support of the view that there are more than two truth values. Among these are arguments based on paradoxes such as the paradox of the liar (which we discussed in chapter 5) and arguments based on Aristotle's problem of future contingents (which we discuss below). Logics that accept these arguments and that reject Aristotle's original definition of a proposition (as that which has exactly one of the two traditional truth values and no others), are called *multi-valued logics*.

As we saw in chapter 5, the paradox of the liar arises from propositions such as "This proposition is false." If this proposition is true, then what it says must be true, and so it must also be false. Similarly, if the proposition is false, then what it says must be false, and so it must also be true. Since, according to our original definition of a proposition, all propositions must be either true or false, it appears that the liar proposition must be both true and false, yet this is clearly impossible.

The problem of future contingents emphasizes a different but related difficulty. Imagine that you are in ancient Athens and that the city has been busy preparing for war. From a hillside on the edge of the city you can see the Athenian navy readying itself for battle. On the horizon you see arriving the lead ships of the Persian navy. The weather is clear and you know that there will be a sea battle tomorrow.

As you discuss these matters with your friends, someone makes the following claim: "Athens will win the sea battle tomorrow." If we accept the traditional definition of a proposition, we know that every proposition must be either true or false. So, just as with the liar paradox, let us consider each of these two possibilities in turn. If the proposition is true (now), then it is already (today) determined that Athens will win the sea battle tomorrow. Similarly, if the proposition is false (now) then it is already (today) determined that Athens will not win the sea battle tomorrow. Yet if this is correct, then it appears that whatever the outcome, the future is already determined. Furthermore, given that there was nothing special about our original proposition—any contingent proposition would have served as well—it appears to follow that everything that happens must happen necessarily. Yet, because we have free will, we know this is false. Not everything that happens does so necessarily. So, just as with the liar paradox, we have discovered a contradiction. How can this paradox be solved?

One thing that is common to both the paradox of the liar and the problem of future contingents is that they both rely on the traditional assumption that there are exactly two truth values, truth and falsehood. In the problem of future contingents, regardless of whether our original (contingent) proposition is true or false, it turns out that the future is determined. Similarly, in the case of the liar paradox, regardless of whether we assume our original proposition to be true or false, contradictory claims follow. What are we to do?

> ## The Problem of Future Contingents
>
> Consider the claim, made today, that
>
> Athens will win the sea battle tomorrow.
>
> Aristotle pointed out that if every proposition is either true or false then this propo-
> sition must be either true or false.[6] So let us consider these two cases in turn. If the
> proposition is true (now), then it is already determined that Athens will win the sea
> battle tomorrow. Similarly, if the proposition is false (now) then it is already determined
> that Athens will not win the sea battle tomorrow. Yet if this is correct, then whatever
> the outcome, this outcome is already determined. Since there was nothing special
> about our original proposition, it also appears to follow that everything that hap-
> pens must happen necessarily. Yet, because we have free will, we know that this is
> false. How can we resolve this contradiction?

One response is to conclude that traditional logic must be modified. In other
words, one response is to introduce a logic that uses more than our two traditional
truth values. The easiest way to introduce such a logic is to reject Aristotle's definition
of a proposition and to redefine propositions as claims which are true, or false, or neither true nor false.

Since claims of future contingents, such as the claim that "Athens will win the sea
battle tomorrow," are not yet determined, they may now be understood as not (yet)
having one of our two original truth values, as being neither true nor false. Similarly,
in the case of propositions such as "This proposition is false," we may conclude that
they, too, are neither true nor false. Is there a way to develop this basic idea? Can we
develop a logic that uses more than two truth values?

One way to do so is to redefine our five classical propositional connectives as
follows:

Conjunction

	$p \wedge q$	T	I	F
	T	T	I	F
p	I	I	I	F
	F	F	F	F

Disjunction

	$p \vee q$	T	I	F
	T	T	T	T
p	I	T	I	I
	F	T	I	F

Negation

$\sim p$	p
F	T
I	I
T	F

Conditional

	$p \supset q$	T	I	F
	T	T	I	F
p	I	T	T	I
	F	T	T	T

Biconditional

	$p \equiv q$	T	I	F
	T	T	I	F
p	I	I	T	I
	F	F	I	T

These definitions of the propositional connectives are due to the Polish logician Jan Łukasiewicz. In them the "I" stands for "indeterminate," the value Łukasiewicz assigns to future contingent propositions. If we order these three truth values such that T > I > F, then we see that a conjunction always takes the smaller of the truth values of its two conjuncts and a disjunction always takes the larger of the truth values of its two disjuncts. Negation is similar to classical negation, except that the negation of an indeterminate proposition is itself defined as being indeterminate.[7]

> **Łukasiewicz's Three-valued Logic**
> In order to solve the problem of future contingents, the Polish logician Jan Łukasiewicz introduces a third, indeterminate truth value, "I." In Łukasiewicz's logic an indeterminate proposition is one that is neither true nor false.

A different, competing definition of the connectives is due to D.A. Bochvar:

	Conjunction		
		q	
$p \wedge q$	T	I	F
T	T	I	F
p I	I	I	I
F	F	I	F

	Disjunction		
		q	
$p \vee q$	T	I	F
T	T	I	T
p I	I	I	I
F	T	I	F

Negation	
$\sim p$	p
F	T
I	I
T	F

	Conditional		
		q	
$p \supset q$	T	I	F
T	T	I	F
p I	I	I	I
F	T	I	T

	Biconditional		
		q	
$p \equiv q$	T	I	F
T	T	I	F
p I	I	I	I
F	F	I	T

Bochvar's definitions of the connectives differ from Łukasiewicz's only with regard to those propositions that involve the truth value I. However this difference is important philosophically. It allows us to interpret the third value as meaning "paradoxical" or "meaningless" rather than "indeterminate." In Bochvar's logic, any proposition that contains a meaningless proposition as one of its constituents will itself be meaningless. This is in contrast to Łukasiewicz's definitions where the truth or falsehood of one component is sufficient to decide the truth value of its molecular proposition.

> **Bochvar's Three-valued Logic**
> In order to solve the liar paradox, the logician D.A. Bochvar introduces a third truth value, "I," which is applied to paradoxical or meaningless propositions. In Bochvar's logic any proposition that contains a meaningless proposition as one of its constituents —such as the liar sentence—is itself meaningless.

To see how these two logics work, consider two propositional forms that we know to be tautologies in classical logic, the law of excluded middle, $p \vee \sim p$, and the law of non-contradiction, $\sim(p \wedge \sim p)$. Using Łukasiewicz's connectives and Bochvar's connectives, we obtain exactly the same truth tables:

	p	*~p*	*p* ∨ *~p*
(1)	T	F	T
(2)	I	I	I
(3)	F	T	T

	p	*~p*	*p* ∧ *~p*	*~(p* ∧ *~p)*
(1)	T	F	F	T
(2)	I	I	I	I
(3)	F	T	F	T

Thus neither the law of excluded middle nor the law of non-contradiction is a tautology in either Łukasiewicz's or Bochvar's logic. However, this does not mean that these two logics are identical. To see this, consider yet a third proposition, $[(A \supset B) \land (B \supset A)] \equiv (A \equiv B)$. Because $[(A \supset B) \land (B \supset A)]$ is equivalent to $(A \equiv B)$, we again know that this proposition is a tautology in classical logic. Is it also a tautology in the three-valued logics of Łukasiewicz and Bochvar?

Using Łukasiewicz's definitions of the connectives we obtain the following truth table:

	A	*B*	*A⊃B*	*B⊃A*	*(A⊃B)∧(B⊃A)*	*A≡B*	*[(A⊃B)∧(B⊃A)]≡(A≡B)*
(1)	T	T	T	T	T	T	T
(2)	T	I	I	T	I	I	T
(3)	T	F	F	T	F	F	T
(4)	I	T	T	I	I	I	T
(5)	I	I	T	T	T	T	T
(6)	I	F	I	T	I	I	T
(7)	F	T	T	F	F	F	T
(8)	F	I	T	I	I	I	T
(9)	F	F	T	T	T	T	T

Here the proposition $[(A \supset B) \land (B \supset A)] \equiv (A \equiv B)$ turns out to be a tautology, just as it is in classical logic.

In contrast, Bochvar's logic yields the following truth table:

	A	*B*	*A⊃B*	*B⊃A*	*(A⊃B)∧(B⊃A)*	*A≡B*	*[(A⊃B)∧(B⊃A)]≡(A≡B)*
(1)	T	T	T	T	T	T	T
(2)	T	I	I	I	I	I	I
(3)	T	F	F	T	F	F	T
(4)	I	T	I	I	I	I	I
(5)	I	I	I	I	I	I	I
(6)	I	F	I	I	I	I	I
(7)	F	T	T	F	F	F	T
(8)	F	I	I	I	I	I	I
(9)	F	F	T	T	T	T	T

Here the final column is no longer a tautology. Because "I" now stands for "meaningless," a molecular proposition that contains a meaningless proposition as one of its components is itself meaningless.

Having seen how these two systems work, let us now return to our original two problems. Do either of these logics help us solve the paradox of the liar or the problem of future contingents?

Łukasiewicz's logic is intended to help resolve the problem of future contingents; Bochvar's logic is intended to help resolve the paradox of the liar. If Łukasiewicz is correct, then the problem of future contingents disappears once we realize that contingent propositions about the future are neither true nor false. If they are neither true nor false, they are consistent with the future being undetermined. If Bochvar is correct, the proposition "This proposition is false" also turns out to be neither true nor false. As a result, we can now accept with impunity the claims that *if* it were true, then it would be false (and, hence, be both true and false), and that *if* it were false, then it would be true (and, hence, again be both true and false). The reason we can do so is that, in fact, neither antecedent is true. Since the liar sentence is neither true nor false, neither of these conditional claims causes us concern. The proposition says of itself that it is false. This is not true, of course, but this is now easily explained since we have accepted the third possibility, namely that it is neither true nor false.

Paradox of the Strengthened Liar

Consider the following proposition:

> This proposition is not true.

Assuming that every proposition is true, false, or neither, what is the truth value of this proposition? Is it true, false, or neither? If it is true, then it is true that it is not true, and so it must be both true and not true. Similarly, if it is false, then it is not true (since being false is one way of not being true), and since it is not true, and it says that it is not true, it must be true (since it is what it says it is). So again, it must be both true and not true. Finally, if it is neither true nor false, then it is not true (since being neither true nor false is one way of not being true), and since it is not true, and it says that it is not true, it must be true (since it is what it says it is). So once again, it must be both true and not true. It follows that in all three cases the proposition turns out to be both true and not true.

However, it is not yet time to celebrate. Lurking in the background is a related paradox, the *paradox of the strengthened liar.* Even if the proposition, "This proposition is false" is no longer a cause for concern, the paradox of the strengthened liar asks us to consider the following proposition: "This proposition is not true." Assuming that every proposition is true, false, or neither, what is the truth value of this proposition? Is it true, false, or neither?

Let us consider the three cases in turn. First, if it is true, then it is true that it is not true, and so it must be both true and not true. This is clearly impossible. Second, if it is false, then it is also not true (since being false is one way of not being true), and since it is not true and it says that it is not true, it must be true (since it is what is says it is). So again, it must be both true and not true, which is again impossible. Finally, if it is neither true nor false, then it is not true (since being neither true nor false is one way of not being true), and since it is not true and it says that it is not true, it must be true (since it is what it says it is). So once again, it must be both true and not true. It follows that in all three cases the proposition turns out to be both true and not true, which is clearly impossible. Our three-valued logics may have solved our original two paradoxes, but this new paradox remains. So whatever their other virtues, it appears that our three-valued logics have not yet provided us with a complete and accurate account of propositions and their logic.[8]

Exercise 7.5

1. Determine whether the following proposi-tions are tautologies, contingencies, or contradictions in Łukasiewicz's three-valued logic:

    (a) $A \vee (B \vee \sim B)$

    (b) $\sim A \supset (A \supset B)$

    (c) $\sim[\sim A \supset (A \supset B)]$

    (d) $\sim[\sim \sim A \vee (A \supset B)]$

    (e) $A \equiv \sim A$

2. Determine whether each proposition in question 1 above is a tautology, contin-gency, or contradiction in Bochvar's three-valued logic.

Summary

In this chapter we have encountered several systems of propositional logic distinct from system *P*. System *RP*, a relatedness logic, restricts the idea of validity as used in sys-tem *P* by introducing the idea of a common subject matter between propositions. In doing so, it attempts to resolve the fallacy of *ignoratio elenchi.*

In system *RP* an *R-negation* ($\neg$) always has the opposite truth value to that of the proposition negated; an *R-conjunction* ($\wedge$) is true when and only when both of its conjuncts are true; an *R-disjunction* ($\vee$) is true when and only when its two dis-juncts are related and at least one of its disjuncts is true; an *R-conditional* ($\rightarrow$) is false when and only when its antecedent is true and its consequent is false or its antecedent and consequent are unrelated to each other; and an *R-biconditional* ($\leftrightarrow$) is true when and only when its two component propositions are related and they share the same truth value.

Unlike system *RP*, the other systems we considered were all extensions of *P*. First, *modal logics* supplement system *P* by adding two new propositional connec-tives, the diamond, $\diamond$, which is read "It is possible that" (or "Possibly") and the box, $\square$, which is read "It is necessary that" (or "Necessarily"). Of the many systems of modal logic developed, systems *S1* to *S5* were of particular interest. Second, *epis-*

temic logics supplement *P* by adding the new connectives, B, read "It is believed that ...," and K, read "It is known that ...." Third, *deontic logics* add the connectives P, read "It may be the case that ..." (or "It is permissible that ..."), and O, "It ought to be the case that ..." (or "It is obligatory that ..."). Unlike the classical connectives of system *P*, none of these connectives are fully *truth-functional*.

Finally, we reviewed two multi-valued logics. In order to attempt to solve the *problem of future contingents*, the Polish logician Jan Łukasiewicz introduces a third, indeterminate truth value, "I." In Łukasiewicz's logic, an indeterminate proposition is one that is neither true nor false. In order to attempt to solve the *liar paradox*, the logician D.A. Bochvar introduces a third truth value, "I," which is applied to paradoxical or meaningless propositions. In Bochvar's logic, any proposition that contains a meaningless proposition, such as the liar sentence, as one of its constituents is itself meaningless. However, it appears that neither logic fully solves the *paradox of the strengthened liar.*

Weblinks

Episteme Links—Logic
www.epistemelinks.com/Topi/LogiTopi.htm

Philosophy in Cyberspace—Logic
www.geocities.com/Athens/Acropolis/4393/logic.htm

Stanford Encyclopedia of Philosophy—Relevance Logic
plato.stanford.edu/entries/logic-relevance/

Advances in Modal Logic
turing.wins.uva.nl/~mdr/AiML/

Notes

1. For further study, see Richard L. Epstein, "Relatedness and Implication," *Philosophical Studies* 36 (1979): 137–173; Douglas N. Walton, "Philosophical Basis of Relatedness Logic," *Philosophical Studies* 36 (1979): 115–136; Michael Dunn, "Relevance Logic and Entailment," in D. Gabbay and F. Guenthner, *Handbook of Philosophical Logic*, Vol. 3, (Dordrecht: Reidel, 1983), 117–224; and Stephen Read, *Relevant Logic*, (New York: Blackwell, 1988).

2. "Alethic" comes from the Greek word *aletheia*, meaning truth. Modalities, as they are understood by logicians, are expressions that qualify the expressions to which they are appended. The alethic modalities qualify the expressions to which they are appended with regard to necessity, possibility, impossibility, and contingency.

3. Twin primes are pairs of prime numbers that are separated by only a single number, for example 5 and 7, 11 and 13, 17 and 19, etc.

4. Of course, it is important to note that the proposition "It is possible that Bill is in Melbourne" is not the same as the proposition "Given that it's not true that Bill is in Melbourne, it is possible that Bill is in Melbourne." The former, we are assuming, is true; the latter false.

5. At least this is true for what is called *propositional knowledge*. Distinguishing between various types of knowledge is the job of that branch of philosophy known as *epistemology*.

6. See Aristotle's *On Interpretation*, bk. 9, 19a, 30.

7. As Susan Haack points out, this three-valued logic can be generalized. If we let $|p|$ stand for "the truth value of p" and represent T by 1, I by 1/2 and F by 0, then Łukasiewicz's connectives can be redefined as follows:

$$|{\sim}p| = df\ 1 - |p|,$$

$$|p \lor q| = df \max \{|p|, |q|\},$$

$$|p \land q| = df \min \{|p|, |q|\},$$

$$|p \supset q| = df \quad \begin{cases} 1 \text{ if } |p| \leq |q|, \text{ or} \\ 1 - |p| + |q| \text{ if } |p| > |q|. \end{cases}$$

These same rules can then be used to define the connectives for 4, 5, 6, ..., n, and infinitely many-valued logics. See Susan Haack, *Philosophy of Logics* (Cambridge: Cambridge University Press, 1978), 206.

8. For further information see Alasdair Urquhart's "Many-valued Logic," in D. Gabbay and F. Guenthner, *Handbook of Philosophical Logic*, Vol. 3 (Dordrecht: Reidel, 1986), 71–116, and Susan Haack's *Deviant Logic, Fuzzy Logic* (Chicago: University of Chicago Press, 1996), ch. 4.

CHAPTER 8

Extending Deductive Logic: II

IN THE last few chapters, we have seen that formal methods can be applied fruitfully to the study of rational inference and the fallacies. In this chapter we will investigate the first system of formal logic ever developed, the traditional logic of Aristotle.

Aristotle's logic (or *term logic*, as it is sometimes called) was, for many centuries, the only systematic account of valid inference that was widely studied. It consists of two main parts: his theory of one-premiss arguments, called his theory of *immediate inference*, and his theory of two-premiss arguments, called his theory of the *syllogism*. After investigating Aristotle's logic, we will see how modern propositional logic can be extended to deal with syllogistic arguments, but with greater generality and depth of treatment. This modern extension of propositional logic is called *predicate logic* or *quantification theory*. It forms the basis for most contemporary logical studies.

1. Aristotle's Categorical Propositions

In chapters 4 and 6 we were introduced to some of the basic concepts of propositional logic. In propositional logic we were concerned with discovering the logical relations that hold between propositions; but we did not analyze the internal logical structure of atomic propositions themselves. Propositions were taken as basic, unanalyzed units. In this chapter our analysis will concentrate, in large part, on the internal structure of these propositions and how this internal structure affects properties of arguments such as validity.

Specifically, we will be concerned with so-called *categorical propositions*. These are propositions such as

All politicians are liars

No politicians are liars

Some politicians are liars

Some politicians are not liars.

We label the forms of these four propositions as follows:

A (Universal Affirmative):	All *S* are *P*
E (Universal Negative):	No *S* are *P*
I (Particular Affirmative):	Some *S* are *P*
O (Particular Negative):	Some *S* are not *P*.[1]

Two of these forms, A and I, are *affirmative*; the remaining two, E and O, are *negative*. Similarly, two of these forms, A and E, are *universal*, while the remaining two, I and O, are *particular*. The labels A, E, I, and O originated in medieval times from two Latin words: *affirmo,* meaning "I affirm," and *nego*, meaning "I deny." "A" and "I", the labels for our two affirmative propositions, are the first two vowels in *affirmo*; "E" and "O", the labels for our two negative propositions, are the first (and only) two vowels in *nego*.

Each categorical proposition includes exactly two nonlogical terms. One term, *S*, is called the *subject* term, the other, *P*, the *predicate* term. Each term stands for (or denotes) a class of objects. For example, the term "politicians" stands for (or denotes) the class of politicians. Alternatively, we say that each term has a given class of objects as its *extension*. In the case of universal propositions, this class of objects may turn out to be empty. In particular propositions, in contrast, the word "some" is interpreted as meaning "at least one."

In natural language, referring terms are typically represented by nouns or noun phrases. However, sometimes adjectives or verbs can be used to stand in their stead. For example, "Some *S* are *P*" might abbreviate "Some politicians are liars," but it might equally well stand for "Some politicians lie" or "Some politicians are people who lie." Similarly, "All *S* are *P*" might stand for "All birds sing" or for "All birds are singing creatures," as well as for "All birds are singers." Whenever adjectives or verbs in a proposition such as "All politicians lie" are replaced with the appropriate noun or noun phrase we say that the proposition has been placed in *standard categorical form* (or, more simply, *standard form*). For example, "All politicians lie" is not in standard form, whereas "All politicians are liars" is.

> **Aristotle's Categorical Propositions**
> Given two referring terms, *S* and *P*, Aristotle identified four types of categorical proposition: *universal affirmative propositions* are propositions of the form "All *S* are *P*"; *universal negative propositions* are propositions of the form "No *S* are *P*"; *particular affirmative propositions* are propositions of the form "Some *S* are *P*"; and *particular negative propositions* are propositions of the form "Some *S* are not *P*." In particular propositions the word "some" is interpreted to mean "at least one." In contrast, in universal propositions the word "all" is interpreted to mean "if there are any, then all." Thus particular propositions, unlike universal propositions, are said to have *existential import*.

Among the many variant ways of stating an A proposition such as "All horses are mammals" are the following: "Each (or every, or any) horse is a mammal," "Horses are mammals," "If something (or anything) is a horse, then it is a mammal," "If something (or anything) is not a mammal, then it is not a horse," "All non-mammals are non-horses," "Only mammals are horses," "No horse is not a mammal," and "Horses are exclusively mammals."

Non-standard Categorical Propositions

Each of our four types of categorical proposition can be expressed in a variety of ways. The most common equivalent forms include the following:

A: Universal Affirmative Propositions

All *S* are *P*

Only *P* are *S*

Each *S* is a *P*

If it's an *S*, then it's a *P*

Any *S* is a *P*

Every *S* is a *P*

S are always *P*

E: Universal Negation Propositions

No *S* are *P*

Every *S* is a non-*P*

If it's an *S*, then it's not a *P*

All *S* are non-*P*

S are never *P*

I: Particular Affirmation Propositions

Some *S* are *P*

At least one *S* is a *P*

Some *P* are *S*

S are sometimes *P*

O: Particular Negation Propositions

Some *S* are not *P*

At least one *S* is not a *P*

Not all *S* are *P*

S are sometimes not *P*

Among the many variant ways of stating an E proposition such as "No spiders are insects" are the following: "Nothing is both a spider and an insect," "Nothing that is a spider is an insect," "There are no spiders that are insects," "Spiders aren't insects," and "If it's a spider, then it's not an insect."

Among the many variant ways of stating an I proposition such as "Some diamonds are gems" are the following: "Some gems are diamonds," "At least one diamond is a gem," "Diamonds are frequently gems," "A few diamonds are gems," and "Most diamonds are gems."

Among the many variant ways of stating an O proposition such as "Some turtles are not land-dwellers" are the following: "Not all turtles live on the land," "Some turtles are not land-dwelling," "Many turtles don't live on the land," "Most turtles are not land-dwellers," and "There are at least some non-land-dwelling turtles."

As helpful as these equivalences are, checklists of idioms can be misleading. For example, "always" usually means "at all moments," but not every time. The sentence "Bill always dials the phone with his left hand" does not mean "Bill dials the phone with his left hand at all moments." Rather, it means that "All moments at which Bill dials the phone are moments at which Bill dials the phone with his left hand." As a general rule of thumb, when standardizing propositions, it is helpful to proceed through each of the following four steps.

Step 1 – Determine the *Quality* of the Proposition

In other words, determine whether the proposition is affirmative or negative. If it is affirmative, we know that it will have to be either an A or an I proposition. If it contains a negation, we know it will have to be either an E or an O proposition. For example, given that the proposition "Copper doesn't conduct electricity" contains a negation, we know immediately that it will be either an E or an O proposition.

Step 2 – Determine the *Quantity* of the Proposition

In other words, determine whether the proposition is universal or particular. If it is universal, we know that it will have to be either an A or an E proposition. If it is particular, we know that it will have to be either an I or an O proposition. In the example above, since the proposition does not refer to only some copper things, we recognize that it must be universal, and hence either an A or an E proposition; and since we already know that it is either an E or an O proposition, it follows that it must be an E proposition.

Step 3 – Identify the Proposition's Two Nonlogical Referring Terms

For example, in a proposition such as "Fish swim," this will involve changing the verb "swim" to the referring term "swimmers" and adding the copula "are." In our previous example, the terms are easy to identify: "copper things" and "things that conduct electricity."

Step 4 – Place the Proposition in Standard Categorical Form

In the case of "Copper doesn't conduct electricity" the result is "No copper things are things that conduct electricity." In the case of "Fish swim" the result is "All fish are swimmers."

What we have said so far conforms fairly closely to the *ancient*, or *Aristotelian*, interpretation of categorical propositions. However, we will now make some assump-

Steps for Standardizing Categorical Propositions
1. Determine the *quality* of the proposition.
2. Determine the *quantity* of the proposition.
3. Identify the proposition's two nonlogical referring terms.
4. Place the proposition in standard categorical form.

tions that depart slightly from that interpretation. These assumptions conform to the *modern* (or *hypothetical*, or *Boolean*) interpretation of standard-form categorical propositions.

The first such assumption concerns how we formalize propositions about individuals. For example, how might we formalize the proposition "Bertrand Russell was a prominent pacifist during the First World War"? This proposition does not immediately appear to conform to any of our four categorical forms. However, recognizing that Bertrand Russell can be identified with the members of the set of people identical to Bertrand Russell, we can reconstruct this proposition as the proposition "All people identical with Bertrand Russell are people who were prominent pacifists during the First World War." The same general idea will work with other propositions about individuals as well. For example, "Bertrand Russell was not a prominent pacifist during the First World War" becomes "No people identical with Bertrand Russell are people who were prominent pacifists during the First World War."

Second, we will assume that propositions of the form "All *S* are *P*" are to be interpreted as meaning "If anything is an *S* then it is also a *P*" and that propositions of the form "No *S* are *P*" are to be interpreted as meaning "If anything is an *S* then it is not a *P*." In other words, the statement "All diamonds are gems" can be understood as meaning "If anything is a diamond, it is also a gem" and the proposition "No diamonds are gems" can be understood as meaning "If anything is a diamond, then it is not a gem."

More technically, we say that universal propositions do not have *existential import*. A proposition has existential import when it implies the existence of something. Thus "Some computers are expensive" (or, more properly, "Some computers are expensive things") has existential import since it implies that there exist both computers and expensive things. In contrast, if we say that universal propositions lack existential import, we are saying that propositions such as "All diamonds are gems" do not imply the existence of either diamonds or gems. How can this be?

According to the ancient (or Aristotelian) interpretation, universal propositions have existential import. In contrast, the modern (or hypothetical) view is that universal propositions are better understood as being equivalent to conditional (or hypothetical) propositions. Thus "All computers are expensive" is equivalent to the conditional claim, "If something is a computer, then it is an expensive thing." This proposition, in turn, no more implies the existence of computers than "All deserters will be shot" (or, more properly, "All deserters are people who will be shot") implies the existence of deserters, or "All cheaters will be punished" (or, more properly, "All cheaters are people who will be punished") implies the existence of cheaters. In fact, we would like to think both that this last proposition is true and that there are, in fact, no students who cheat![2]

Exercise 8.1

1. Identify each of the following propositions as having the form A, E, I, or O:

    (a) The monkey has a tail.

    (b) Men are not selfish by nature.

    (c) Only people over eighteen are allowed inside.

    (d) Copper conducts electricity.

    (e) The gods have no mercy.

    (f) Many politicians are not honest.

    (g) An investment broker is in a good position when interest rates are high.

    (h) Most elements are not inert.

    (i) Anyone who loves music loves Mozart.

    (j) Some people who love music will not be pleased with this score.

2. Identify each of the following propositions as having the form A, E, I, or O, then place it in standard categorical form:

    (a) Everyone who works at the *Daily Planet* lives in Metropolis.

    (b) There is more than one reporter who is a crime-fighter.

    (c) Not every reporter is a disguised crime-fighter.

    (d) No superheroes who change their clothes in a telephone booth can be welcomed into the pantheon of superheroes.

    (e) Superheroes have been known to take bribes.

    (f) Superheroes have been known not to take bribes

    (g) Superheroes have never been known to take bribes.

    (h) Only dogs who misbehave bite.

    (i) Bill likes dogs.

    (j) Sue likes Bill's dog.

3. For each of the propositions listed in question 2 above, does it have existential import according to the ancient (or Aristotelian) interpretation?

4. For each of the propositions listed in question 2 above, does it have existential import according to the modern (or hypothetical) interpretation?

2. Immediate Inference

How can we determine whether propositions such as "No S are P" and "All S are non-P" are equivalent? Aristotle attempted to answer this question by identifying the various relations that hold between A, E, I, and O propositions. This theory of relations has come to be known as Aristotle's *theory of immediate inference*. Among the relations that Aristotle identified are *conversion*, *contraposition*, *obversion*, *contradiction*, *contrariety*, and *subcontrariety*.

Given a categorical proposition, the *converse* of that proposition is obtained by interchanging that proposition's subject and predicate terms. It turns out that all E and I propositions, but not all A and O propositions, are formally equivalent to their

Aristotle's Logic
Aristotle's logic, or theory of validity, is usually divided into two parts: his theory of one-premiss arguments, called his *theory of immediate inference*, and his theory of two-premiss arguments, called his *theory of the syllogism*.

converses. For example, given the A proposition "All dogs are mammals," we can create its converse, "All mammals are dogs." Since the first of these two propositions is true and the second is false, it follows that they cannot be equivalent. In contrast, given the I proposition "Some dogs are mammals," we can create its converse, "Some mammals are dogs." Both of these two propositions are not only true, if one is true the other must be true, and if one is false the other must be false. Hence they are equivalent.

Conversion

The *converse* of a categorical proposition is obtained by interchanging the proposition's subject and predicate terms.

Form	Proposition	Converse
A	All *S* are *P*	All *P* are *S*
E	No *S* are *P*	No *P* are *S*
I	Some *S* are *P*	Some *P* are *S*
O	Some *S* are not *P*	Some *P* are not *S*

It turns out that all E and I propositions (but not all A and O propositions) are logically equivalent to their converses.

Similarly, for any arbitrary categorical proposition, the *contrapositive* of that proposition may be obtained by first converting it, and then attaching a "non" to each of its nonlogical terms (or categories). It turns out that all A and O propositions, but not all E and I propositions, are formally equivalent to their contrapositives. For example, given the A proposition "All historians are parents," we can create its contrapositive, "All non-parents are non-historians," and this is clearly just another way of saying that "All historians are parents." In contrast, given the E proposition "No historians are parents," we can create its converse, "No non-parents are non-historians." These two propositions turn out not to be equivalent at all.

Contraposition

The *contrapositive* of a categorical proposition is obtained by first converting it and then attaching a "non" to each of its two nonlogical terms.

Form	Proposition	Contrapositive
A	All *S* are *P*	All non-*P* are non-*S*
E	No *S* are *P*	No non-*P* are non-*S*
I	Some *S* are *P*	Some non-*P* are non-*S*
O	Some *S* are not *P*	Some non-*P* are not non-*S*

It turns out that all A and O propositions (but not all E and I propositions) are logically equivalent to their contrapositives.

Thirdly, for any arbitrary categorical proposition, the *obverse* of that proposition may be obtained by first attaching a "non" to the predicate term, and then changing the proposition from affirmative to negative, or from negative to affirmative. It turns out that all A, E, I, and O propositions are formally equivalent to their obverses. For example, given the A proposition "All politicians are taxpayers," we can create its obverse, "No politicians are non-taxpayers," and this is clearly just another way of saying that "All politicians are taxpayers." In the case of the I proposition "Some politicians are taxpayers," the obverse, "Some politicians are not non-taxpayers" is again clearly equivalent to our original. The same is true for E and O propositions as well.

Obversion

The *obverse* of a categorical proposition is obtained by first attaching a "non" to the predicate term, and then changing the statement from affirmative to negative, or from negative to affirmative.

Form	Proposition	Obverse
A	All *S* are *P*	No *S* are non-*P*
E	No *S* are *P*	All *S* are non-*P*
I	Some *S* are *P*	Some *S* are not non-*P*
O	Some *S* are not *P*	Some *S* are non-*P*

It turns out that all A, E, I, and O propositions are logically equivalent to their obverses.

These three relations between categorical propositions can be made more clear by the use of a diagrammatic method devised by the nineteenth-century British logician John Venn. In Venn's diagrams, circles are used to represent classes or categories of objects. When a class is known to be empty, it is shaded. When a class is known to have at least one member, an X is placed within the circumference of its corresponding circle.

Four regions can then be represented by a diagram involving two overlapping circles:

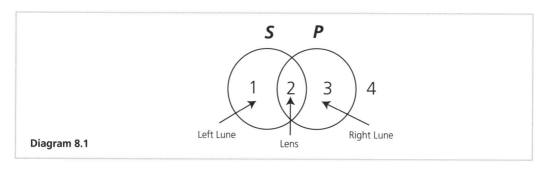

Diagram 8.1

In this diagram, region 1 (the left lune) represents objects that are *S* but not *P*; region 2 (the lens) represents objects that are both *S* and *P*; region 3 (the right lune) represents objects that are *P* but not *S*; and region 4 (the remainder) represents objects that are neither *S* nor *P*. For example, if *S* stands for the class "Greeks" and *P* for the class "generals," the lens will represent the class of Greek generals; the left lune will represent the class of Greek non-generals; the right lune will represent the class of non-Greek generals; and the remainder of the diagram, which is outside both circles, will represent the class of non-Greek non-generals.

A, E, I, and O propositions may all be represented using diagrams of this type. For example, in diagram 8.2 we see that shading is used to indicate A and E propositions, while X's are used to indicate I and O propositions.

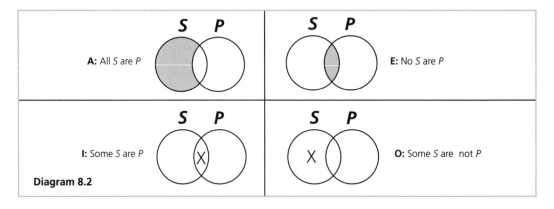

Diagram 8.2

In a Venn diagram, whiteness means nothing but lack of information. In the diagram for an E proposition, for example, both the lunes are empty, or blank. This is not because we deny that there are some *S* that are not *P*, or some *P* that are not *S*. Rather, they are blank because the proposition "No *S* are *P*" gives us no information about whether there are some *S* that are not *P*, or some *P* that are not *S*.

The symmetry of the two diagrams used to represent E and I propositions shows that the terms in E and I can be reversed. That is, all E and I propositions turn out to be equivalent to their converses. In yet other words, "No *S* are *P*" is equivalent to "No *P* are *S*" and "Some *S* are *P*" is equivalent to "Some *P* are *S*." This is clearly not the case for the terms in A and O propositions. Hence "All Greeks are men" is not to be confused with "All men are Greeks" and "Some men are not Greeks" is clearly not equivalent to "Some Greeks are not men."

Put another way, if we draw the Venn diagrams for the converses of arbitrary A, E, I, and O propositions, as in diagram 8.3, we will see that our original Venn diagrams for E and I propositions (in diagram 8.2) turn out to be identical to those of their converses. In contrast, the diagrams for the A and O propositions turn out to be quite different from those of their converses.

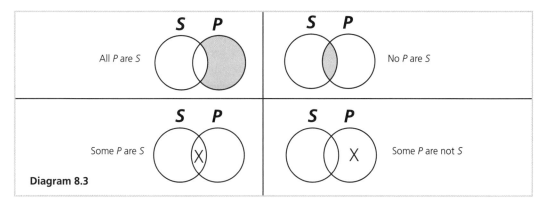

Diagram 8.3

Much the same is true in the case of contraposition and obversion. As a comparison between diagrams 8.2 and 8.4 shows, the Venn diagrams for A and O propositions turn out to be equivalent to their contrapositives, yet this is not the case for E and I propositions.

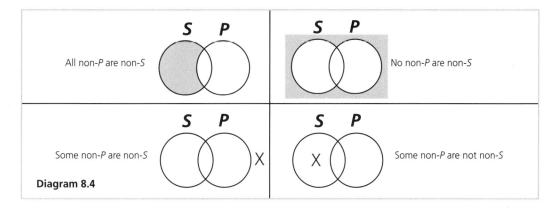

Diagram 8.4

As a comparison between diagrams 8.2 and 8.5 also shows, the Venn diagrams for A, E, I, and O propositions all turn out to be equivalent to their obverses.

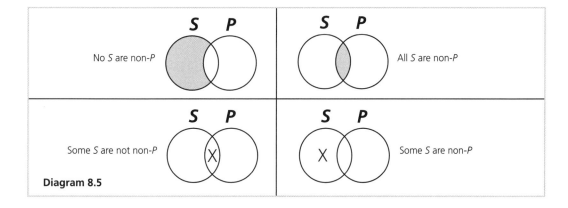

Diagram 8.5

We can also see from diagram 8.2 that A and O propositions are inconsistent with each other. An A proposition is true if and only if its corresponding O proposition is false, since where an A proposition has shading, the O proposition has an X, and vice versa. Similarly, E and I propositions are mutually contradictory. This leads us to notice Aristotle's three types of negation: contradiction, contrariety, and subcontrariety.

The *contradictory* (or *contradiction*) of a categorical proposition is the explicit denial (or negation) of that proposition. In other words, a proposition and its contradiction always have opposite truth values; if one is true, the other is false, and if one is false, the other is true. With this definition in mind, it turns out that both A and O propositions are contradictory, and E and I propositions are contradictory.

Three Types of Negation

Aristotle identifies three types of negation: contradiction, contrariety and subcontrariety. The *contradiction* of a proposition is the direct denial of that proposition. Given two *contradictory* propositions, at most one can be true and at most one can be false. In contrast, both *contrariety* and *subcontrariety* are weaker types of negation. Given two *contrary* propositions, at most one can be true, although both may be false. Given two *subcontrary* propositions, at most one can be false, although both may be true.

In contrast, *contrariety* and *subcontrariety* are defined as follows: given two contrary propositions, at most one can be true, although both may be false, and given two subcontrary propositions, at most one can be false, although both may be true.

For example, consider the following pair of propositions:

(1) All human differences are determined by the environment

(2) Not all human differences are determined by the environment.

These two propositions are contradictions since they must have opposite truth values. If one is true, the other must be false, and vice-versa.

In contrast, the two propositions

(1) All human differences are determined by the environment

(3) No human differences are determined by the environment

are not contradictions but contraries. In other words, at most one of these two propositions may be true, although both may turn out to be false.

Finally, consider the two propositions:

(4) Some human differences are determined by the environment

(5) Some human differences are not determined by the environment.

These two propositions turn out to be subcontraries. In other words, at most one of the two may be false, although both may be true.

All of this information is summarized in what has come to be known as the *square of opposition*. In the square of opposition, each of the four categorical propositions (A, E, I, and O) is the contradictory of the proposition diagonally opposite it. Each of the two top propositions (A and E) is a contrary of the other, and each of the bottom two propositions (I and O) is a subcontrary of the other.

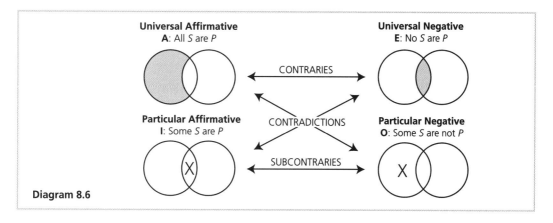

Diagram 8.6

Recalling that two propositions are inconsistent with one another if and only if it is not possible that they both be true together, it turns out that contradiction and contrariety are both types of inconsistency, while subcontrariety is not.

Exercise 8.2

1. Place each of the following propositions in standard form. Then construct its converse, contrapositive, and obverse:

   (a) Some taxpayers vote.

   (b) All taxpayers are citizens.

   (c) No politicians pay taxes.

   (d) Some taxpayers pay their taxes in installments.

   (e) Some taxpayers don't pay their taxes in installments.

2. Give an example of a pair of categorical propositions that satisfies each of the following relations:

   (a) contradiction

   (b) contrariety

   (c) subcontrariety.

3. The Syllogism

It is now time to turn to Aristotle's theory of two-premiss arguments, his *theory of the syllogism*. Consider, for a moment, the following pair of arguments:

All whales are mammals
All mammals are warm-blooded creatures
_____

Therefore, all whales are warm-blooded creatures

and

No actors are lawyers
Some taxpayers are lawyers
_____

Therefore, some taxpayers are not actors.

Although both of these arguments are valid, classical propositional logic will be of no use in showing this, since the only way we can formalize the form of these arguments in classical propositional logic is as follows:

(P1) p
(P2) q
_____

(C) r

and

(P1) $\sim s$
(P2) t
_____

(C) $\sim u$.

In contrast, Aristotle's theory of the syllogism provides a way of showing these arguments to be formally valid.

Traditionally, a syllogism is defined as an argument in which there are no redundant premisses, in which no premiss is repeated as a conclusion, and in which the conclusion is a consequence of the premisses, jointly construed. It follows that syllogisms in this sense are always valid and that it is the job of Aristotle's theory of the syllogism to distinguish syllogisms from other, fallacious arguments.

However, over the centuries, the term "syllogism" has evolved to include not just valid arguments, but any argument composed of three categorical propositions containing three nonlogical referring terms and constructed in such a way that each term appears in exactly two of the three propositions. Thus, under this definition, it is the job of Aristotle's logic to determine, for any arbitrary syllogism, whether or not it is valid.

The Syllogism

Originally defined as an argument in which there are no redundant premisses, in which no premiss is repeated as a conclusion, and in which the conclusion is a consequence of the premisses, jointly construed, syllogisms in Aristotle's sense are always valid.

However, over the centuries, the term "syllogism" has evolved to include not just valid arguments, but any argument composed of three categorical propositions containing three nonlogical referring terms and constructed in such a way that each term appears in exactly two of the three propositions. Under this definition, it is the job of Aristotle's logic to determine, for any arbitrary syllogism, whether or not it is valid.

For example, consider again the argument:

All whales are mammals
All mammals are warm-blooded creatures

_____

Therefore, all whales are warm-blooded creatures.

This argument contains exactly three propositions, which in turn contain exactly three nonlogical, referring terms: "whales," "mammals," and "warm-blooded creatures."

The predicate term of the conclusion is called the *major term* of the syllogism. The subject term of the conclusion is called the *minor term*. The third term, which occurs in both premises but not in the conclusion, is called the *middle term*. Thus in this argument "warm-blooded creatures" is the major term, "whales" is the minor term, and "mammals" is the middle term.

As was the case with Aristotle's theory of immediate inference, Venn diagrams provide us with a straightforward test for validity. However, because each syllogism contains three terms, we will need to use three intersecting circles rather than two. For a valid syllogism the conclusion will be diagrammed automatically whenever the two premises have been diagrammed.

Major, Minor, and Middle Terms
In a syllogism, the three referring terms are identified by their positions. The *major term* is found in the predicate of the conclusion; the *minor term* is found in the subject of the conclusion; and the *middle term* is found in both of the premises but not in the conclusion.

Letting F = whales, G = mammals, and H = warm-blooded creatures, we can formalize the above argument as follows:

(P1) All F are G
(P2) All G are H

_____

(C) All F are H.

We now diagram the first premise by shading the area in F that lies outside the circumference of G.

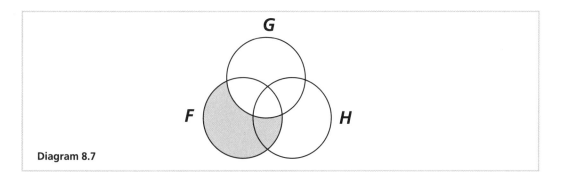

Diagram 8.7

Then we diagram the second premise by shading the area in G that lies outside H.

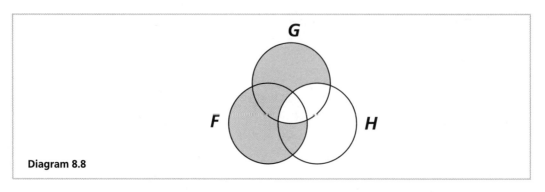

Diagram 8.8

Examining diagram 8.8, we can now see that the conclusion "All *F* are *H*," is already represented on the diagram: all the area in *F* that lies outside *H* is shaded, meaning that the only *F* things that may exist must be in *H*. In other words, the information contained in the conclusion was already contained in the premisses. Hence it is impossible for the premisses to be true and, at the same time, the conclusion to be false. We therefore conclude that the argument is valid.

Consider another example:

All philosophers are liars
Some Greeks are philosophers
_____

∴ Some Greeks are liars.

Letting *F* = Greeks, *G* = philosophers, and *H* = liars, we obtain the following formalization:

(P1) All *G* are *H*
(P2) Some *F* are *G*
_____

(C) Some *F* are *H*.

Once again, we are then able to construct the corresponding Venn diagram as follows:

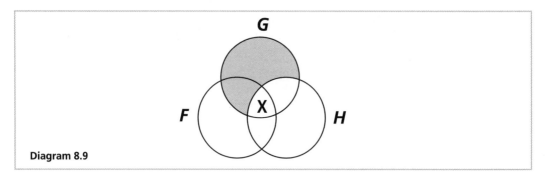

Diagram 8.9

Once again, this argument is seen to be valid since, once the information given in the premisses is placed in the diagram, the information contained in the conclusion automatically appears there as well.

This example also illustrates why it is helpful to diagram universal premisses before diagramming particular premisses. If we had inscribed the second premiss—Some *F* are *G*—on the diagram first, we would have had to inscribe it on the line that divides the lens area between *F* and *G*, as in diagram 8.10:

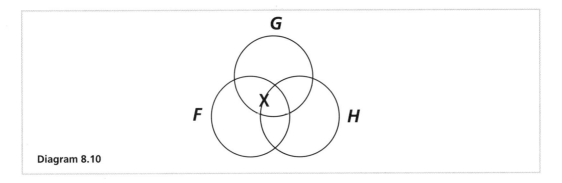

Diagram 8.10

This would be necessary because all we know at this point is that the class represented by the lens area dividing *F* and *G* has at least one member. What we do not know is whether this member is in the left-hand side or the right-hand side of the lens. By placing our X directly on the line, we indicate that, for all we know, it may be in either area, or both. However, if we inscribe the universal premiss—All *G* are *H*—first, we see that the upper half of the lens area between *F* and *G* is empty:

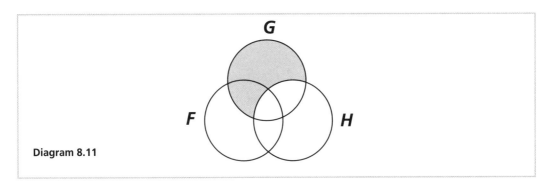

Diagram 8.11

As a result, our need to resort to the strategy of putting the X on the line is obviated. We now know that the X can go only in the right-hand side of the *F*–*G* lens, as in diagram 8.9. A general rule, therefore, is always to diagram universal premisses before particular premisses.

Here is an example where the Venn diagram method demonstrates that an argument is formally invalid. Consider the argument

All Mennonites are pacifists
No Muslims are Mennonites

_____

No Muslims are pacifists.

Then let F = Muslims, G = Mennonites, and H = pacifists. This allows us to formalize the argument as

(P1) All G are H
(P2) No F are G

_____

(C) No F are H

and then diagram it as

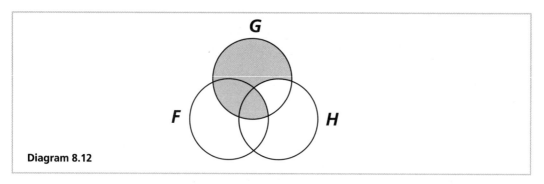

Diagram 8.12

This argument is formally invalid since the conclusion, "No F are H," is not automatically included on the diagram once the information contained in the premises has been placed there. In this case the lens area between F and H is not entirely shaded, so the proposition "No F are H" need not be true.

In summary, in order to use Venn diagrams to test for validity, the following steps should be followed:

Step 1 – Identify the Premisses and Conclusion

As with any argument, it is important to identify both the premisses and the conclusion before attempting to evaluate a syllogism. If the argument is a syllogism, it will contain exactly three categorical propositions: two premisses and one conclusion.

Step 2 – Identify the Three Referring Terms

In a syllogism there will be exactly three nonlogical referring terms. Each term will appear in two of the argument's three propositions. The predicate term of the conclusion is called the *major term*. The subject term of the conclusion is called the *minor term*. The third term, which occurs in both premisses but not in the conclusion, is called the *middle term*.

Step 3 – Formalize the Argument

Having identified the premisses and the conclusion as well as the major, minor, and middle terms, each proposition must be placed in standard categorical form. The argument can then be formalized by abbreviating each term (or category of object) with an upper case letter.

Step 4 – Construct and Label Three Intersecting Circles

These three circles will represent the three terms of the argument. Each circle must be labelled with the letter that stands for that term.

Step 5 – Inscribe the Contents of the Two Premisses onto the Diagram

When a class or category is known to be empty, the appropriate area of the diagram is shaded. When a class or category is known to have at least one member, an X is placed within the appropriate area of the diagram. If one premiss is universal and another is particular, always inscribe the universal premiss first.

Step 6 – Test for Validity

Finally, examine the completed diagram to see whether the conclusion has automatically been included. If so, the argument is formally valid; if not, the argument has not been proved to be valid.

Steps for Testing for Validity Using Venn Diagrams

1. Identify the Premisses and Conclusion
2. Identify the Three Referring Terms
3. Formalize the Argument
4. Construct and Label Three Intersecting Circles
5. Inscribe the Contents of the Two Premisses onto the Diagram
6. Test for Validity

Venn diagrams provide an effective means for testing syllogisms for formal validity. However, there is also a second way to test for formal validity. This is a method that involves five basic rules. In order to be valid, a syllogism must satisfy each of these rules. However, before introducing these rules, we first need to understand what it means for a term in a categorical proposition to be distributed.

We say that a referring term is *distributed* in a categorical proposition if and only if the proposition makes a claim about every item within that term's extension. For example, in an A proposition such as "All politicians are taxpayers," the subject term, "politicians," is distributed while the predicate term, "taxpayers," is not. In other words, the proposition tells us something about all politicians (namely, that they are all taxpayers), but it does not tell us something about all taxpayers. (Some taxpayers, we know, will be politicians, but are there others who are not? We are not told.)

In an E proposition such as "No politicians are taxpayers," it turns out that both the subject term, "politicians," and the predicate term, "taxpayers," are distributed. In other words, the proposition tells us something about all politicians (namely, that they are never taxpayers) and something about all taxpayers (namely, that they are never politicians).

In an I proposition such as "Some politicians are taxpayers" it turns out that neither the subject term, "politicians," nor the predicate term, "taxpayers," is distributed. In other words, the proposition does not give us information about all politicians or about all taxpayers. We are told that some politicians are taxpayers, and hence that some taxpayers are politicians, but that is all.

Finally, in an O proposition such as "Some politicians are not taxpayers" the subject term, "politicians," is not distributed while the predicate term, "taxpayers," is. In other words, the proposition (surprisingly!) tells us something about all taxpayers (since some politicians turn out to be distinct from *all* taxpayers), but it does not do this for all politicians. (Some politicians, we know, will be taxpayers, but what about the others?)

Understanding how distribution works helps us to distinguish between valid and invalid syllogisms. For example, in the invalid syllogism

All astronauts are taxpayers
Some taxpayers are people in debt

Therefore, some astronauts are people in debt

it turns out that the middle term, "taxpayers," is not distributed. This is no accident. If there is no premiss in which the middle term is distributed, then that syllogism is invalid. Syllogisms such as the one above, which contain an undistributed middle term, are said to commit the *fallacy of undistributed middle*.

It is this kind of observation that leads to our five rules for validity, as set out below:

Rule 1 – Distribution of the Middle Term

For a syllogism to be valid, the middle term must be distributed in at least one premiss.

Rule 2 – Distribution of the Major and Minor Terms

For a syllogism to be valid, no term may be distributed in the conclusion unless it is also distributed in a premiss.

Rule 3 – Affirmative Premiss Requirement

For a syllogism to be valid, there must be at least one affirmative premiss.

Rule 4 – Negative Premiss Requirement

For a syllogism to be valid, the conclusion will be negative if and only if there is exactly one negative premiss.

Rule 5 – Particular Premiss Requirement

For a syllogism to be valid, if the premisses are both universal then the conclusion must be universal as well.[3]

> ## Rules for Testing for Valid Syllogisms
>
> All valid syllogisms must have the following characteristics:
>
> 1. A middle term that is distributed at least once,
>
> 2. Major and minor terms that are distributed in their premisses if they are distributed in the conclusion,
>
> 3. At least one affirmative premiss,
>
> 4. A negative conclusion if and only if one of the premisses is negative, and
>
> 5. A particular premiss if the conclusion is particular.

For an example of how these rules work, consider the following argument:

> All software that is in the public domain may be copied without permission or fee. But that can't be done with software under copyright. So software under copyright must not be in the public domain.

In order to evaluate this argument, we first let P = items of software that are in the public domain, C = items of software that are under copyright, and W = things that may be copied without permission or fee. We then identify the relevant categorical propositions and formalize the argument as follows:

(P1) All P are W
(P2) No C are W
_____

(C) No C are P.

We now check this argument using our five rules. First, we know that in order for a syllogism to be valid, the middle term must be distributed in at least one premiss. In this case the middle term, W, is distributed in (P2). Second, no term may be distributed in the conclusion unless it is also distributed in at least one premiss. Here both the major and minor terms are distributed in the conclusion, but they are also distributed in their respective premisses. Third, there must be at least one affirmative premiss. Premiss (P1) satisfies this requirement. Fourth, the conclusion may be negative if and only if there is exactly one negative premiss. In this case (C) is negative, but so is exactly one of our two premisses, (P2). Finally, if the premisses are both universal, then the conclusion may not be particular. This last requirement is also satisfied, since all three propositions are universal. This shows that the argument is valid.

Here is another example:

> Despite what you may have heard, no computer software is completely reliable. Since this is so, and since things that are completely reliable are always very expensive, if follows that some computer software is not very expensive.

Here we let C = items of computer software, R = completely reliable things, and E = very expensive things. The argument can then be formalized as follows:

(P1) No *C* are *R*
(P2) All *R* are *E*

(C) Some *C* are not *E*.

In this case the argument is invalid. We can see this immediately by observing that both Rule 2 and Rule 5 are broken. In other words, the major term, *E*, is distributed in the conclusion but not in the premises, and the conclusion is particular even though both premises are universal.

One final example is as follows:

> If a person doesn't understand that computers require software as well as hardware, then that person can't understand what causes computers to crash. Strange as it may seem, then, there are many adults who don't know what causes computers to crash, since a survey a year or so ago showed that many adults don't know that computers require software as well as hardware.

Here we let *S* = people who don't understand that computers require software as well as hardware, *C* = people who don't understand what causes computers to crash, and *A* = adults. The argument can then be formalized as follows:

(P1) All *S* are *C*
(P2) Some *A* are *S*

(C) Some *A* are *C*.

This argument turns out to be valid, and we can once again prove this by confirming that all five of our rules for valid syllogisms hold. First, we know that in order for the syllogism to be valid, the middle term must be distributed in at least one premiss. In this case, the middle term, *S*, is distributed in (P1). Second, no term may be distributed in the conclusion unless it is also distributed in at least one premiss. In this case, neither the major nor the minor term is distributed in the conclusion, so they need not be distributed in the premises. Third, there must be at least one affirmative premiss. In this argument both premises satisfy this requirement. Fourth, the conclusion may be negative if and only if there is exactly one negative premiss. In this case, all three propositions are positive. Finally, if the premises are both universal, then the conclusion may not be particular. This last requirement is also satisfied since in this case we have both a particular conclusion and exactly one particular premiss. It follows that the argument is valid.

Flashback on...

The *Port Royal Logic*

THE *PORT Royal Logic* is the popular name for the influential seventeenth-century textbook of logic, *La Logique, ou l'art de penser* (1662), and for the system of logic contained therein. Written by Antoine Arnauld (1612–1694) and Pierre Nicole (1625–1695), and in part based upon manuscripts of Blaise Pascal (1623–1662), the book marks the beginning of the modern period in logic. As such, it represents the first systematic attempt develop logic beyond its Aristotelian beginnings.

The name "Port Royal" is also used in conjunction with the group of Cartesian scholars associated with Arnauld and Nicole and with another book, the *Grammaire générale et raisonnée* (the *Port Royal Grammar*, 1660), written by Arnauld and Lancelot. The common name comes from the Cistercian abbey, *Port Royal-des-Champs*, with which Arnauld and the others were associated. Founded south of Versailles in 1204, the abbey was moved to Paris in 1626 where it became home of the Jansenist community. The abbey was closed in 1662 after the Jansenist movement was condemned by the Pope and the movement's members were required to sign a renunciation.

With their writings still influential during the eighteenth and nineteenth centuries, the Port Royal group brought a fresh vigour to the study of logic and semantics. The *Port Royal Grammar* introduced the notion of a universal grammar and set the stage for modern linguistic analysis. The *Port Royal Logic* emphasized the need for clarity of thought and, by abandoning the essential medieval connection between logic and semantics, marked the beginning of modern logic. However, the group's best-remembered contribution is the now famous distinction between a term's extension and its comprehension (or what Sir William Hamilton later called its "intension"). Although the distinction had been anticipated well before the seventeenth century, Arnauld was the first to use it systematically.

Arnauld himself was the twentieth child of his father and was born in Paris in 1612. His father, also named Antoine, was a prominent lawyer who succeeded his own father as Procureur General to Queen Catherine dè Medici. Antoine senior was an outspoken critic of the Jesuits, calling for their expulsion from France in 1594. In 1641 the youngest Arnauld was ordained and admitted to the degree of doctor of theology. On the death of Cardinal Richeleu, who had opposed it, he entered the Sorbonne in 1643.

A leading exponent of the views of Cornelius Jansen (1585–1638), the Dutch bishop of Ypres, Arnauld and his followers proposed a return to St. Augustine's teachings about grace. They also espoused a strong form of predestination. Arnauld's sister was also the abbess of the convent of Port Royal des Champs, a leading centre of Jansenist thought. In 1656 Arnauld lost his post at the Sorbonne and, together with other Jansenists, endured Jesuit persecution for several years following. He died in exile in Brussels in 1694. Fifteen years later, in 1709, Port Royal-des-Champs was burned to the ground by order of Louis XIV.

Exercise 8.3

1. Formalize each of the following arguments. In each case, indicate what the symbols represent, then prove each argument to be formally valid or formally invalid using Venn diagrams.

(a) All logic classes are extremely interesting. So some classes that are offered in the spring are extremely interesting, since some logic classes are offered in the spring.

(b) There are a few logic classes that are not very interesting even though this is not true of any history class. So no logic classes are history classes.

(c) Some logic professors aren't very kind even though all history professors are. So it follows that no logic professors are history professors.

(d) There's no such thing as an ambitious mathematician, since only ambitious people are politicians and no mathematicians are politicians.

(e) Some students are not scientists and some writers are not students, so some writers are not scientists.

(f) There are a few actors who are not egomaniacs, but the genuine thespian is, without exception, an egomaniac. Hence all genuine thespians are actors.

(g) There's no such thing as a delinquent who isn't maladjusted. And, of course, many rich kids are delinquents. So there are some rich kids who are maladjusted.

(h) Not all people who are irrational are illogical, since nobody who is illogical is confused and many people are both irrational and confused.

(i) No artists are rational, since no painters are rational and no artists are non-painters.

(j) All of our local Internet service providers are important for the future well being of our community, even though some institutions that are important for our future well being are facing financial difficulties just now. It follows that some of our Internet service providers must also be facing financial difficulties.

2. Formalize each of the following arguments. In each case, indicate what the symbols represent, then prove each argument to be formally valid or formally invalid using the rules for valid syllogisms.

(a) Salespeople love to sell their product. So salespeople are always well paid, because anyone who loves to sell their product is well paid.

(b) Salespeople are often unscrupulous, since most salespeople tell lies and all liars are unscrupulous.

(c) All men are basically cowards, and all men are mortal. So it follows that all cowards are mortal as well.

(d) All men are basically cowards; so it follows that Bill is a coward.

(e) Not all adults know the dates of the Industrial Revolution. But everyone who knows the dates of the Industrial Revolution is well educated. So not all adults are well educated.

(f) Not all adults know the dates of the Industrial Revolution. But only people who know the dates of the Industrial Revolution are well educated. So not all adults are well educated.

(g) Sue knows the dates of the Industrial Revolution. And someone who knows the dates of the Industrial Revolution is well educated. So Sue is well educated.

(h) Most adults are drug users, because caffeine and nicotine are drugs.

(i) Nothing that contains all the genetic information necessary to form a complete human being could ever be considered to be mere property. But we all know that a fertilized human egg contains all the genetic information necessary to form a person. So a fertilized egg cannot, by any stretch of the imagination, be viewed as mere property.

(j) "Speculative opinions ... and articles of faith ... which are required only to be believed, cannot be imposed on any church by the law of the land; for it is absurd that things should be enjoined by laws which are not in men's power to perform; and to believe this or that to be true does not depend upon our will."[4]

4. Predicate Logic

Predicate logic (or *quantification logic*) is that branch of modern logic that studies words such as "all" and "some." As such, it studies syllogistic arguments, but with greater generality and depth of treatment than Aristotle's logic. In this sense it is an extension of both classical propositional logic and Aristotle's theory of the syllogism. It is in large measure a creation of one man, the nineteenth-century German logician Gottlob Frege.

Consider an argument such as

All human beings are mortal creatures
Socrates is a human being

_____

Therefore, Socrates is a mortal creature.

If we were to represent the logical form of this argument in system *P*, we would obtain something like the following:

(P1) *p*
(P2) *q*

_____-

(C) *r*.

However, this formalization does not help exhibit the argument's validity. In contrast, predicate logic analyzes the internal structure of atomic propositions by introducing upper case letters such as *P*, *Q*, *R*, ..., to stand for *predicate constants* and lower case letters such as *a*, *b*, *c*, ..., to stand for *individual constants*.

For example, if *L* abbreviates the two-place predicate "... loves ___," *a* abbreviates the name "Sue," and *b* abbreviates the name "Bill," then the proposition "Sue loves Bill" can be formalized as "*Lab*" and the proposi-

> **Predicate Logic**
> *Predicate logic* (or *quantification logic*) is a branch of modern logic that studies words such as "all" and "some." As such, it includes the study of both classical propositional logic and Aristotle's logic of the syllogism.

Flashback on...
Gottlob Frege (1848–1925)

AS THE primary inventor of predicate logic, Gottlob Frege is generally credited with being the greatest logician of the nineteenth century. Along with George Boole and Charles Peirce, he is one of the three founders of modern mathematical logic. In addition, he is generally recognized as being the first modern philosopher of mathematics and, together with Ludwig Wittgenstein, one of the founders of modern philosophy of language.

Born in Weimar, Germany, Frege received his doctorate from Göttingen in 1873. That same year, he was appointed professor of mathematics at the University of Jena, a position that he retained until his retirement in 1918.

Frege's many important contributions to modern logic include the introduction of quantifiers and the rigorous formalization of both propositional and predicate logic. In the philosophy of mathematics Frege is remembered as the founder of modern logicism, the view that mathematics is, in some important sense, reducible to logic. In the philosophy of language he is remembered for his introduction of the distinction between a referring term's sense and its reference.

Frege's logical studies resulted originally from a desire to rigorize the notion of proof in mathematics. In his 1879 *Begriffsschrift* (meaning "concept-writing"), Frege developed the first formally adequate notation for quantification, and thereby succeeded in providing the first successful formalization of predicate logic. In his 1884 *Die Grundlagen der Arithmetik* (*The Foundations of Arithmetic*), he introduced a feasible definition of number on the basis of set theory. His *Die Grundgesetze der Arithmetik* (*The Basic Laws of Arithmetic*, 1893, 1903) was a more detailed attempt at completing the logicist goal of deriving arithmetic from logic. When the second volume of the *Grundgesetze* was in press, Frege received a letter from the British philosopher Bertrand Russell informing him that his axioms were inconsistent. Although Frege attempted to revise the work by adding an appendix that discussed Russell's discovery, he eventually abandoned the project. A projected third volume, which was to deal with geometry, never appeared. Frege's later unpublished work shows that Russell's discovery had convinced him of the falsehood of logicism, and that he had opted instead for the view that all of mathematics, including number theory and analysis, was reducible to geometry.

During his life, most of Frege's work was met with indifference or hostility on the part of his contemporaries. This indifference was typified by a rather caustic review of the *Begriffsschrift* by Georg Cantor, who had not even bothered to read the book. However, a more important reason was the difficulty of working with Frege's idiosyncratic and cumbersome notation. It was not until Giuseppe Peano and Bertrand Russell were able to replace Frege's notation with their own that his discoveries began to receive the prominence they deserved.

tion "Bill loves Sue" can be formalized as "*Lba*." (Note that unlike many natural languages, in this language we place the predicate first, followed by its individual constants.)

Propositions written this way can now be joined together using the familiar connectives of propositional logic. For example, "Sue loves Bill and Bill loves Sue" is written "*Lab* ∧ *Lba*," "If Sue loves Bill then Bill loves Sue" is written "*Lab* ⊃ *Lba*," and "If Sue loves Bill then Bill loves Sue and himself" is written "*Lab* ⊃ (*Lba* ∧ *Lbb*)."

In order to complete this logic, we also need to introduce lower case letters, *x*, *y*, *z*, ..., which stand for *individual variables*, and two additional symbols known as *quantifiers*. Given the individual variables *x*, *y*, *z*, ..., it is possible to construct *propositional forms* for atomic sentences. For example, if *L* is again introduced to abbreviate the two-place predicate "... loves ___," then *propositional forms* may be constructed as follows: "*Lxy*" can be used to represent "*x* loves *y*," "*Lyx*" can be used to represent "*y* loves *x*," and "*Lxx*" can be used to represent "*x* loves *x*" (or "*x* loves him- or herself"). It is worth noting that unlike the proposition *Lab*, which will be true or false, the corresponding propositional form *Lxy* will be neither true nor false.

This distinction, of course, is similar to the distinction between propositional constants (*A*, *B*, *C*, ...) and propositional variables (*p*, *q*, *r*, ...) made in chapters 4 and 6. The only difference is that the formula "*Lab*" shows the internal structure of an atomic proposition in a way that the symbol "*A*" does not, and the formula "*Lxy*" shows the internal structure of an atomic propositional form in a way that the symbol "*p*" does not. We say that in propositional forms such as *Lxy*, the variables *x* and *y* are *free*.

Finally, we can introduce our two quantifiers, ∀, called the *universal quantifier*, and ∃, called the *existential quantifier*. When supplemented with an individual variable such as *x*, the first of these two quantifiers is written (∀*x*) and is read "For all *x* ...." A proposition such as "(∀*x*)*Fx*" is then read "For all *x*, *x* is an *F*," or "All *x*'s are *F*'s," or, more simply, "Everything is an *F*." The existential quantifier is similarly written (∃*x*) and is read "There is at least one *x* such that ...." A proposition such as "(∃*x*)*Fx*" is then read "There is at least one *x* such that *x* is an *F*," or "Some *x*'s are *F*'s," or, more simply, "Something is an *F*." In contrast to the variables in a propositional form such as "*Lxy*," which are free, we say that the variables in a proposition such as "(∃*x*)*Fx*" are *bound*.

It is also worth noting that one way to understand the existential quantifier is that it may be defined in terms of the universal quantifier as follows:

$$(\exists x)Fx =df \sim (\forall x)\sim Fx.$$

In other words, (∃*x*)*Fx* says the same thing as "It is not the case that all *x*'s are not *F*'s," or "Not all *x*'s are non-*F*'s."

The Universal and Existential Quantifiers

Predicate logic makes use of two symbols, ∀ and ∃, known as *quantifiers*. The first of these two symbols, when supplemented with an individual variable such as *x*, is written (∀*x*) and is read "For all *x* ...." A proposition such as "(∀*x*)*Fx*" is then read "For all *x*, *x* is an *F*" or, more simply, as "Everything is an *F*." The existential quantifier is similarly written (∃*x*) and is read "There is at least one *x* such that ...." A proposition such as "(∃*x*)*Fx*" is then read "There is at least one *x* such that *x* is an *F*" or, more simply, as "Something is an *F*."

Atomic propositions may now be formalized in a way that was not possible using only propositional logic. For example, letting "Mx" stand for "x has mass," and "Sx" stand for "x occupies space," we can obtain the following formalizations:

- Something has mass $\qquad\qquad\qquad\qquad\qquad\qquad\qquad$ $(\exists x)Mx$

- Everything has mass $\qquad\qquad\qquad\qquad\qquad\qquad\qquad$ $(\forall x)Mx$

- Something with mass occupies space $\qquad\qquad\qquad$ $(\exists x)(Mx \land Sx)$

- Everything with mass occupies space $\qquad\qquad\qquad$ $(\forall x)(Mx \supset Sx)$

- Everything has mass and occupies space $\qquad\qquad$ $(\forall x)(Mx \land Sx)$

- Everything has mass and some things occupy space $\quad$ $(\forall x)Mx \land (\exists y)Sy$

- Some things have mass and some
  other things occupy space $\qquad\qquad$ $(\exists x)(\exists y)((Mx \land Sy) \land \sim(x = y))$

- Some things have mass and occupy space and some
  things occupy space without having mass $\quad$ $(\exists x)(Mx \land Sx) \land (\exists y)(Sy \land \sim My)$

- At least two things have mass $\qquad\qquad$ $(\exists x)(\exists y)((Mx \land My) \land \sim(x = y))$

- Exactly two things have mass
  $(\exists x)(\exists y)([(Mx \land My) \land \sim(x = y)] \land ((z)[Mz \supset ((z = x) \lor (z = y))]))$

Constructing these formulas can be tricky. For example, it is important to recognize that the formula $[(\exists x)Mx \land (\exists y)Sy] \land \sim(x = y)$ will not do as a formalization of the proposition "Some things have mass and some other things occupy space." The reason is that, like the negation symbol, $\sim$, quantifiers such as $(\exists x)$ and $(\exists y)$ have the most limited scope of application possible. Thus, just as in the formula $\sim A \land B$ the tilde applies only to A and not to $A \land B$, in the formula $[(\exists x)Mx \land (\exists y)Sy] \land \sim(x = y)$ the quantifier $(\exists x)$ applies only to Mx and not to $Mx \land (\exists y)Sy \land \sim(x = y)$. The result is that the formula $[(\exists x)Mx \land (\exists y)Sy] \land \sim(x = y)$ contains two free variables, namely the x and the y in the subformula $\sim(x = y)$. Our original formula is thus a *propositional form* as opposed to a *proposition*. As a result, it cannot serve as a formalization of the proposition "Some things have mass and some other things occupy space."

In one sense, existential quantification may be thought of as a type of infinite disjunction and universal quantification may be thought of as a type of infinite conjunction. For example, an existential statement, $(\exists x)Fx$, means that there is at least one

---

Alternative Notations

Universal Quantifier: For every x

$\qquad \forall x \qquad\qquad \land x \qquad\qquad \Pi x \qquad\qquad (x)$

Existential Quantifier: There is at least one x

$\qquad \exists x \qquad\qquad \lor x \qquad\qquad \Sigma x$

thing in the universe that has property F. In other words, suppose that the universe consists of only a finite set of n objects, $a_1, a_2, \ldots a_n$. Then $(\exists x)Fx$ means exactly the same thing as $Fa_1 \lor Fa_2 \lor \ldots \lor Fa_n$. Either object a_1 has property F, or object a_2 has F, or object a_3 has F, and so on. Similarly, to say $(\forall x)Fx$ is simply to say that a_1 has F, and a_2 has F, and a_3 has F, and so on.

Reconstruction of Aristotle's four categorical propositions using the notation of predicate logic can now be done as follows:

A : All S are P $(\forall x)(Sx \supset Px)$

E : No S are P $(\forall x)(Sx \supset {\sim}Px)$

I : Some S are P $(\exists x)(Sx \land Px)$

O : Some S are not P $(\exists x)(Sx \land {\sim}Px)$.

It is important to note that the constants S and P are playing very different roles in these four pairs of propositions. In the propositions on the left, S and P are functioning as *term constants*. That is, they represent referring terms such as "Greeks" and "mortals." In the propositions on the right, they are functioning as *predicate constants*. That is, they represent predicates such as "is Greek" or "is a mortal."

Having seen these equivalences, we can now reconstruct our original square of opposition as follows:

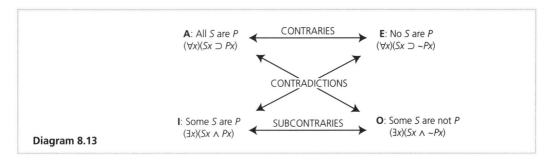

Diagram 8.13

It is also interesting to note that we can use the interdefinability of the quantifiers plus some truth-functional equivalences to make explicit the fact that the diagonal lines indicate contradictions. We do so as follows: We know that the A-proposition $(\forall x)(Sx \supset Px)$ is equivalent to ${\sim}(\exists x){\sim}(Sx \supset Px)$ because $(\forall x)\varphi$ is always equivalent to ${\sim}(\exists x){\sim}\varphi$ no matter what expression we substitute for φ.[5] But since we can show, by a truth table, that ${\sim}(p \supset q)$ is equivalent to $(p \land {\sim}q)$, we can substitute $(Sx \land {\sim}Px)$ for ${\sim}(Sx \supset Px)$ in ${\sim}(\exists x){\sim}(Sx \supset Px)$, getting ${\sim}(\exists x)(Sx \land {\sim}Px)$. So we know by this reasoning that $(\forall x)(Sx \supset Px)$ is actually equivalent to ${\sim}(\exists x)(Sx \land {\sim}Px)$. Also, intuitively, this equivalence holds since "All marbles are round" is equivalent to "There are no marbles that are not round." But observe that our new transformation of the A-proposition, ${\sim}(\exists x)(Sx \land {\sim}Px)$, is simply the negation of the O-proposition, $(\exists x)(Sx \land {\sim}Px)$. Hence the A- and O-propositions are negations or contradictories. By similar equivalences it can be shown that E- and I-propositions are also contradictories.

Finally, it is worth noting that predicate logic can be helpful in dealing with the fallacies. In this context it is useful to revisit a fallacy we discussed in chapter 5, the fallacy of equivocation. Consider the argument

Everything has a cause

Therefore, there is something that causes everything.

As we saw, this argument might be taken as providing good reason for believing in the existence of a single cause, God. However, once we consider the quantificational structure of this argument we see that it is really two arguments masquerading as one. For example, if we let *a* represent a specific individual, and *Cxy* represent the predicate "*x* causes *y*," then we see that we might represent our original argument either as

(P1) $(\forall x)(\exists y)Cyx$

(C) $(\exists y)(\forall x)Cyx$

or as

(P1') $\quad (\forall x)Cax$

(C') $\quad (\exists y)(\forall x)Cyx.$

The classical pattern of equivocation is now evident. The first of these two arguments has a plausible premiss but is invalid. The second is valid, but the premiss is, without further evidence, implausible. The equivocator seeks both the true premiss and valid argument. Following the classical pattern of equivocation, the equivocator in effect blurs these two arguments together as if they were one.

Exercise 8.4

1. Reconstruct each of the following propositions in the language of predicate logic:

   (a) Socrates is wise.

   (b) Socrates lives in Athens.

   (c) If Socrates is wise then he lives in Athens.

   (d) Some Athenians are wise.

   (e) If Socrates is wise, then some Athenians are wise.

   (f) No Athenians are Spartans.

   (g) No Athenians are non-Athenians.

   (h) Some Athenians are not brave.

   (i) All Athenians are rich.

   (j) All Athenians are wise or all Athenians are rich.

   (k) All Athenians are wise or rich.

   (l) All Athenians are wise or no Athenians are wise.

   (m) Some Athenians are wise and some are not.

   (n) If all Athenians are rich then at least some Athenians are wise.

   (o) If all Athenians are rich then at least some Athenians are wise and Socrates is both wise and rich.

Summary

In previous chapters we have seen that classical propositional logic studies its target properties by manipulating propositions with very elementary grammatical structures. Another way of saying this is that system *P* does its business using only a minimal supply of logical constants; namely, the truth-functional connectives. This means that the logical forms of *P* are a considerable abstraction from the natural language constructions whose forms they study. Despite this, there is a benefit in this sort of minimalism: It contributes significantly to the *mechanization* of *P*.

In this chapter we have considered two separate ways of expanding our study of validity. The first is to use Aristotle's term logic, including his theory of one-premiss arguments, called his theory of *immediate inference*, and his theory of two-premiss arguments, called his theory of the *syllogism*. The second is to supplement modern propositional logic with a series of additional constants and variables together with two new symbols representing the universal and existential quantifiers. This expanded logic, called *predicate logic* or *quantification theory*, is so powerful that it forms the basis for most contemporary logical studies.

Weblinks

A Survey of Venn Diagrams
www.combinatorics.org/Surveys/ds5/VennEJC.html
The Syllogistic Machine
home3.swipnet.se/~w-33039/Syllog.machine.html
Episteme Links—Gottlob Frege
www.epistemelinks.com/Pers/FregPers.htm
Stanford Encyclopedia of Philosophy—Gottlob Frege
plato.stanford.edu/entries/frege/

Notes

1. Note that here we are using upper case letters to stand for referring terms, not propositions.

2. Note that it follows from what we have said here that if ordinary language statements about real-life individuals are intended to have existential import they will have to be understood as encompassing two categorical propositions: a universal proposition that does not have existential import and a particular proposition that does. Thus, if we intend the statement "Bill is a taxpayer" to have existential import we will have to represent it as a conjunction of the two categorical propositions, "All people identical with Bill are taxpayers" and "Some people identical with Bill are taxpayers."

3. Note that this rule assumes the modern (or hypothetical) interpretation for A and E propositions.

4. John Locke, *A Letter Concerning Toleration* (Buffalo: Prometheus, 1990), 55.

5. Here the symbol φ is functioning as a variable for propositional forms, which themselves contain whatever free variable is contained within the quantifier.

CHAPTER 9

Inductive Logic

WE HAVE seen that deductively valid arguments are truth-preserving. In other words, any deductively valid argument with true premises will also have a true conclusion. In yet other words, deductive arguments have a very strong consequence relation. In fact, it is hard to imagine how it could be any stronger: if the premises of such an argument are true, it is not just *probable* that the conclusion will be true; the conclusion *must* be true.

In this chapter we will look at arguments in which the consequence relation is not as strong as in valid arguments, arguments in which the consequence relation is not truth-preserving. These arguments are called *inductive* (or *ampliative*) *arguments*. Inductive arguments are not conclusive in the way that deductive arguments are. Even so, we can distinguish between good and bad inductive arguments, depending on how *probable* the conclusion is, given the argument's premises. At the same time, some of the trickiest fallacies crop up in inductive reasoning, especially in arguments involving statistical claims or generalizations. In this chapter we will try to understand not just why good inductive arguments are reliable, but also why bad inductive arguments are not.

1. Induction and Fallibility

Deductive and inductive logic both study arguments in the narrow sense. That is, they both study sequences of propositions, one of which is the conclusion and the remainder of which are the premises. As was the case with deductive arguments, our interest in inductive arguments will focus on the logical relationship between premises and conclusions. What is this relationship, and how does it differ from the relationship between the premises and conclusion of a deductive argument?

A *deduction* is a good one if its premises conclusively verify its conclusion; that is, an argument is valid provided that it is not possible for its premises to be true and its conclusion false. In contrast, an *induction* is a good one and is said to be *inductively strong* whenever, given the truth of the premises, it is *highly likely* (or *highly probable*) but not certain that the conclusion will be true as well. Similarly, an argument or inference is *inductively weak* if and only if, assuming that the premises are true, it is *highly unlikely* (or *highly improbable*) that the conclusion will be true as well.

In addition, arguments and inferences in which it is likely, but not *highly* likely that the conclusion is true are said to be *moderately strong*. Arguments and inferences in which it is unlikely, but not *highly* unlikely that the conclusion is true are said to be *moderately weak*. Thus the basic idea behind an inductive argument is this: an induction has a strong consequence relation only to the extent that its premises increase the likelihood of its conclusion.

Inductive Strength

An argument or inference is *inductively strong* if and only if, assuming that the premisses are true, it is *highly likely* (or *highly probable*) but not certain that the conclusion will be true as well. An argument or inference is *inductively weak* if and only if, assuming that the premisses are true, it is *highly unlikely* (or *highly improbable*) that the conclusion will be true as well.

Arguments and inferences in which it is likely, but not *highly* likely that the conclusion will be true are said to be *moderately strong*. Arguments and inferences in which it is unlikely, but not *highly* unlikely that the conclusion will be true are said to be *moderately weak*.

For example, if we know that Bill has three siblings, this is some evidence in support of the claim that he has two brothers. Of course, this does not provide us with strong or conclusive evidence that he has two brothers, but it is some evidence nevertheless. If, in addition, we know that Bill has at least one brother, Tom, then this provides us with further evidence. Finally, if we also know that Sue, Bill's best friend, has told us that Bill has two brothers, then the evidence is becoming very strong indeed. It is still not conclusive, but it is compelling. Thus, all three of the arguments

Bill has three siblings
_____

Therefore, Bill has two brothers

Bill has three siblings
Bill has at least one brother, Tom
_____

Therefore, Bill has two brothers

and

Bill has three siblings
Bill has at least one brother, Tom
Sue, Bill's best friend, has told us that Bill has two brothers
_____

Therefore, Bill has two brothers

are inductive, but only the last is inductively strong.

One of the simplest types of inductive argument is *induction by simple enumeration*. In an induction by simple enumeration, evidence is offered in support of a general conclusion by listing (or enumerating) as many positive instances of the general claim as possible. Thus, every proposition describing a positive instance of a generalization gives that generalization some (non-zero) degree of *confirmation*. In other words, every time we see a white swan this increases the probability of the claim "All swans are white."[1]

For example, if the conclusion we wish to defend is the claim that no planet in our solar system, other than Earth, is inhabited by intelligent beings, then we might begin to defend this claim with the argument

> Mercury is not inhabited by intelligent beings
> Venus is not inhabited by intelligent beings
> Mars is not inhabited by intelligent beings
> _____
> Therefore, no planet in our solar system, other than Earth, is inhabited by intelligent beings.

This is not a bad start, since the premisses provided some support for the conclusion, but the argument can be strengthened by enumerating even more confirming instances, as follows:

> Mercury is not inhabited by intelligent beings
> Venus is not inhabited by intelligent beings
> Mars is not inhabited by intelligent beings
> Jupiter is not inhabited by intelligent beings
> Saturn is not inhabited by intelligent beings
> Uranus is not inhabited by intelligent beings
> Neptune is not inhabited by intelligent beings
> Pluto is not inhabited by intelligent beings
> _____
> Therefore, no planet in our solar system, other than Earth, is inhabited by intelligent beings.

This is now a very strong induction, since the premisses have enumerated all the various planets in our solar system other than Earth. The argument will still not be valid, though, until we add one final premiss:

> Mercury is not inhabited by intelligent beings
> Venus is not inhabited by intelligent beings
> Mars is not inhabited by intelligent beings
> Jupiter is not inhabited by intelligent beings
> Saturn is not inhabited by intelligent beings
> Uranus is not inhabited by intelligent beings
> Neptune is not inhabited by intelligent beings
> Pluto is not inhabited by intelligent beings
> These are all the planets in our solar system, other than Earth
> _____
> Therefore, no planet in our solar system, other than Earth, is inhabited by intelligent beings.

Because this argument is now truth-preserving, it is conclusive in a way that induc-tive or ampliative arguments are not.

In addition to the strength of their consequence relation, inductively strong arguments differ in two important respects from deductively valid ones. First, they dif-fer with regard to a logical property called *monotonicity*. Second, they differ with regard to *fallibility*. We will consider each in turn.

An argument (or inference or logic) is said to be *monotonic* if and only if the addition of a new premiss will never require the elimination of a previously established conclusion. In other words, if the discovery of additional information can only sup-plement, but never overturn, a previously accepted conclusion, the argument (or inference or logic) under consideration is monotonic. It is *non-monotonic* if and only if it is not monotonic.

In the case of a valid argument, we know that if we supplement its premisses in any way at all, the resulting argument will remain valid. For example, consider the argument

> Bill has (at least) three brothers
> _____
> Therefore, Bill has (at least) three siblings.

No matter how we might choose to supplement the premiss for this argument, the resulting argument will still be valid. For example, learning that Bill also has two sis-ters, or that he has no sisters, or that he lives in an igloo, or that he is a malamute sled dog, will never overturn this conclusion. The only way to overturn it is to reject (rather than supplement) our original premiss set. Thus, validity is a monotonic property.[2]

In contrast, it is easy to see that inductively strong arguments are not monoto-nic. For example, consider the argument:

> The burglary in Toronto has Bill's *modus operandi*
> Bill was seen in the neighbourhood of the burglary only last week
> Two days after the burglary Bill was seen talking to a well-known fence
> Much of the stolen property was recovered from that fence
> _____
> Therefore, Bill is guilty of the burglary.

This is not a bad inductive argument. However, let us now augment the premisses as follows:

> The burglary in Toronto has Bill's *modus operandi*
> Bill was seen in the neighbourhood of the burglary only last week
> Two days after the burglary Bill was seen talking to a well-known fence
> Much of the stolen property was recovered from that fence
> At the time of the burglary, Bill was under arrest in Halifax
> _____
> Therefore, Bill is guilty of the burglary.

Not only does this new argument not have the same high degree of inductive strength as the original, it is now a very weak argument indeed. In other words, where before we had good reasons for accepting the conclusion, now we have a good reason for rejecting it. We conclude that, unlike deductive arguments, inductive arguments are non-monotonic.

Related to the issue of monotonicity is the issue of *fallibility*. Validity, we know, is a truth-preserving property. This means that in a valid argument, if the premisses

---

Hume's Problem of Induction

How can we obtain knowledge of the unobserved? For example, consider the case of an opaque urn that contains 100 marbles. If we withdraw 40 of these marbles and observe that they are all yellow, does this tell us anything about the remaining 60? After all, the remaining 60 are not only unobserved, they are totally distinct from the marbles we have already seen. What makes us think that by observing some marbles we have any information at all about the unobserved marbles that remain in the urn?

The Scottish enlightenment philosopher David Hume (1711–1776) was the first to raise this question.[3] In effect, Hume asked whether inductively strong arguments can ever exist or, to put it another way, whether it is ever rational to rely upon inductive (or ampliative) inferences. Because inductive arguments are always inconclusive, in some way their conclusions will always amplify or go beyond the information given in their premisses.

How can we say that such arguments or inferences are ever justified? If they could be justified deductively, they would not be ampliative. On the other hand, trying to justify them inductively appears to be viciously circular. In other words, it appears to assume the very point at issue, namely that inductive reasoning may, on occasion at least, be reliable.

If Hume's skepticism about induction is right, all rational inferences will have to be deductive. In other words, contrary to what probability theory tells us, no arguments or inferences can ever be inductively strong. Yet if this is so, it will also turn out that we can have little if any knowledge of the unobserved, surely an unpalatable conclusion if ever there were one.

---

are true, then the conclusion must be true as well. Inductively strong arguments lack this property. Thus, even in inductively strong arguments where we know the premisses to be true, it is always possible that the conclusion might be false. In other words, inductive arguments are fallible in a sense in which deductive arguments are not. As the arguments above show, until we have conclusive evidence in favour of a conclusion, we may always have to revise our beliefs.

Despite these differences, inductive arguments appear to be an utterly indispensable tool for rational inference. Every principle of human personality ("frustration breeds aggression"), every principle of the marketplace ("if demand is inelastic, an increase in supply will cause a larger fall in market price than an increase in amount sold"), every principle of experimental science ("copper conducts electricity"), and every rule of thumb ("red sky at night, sailor's delight"), involves induction. Induction is what allows us to form generalizations from the scattered, particular fragments of everyday experience—from what the philosopher William James called "the buzzing, booming confusion" of our everyday lives.

A Related Challenge

Given the limitations of induction by simple enumeration, we know that the following argument form is not valid, even for suitably large choices of *n*:

(P1) S_1 is P
(P2) S_2 is P
        ...
(Pn) S_n is P
———————————
(C)   All S are P.

The argument may be inductively strong and, if the premisses are true, it may turn out to be a very good argument, but since it is still possible for the conclusion to be false even though the premisses are true, it cannot be valid.

Despite this, we may hypothesize that by suitably weakening the conclusion, we may be able to turn the argument into a valid one, as follows:

(P1) S_1 is P
(P2) S_2 is P
        ...
(Pn) S_n is P
———————————————
(C)   *Probably* all S are P.

In fact, this second argument is not valid either. Why not?

Exercise 9.1

1. For each of the following arguments, determine whether its consequence relation is weak, moderately weak, moderately strong, or strong:

   (a) Bill has at least one brother, and Sue has told us that Bill is secretive about whether he has any other brothers or sisters. So he must have at least three siblings.

   (b) Bill has two brothers, and he has told us that he has no other siblings. Therefore he has exactly two siblings.

   (c) Bill has at least five brothers and sisters, so given that most families don't have more than six children, these are likely his only siblings.

   (d) Bill has two brothers. So he likely has some sisters as well.

   (e) Bill has two brothers. Therefore he has three siblings.

2. Give an example of an inductively strong argument with false premisses and a false conclusion, or else explain why this is impossible.

3. Give an example of an inductively strong argument with false premisses and a true conclusion, or else explain why this is impossible.

4. Give an example of an inductively strong argument with true premisses and a false conclusion, or else explain why this is impossible.

2. The Elements of Probability Theory

One way to approach the study of induction is through probability theory. In probability theory, all propositions are assigned a real number somewhere on the interval from 0 to 1. This number is used to represent each proposition's likelihood or degree of probability. It then turns out that, if we know the probability of some propositions, we can calculate the probability of other propositions as well.

For example, say Sue tosses a fair die. Because it is fair, we know that each of the six sides has an equal chance of ending up on top. Thus, the proposition "Sue tossed a three" (meaning "Sue tossed the die in such a way that the third side ended up on top") has a probability of 1/6. In other words, the conclusion of the argument

Probability

For any proposition, p, the probability of p, written Pr(p), is a real number somewhere on the interval from 0 to 1. The probability of a tautology, Pr(T), is 1; the probability of a contradiction, Pr(F), is 0; and the probability of a contingent proposition, Pr(C), lies between 0 and 1.

Sue tossed a fair, six-sided die

_____

Therefore, Sue tossed a three

has a probability of 1/6, given the truth of the argument's premiss. In yet other words, if we let P = "Sue tossed a fair, six-sided die" and Q = "Sue tossed a three," we say that the *conditional probability* of Q given P equals 1/6.

At the extremities of probability theory are the tautologies and contradictions of classical propositional logic. For example, the tautology "Either a three will come up or not" is given the value 1. In contrast, a contradiction such as "A three will come up and a three will not come up" is given the value 0. Contingent propositions, in turn, will have values represented by real numbers somewhere on the interval between 0 and 1.

Writing "The probability of p is x" as "Pr(p) = x" and "The conditional probability of q given p is x" as "Pr($q|p$) = x," we can now introduce several rules governing molecular propositions involving negation, disjunction, and conjunction. For example, since contradictions represent impossible propositions, we know that their probability will always be 0. In other words,

for all propositions p, Pr($p \land {\sim}p$) = 0.

Similarly, since tautologies are a type of necessary truth, we know that their probability will always be 1. In other words,

for all propositions p, Pr($p \lor {\sim}p$) = 1.

These claims then lead us to a corresponding rule for negation, namely that

for all propositions p, Pr(${\sim}p$) = 1 – Pr(p).

These three rules can now be used to calculate new probabilities.

For example, since we know that Pr(Q) = 1/6, we can now calculate the probability of Sue not tossing a three. We do so using our rule for negation, as follows:

$$
\begin{aligned}
\mathrm{Pr}(\sim Q) \quad &= 1 - \mathrm{Pr}(Q) \\
&= 1 - 1/6 \\
&= 5/6.
\end{aligned}
$$

Similarly, we can determine that $\mathrm{Pr}(Q \wedge \sim Q) = 0$ and $\mathrm{Pr}(Q \vee \sim Q) = 1$.

We can also calculate the probability of a disjunction such as "Sue tossed a three or Sue tossed a six." To do so, we first note that a pair of propositions will be *mutually exclusive* whenever it is not possible for them to be true together. We then observe that

for all propositions p and q, if p and q are mutually exclusive,

then $\mathrm{Pr}(p \vee q) = \mathrm{Pr}(p) + \mathrm{Pr}(q)$.

For example, we may assume that it is not possible for a fair die to show two faces uppermost on one throw. Hence "Sue tossed a three" and "Sue tossed a six" may be treated as mutually exclusive. Thus, if R = "Sue tossed a six," we see that $\mathrm{Pr}(Q \vee R) = \mathrm{Pr}(Q) + \mathrm{Pr}(R) = 1/6 + 1/6 = 1/3$.

Since we will also want to be able to calculate the probability of two propositions that are not mutually exclusive, we will also need a formula that expresses this probability. We construct it as follows:

for all propositions p and q, $\mathrm{Pr}(p \vee q) = \mathrm{Pr}(p) + \mathrm{Pr}(q) - \mathrm{Pr}(p \wedge q)$.

To illustrate this equation, consider the chance of Sue obtaining either an odd number or a number greater than three on a single throw. Letting S = "Sue tossed an odd number" and T = "Sue tossed a number greater than three," we conclude that $\mathrm{Pr}(S) = 3/6 = 1/2$ and $\mathrm{Pr}(T) = 3/6 = 1/2$. We may think that our earlier rule—add the two fractions—will now give us the required disjunctive probability, but adding the fractions in this case yields a probability of 1, and this result is clearly incorrect. After all, there is still the possibility of obtaining an even number less than three, namely two. As a result, $\mathrm{Pr}(S \vee T)$ must be less than 1. Thus, to solve for $\mathrm{Pr}(S \vee T)$, we first need to calculate $\mathrm{Pr}(S) + \mathrm{Pr}(T)$; then we must subtract $\mathrm{Pr}(S \wedge T)$. The result is $1/2 + 1/2 - 1/6 = 5/6$.

Next, it turns out that the conjunctive probability of two propositions, p and q, may be defined as their product, provided that the two propositions are probabilistically independent of each other. In other words,

for all propositions p and q, if p and q are probabilistically independent,
then $\mathrm{Pr}(p \wedge q) = \mathrm{Pr}(p) \times \mathrm{Pr}(q)$.

Probabilistic independence in turn may be defined using conditional probability as follows: propositions p and q are (probabilistically) independent if and only if $\mathrm{Pr}(q|p) = \mathrm{Pr}(q)$.

For example, assume that you have two dice. Because the throw of one die does not influence the throw of the other, the probability that both will come up three is calculated by multiplying together the probabilities that each will come up three. That is, $1/6 \times 1/6 = 1/36$. Generally, we can see that the probability values of conjunctive propositions tend to diminish as more conjuncts are added.

It is important to understand the difference between *probabilistic independence* and *mutual exclusiveness*. The statements "Wayne Gretzky was in Portage La Prairie on June 8" and "This die will come up three" may be presumed to be probabilistically independent of each other, but they are not mutually exclusive. They are probabilistically independent because neither influences the probability of the other, but they are not mutually exclusive because it is quite possible that they might both be true together. On the other hand, the propositions that, on the same toss, "This die will come up three" and "This die will come up four" are mutually exclusive, but they are by no means independent. The outcome of one proposition clearly affects the probability of the other. Indeed, if one proposition is true, the probability of the other will have to be zero.

Conditional Probability, Mutual Exclusivity, and Independence

Three important ideas in the theory of probability are conditional probability, mutual exclusivity, and (probabilistic) independence. We define them as follows. First, for any two propositions, p and q, the *conditional probability* of p given q, written $\Pr(p|q)$, is defined as

$\Pr(p|q) = \Pr(p \wedge q) / \Pr(q)$, provided $\Pr(q) \neq 0$.

Second, propositions p and q are *mutually exclusive* provided that it is not possible for them to be true together. In other words, p and q are mutually exclusive provided that

$\Pr(p \wedge q) = 0$.

Finally, p and q are *(probabilistically) independent* provided that knowledge of one does not affect the probability of the other. In other words, p and q are (probabilistically) independent provided that

$\Pr(p|q) = \Pr(p)$.

It is easy to overlook probabilistic dependencies in estimating conjunctive probabilities. This mistake is called the *fallacy of independence*. For example, let us calculate the chance of drawing two red cards from an ordinary deck of fifty-two playing cards. It might seem logical to multiply 1/2 by 1/2, since half the cards in the deck are red, but if we do not replace the first card in the deck before the second is drawn, this calculation will be mistaken. Unless we replace the first card, the second draw is not independent of the first. At the time of the second draw, one card has been removed from the deck: this affects the probability of selecting a red card on the second draw. Thus, if we want to calculate the probability of a conjunction of two propositions that are not probabilistically independent, we need to keep in mind their combined conditional probability. In other words,

for all propositions p and q, $\Pr(p \wedge q) = \Pr(p) \times \Pr(q|p)$.

For example, if we want to calculate the probability of drawing two red cards in a row, we can do so as follows: letting R_1 = "The first card drawn is a red card" and R_2 = "The second card drawn is a red card," we obtain $\Pr(R_1 \wedge R_2) = \Pr(R_1) \times \Pr(R_2|R_1) = 1/2 \times 25/51 = 25/102$. It is interesting to note that once we have defined conjunctive probability in this way, conditional probability may also be defined as follows: for all propositions p and q, $\Pr(p|q) = \Pr(p \wedge q) / \Pr(q)$.

Rules of Probability

Contradiction Rule
　For all propositions p, $\Pr(p \wedge \sim p) = 0$

Tautology Rule
　For all propositions p, $\Pr(p \vee \sim p) = 1$

Negation Rule
　For all propositions p, $\Pr(\sim p) = 1 - \Pr(p)$

Restricted Disjunction Rule
　For all propositions p and q, if p and q are mutually exclusive, then
　$\Pr(p \vee q) = \Pr(p) + \Pr(q)$

Generalized Disjunction Rule
　For all propositions p and q, $\Pr(p \vee q) = \Pr(p) + \Pr(q) - \Pr(p \wedge q)$

Restricted Conjunction Rule
　For all propositions p and q, if p and q are probabilistically independent, then
　$\Pr(p \wedge q) = \Pr(p) \times \Pr(q)$

Generalized Conjunction Rule
　For all propositions p and q, $\Pr(p \wedge q) = \Pr(p) \times \Pr(q|p)$

Having these rules also allows us to prove a well-known theorem of probability called *Bayes' theorem*. First proved in 1763 by Thomas Bayes,[4] Bayes' theorem allows us to calculate so-called inverse probabilities. That is, if we know some conditional probabilities, such as $\Pr(p|q)$ and $\Pr(p|\sim q)$, Bayes' theorem lets us calculate the inverse probability, $\Pr(q|p)$. In other words, if we know, say, the probability that a customer has purchased a particular product if he shops in your store, and the probability that he has purchased that same product if he does not shop in your store, we will be able to calculate the probability that he shops in your store if he buys that particular product. Provided that we can obtain the required conditional probabilities (for example, through an independent telephone survey), we will be able to calculate the required inverse probability using the following formula:

$$\Pr(q|p) = \frac{\Pr(q) \times \Pr(p|q)}{[\Pr(q) \times \Pr(p|q)] + [\Pr(\sim q) \times \Pr(p|\sim q)].}[5]$$

For example, if we let P = "Sue has purchased product x" and Q = "Sue shops in your store," and we know that $\Pr(Q) = 0.1$, $\Pr(P|Q) = 0.5$, and $\Pr(P|\sim Q) = 0.7$, then we know immediately that $\Pr(\sim Q) = 0.9$ and we can calculate $\Pr(Q|P)$ as follows:

$$\Pr(Q|P) = \frac{\Pr(Q) \times \Pr(P|Q)}{[\Pr(Q) \times \Pr(P|Q)] + [\Pr(\sim Q) \times \Pr(P|\sim Q)]}$$

$$= \frac{0.1 \times 0.5}{[0.1 \times 0.5] + [0.9 \times 0.7]}$$

$$= 0.05$$

In other words, people who purchase product x are only half as likely to shop in your store as are people generally.

Bayes' Theorem

First proved by Thomas Bayes in 1763, Bayes' theorem allows us to calculate so-called *inverse* probabilities. That is, if we know the values of the conditional probabilities $\Pr(p|q)$ and $\Pr(p|\sim q)$, together with the prior probabilities $\Pr(q)$ and $\Pr(\sim q)$, Bayes' theorem lets us calculate $\Pr(q|p)$. The theorem itself is stated as follows:

$$\Pr(q|p) = \frac{\Pr(q) \times \Pr(p|q)}{[\Pr(q) \times \Pr(p|q)] + [\Pr(\sim q) \times \Pr(p|\sim q)].}$$

Bayes' theorem can be proved from our earlier rules of probability as follows: we know from our generalized conjunction rule that $\Pr(p \wedge q) = \Pr(p) \times \Pr(q|p)$; thus

$$\Pr(q|p) = \frac{\Pr(p \wedge q)}{\Pr(p).}$$

Because p is logically equivalent to $(p \wedge q) \vee (p \wedge \sim q)$, it follows that

$$\Pr(q|p) = \frac{\Pr(p \wedge q)}{\Pr([p \wedge q] \vee [p \wedge \sim q]).}$$

Then, from our restricted disjunction rule it follows that

$$\Pr(q|p) = \frac{\Pr(p \wedge q)}{\Pr(p \wedge q) + \Pr(p \wedge \sim q).}$$

Finally, from our generalized conjunction rule (together with commutation) it follows that

$$\Pr(q|p) = \frac{\Pr(q) \times \Pr(p|q)}{[\Pr(q) \times \Pr(p|q)] + [\Pr(\sim q) \times \Pr(p|\sim q)].}$$

In this context it is worth noting one other fallacy common in inductive reasoning. This is the fallacy of confusing *prior* and *posterior* probabilities. Suppose that we have drawn a black card from an ordinary deck of fifty-two playing cards; suppose, also, that we now wish to calculate the probability of drawing a second black card. If we assume that the card we have drawn has been replaced in the deck, and that the deck has been reshuffled, we might be tempted to think that the probability of drawing a second black card will be $1/2 \times 1/2 = 1/4$. However, we must keep in mind that we know we have already drawn one black card. Our original proposition would have been something like "I will draw one black card from this deck; then I will draw a second black card from this deck," but the first part of this proposition has already come true. So it now has a probability of 1. Thus the correct calculation will be $1 \times 1/2 = 1/2$. In other words, if one black card is already drawn, we can base our calculations on the second draw only. It is, after all, the only remaining unknown; and it now may be treated as independent of the previous draw.

Stephen Campbell tells an amusing story of someone who confused prior and posterior probabilities.[6] The story is about a man who packed a bomb in his luggage for protection on plane trips. The man reasoned that the chances of two people carrying a bomb on board the same plane were extremely low. After all, the chance of one person carrying a bomb is low; thus the chance of two people doing it will be even lower. However, as Campbell points out, the man who takes the bomb along knows with certainty that he has it with him. Thus, if we take this knowledge into account, the chances of another person bringing a bomb on board the plane will remain unchanged.

The Raven Paradox

Consider the generalization "All ravens are black." As we saw when discussing induction by simple enumeration, it is a fundamental principle of confirmation theory that every true positive instance of a generalization gives it some non-zero degree of confirmation. For example, if Tweety is a raven and Tweety is black, the proposition "Tweety is a raven and Tweety is black" will be a confirming instance of the generalization "All ravens are black." It is also generally assumed that confirmation is closed under equivalence. In other words, if one proposition, such as "Tweety is a raven and Tweety is black," confirms another, then any proposition equivalent to the first will also confirm the second, and it will do so to the same degree or extent as the first.

In the notation of predicate logic, "All ravens are black" can be written as $(\forall x)(Rx \supset Bx)$, and by the law of contraposition, this proposition will be equivalent to $(\forall x)(\sim Bx \supset \sim Rx)$. However, any non-black, non-raven will now confirm not only $(\forall x)(\sim Bx \supset \sim Rx)$, but also $(\forall x)(Rx \supset Bx)$. In other words, not just black ravens, but green trees, white shoes, and red herrings will all confirm the proposition "All ravens are black"! How can this be?[7]

Exercise 9.2

1. Given a standard deck of fifty-two playing cards containing four suits (two of which, clubs and spades, are black, and two of which, diamonds and hearts, are red), calculate the probability of drawing each of the following:

    (a) an ace

    (b) a black ace

    (c) an ace or a non-spade

    (d) a red card or a face card or an ace

    (e) a red face card

    (f) an ace on the first draw, then, without replacing the first card drawn, an ace on the second draw

    (g) an ace on the first draw, then, without replacing the first card drawn, a red jack on the second draw

    (h) a black ace on the first draw or, after replacing the first card drawn, an ace on the second draw

    (i) a black ace on the first draw or, after replacing the first card drawn, a heart that is not an ace on the second draw

    (j) an ace on the first draw then, after replacing the first card drawn, a spade on the second draw.

2. Given an urn that contains exactly 50 blue marbles, 30 green marbles, and 20 yellow marbles, calculate the following:

    (a) the probability of drawing a marble that is green

    (b) the probability of drawing a marble that is blue or green

    (c) the probability of drawing a marble that is blue or green or yellow

    (d) the probability of drawing a marble that is not yellow

    (e) the probability of drawing a marble that is blue and, after replacing it, a marble that is yellow

    (f) the probability of drawing a marble that is blue and, after replacing it, a marble that is yellow and, after replacing it, a marble that is not green

    (g) the probability of drawing a marble that is blue and, without replacing it, a marble that is yellow

    (h) the probability of drawing a marble that is blue and, without replacing it, a marble that is yellow and, without replacing it, a marble that is not green

    (i) the probability of drawing a marble that is blue and, after replacing it, a marble that is not blue

    (j) the probability of drawing a marble that is blue and, after replacing it, a marble that is not yellow and, without replacing it, a marble that is not green.

3. Sue has begun working for an insurance company and she has been told that 60 percent of drivers are male and that 73 percent of drivers are involved in an accident at some point in their lives. She has also been told that this figure rises to 75 percent for men and drops to 70 percent for women. What is the probability that the next person who arrives in Sue's office to complete an accident report form is a man?

4. Bill's brother, Tom, is married to Renée. Because they have been married only a short time, they do not yet want to have children. As a result, they use a method of contraception that is advertised as being 90

percent effective. However, recently Renée has obtained a positive result on a home pregnancy test. Given that the test claims to be able to detect 85 percent of all pregnancies and that it yields a false positive only 5 percent of the time, what is the probability that Renée is pregnant?

5. Two propositions, p and q, are independent if and only if $\Pr(p) = \Pr(p|q)$. Is the relation of independence reflexive? Is it symmetric? Is it transitive?

3. Hasty Generalization and Related Fallacies

One of the most widespread and pervasive inductive fallacies is *over-generalization* or, as it is often called, *hasty generalization*. How often does so-called popular wisdom such as "It never rains but it pours" or "It takes one to know one" go unchallenged in the face of obvious evidence to the contrary?

Traditionally, this sort of fallacy, in which an unwarranted induction is made on the basis of a few particular observations, is called *secundum quid*, meaning "in a certain respect." In other words, what is true in a certain respect need not be true in all relevant respects, or in the more general case.

Unfortunately, there are difficulties inherent in trying to develop a more detailed definition of *secundum quid*. The reason is that there appears to be no general method for knowing exactly when all the necessary qualifications of a general proposition have been made, or when all the loopholes in a generalization have been plugged. Even so, that branch of probability and statistics known as *sampling theory* helps shed some light on this difficult subject.

Consider an urn containing a large number of marbles. We are told that some of the marbles are black and some are white. The best way to find out how many marbles are black and how many are white would be to remove the marbles from the urn and count them. Sometimes, however, this may be inconvenient or even impossible. If so, we will have to make a conjecture about the proportion of black to white marbles on the basis of less than perfect evidence.

In real-life situations, complete access to data is rarely available. Fortunately, there are often indirect methods of obtaining access to the information we need. For example, in the case of our urn, we might pull out a handful of marbles and count the proportion of black marbles to white marbles. If the marbles in the urn are mixed so that the proportion of black marbles to white marbles is approximately the same throughout, and if the sample is large enough and has been selected properly, then we will be able to get a good idea of the composition of the entire population of marbles in the urn.

These are big *ifs*, to be sure. For example, if we picked just one marble, and it were black, we would certainly not be justified in concluding that all the marbles in the urn were black. Because of our small sample size, such a generalization would

The Paradox of the 99-foot Man

As we saw earlier in this chapter, it is a fundamental assumption underlying the theory of induction by simple enumeration that every true positive instance of a generalization gives that generalization some non-zero degree of confirmation. For example, as we saw in our discussion of the Raven Paradox, if Tweety is a raven and Tweety is black, then the proposition "Tweety is a raven and Tweety is black" will be a confirming instance of the generalization "All ravens are black."

Now consider the claim that no person is over one hundred feet tall. Of course we know this to be true. Think of all the people you have encountered in your life. Not one was over ten feet tall, let alone over one hundred feet tall. So we all have a very large number of confirming instances, and no disconfirming instances, of the claim "No person is over one hundred feet tall."

But now ask yourself what would happen if you saw a 99-foot man. According to what we have said about confirmation, this should be one more confirming instance of the claim "No person is over one hundred feet tall." But far from increasing our confidence that this claim is true, this observation will in fact decrease our confidence about this claim. After all, if someone could grow to be 99 feet tall, isn't it likely that by taking a few more vitamins he could grow to be 101 feet tall?

If this is correct, we have an example of a confirming instance that fails to increase the probability of its corresponding generalization. How are we to resolve this puzzle? Does this mean that we have to give up our belief in the reliability of induction?

be virtually meaningless. Similarly, if we picked a large enough sample but purposely selected only black marbles, ignoring the white ones, someone might mistakenly conclude that all the marbles were black; but by relying upon such an unrepresentative sample he or she could hardly be said to be acting rationally. Or, suppose that all the black marbles are at the top of the urn and all the white ones are at the bottom. If we then take our sample from the top only, it would again be misleading to generalize from the composition of our sample to the composition of the population as a whole. Thus, the fallacy of *secundum quid* may be said to have occurred in any of these cases.

The *Secundum Quid* Fallacy

The fallacy of *secundum quid*, or *hasty generalization*, occurs whenever an unwarranted induction is drawn on the basis of a few particular observations, rather than on the basis of a fair and reasonable sample or on the basis of a balanced and representative sampling of data.

Avoiding *secundum quid* in these and related contexts requires that we learn something about sampling theory. Specifically, it requires that we learn to avoid the *fallacy of insufficient statistics* and the *fallacy of biased statistics*. The first of these two fallacies occurs when the sample chosen is so small that to generalize from it to the entire population is virtually meaningless. In everyday argument, the basis of a generalization is often quite slim. We are told, for example, that a given test group for a new toothpaste had many fewer cavities. However, until the size of the test group has been specified, this type of information is not very informative. If the test group were small enough, any generalization about the entire population would be worthless.

At the same time, even if the sample is large enough, we must also avoid the fallacy of biased statistics. This fallacy occurs when a generalization is based on a sample that does not represent the population as a whole, or when the sample does not tell us enough about the particular factor we are attempting to analyze. In our urn illustration, for example, we saw that if we picked only black marbles, our sample would not tell us much about the population of the urn as a whole. Similarly, if all the black marbles were at the top of the urn and we took marbles only from the top, our sample again would not be sufficiently representative. Thus, if there is variegation in the population, a fair sample must reflect these varieties.

The simplest kind of fair sample is called a *random sample*. In a random sample, each member of the population has an equal chance of being selected. As a result, if the sample is large enough, it is likely to be representative of the population as a whole. However, where there are regular and well-understood variations in the population, a *stratified random sample* may also be used. For a stratified random sample, the population must first be classified into mutually exclusive subgroups (or *strata*). Then, independent random samples are drawn from each of these subgroups.

As it turns out, the fallacy of insufficient statistics and the fallacy of biased statistics are two sides of the same counterfeit coin. In other words, a very small sample, in proportion to a total population, is much more likely to be biased. If the sample is small there is a greater risk of error; and if the sample is small enough any statistical generalization derived from it will be virtually worthless.

In this context it is worth stressing that it will be a mistake to infer that what is true of a large sample must also be true of a smaller sample. An example of coin flipping might help illustrate why this is so. First, we know that if a penny is "fair"— that is, if heads and tails are equally probable on each throw—then, given a large number of tosses, the chances are reasonably good of getting roughly equal proportions of heads and tails. However, it does not follow that the chances will also be reasonably good of getting half heads and half tails in a small number of tosses.

Having a fair coin also means that each outcome in a sequence is independent from its predecessors or successors. In other words, if you get a head on this toss, it does not follow that it is more likely you will get a tail (or a head for that matter) on the next toss. Each toss will be independent of the previous one. Even so, it is natural for many of us to regard such sequences as "self-correcting." For example, given a run of tails, we may often expect that the next toss is more likely to be heads. This is a fallacy, and it is a common one with a recognized name, the *gambler's fallacy*.

In part, the gambler's fallacy consists of confusing a single member of a sequence with the sequence as a whole. Statistics tells us that a large sequence of heads, H H H ... H, is slightly less probable than a similar large sequence of heads that contains a single tail, H H H ... T; but if instead of applying this probability to the outcomes as a whole we apply it to just one throw, say, the last one, we are bound to be misled. On the final single throw, for example, the chance of getting heads is just the same as the chance of getting tails: 1/2. For each single toss, we must disregard what has gone before.

The Gambler's Fallacy

The *gambler's fallacy* occurs whenever we confuse the probability of a single member of a sequence with the probability of that sequence as a whole. For example, it occurs whenever we believe that a string of independent coin tosses will be "self-correcting" and that, given a run of tails, say, it is more likely that the next toss will be heads.

By applying our previously defined notions of conditional and conjunctive probability, we can put this point another way. As we have seen, the gambler expects that, given a certain outcome on one toss (or on a series of tosses), it is more likely that he will get a certain outcome on the next toss. In other words, if T_2 = "Tails comes up on the second toss" and H_1 = "Heads comes up on the first toss," then he believes that $Pr(T_2|H_1) > Pr(T_2)$. He believes that the conditional probability of T_2 given H_1 is greater than the probability of T_2 taken by itself. In other words, his belief is a denial of the claim that T_2 and H_1 are independent. Even so, we know that it is reasonable to assume that each toss must be independent of the next. Thus, if the tosses really are independent, our gambler is bound to be mistaken!

In theory, of course, the gambler may concede that each toss of a fair coin is independent of the next, but it may be hard for him to adhere consistently to this assumption given his expectation that sequences of events tend to be "self-correcting."

What is the psychology behind these fallacies? Why are they so widespread? According to some writers, many of us have a strong tendency to think that samples of a population are more representative of that population than a careful analysis would indicate. When subjects are instructed to predict the proportion of heads in a random sequence of fair tosses, for example, they usually produce sequences that are far closer to 1/2 than the laws of chance would allow for short sequences. That is, subjects tend to have unrealistically high expectations about the "fairness" of the coin, especially for short sequences of tosses.

Goodman's New Riddle of Induction

"All emeralds are green," we know, will be confirmed every time we observe a green emerald. In other words, as we noted earlier, every true positive instance of a generalization gives it some, possibly small, degree of support. However, as the American philosopher Nelson Goodman has pointed out, the observation of a green emerald supports other, contrary generalizations as well.

For example, consider the new colour words "grue" and "bleen," which we define as follows:

(D1) Object *x* is *grue* =df *x* is green and *x* has been inspected, or *x* is blue and *x* has not been inspected

(D2) Object *x* is *bleen* =df *x* is blue and *x* has been inspected, or *x* is green and *x* has not been inspected.

If we have observed, say, 1,000 emeralds, and if they have all been green, these observations will support the claim "All emeralds are green." However, these same observations also support the contrary claim "All emeralds are grue," and they do so to exactly the same degree or extent! What is even more disturbing is that these two generalizations have different, incompatible consequences. According to the claim "All emeralds are grue," emeralds not yet examined are blue, whereas according to the claim "All emeralds are green," emeralds yet to be examined are green. Yet how can this be?

One objection we might make is that the introduction of colour terms such as "grue" and "bleen" will be inappropriate since objects such as emeralds simply do not change colour, and being grue seems to suggest that emeralds somehow change their colour from blue to green upon inspection.

In response, someone who has hypothesized that all emeralds are grue has at least two replies. First, he might note that many objects do in fact change their colour: green deciduous forests turn red in the autumn and chameleons alter their colour depending upon a variety of factors, including ambient temperature. Even more significantly, he might reply that in claiming that all emeralds are grue, he is not suggesting that they change their colour at all. In fact, he is claiming just the opposite! Being grue (and not bleen), all emeralds have the same colour, and it is only people who mistakenly use words like "green" and "blue" who are deceived into thinking that emeralds change their colour upon inspection!

Having thus made little progress with our first objection, we might now try a second. It is inappropriate, we might say, to define colour words as in definitions (D1) and (D2) above, since "grue" and "bleen" are clearly artificial in a way that "green" and "blue" are not. "I couldn't agree more," the advocate of grue and bleen might reply. "Except it is not 'grue' and 'bleen' that are artificial, but 'green' and 'blue.' After all, it is these two colour words that have been defined artificially using 'grue' and 'bleen' as follows:

> "(D3) Object x is *green* =df x is grue and x has been inspected, or x is bleen and x has not been inspected
> "(D4) Object x is *blue* =df x is bleen and x has been inspected, or x is grue and x has not been inspected."

Green and blue are thus no more highly confirmed natural properties of the world than grue and bleen! Yet surely this cannot be right.[8]

Another related tendency is to think that short sequences of tosses are "self-correcting." For example, many people think that, after a string of heads in a sequence of tosses, there should be a trend towards tails. Tversky and Kahneman, for example, suggest that this phenomenon lies at the heart of the gambler's fallacy:

> The gambler feels that the fairness of the coin entitles him to expect that any deviation in one direction will soon be canceled by a corresponding deviation in the other. Even the fairest of coins, however, given the limitations of its memory and moral sense, cannot be as fair as the gambler expects it to be.[9]

Thus, the fallacy would seem to be based on the illegitimate belief that what is true of a large number of things must also be true of a small number of things. Very large numbers can, under the right conditions, be highly representative of the population from which they are drawn, but it is unrealistic to expect that what we learn from large samples can be obtained from small samples as well.

The Lottery Paradox

Imagine a lottery with a large number of tickets and with exactly one winning ticket. Since the ratio of losing tickets to winning tickets is high, it is reasonable to believe that, for any particular ticket, it will not be the winning ticket. In other words, a rational person will be justified in believing that "Ticket 1 is not the winning ticket," and that "Ticket 2 is not the winning ticket," and that "Ticket 3 is not the winning ticket," and so on for all the tickets in the lottery.

However, given the rule of Conjunction in propositional logic, it appears to follow that a rational person will also be justified in believing that "Ticket 1 is not the winning ticket, and ticket 2 is not the winning ticket, and ticket 3 is not the winning ticket, and so on for all the tickets in the lottery," but this is clearly inconsistent with what we know, namely that one of the tickets will be the winning ticket. How can we resolve this inconsistency?

One way is to deny the suggestion that it is reasonable to believe that, say, "Ticket 1 is not the winning ticket," and to suggest instead that it is reasonable only to believe that "Ticket 1 is *probably* not the winning ticket." The resulting conjunction would then be "Ticket 1 is probably not the winning ticket, and ticket 2 is probably not the winning ticket, and ticket 3 is probably not the winning ticket, and so on for all the tickets in the lottery," and this is not inconsistent with the claim that "There is exactly one winning ticket."

However, this solution comes at a cost: it means that rarely, if ever, will we be able to say that we know things with logical certainty. After all, the probability that "Ticket *n* is not the winning ticket" is much higher than for many other claims that we make in our day-to-day lives. Logical certainty, it seems, is a very rare commodity.

The psychology of small numbers in turn suggests that beliefs about biased and inadequate statistics represent forms of inference that are virtually irresistible in everyday argumentation and even scientific research. Tversky and Kahneman suggest that, too often, psychological studies are based on ridiculously small samples. Of course small samples can result in frustrated scientists and inefficient research. It is little wonder, then, that the fallacy of inadequate statistics is so prevalent in the less structured milieu of everyday reasoning and decision-making.

Before leaving the topic of statistics, it is worth taking a moment to discuss one final fallacy associated with the pictorial representation of this type of information. Charts, graphs, and other types of diagrams are frequently found wherever statistics are used. However, pictorial representations of these kinds can turn out to be deceptive. Suppose, for example, that we have a set of figures indexed on a scale from 1 to 10; suppose, too, that these figures show an even rise from 7 to 8 between January and December. For example, the figures could represent an increase in profits per average share for a local software company during the last calendar year. As depicted in diagram 9.1, we see that between January and December profits rose from $70 to $80 per share.

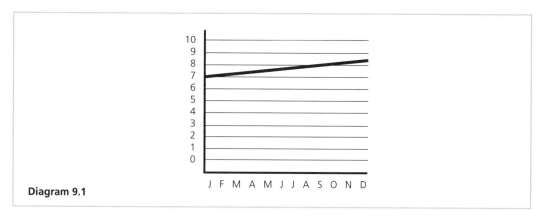

Diagram 9.1

However, an easy way to make this information look more impressive without altering the figures is to remove the "unnecessary" blank space. Diagram 9.2 gives the result:

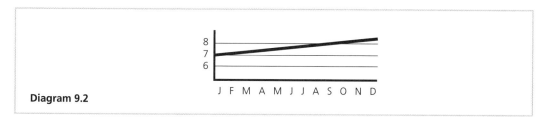

Diagram 9.2

This looks impressive, but if we want to make it look even more so, we can now also change the scale in the graph as follows:

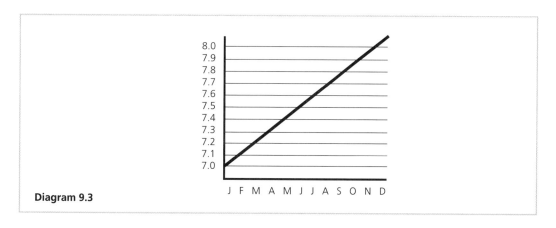

Diagram 9.3

This graph looks very impressive indeed. It gives the appearance that our shareholders' profits are shooting up at a terrific rate. Of course, in giving this impression of a dramatic rate of increase we have not tampered with the statistics themselves in any way. All we have done is manipulated the scope and scale of the graph. We have made it look as if profits are skyrocketing, although the graph indicates only what it showed before— that during the past calendar year profits per share have increased from $70 to $80.

This type of technique of modifying information is dishonest, but it is also ubiquitous, and it can be applied to any graph. Variations on this theme are well known, and bar graphs, pictograms, and other suggestive yet conceptually fuzzy forms of illustration often find their way into statistical presentations. In many circumstances we will not want to take the time to digest a welter of complex numerical tabulations; as a result, we will be quite happy to see statistical information neatly summed up in an appealing graph or picture. Even so, if we are genuinely interested in discovering the truth behind these types of pictures, a healthy distrust of pretty pictures is not a bad attitude to foster. The attractively packaged conclusion may be quite fallacious, just as the attractively packaged product it was designed to promote may be a bad buy.[10]

4. A Causal Fallacy

Post hoc, ergo propter hoc is Latin for "after this, therefore because of this." The *post hoc* fallacy therefore occurs whenever we observe that one event, E_2, follows another, E_1, in temporal sequence, and then hastily conclude that E_1 causes E_2.

   Post hoc is sometimes also described as the fallacy of arguing from correlation to causation, but here we must tread carefully. A correlation between two classes of events is often evidence that they are causally related. However, as we know, correlations need not be conclusive in this regard. In theory, there is nothing wrong with an argument from correlations to causes. Rather, the fallacy occurs when we leap too quickly to a causal conclusion on the basis of such data. Because there are a number of factors that may be overlooked in this regard, there are several versions of the *post hoc* fallacy that are worth studying.

Post hoc, ergo propter hoc

The *post hoc* fallacy occurs whenever we observe that one event, E_2, follows another, E_1, in temporal sequence, and then hastily conclude that E_1 causes E_2. Latin for "after this, therefore because of this," *post hoc, ergo propter hoc* is also used to describe the related fallacy of arguing from correlation to causation. However, because some correlations indicate legitimate causal relations, identifying genuine instances of this fallacy can be tricky.

   Under some circumstances, of course, it is tempting to conclude that because E_2 follows E_1, E_1 must have caused E_2. For example, if after taking a dose of Sinus Blast Sue's cold clears up, it may be natural for her to conclude that it was the Sinus Blast that caused her cold to disappear; but without further testing, this one instance of a correlation remains rather weak evidence in favour of this conclusion. Perhaps the cold would have cleared up by itself, or even sooner, if Sue had not taken Sinus Blast.

   Similarly, it is sometimes easy to mistakenly reverse the order of cause and effect. When driving to work Bill may regularly experience car trouble on those days when he is running low on oil. Hearing the car engine sputter, he may conclude that running low on oil is somehow causing the engine to malfunction. In reality, it may be that it is the engine trouble that causes the decrease in his car's oil level. Until he does further testing, it is simply impossible to know.

Similarly, it is sometimes tempting to conclude that an event, E_1, is the cause of another event, E_2, when both in fact are effects of a common third factor, E_3. Noticing a strong correlation between her dry lawn and the number of crickets in her garden, Sue may conclude that the crickets prefer to eat dry grass. In fact, it may be that both the dry grass and the increase in crickets result from a common cause—the summer's warm sunshine.

Alternatively, we may fail to notice that there is an unrecognized form of intermediate causation between E_1 and E_2. For example, while driving in traffic, Bill might repeatedly observe that whenever he applies the brakes in winter weather his defroster fan squeaks. He concludes that the brakes are connected to the fan. A more mechanically sophisticated observer might conclude that applying the brakes causes deceleration of the vehicle, which tilts the fan mechanism, which in turn causes the squeak.

Despite all these examples, it is not easy to offer a more detailed analysis of the fallacy of *post hoc*. The reason is that there is no widespread agreement on how to analyze the concept of causation and how causation in fact differs from correlation. Consequently, no established theory of what, precisely, is wrong about *post hoc* reasoning can be offered. We seem to understand intuitively what causation is at a practical level, but numerous philosophical critiques of the concept show that it is highly elusive and unstable at the level of theoretical analysis.

Thus we conclude our discussion with a negative finding: whatever causation is, we need to be aware of the numerous pitfalls we can encounter if we conclude too quickly that A causes B just because there is a correlation of some sort between A and B. The danger of *post hoc* lurks in any causal interpretation we might seek to impose on statistical data. Statistical data often suggest causal relationships, but we need to be careful: it is dangerous to leap to a suggested conclusion too quickly.

Exercise 9.3

1. Identify the fallacy in each of the following arguments:

    (a) They say that studying helps you understand this material. But it doesn't work for me. I studied all last night and it's no clearer now than it was before.

    (b) The last three times I've tried to go golfing, I've been caught in the rain. So this time I'm sure things will begin to average out and I'll be able to complete a round without getting wet.

    (c) That restaurant serves the healthiest food; every time I go there I leave feeling great.

    (d) Our team is bound to lose on Friday when we go to watch them. Every time I've attended a game, they've lost.

    (e) I wouldn't trust that store's salespeople. The last time I was measured for a shirt there, the salesperson got the size wrong.

Summary

Unlike deductively valid arguments, inductively strong arguments are *non-monotonic*. This means that even strong inductive arguments may be weakened and their conclusions may be overturned by the addition of new premises. As a result, inductively strong arguments are fallible in a way that deductive arguments are not.

Even so, it is possible to distinguish between good and bad inductive arguments. We say that an argument (or inference) is *inductively strong* if, assuming that its premisses are true, it is *highly likely* (or *highly probable*) that its conclusion will be true as well. An argument or inference is *inductively weak* if, assuming that the premisses are true, it is *highly unlikely* (or *highly improbable*) that the conclusion will be true as well.

When studying inductive arguments, it is customary for logicians to exploit the resources of the probability calculus. Thus, after observing that the probability of a tautology, $\Pr(T)$, is 1, that the probability of a contradiction, $\Pr(F)$, is 0, and that the probability of a contingent proposition, $\Pr(C)$, lies between 0 and 1, we introduced several rules of probability that allow us to calculate the probability of an argument's conclusion given knowledge of its premises.

Even so, several difficulties remain. Hume's problem of induction, the raven paradox, the lottery paradox, and Goodman's new riddle of induction all indicate that we may have not fully understood the way inductive inference operates.

Also of interest are several common fallacies associated with inductive inference. The fallacy of *secundum quid*, or hasty generalization, occurs whenever an unwarranted induction is drawn on the basis of a few particular observations, rather than on the basis of a fair and reasonable sample or on the basis of a balanced and representative collection of the evidence.

A related fallacy, the *post hoc* fallacy, occurs whenever we observe that one event, E_2, follows another, E_1, in temporal sequence, and then hastily conclude that E_1 causes E_2. Latin for "after this, therefore because of this," *post hoc, ergo propter hoc* is also used to describe the related fallacy of arguing from mere correlation to causation. However, as we noted, because some correlations indicate genuine causal relations, identifying genuine instances of this fallacy can be tricky. To some extent, modern statistics helps us steer clear of this mistake. It allows us to discover statistically significant correlations, and it permits us to attribute causal significance to these correlations.

Weblinks

History of Mathematics—History of Probability and Statistics
aleph0.clarku.edu/~djoyce/mathhist/statistics.html

The Nizkor Project—*Post Hoc* Fallacy
www.nizkor.org/features/fallacies/post-hoc.html

Notes

1. In contrast, we say that every proposition describing a negative instance of a generalization gives that generalization some (much higher) degree of *falsification*. In other words, every time we see a non-white swan, this decreases (quite dramatically!) the probability that the proposition "All swans are white" is true.

2. One possibility may be puzzling. What if we supplement (rather than replace) our original premiss with the additional premiss "Bill has no brothers"? Will this make the argument invalid? In fact, it won't. As we saw in chapter 6, all arguments with inconsistent or contradictory premisses turn out to be valid.

3. See David Hume's 1739 *Treatise of Human Nature* (Book I, Part IV, Section I) and his *Enquiry Concerning Human Understanding* (Section V), first published in 1748 under the title *Philosophical Essays Concerning Human Understanding*.

4. See Thomas Bayes, "An Essay towards Solving a Problem in the Doctrine of Chances," reprinted in E. S. Pearson and M. G. Kendall, *Studies in the History of Statistics and Probability* (London: Charles Griffin and Co., 1970), 131–153.

5. This version of Bayes' theorem is the simplified version. The more general version, which allows us to substitute more than two values for q, is as follows:

$$Pr(q|p) = \frac{Pr(q) \times Pr(p|q)}{[Pr(q_1) \times Pr(p|q_1)] + \ldots + [Pr(q_n) \times Pr(p|q_n)]}$$

6. Stephen K. Campbell, *Flaws and Fallacies in Statistical Thinking* (Englewood Cliffs: Prentice-Hall, 1974), ch. 11.

7. Carl Hempel, "Studies in the Logic of Confirmation," *Mind* 54 (1945), 1–26, 97–121.

8. Nelson Goodman, *Fact, Fiction and Forecast*, 4th ed. (Cambridge, Mass.: Harvard University Press, 1983), ch. 3.

9. Amos Tversky and Daniel Kahneman, "Belief in the Law of Small Numbers," *Psychological Bulletin* 76 (1971), 106.

10. For example, see the classic little book by Darrell Huff, *How to Lie With Statistics* (New York: Norton, 1954). Also see Leo Groarke, "Logic, Art and Argument," *Informal Logic*, 18 (1996), 105–129.

CHAPTER 10

Arguing in a Circle

HAVING now spent several chapters considering arguments in the narrow sense, it is time to revisit arguments in the broad sense. In doing so we will want to ask whether sound arguments are always good arguments. If an argument is sound, then it is valid and it has true premises; and because all valid arguments are truth-preserving, it follows that the conclusions of sound arguments will always be true. Is this all it takes for an argument to be a good one?

In this chapter we examine this question by considering the fallacy of *begging the question*, or *arguing in a circle*, or *petitio principii*. We conclude that, at least with arguments in the broad sense, where arguments are used to help advance knowledge, there is more to being a good argument than just being sound.

1. The Fallacy of Begging the Question, or Arguing in a Circle

It is important to appreciate that an argument is rarely either just good or just bad. Frequently, the same argument can be good in one sense but not in another. For example, as we have seen, some inductive arguments are good arguments even though they are not valid. Similarly, just because an argument is valid is no guarantee that it will also be sound.

An example is contained in this simple argument:

Bill is in Montreal

Therefore, Bill is in Montreal.

How should we evaluate this argument? It is clear that it is valid; and if its premiss is true, it will be sound as well. Nevertheless, nearly everyone will also agree that it is not a good argument, at least in the broad sense. The reason is that it commits the fallacy of *begging the question*. That is, it assumes the very point that it is trying to prove.

Also called the fallacy of *arguing in a circle* (*circulus probandi*) or *petitio principii* (we shall use these various terms interchangeably), this fallacy occurs whenever an argument attempts to "pull itself up by its own bootstraps" by assuming its own conclusion.

This fallacy is important, partly because circular arguments can be tricky to identify. It is also important since it may turn out that all valid arguments are circular. After all, another way of explaining validity is to note that, in a valid argument, nothing is contained in the conclusion that is not already contained in, or implied by, the premises. Thus, the difference between arguing validly and arguing in a circle may turn out to be vanishingly small.

> **The Fallacy of Begging the Question or Arguing in a Circle**
> The fallacy of *begging the question* (or as it is also known, the fallacy of *arguing in a circle*, or *petitio principii*) occurs whenever an argument illegitimately assumes or presupposes the very proposition that it is supposed to be proving.

This claim, that all valid arguments are circular, appears to have first been made by the Greek logician Sextus Empiricus.[1] Working near the end of the second century, Sextus was a leading logician in the Stoic school in ancient Greece. His claim is a startling one. If correct, it means that no valid argument will ever serve as a reliable means of justifying its conclusion!

However, before we evaluate this claim, let us try to get a better idea of the fallacy itself. Suppose Sue, a skeptical agnostic, and Bill, a devout believer, are conducting a theological dispute as follows:

Sue: What reasonable grounds could we have for believing that God exists?

Bill: It says so, quite clearly, in the Bible.

Sue: Of course. But how can we be assured that what the Bible says is, in this respect, accurate?

Bill: The Bible is the word of God. We can trust it completely, especially in a case like this, where its message is obvious.

Sue: Hold on a second!

At this point Sue has likely noticed that Bill is assuming the very proposition he has set out to prove. We can see this if we reconstruct Bill's argument using the following two sub-arguments:

(P1) Anything written in the Bible is the word of God
(P2) The word of God can be trusted completely
_____
(C1) Anything written in the Bible can be trusted completely

(C1) Anything written in the Bible can be trusted completely
(P3) The claim "God exists" is written in the Bible
_____
(C2) The claim "God exists" can be trusted completely.

Schematically, we might represent these two sub-arguments as follows:

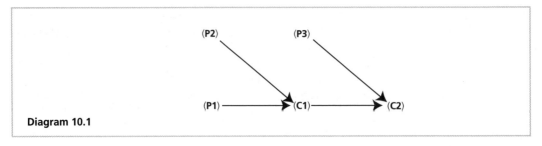

Diagram 10.1

The problem is that (P1) appears to presuppose (C2), the very claim that (P1) is being used to prove. In other words, taking the Bible as an authoritative source of the word of God clearly presupposes the existence of God. Bill's original premiss, it would seem, can hardly escape being based, at least in part, on his conclusion. But how can this be if he is supposedly less certain of his conclusion than he is of his premisses?

To put this point even more explicitly, we note that (C2) is supposed to be based (in part) on (C1), and (C1) is supposed to be based (in part) on (P1); but because (P1) in turn presupposes (C2), we have the following circular state of affairs:

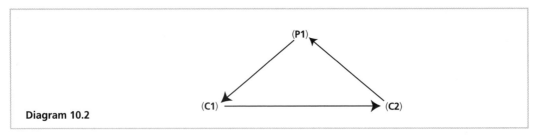

Diagram 10.2

Small wonder that Sue hesitates. She is suspicious that somehow Bill's argument has gone astray, and so it has.[2]

Flashback on...
Aristotle's Version of *Petitio Principii*

ARISTOTLE was the first thinker to offer a systematic analysis of the fallacy of *petitio principii* or, as he is often translated, the fallacy of *begging the question*. He is quite clear in classifying it as a fallacy; and since, for Aristotle, a fallacy is an argument that appears to be a syllogism but is not, it will be useful to revisit the definition of "syllogism." In his book the *Topics* (100a, 25–26), Aristotle writes, "A syllogism is an argument in which, certain things being laid down,

something other than these necessarily comes about through them." We can see in this an awareness that in a syllogism (i) the premisses necessitate (i.e., logically entail) the conclusion; and (ii) the conclusion does not repeat any premiss.

It may now strike us as obvious what Aristotle's account of circularity will be. Surely it will be the fallacy involved in violating condition (ii). However, Aristotle recognizes not just one but five ways in which an argument may be circular, or in which a question may be begged.

Modern readers are likely to regard the name "begging the question" as somewhat unclear and perhaps a trifle theatrical. But begging in this context is not intended to refer to a type of supplication. Rather, it is something any questioner does in the course of attempting to refute an opponent's thesis. Before refuting a thesis, the questioner must ask his opponent what premisses they agree on. Begging the question is thus a mistaken way of questioning one's opponent on this matter. In other words, it is a mistaken way of selecting propositions that are to serve as premisses in a would-be refutation or syllogism.

For Aristotle, the *original question* of a refutation is the respondent's thesis, *T*. A question is then "begged in the first way" if the questioner begs the point that he himself must try to derive, namely, not-*T*. Even if, says Aristotle, you get your opponent to admit that the argument

> Not-*T*
> ___
> Not-*T*

is sound, this will not be sufficient to prove not-*T*.

In the second way of begging the question, Aristotle calls into question arguments in which the conclusion follows from a single general premiss, as with

> All humans are mortal
> _____
> Therefore, some humans are mortal.

Interestingly enough, Aristotle is in no doubt that the premiss *implies* the conclusion. What he does not like is the idea that this argument is a syllogism. Here his reasoning turns on a technicality in the definition of refutation that we have not yet brought to light. For Aristotle, in a successful refutation, every premiss must be consistent with the respondent's original thesis, *T*. Thus it is only the premisses collectively that imply the thesis' contradictory, not-*T*.

The third way of begging the question can be illustrated with the following argument:

> Socrates, who is Greek, loves to argue
> _____
> Therefore, all Greeks love to argue.

Here the problem is that anyone doubting that Socrates loves to argue will also doubt that all Greeks love to argue.

The fourth way of begging the question is a bit tricky. On the face of it, there appears to be nothing wrong with an argument of the form

> p
> q
> _____
> Therefore, p and q.

Certainly, arguments of this form will be valid. So perhaps the fault is that the conclusion violates the non-circularity condition on syllogisms twice over, by repeating both premisses in the conclusion. Curiously, this appears not to have been Aristotle's own diagnosis. As we have already seen, he insisted that syllogisms must be constructed entirely from categorical propositions. Since no compound statement is a categorical proposition in Aristotle's sense, the fault is that the conclusion is not technically a proposition.

Finally, the fifth way of begging the question has a distinctly modern ring to it. Like the first, it is really a variation of the non-circularity condition on syllogisms. Specifically, it bans arguments of the form

> p
> q
> _____
> Therefore, r

in which r is equivalent to p or to q.

Of course, when Aristotle indicates that these five types of argument are defective, he does not mean that they are invalid. He means only that they are not syllogisms. In fact, it is precisely because question-begging arguments are valid that they may also seem to be what they are not; namely, syllogisms. Hence question-begging arguments are near-perfect specimens of what Aristotle understands by "fallacy."

To sum up, in Aristotle's usage, *petitio principii* or begging a question is simply a mistaken form of premiss-selection. Of the five ways of begging the question that Aristotle lists, the first and fifth are straightforward violations of the non-circularity condition on syllogisms. They would be recognized by any modern reader as question-begging precisely because they involve an element of circularity. We may also say that the second way of begging the question has something of a modern sound to it since a conclusion that comes from a single premiss in one step may strike us as fairly close to a circular argument. Of the two remaining ways, the third, in which there is a generalization from a single case, will seem to the modern reader to be more like the fallacy of hasty generalization than a fallacy of circularity, and the fourth will appear as the violation of a simple technical requirement that may or may not be of interest outside of Aristotle's specific logical system.

Having considered this example, it is now worth noting that both historical and contemporary textbooks typically emphasize two types of *petitio*. The first is called the *dependency version*; the second is called the *equivalence version*. According to the dependency version, an argument is circular whenever the conclusion is presupposed by some premiss, in the sense that the premiss depends on the conclusion as part of the evidence that supports it. Proponents of the dependency conception often express this idea in terms of what is or is not inferred from a conclusion. In other words, an argument is non-circular only if one knows that each premiss is true without having to infer it from the conclusion, or from some statement that can only be known by inference from the conclusion. It is easy to see how the dependency conception is exemplified in our earlier example. There, premiss (P1) could only be known to be true by an inference that would depend (at least in part) on (C2), the conclusion of the argument.

> ### Two Versions of the Fallacy of *Petitio Principii*
>
> The fallacy of *petitio principii* is regularly said to come in two versions. According to the *dependency version*, an argument is circular whenever the conclusion is presupposed by some premiss, in the sense that the premiss depends on the conclusion as part of the evidence that supports it. According to the *equivalence version*, an argument is circular whenever the conclusion itself is tacitly or explicitly assumed as one of the premisses.

According to the *equivalence version*, an argument is circular whenever its conclusion is tacitly or explicitly assumed as one of its premisses. That is, it is circular whenever the conclusion is equivalent, or identical, to a given premiss. Here is the American logician Irving Copi's discussion of the equivalence conception:

> If one assumes as a premiss for an argument the very conclusion it is intended to prove, the fallacy committed is that of *petitio principii*, or begging the question. If the proposition to be established is formulated in exactly the same words, both as premiss and as conclusion, the mistake would be so glaring as to deceive no one. Often, however, two formulations can be sufficiently different to obscure the fact that one and the same proposition occurs both as premiss and conclusion.3

An example will help. Consider the following argument: "To allow every man unbounded freedom of speech must always be, on the whole, advantageous to the state; for it is highly conducive to the interests of the community that each individual should enjoy a liberty, perfectly unlimited, of expressing his sentiments."⁴ If you think about this argument, you will see that the premiss (the part after "for") is nothing but the conclusion restated in different words.

Exercise 10.1

1. Determine whether each of the following contains an example of *petitio principii*. If so, is it the dependency or the equivalence version of the fallacy?

    (a) Theism is universal since everyone, deep down, believes in God.

    (b) Theism is universal since everyone, deep down, believes that the world could not have existed without a creator, and the only thing capable of creating the world is God.

    (c) The best jobs are those that pay the highest salaries, because the only good thing about a job is the money you can make from it.

    (d) Free trade will be good for this country and the reason is patently obvious: Unrestricted commercial relations will bestow on all sections of our nation the benefits that result when there is an unimpeded flow of goods between countries.

    (e) In response to the question of why a politician lost her seat in a recent election, Bill replied, "Because she didn't get enough votes."

2. Sextus' Puzzle

The nineteenth-century logician Augustus De Morgan was a staunch defender of formal logic. As a result, he had some original and useful thoughts on the subject of the fallacies. In keeping with his championship of formal logic, De Morgan preferred the equivalence conception as an account of the *petitio*: "strictly speaking," says De Morgan, "there is no formal *petitio* except when the very proposition to be proved, and not a mere synonym of it, is assumed."⁵

In contrast, De Morgan's contemporary, Alfred Sidgwick, was skeptical about whether an account of *petitio* would be adequate if it confined itself only to formal cases such as

$$p$$
$$\overline{}$$
$$\therefore p$$

and

$$p \wedge q$$
$$\overline{}$$
$$\therefore p.$$

These cases are indeed circular, but they are also trivial. As a result, says Sidgwick, "nothing appears to be really gained by restricting the name to so small a compass as this and there is no doubt that such a restriction would be very much at variance with the popular acceptation of the term."[6]

Thus a general question can be raised about the limits of formal logic as a tool for the study of the *petitio*. Can circular arguments be identified and explained solely as a result of their logical form? If so, and if circular arguments turn out to be fallacious because of their form, does it follow that Sextus Empiricus was right and that all valid arguments are circular?

This possibility occurred to Aristotle, who considered and rejected the idea in his book *Posterior Analytics*.[7] As John Stuart Mill explains, the claim that a syllogism always begs the question is "fundamentally erroneous" since it misrepresents "the true character of the syllogism."[8] Mill does note that when a syllogism is offered as a proof, and when a general premiss (e.g., "All *A* are *B*") is analyzed in conformity with the received opinion of his day, it is indeed question-begging. However, he took this merely to be a *reductio ad absurdum* of the then-received view of general propositions.

Are All Valid Arguments Circular?

Can all circular arguments be identified and explained solely as a result of their logical form? If so, does it also follow that the ancient Greek logician Sextus Empiricus was right in claiming that all valid arguments are formally valid only because they assume the very proposition that they are trying to prove? And if all valid arguments are circular, does it follow that no valid argument can ever serve to justify its conclusion?

Many logicians, including Aristotle, John Stuart Mill, and Augustus De Morgan have denied this, arguing that no valid argument with non-superfluous, multiple premises will be circular. Thus it is this subset of the valid arguments that, if sound, will justify their conclusions.

According to the then-received view, a general proposition (such as "All men are mortal creatures") is strictly equivalent to the conjunction of all (and only) its positive instances, namely "(Aristotle is a human and Aristotle is a mortal creature) and

(Plato is a human and Plato is a mortal creature) and (Socrates is human and Socrates is a mortal creature) and ...." It follows that in the syllogism

All men are mortal creatures
Plato is a man

Therefore, Plato is a mortal creature

the conclusion will have already been asserted in one of the conjuncts of the first premiss, namely in the conjunct "Plato is human and Plato is a mortal creature."

Something like this argument had been known even in ancient times, and De Morgan, no doubt aware of its implications, was ready to concede that it was "ingenious." Nevertheless, like Mill, he offered a way of bypassing these difficulties with what we shall call "De Morgan's Deadly Retort":

> The whole objection [i.e., that all valid arguments are circular] tacitly assumes the superfluity of the minor [i.e., the second premiss]; that is, tacitly assumes we know Plato to be a man, as soon as we know him to be Plato.[9]

In other words, De Morgan grants that, if the conclusion is false, then the major (first) premiss must also be false—but only on the assumption that the minor (second) premiss is true. That is, he grants that the argument is in a sense circular, but only on the assumption that Plato is not a dog, for example, or a computer program. But, if so, then the conclusion depends on more than just the first premiss and neither premiss, individually, begs the question.

De Morgan then concludes that the most favourable account of *petitio* refers to what is assumed in *one* premiss: "The most fallacious *pair* of premisses, though expressly constructed to form a certain conclusion, without the least reference to their truth, would not be assuming the question or *an* equivalent."[10]

Thus De Morgan illuminatingly connects the phenomenon of *petitio* to the number of premisses of an argument.[11] Since syllogisms are always multi-premissed, we can state De Morgan's thesis succinctly as follows: No syllogism is circular; or using the vocabulary of modern logic: No valid argument with more than one premiss, and no superfluous premisses, is circular.

We may now define the notion of a *superfluous premiss*. A premiss in a valid argument is superfluous if and only if the argument is still valid when that premiss is deleted. Take, for example, an argument of the form

$p \supset q$
p

$\therefore q.$

Is the second premiss, p, superfluous? Let us try deleting it. The result is

$p \supset q$

$\therefore q$

which is not valid. In the same manner, we learn that the first premiss is non-superfluous. Thus all *Modus Ponens* arguments are multi-premiss arguments without superfluous premisses.[12]

In contrast let us look at the argument form

$$p$$
$$q$$
_____
$$\therefore p.$$

Here we can see that the first premiss is not superfluous, but the second one is, for if we delete *q* we are left with "*p*, therefore *p*," which is clearly a valid argument form.

Now we reach the heart of the matter. Is De Morgan correct that no valid argument with more than one premiss, and no superfluous premiss, is circular? Two worries come immediately to mind. First, in modern logic any multi-premiss argument may be recast as a one-premiss argument, simply by using the rule of Conjunction to join the several premisses into one. This means that the distinction between non-circular, multi-premiss arguments and circular, one-premiss arguments may be artificial.

Second, isn't it possible, we might ask, that an argument satisfying De Morgan's conditions might still be circular? For example, isn't it possible that while justifying the premisses themselves, one might unknowingly commit a *petitio*? Consider, for example, an argument in the form of a disjunctive syllogism,

$$p \lor q$$
$$\sim p$$
_____
$$\therefore q.$$

If we delete *p* ∨ *q*, we are left with "~*p*, therefore *q*," which is clearly not formally valid. If we delete ~*p* we are left with "*p* ∨ *q*, therefore *q*," which is also not formally valid. Neither premiss is superfluous. Even so, might it not be the case that in the process of justifying one of these premisses, *p* ∨ *q*, say, we will have mistakenly relied upon *q*? (After all, we know that *p* ∨ *q* follows from *q* by the rule of Addition.) If so, will this not be a counter-example to De Morgan's thesis? Is there any way to know in advance that formal logic will rule out such situations?

Exercise 10.2

1. Find any superfluous premisses in the following argument forms:

(a) $p \supset q$, $\sim q \supset \sim p$, p, therefore q

(b) $p \lor q$, $\sim p$, $\sim q$, therefore q

(c) $p \supset q$, $\sim p$, $p \lor q$, therefore q

(d) $p \supset \sim q$, $r \supset \sim s$, $p \lor r$, $\sim s$, therefore $\sim q \lor \sim s$

(e) $p \supset q$, $\sim q$, $p \lor q$, therefore $\sim p \lor \sim q$

(f) $\sim r$, $s \supset r$, $(\sim s \lor t) \supset (p \supset q)$, therefore $\sim q \supset \sim p$

(g) $p \supset (q \land r)$, s, $q \supset s$, $\sim r$, therefore $s \land \sim p$

(h) $p \supset (q \land r)$, $p \supset (s \land t)$, $t \supset \sim r$, therefore $\sim p$

(i) $p \supset \sim q$, q, therefore $q \supset \sim p$

(j) r, q, therefore $r \wedge (q \vee \sim q)$

2. Sextus Empiricus held that all valid arguments are circular since they assume the very propositions that they are trying to prove. In contrast, Augustus De Morgan denied this, arguing that no valid argument with non-superfluous, multiple premisses will be circular. For each of the following arguments, would Sextus judge it to be circular? Would De Morgan?

(a) Theism is universal since everyone, deep down, believes in God.

(b) Theism is universal since everyone, deep down, believes that the world could not have existed without a creator, and the only thing capable of creating the world is God.

(c) The best jobs are those that pay the highest salaries, because the only good thing about a job is the money you can make from it.

(d) If unemployment continues to rise, taxes will increase. If taxes increase, then money will become scarce. So, if unemployment continues to rise, money will become scarce.

(e) Galileo died the year Newton was born. So it follows that Newton was born the year that Galileo died.

3. De Morgan's Defence

Even though we have shown that arguments in the form of disjunctive syllogism are not circular, how can we reply to the two worries raised at the end of the last section? First, if all multi-premiss arguments can be recast as one-premiss arguments, can De Morgan defend his distinction between non-circular, multi-premiss arguments and circular, one-premiss arguments? Second, even in multi-premiss arguments, how can we be sure that the premisses have been justified in a non-circular way? That is, what guarantee do we have that the ultimate justification of these premisses does not rely upon the conclusion?

In response to the first of these two worries, the modern defender of De Morgan will likely reply that there is an important difference between multi-premiss arguments in the broad sense, and these same arguments after they have been recast as single-premiss arguments. The difference is that the premiss of any argument in the broad sense will itself have to be justified in a real-world, epistemic context. But if so, distinguishing between an argument's various individual premisses allows us to distinguish between these various justifications, and it is exactly this point that is crucial for distinguishing between circular and non-circular arguments.

With regard to the second of these worries, we can point out that, if it is true that arguments of the form

$p \vee q$

$\sim p$

___

q

contain premisses that have been justified in a circular way, then this argument form alone will not completely describe the postulated circular argument. In such a case the argument will contain an additional part, for example

$$q$$
$$\overline{}$$
$$p \lor q.$$

If we then look at this new argument as a whole, we see that it really consists of two stages, namely

$$q$$
$$\overline{}$$
$$p \lor q$$

and

$$p \lor q$$
$$\sim p$$
$$\overline{}$$
$$q.$$

First we have the premiss q, then the intermediate conclusion, $p \lor q$. The intermediate conclusion is then used as premiss for the next stage of the argument, which is a disjunctive syllogism. However, this new, more detailed representation of the form of the argument reveals its circularity in a purely formal manner. The statement q appears as both a premiss and a conclusion of the larger argument, the argument that contains both stages. In short, it seems that De Morgan is vindicated. If the argument really is a *petitio*, then we can show that the conclusion is in fact identical to a premiss and not "a mere synonym," just as De Morgan postulated. A circular argument might initially appear to have the form of, say, disjunctive syllogism, but a deeper analysis of its full logical form will reveal that the conclusion is being smuggled in as a premiss, and the argument is revealed to be a classical equivalence *petitio* of a purely deductive sort.

De Morgan's defence can thus be stated in a general way, and we can combine it with his preference for the equivalence conception of *petitio*. In other words, it is De Morgan's position that in any circular argument there will exist a chain of reasoning back to a point at which the conclusion is repeated as a premiss. Just as we may discover that the premiss of one argument is really the conclusion of another argument,

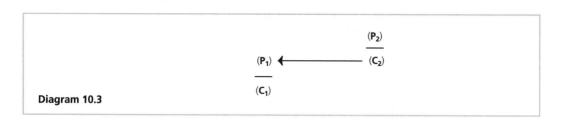

Diagram 10.3

we may also discover that this chain of reasoning continues indefinitely to some premiss, P_i.

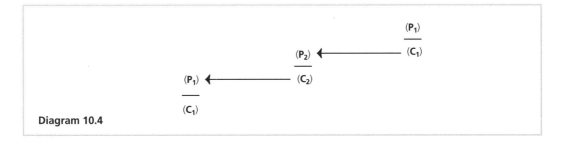

Diagram 10.4

However, in any case in which our argument is circular, P_i will turn out to be equivalent to our conclusion, C.

In arguments, it happens often that a critic or skeptic may not be satisfied with your premiss, and may ask for some additional premiss that could be used as a basis for your original premiss. This process is called *dialectical regression*. In effect, the larger, major argument is composed, in chain-like fashion, of a number of smaller arguments or links. Presumably, De Morgan would suggest that arguments (and their logical forms) must be viewed from a "macroscopic" perspective as well as from the usual "microscopic" perspective we are accustomed to. In a macroscopic representation of the form of the argument, we will find a clear line of demarcation between the circular and non-circular arguments, provided that we push the regression back far enough to encompass the circle. So we now see that disjunctive syllogism is not an exception to De Morgan's thesis, and it would seem that we can deal with *petitio* exclusively in terms of classical logical forms. So concludes De Morgan's defence.

However, by introducing the notion of step-like sequences of arguments, does De Morgan's defence successfully show that the equivalence version of the *petitio* is to be preferred over the dependence version? The answer depends on how we interpret the arrows used in the above diagrams. Suppose we have a circular argument. If we follow the step-by-step process of isolating those propositions that our premisses are based upon, we will eventually come to our original conclusion. In other words, if we push backwards far enough, we will eventually find the conclusion of the argument at some previous stage. At least, so it appears from the point of view of the equivalence conception of the *petitio*.

But the very same phenomenon can also be interpreted as an instance of the dependency conception. Under this conception, we naturally think of the conclusion as evidentially dependent on the premisses. But by a series of steps, we might also find that a premiss is evidentially dependent on some previous evidential base, which depends on yet another proposition, and so on until, by a series of steps, we arrive back at the original conclusion. If so, we will have shown that these two conceptions of the *petitio* are largely the same, and that even the dependency conception need not be viewed as allowing valid arguments to fall prey to Sextus' objection.

In other words, returning to our original example,

All men are mortal creatures
Plato is a man

Therefore, Plato is a mortal creature

we now see that this argument may or may not be circular depending on how the first premiss is to be verified. If the arguer has some independent way of verifying the first premiss, say, by an appeal to general biological laws that involve no specific reference to the particular individual "Plato," it seems hard to claim that the argument is circular. On the other hand, if the arguer is thinking of the first premiss as a finite enumeration of all men, then the conclusion itself would have to be a part of the evidentiary basis for this premiss. In this case, the charge of *petitio* will be very much to the point.

Flashback on...
Augustus De Morgan (1806–1871)

ALMOST an exact contemporary of John Stuart Mill (1806–1873), Augustus De Morgan was born in Madura, India, to a British military family. In 1827 he graduated fourth in his class in mathematics at Trinity College, Cambridge. (In Cambridge parlance, he was "fourth wrangler," a considerable distinction.) Religious skepticism caused him to be denied an appointment at Cambridge, but it was no bar to his being appointed the founding holder of the chair of mathematics at the fledgling University of London.

One of the leading mathematicians of his day, De Morgan did important work in the foundations of algebra and in mathematical methodology. He was also a pioneer of modern logic, anticipating George Boole's algebraic approach to propositional logic and C.S. Peirce's "logic of relatives." In the present day, every beginning student of logic recognizes De Morgan from the equivalences that establish the duality of conjunction and disjunction and that bear his name. He is perhaps second best known for his

relatively early book *Formal Logic*, which was published in 1847. De Morgan's more mature writings appeared in the *Cambridge Philosophical Transactions* from 1846 to 1862. A brief account of these works was published in 1860 under the title *Syllabus of a Proposed System of Logic*.

Chapter 13 of *Formal Logic*, some fifty pages in all, is devoted to the fallacies. There De Morgan is famously of the view that "there is no such thing as a classification of the ways in which men may arrive at an error: it is much to be doubted whether there ever *can be*."[13] He then goes on to add: "As to mere inference, the main object of this work, it is reducible to rules: these rules being all obeyed, an inference, as an inference, is good; consequently a bad inference is a breach of one or more of these rules."[14]

What De Morgan means is that although all deductive errors can be identified and classified through a complete and sound system of deductive logic, this alone is insufficient for the elimination of all error. If all that is wanted is a theory of *deductive* fallacies, says De Morgan, then there is no need for a separate theory of fallacies. A deductive fallacy is just a breach of a rule of inference. If such a claim sounds odd to modern ears, it is useful to bear in mind that De Morgan means by "inference" what we today mean by "syllogism" in Aristotle's sense. Thus, De Morgan's point is that even if a special theory of deductive (i.e., syllogistic) fallacies is unnecessary, there is still another kind of fallacy whose study must take us beyond deductive logic. As he puts it, "there are many points connected with the matter of premisses to which it is very desirable to draw a reader's attention."[15]

A case in point is ambiguity. Depending on how the premiss "Bill is a bachelor" is taken—whether as saying that Bill has yet to wed or as saying that he is the holder of a first-level university degree—an argument to the conclusion "Therefore, Bill has no wife" may or may not be correct.

Most of what De Morgan has to say about this kind of fallacy is fairly familiar. However, his treatment of *petitio principii* is an exception. Sextus Empiricus had long since laid the charge that all syllogisms beg the question[16] and, by and large, De Morgan is attracted to the view that question-begging is a kind of syllogistic error. De Morgan realizes that if the charge of Sextus Empiricus were justified, this ought to be discernible in the formal structure of any syllogism. De Morgan considers the following standard example:

> All men are mortal
> Plato is a man
> _____
>
> Therefore, Plato is mortal.

According to Sextus, this argument exemplifies what we have called the "dependency conception" of circularity. That is, in order to know the first premiss we must first know the conclusion. In answer to this, De Morgan insists that begging the question is definable only for pairs of *single* propositions, one of which is a premiss and the other a conclusion. By these lights,

> Plato is a bachelor
> _____
>
> Therefore, Plato has yet to marry

would be valid but question-begging, since its (single) premiss is repeated in the conclusion.

It is easy to see that De Morgan is now well positioned to reply to Sextus's criticism. De Morgan can say that it is not true that the only way to know the first premiss of our earlier argument is by prior knowledge of the conclusion, since many people who have never heard of Plato know that all men are mortal. In fact, says De Morgan, "the whole objection tacitly assumes the superfluity of the minor [i.e., the second premiss]; that is, tacitly assumes we know Plato to be a man, as soon as we know him to be Plato."[17] More importantly, since on this view question-begging is definable only for one-premiss arguments, it cannot be true that the conclusion is question-begging in relation to the two premisses together. Jointly, these two points are what we call "De Morgan's Deadly Retort." Perhaps the retort is not conclusive against Sextus, but it does show that his challenge is not as one-sided as it may have first appeared.

Exercise 10.3

1. For each of the following, construct an evidential base (i.e., a background context) in which it is plausible to think that Bill argues in a circle. Then construct a second evidential base (i.e., a second background context) in which it is plausible to think that he does not.

    (a) When Bill is asked by his bank manager for a credit reference, the following dialogue results:

Bill: "My friend Sue will vouch for me."

Manager: "But how do I know I can rely on a reference from Sue?"

Bill. "Oh, no problem—I can vouch for Sue myself."

(b) When Bill is asked by Sue why a mutual friend, Alan, committed suicide, he answers, "Alan committed suicide because he had a death wish."

Summary

We began this chapter by asking whether sound arguments are always good arguments. Since all sound arguments are valid and have true premises, and since all valid arguments are truth-preserving, it follows that the conclusion of every sound argument is true. Even so, sound arguments of the form "*p*, therefore *p*" can hardly be used to justify our belief in *p*. Thus, at least in the broad sense, good arguments must always be *non-circular*. It is for this reason that we say that the fallacy of *arguing in a circle* (or as it is also known, the fallacy of *petitio principii*, or *begging the question*) occurs whenever an argument illegitimately assumes or presupposes the very proposition that it is supposed to be proving.

Throughout history, two versions of this fallacy have often been identified. According to the *dependency conception*, an argument is circular whenever the conclusion is presupposed by some premiss, in the sense that the premiss depends on the conclusion as part of the evidence that supports it. According to the *equivalence conception*, an argument is circular whenever the conclusion itself is tacitly or explicitly assumed as one of the premises.

Can all circular arguments be identified and explained solely as a result of their logical form? If so, does it also follow that the ancient Greek logician Sextus Empiricus was right in claiming that all formally valid arguments are valid only because they assume the very proposition that they are trying to prove? Many logicians, including Aristotle, John Stuart Mill, and Augustus De Morgan, have disagreed with Sextus on this point, arguing that no valid argument with non-superfluous, multiple premises will be circular. At the same time, we also saw some evidence to the effect that the difference between the dependency version and the equivalence version of the fallacy may not turn out to be significant. If so, this helps further justify our confidence in the claim that not all valid arguments fall prey to the fallacy of *petitio principii*.

Weblinks

Stanford Encyclopedia of Philosophy—Informal Logic
plato.stanford.edu/entries/logic-informal/
The Nizkor Project—Begging the Question
www.nizkor.org/features/fallacies/begging-the-question.html

Notes

1. Sextus Empiricus, *Outlines of Pyrrhonism*, ch. 17.

2. Of course, Sue might have other reservations about Bill's argument as well. The argument seems, at least in part, to be an argument from authority (the authority of scripture), and so it might also fall prey to the *ad verecundiam* fallacy.

3. Irving M. Copi, *Introduction to Logic*, 7th ed., (New York and London: Macmillan Publishing Co. and Collier Macmillan Publishers, 1986), 101.

4. From Richard Whately, *Elements of Logic* (London, 1826); reprinted in Irving M. Copi, *Introduction to Logic*, 7th ed., (New York and London: Macmillan Publishing Co. and Collier Macmillan Publishers, 1986), 101.

5. Augustus De Morgan, *Formal Logic* (London: Taylor and Walton, 1847), 254.

6. Alfred Sidgwick, *Fallacies* (New York: D. Appleton & Co., 1884), 194.

7. Aristotle, *Posterior Analytics*, 72b, 5–73a, 20.

8. John Stuart Mill, *A System of Logic*, bk. 2, ch. 3, §1.

9. Augustus De Morgan, *Formal Logic* (London: Taylor and Walton, 1847), 254.

10. Ibid., 257.

11. In ancient times, the Stoics argued about a related issue when they argued about whether there can exist a one-premiss argument. Antipater of Tarsus (fl.c.150 BCE) led the group that stood for the existence of one-premiss arguments such as "Socrates is a father, therefore Socrates is male." The opposition maintained that this argument should be amplified to read "If Socrates is a father, then Socrates is male; Socrates is a father; therefore Socrates is male." See William and Martha Kneale, *The Development of Logic* (Oxford: Clarendon Press, 1962), 163.

12. As stated, this is not quite correct. For example, alert readers may have noticed that even *Modus Ponens* arguments will have superfluous premisses if the conclusion is a necessary truth. Similarly, if p and q are identical, then the conditional premiss, $p \supset q$, will also be superfluous. But what we can say is that all *Modus Ponens* arguments that are valid *qua modus ponens* arguments (i.e., that are valid because of the form, *Modus Ponens*) are multi-premiss arguments without superfluous premisses.

13. Augustus De Morgan, *Formal Logic* (London: Taylor and Walton, 1847), 237.

14. Ibid.

15. Ibid.

16. Sextus Empiricus, *Outlines of Pyrrhonism*, ch. 17.

17. Augustus De Morgan, *Formal Logic* (London: Taylor and Walton, 1847), 259.

CHAPTER 11

Arguments from Authority

IN MANY contexts, the fallacious appeal to arguments from authority is ever-threatening. The bold assertion, "Authority X says so!" is often an argument clincher. Yet too often it is effective in countering an opponent's argument for the wrong reasons. In fact, it is often difficult to know how best to deal with the citation of authorities. As a result, numerous logic texts indicate that any appeal to authority is fallacious.

In contrast, we will try to show in this chapter that appeals to authority are sometimes appropriate and sometimes not. After examining why this is so we will develop some guidelines for dealing with arguments from authority. We will also consider a number of related issues having to do with consistency, and we will discuss how, in many cases, appeals to authority can legitimately assist us in our search for truth.

1. Five Conditions Governing Arguments from Authority

Albert Einstein was often criticized for his involvement in non-scientific matters. Being a sincere man, he would try to give honest answers to questions from reporters about political, ethical, or religious matters. But because he was not an expert in these areas, some people thought that he should not speak out publicly about them. Even so, because of his prestige as an authority in physics, many others tended to take his pronouncements in these areas very seriously, and his remarks often made headlines. So it is with experts. We value their opinions in certain areas because of their expertise in these areas, but by a kind of "halo effect" their pronouncements in other areas, which may be altogether unconnected to their areas of expertise, are escalated in credibility. Appealing to expertise is not wrong, but such appeals can go wrong in numerous ways if we are not careful. The problem is aggravated by the narrowness of many fields of expertise.

Even the most impeccable appeal to expertise must be limited, for experts can be, and sometimes are, mistaken. For example, in the Middle Ages, the writings of Aristotle were very often taken as sacrosanct; his was the last word on many subjects. Yet subsequent developments in experimental science have tended to erode

Aristotle's authority. Thus, perhaps there is some truth in the observation that, ever since the erosion of Aristotle's authority, Western society has tended to be suspicious of authorities.

In the modern world there are many highly specialized fields of knowledge. Often, because of lack of time or resources, we are forced to accept the opinions of suitably qualified experts. You may question your physician's diagnosis, or ask for a second or third opinion, but in the end you listen to your doctors. In short, it is rational to trust the diagnosis of a well-qualified practitioner who has more authority on this matter than to trust your own inexpert speculations. Without the years of education and research required, it is difficult to understand many advanced subjects. So, if a body of experts tends to agree on certain propositions in those subjects, it is reasonable to think that they are likely to be right.

An appeal to authority is rarely—if ever—conclusive in every way, but it does alter the preponderance of evidence and the burden of proof. If we have to make a significant diplomatic or political decision regarding a particular nation, it is wise to take into account the testimony of someone who knows the relevant facts about the culture and current affairs of that nation. It makes better sense to be guided by advice and information from knowledgeable sources than to make a decision on the basis of ignorance or uninformed guesswork. However, some experts are more reliable than others, and some would-be experts are no experts at all. Many an appeal to expertise can mislead. When it does, we say that we have an example of the *ad verecundiam* fallacy.

In fact, several things can go wrong when appealing to authorities. Thus, what many logic textbooks call the *ad verecundiam* is, in reality, an umbrella term for several more specific errors of argument. Below, we cite five conditions that must be met for any legitimate appeal to arguments from authority. Each condition represents one particular way in which such an appeal can go wrong.

The Fallacy of Arguments from Authority

An *ad verecundiam* fallacy occurs whenever a conclusion is drawn, or invited to be drawn, on the basis of a deficient appeal to, or use of, the expert opinion of an authority.

Five Conditions for Legitimate Arguments from Authority

1. The authority must have special competence in an area, and not simply glamour, prestige, or popularity.

2. The judgment of the authority must be within his or her special field of competence, not in some other area.

3. The authority must be interpreted correctly.

4. Direct evidence must be available, at least in principle.

5. A consensus technique is required for adjudicating disagreements among equally qualified authorities.

Condition 1 – The Authority Must Have Special Competence in an Area, and Not Simply Glamour, Prestige, or Popularity

Many of the appeals to authority typically seen in the media and elsewhere are really appeals to prestige or popularity. Thus, it is sometimes difficult to decide when a putative expert actually has the required special competence. This difficulty cannot be overemphasized. In many areas, it may be doubtful that there are any genuine authorities. In other areas, the means of evaluating the degree of expertise may be meagre or only poorly understood. Even in those areas where criteria of special competence are relatively exact, there can be difficulty in rating the degree of expert competence. Even so, for all its roughness, a provisional method of rating competence might be based on the following three criteria:

- access to a record of previous predictions on the subject at hand in order to judge how successful a given authority has been in the past.

- access to a record of hypothetical predictions whenever a record of previous predictions is not available. This might include some type of test or examination that the purported expert may have undergone that was designed to rate the expert's degree of competence in this area.

- access to a record of other types of qualifications, including degrees, professional qualifications, testimony of colleagues or other experts, or to a record of familiarity with the area of expertise. Such criteria, it is expected, will vary considerably from area to area.

We can now ask a number of specific questions based upon these three criteria. First, if holding an important post or position is relevant to expertise in a particular area, we can ask whether an appointment to that post is a desirable one and, if so, how the appointment was made. Was the expert appointed by a committee of experts, or was the appointment based on politics or popularity? Second, if a degree is relevant, what school is the degree from? Is it an earned degree or an honourary one? What are the parameters that determine a good school in this area? Third, what sort of awards or grants has this person won to sponsor his or her research? Have they been merit-based awards, or other types of awards? Fourth, has the expert published findings in books or journals? If in journals, have these publications been refereed by other qualified experts? If the expert has published books, have they been favourably reviewed by other experts, including experts who can be expected to be opposed to the published views? Do other experts in the area refer to or acknowledge this expert's findings? Fifth, what do the expert's professional colleagues think about him or her? Are the colleagues generally thought to be honest and reliable?

Condition 2 – The Judgment of the Authority Must Be within His or Her Special Field of Competence, Not in Some other Area

Typically, the most blatant of fallacious appeals to authority occur when a legitimate expert in a given area makes a judgment that does not fall within his or her field of expertise. Yet if added credibility is given to his or her judgment simply because he or she is an expert in some area, we say that a fallacy has occurred. Of course, in many cases it may be difficult to decide whether your question actually falls within a domain that admits of some particular kind of expertise. Even in areas in which the judgment of an expert is considered more valuable than the judgment of a layperson, a great deal of subjectivity may still remain.

An economic anecdote will serve as an example. The famous economist John Maynard Keynes "was having dinner with Professor Max Planck, the mathematical genius who was responsible for the development of quantum mechanics, one of the more bewildering achievements of the human mind. Planck turned to Keynes and told him that he had once considered going into economics himself. But he had decided against it—it was too hard.... Keynes repeated the story with relish to a friend back at Cambridge. 'Why, that's odd,' said the friend. 'Bertrand Russell was telling me just the other day that he'd also thought about going into economics. But he decided it was too easy.'"[1]

Condition 3 – The Authority Must Be Interpreted Correctly

In an appeal to authority, common pitfalls include misquotation, misrepresentation, and inadequate explanation of an expert's expressed opinion. Subtle changes in emphasis can be misleading and important. If the claim is in the form of a direct quotation, it must be quoted in its proper context. In this context, De Morgan warns us of six problems relevant to the citing of sources:

1. "It is not uncommon, in disputation, to fall into the fallacy of making out conclusions for others by supplying missing premises. One says that A is B; another will take for granted that he must believe B is C, and will therefore consider him as maintaining that A is C."[2]

2. "Again, as to subjects in which men go in parties, it is not very uncommon to take one premise from some individuals of a party, another from others, and to fix the logical conclusion of the two upon the whole party: when perhaps the conclusion is denied by all, some of whom deny the first premise by affirming the second, while the rest deny the second by affirming the first."[3]

3. "Quotation is [not] obligatory, though highly desirable: but the reader must remember, when there is only citation, that it is not the author cited who speaks, but the person who brings [the author] forward ... If the citer be honest, the passage in question exists: if judicious, it is to the effect stated.

Consequently whenever the citer's honesty or judgment is expressly in question, no mere citation is admissible."[4]

4. "Perhaps the greatest and most dangerous vice of the day, in the matter of reference, is the practice of citing citations, and quoting quotations, as if they came from the original sources, instead of being only copies."[5]

5. "Moreover, it is dangerous to truth to shorten without notice, in as much as those who quote the quotation will be apt to do the same thing; that is, thinking they have the whole passage, to shorten it further.... Unjustifiable as unnoted omissions may be, still more so are additions and alterations."[6]

6. "Omission of context, preceding or following the quotation, may alter its character entirely: and this is one of the most frequent of the fallacies of reference, both intentional and unintentional."[7]

There is also the danger that an outdated opinion may be cited. If an expert has changed his or her mind, the earlier opinion loses much of its force. In other cases, the appeal to authority may be misleading if certain qualifications added by the expert are omitted or suppressed. These qualifications are particularly important where the expert's assessment of probability is a conditional one. An expert might make an argument conditional on several contingencies. If these contingencies are not preserved when reporting that expert's judgment, the report is misleading. Also, if the authority delivers a judgment using technical terminology, that terminology might have to be rendered into a more readily intelligible form. This can be especially important when a panel of experts is attempting to come to an agreement on an interdisciplinary matter. Injudicious technical jargon can be disruptive and should be avoided. Yet, in doing so, we need to be careful. Many fallacious appeals to authority trade on ambiguities, vagueness, or misunderstanding arising from the translation of technical terminology into more accessible language.

Condition 4 – Direct Evidence Must Be Available, at Least in Principle

For an appeal to authority to be adequate, the authority must base his or her judgment on actual, relevant, and objective evidence within the area concerned. This evidence need not be fully available to the layperson; but where there is doubt, the layperson or other expert must, in principle, be able to investigate. In other words, no chain of appeals to authority can regress forever. Eventually some evidence other than appeals to authority must be cited. Every authority must be able to cite some non-authoritative evidence that his or her judgment is objective and well founded.

For example, suppose we have a panel of experts in a given domain of experience; suppose also that the judgment of one panel member on a certain question falls well outside the range of consensus. In an evaluation of that particular judgment, evidence must be made available for the evaluation of the other experts on the panel. Similarly, where we have reason to believe that some panel members may not be trustworthy, we should call for an evaluation of the degree to which their judgments are based on the relevant evidence.

Condition 5 – A Consensus Technique Is Required for Adjudicating Disagreements among Equally Qualified Authorities

An obvious problem with expert consultation is that authorities are notorious for their ability to disagree. Yet since two (or more) heads are better than one, when faced with disagreement, the rational method for obtaining the required information (inconclusive though it may be) is to search for consensus. In fact, the repeated search for consensus, after mutual inspection of the grounds for disagreement, may have a convergence effect. Exactly how to establish consensus, or how to deal with inconsistency, is something that we consider later in this chapter.

Exercise 11.1

1. Identify any errors or shortcomings in the following appeals to authority:

    (a) In a press release, an eminent obstetrician states that wantonly doing away with the unborn by allowing abortion on demand violates the principle of the sacredness of human life. She is the author of four books on obstetrics and is a fellow of the Royal College of Physicians and Surgeons. Hence we can say with authority that abortion must be wrong.

    (b) A noted art historian claims in a recent newspaper article that *Frog Recumbent* is the finest statue in Western art. This seems odd, but he is an expert and so he must be right.

    (c) In a series of high-profile television advertisements, a famous baseball player recommends purchasing your next vehicle

    from a particular company. Not only will such a purchase be economical, he tells us, but this company makes the best sport utility vehicle in its class.

    (d) The famous philosopher Socrates was noted for his injunction "Know thyself." Here we have an early exponent of psychiatric examination and therapy.

    (e) The government has recently claimed that no financial improprieties occurred during the last election campaign. In fact, prior to sealing the relevant records, not just one but several government economists and accountants reviewed these documents. They all concluded that everything was in order. Given their unanimity of opinion, it is difficult to believe that they could be mistaken.

2. A Case Study

Professors Robert Gordon Shepherd and Erich Goode conducted a study to discover whether scientists whose work is cited by the press are those who have undertaken original research on a given subject.[8] Since they needed a topic that was of interest both to scientists and the general public, they chose to examine the work of scientists who were conducting research on marijuana use. Among other things, these scientists have debated whether marijuana causes brain damage, and these findings have regularly been of public interest.

Shepherd and Goode based their study on a sample of 271 scientific articles and 275 newspaper and magazine articles published over a five-year period. The scientific articles were selected from *Index Medicus*; the newspaper and magazine articles were chosen from a range of well-known newspapers and magazines. To gauge the standing of a scientist and his or her work in the scientific community, Shepherd and Goode calculated the number of citations that each scientist had received in the *Science Citation Index*. They then studied two types of popular articles on marijuana, both of which involved scientific experts. First there were "news stories," which reported the results of specific scientific studies; second, there were "summary articles," which summarized the state of research on marijuana-related issues.

Their findings were interesting. Shepherd and Goode discovered that there were very few news-story articles, and even fewer scientific publications mentioned in the news stories, but that those publications that were cited did represent research that was well-known in the scientific community. It would appear that in the period under investigation, even topical scientific research received very little attention from the press, but what coverage it did receive was of high quality when measured by the frequency of citation by other scientists.

However, most of the popular articles studied were of the summary type. Here, the correlation between citations in the press and those in scientific journals formed a dismal picture. Of the ten marijuana researchers most often cited in the scientific literature, only one appeared in the list of the ten most publicized authorities in the press. Of the ten press "authorities," seven had not published anything at all in the scientific literature. The results indicated that the press was not always interested in seeking out the views of the most scientifically influential researchers. Spokespersons cited in the press were often selected because they were the administrative heads of health-related agencies, faculties, or institutes.

One relevant factor seems to be that the administrator or director is thought by the public to be the "boss" of the organization; his or her title is thus most effective as a citation since it carries with it the weighty endorsement of authority. Why quote a mere working scientist when you can quote the head of a whole institute?

According to Shepherd and Goode, there is another factor that contributes to the press' tendency to rely on "authorities" who are not really authorities in a specific area of research at all. They theorize that it is not easy for most non-experts to distinguish between the specialized scientific disciplines involved. Being a doctor, for example, seems to make any physician an "instant expert" on all aspects of medical treatment and drug use.

The irony of it, Shepherd and Goode conclude, is that reporters generally pride themselves on going directly to primary sources when they write their stories. In other areas ranging from athletics to literature, they will interview the players and the novelists themselves, but to report scientific research involves much more work and study. The reporter must go to the library and search out technical reports, research indexes, and so forth. It saves time—and possibly fruitless effort—simply to talk to someone who is conspicuous, someone with credentials, or someone that the public will readily acknowledge to be an expert.

Flashback on...
The *Ad Verecundiam*

IF YOU have consulted the flashback on the *ad hominem* in chapter 1, and the flashback on the *ad ignorantiam* in chapter 3, you will have seen that John Locke, in his *An Essay Concerning Human Understanding*, called attention to certain arguments with these words, "it may be worth our while a little to reflect on *four sorts of arguments*, that men in their reasonings with others do ordinarily make use of, to prevail on their ascent; or at least so to awe them, as to silence their opposition."[9] Two of these arguments are the *ad hominem* and the *ad ignorantiam*, but first on Locke's list is a kind of argument for which he coined the term "*ad verecundiam*." Says Locke, when speaking against those whose

> learning, eminency, power, or some other cause has gained a name, and settled their reputation in the common esteem with some kind of authority ... 'tis thought a breach of modesty for others to derogate any way from it, and question the authority of men, who are in possession of it. This is apt to be censured, as carrying with it too much of pride, when a man does not readily yield to the determination of approved authors, which is wont to be received with respect and submission by others: and 'tis looked upon as insolence, for a man to set up, and adhere to his own opinion, against the current stream of antiquity; or to put it

in the balance against that of some learned doctor, or otherwise approved writer. Whoever backs his tenets with such authorities, thinks he ought thereby to carry the cause, and is ready to style it impudence in any one, who shall stand out against them. This, I think, may be called *argumentum ad verecundiam*.[10]

Here, as with Locke's *ad hominem* and *ad ignorantiam*, the *argumentum ad verecundiam* is not a fallacy. Of course it would be a fallacy if it we were required to accept something as true on the basis of "an authority insufficient to assure us of this truth [i.e., insufficient to show its truth]," as the Port Royal logicians nicely put it in their book, *Logic or the Art of Thinking* (1662), and which has the ring of the modern analysis about it. In contrast, for Locke, whether an *ad verecundiam* argument succeeds or fails depends on the extent to which it persuades an opponent to concede the proposition in question, or to silence his opposition to it. Indeed, the word *verecundiam* does not even mean "authority," but rather "modesty." For Locke, argument in this sense is thus a matter of the deference that our modesty as reasoners allegedly requires.

The basic structure of Locke's *ad verecundiam* is this: two parties are disputing a proposition, *p*; at some point the proponent of *p* then makes the following argument:

▶

Proposition p is endorsed by people who are experts on this matter

_____

Therefore, it is immodest of you, indeed it is a kind of insolence, to persist in your opposition; for, in resisting p, you resist the eminency and expertise of these "learned doctors."

There can be no suggestion that Locke thinks this type of argument actually proves the opponent of p to be immodest. Locke himself displayed plenty of resistance toward the philosophical doctrines of the "learned doctors" of the medieval period. He would not think it immodest to oppose anyone, provided that he had good reason to think them wrong.

His point, therefore, is entirely tactical. He is pointing out that this is a method whose function is to subdue one's opponent, to get one's opponent to believe that his resistance to p would be immodest. Whether such an argument is appropriate will therefore depend upon the details of each individual case.

The modern ad verecundiam thus bears little resemblance to the argument Locke refers to by the same name. This is not, however, to suggest that it is a strictly modern invention. In fact, a good resemblance of the modern version of the ad verecundiam can be found in the Port Royal logicians' "sophisms of authority and manners," as presented in their Logic or the Art of Thinking (see part 3, chapter 8). As mentioned previously, sophisms of authority involve inferences to the effect that something is true on "an authority insufficient to assure us of this truth [i.e., insufficient to show its truth]." However, the Port Royalists distinguished two subcases of this fallacy, neither of which is strictly identical to the modern ad verecundiam. In the first subcase, the fallacy of authority results from acceding to "doctrines spread by sword and bloodshed," which is more akin to the modern ad baculum fallacy. In the second subcase, it is the fallacy of yielding to an argument of the form, "the majority hold this opinion; therefore, it is the truest," an error that is more akin to the modern ad populum.

In contrast, so-called "sophisms of manner" have more to do with the modern ad verecundiam than do sophisms of authority. The Port Royal logicians conceded, "Granted, if any error is pardonable it is the error of excessive deference to the opinion of a good man." Even so, they continue, "an absurd yet more common delusion is that of deferring to a man because of his birth, wealth, or high office."

How can it be that Locke's ad verecundiam is not a fallacy, while the Port Royalist sophism of manner is? After all, the abstract structure of Locke's ad verecundiam and the Port Royalist's sophism of manner appears to be the same:

Authority X asserts that p

_____

Therefore, it is appropriate to accede to p.

What the Port Royalists condemn, and Locke does not, seems to be the same thing, namely accepting a proposition on the basis of the stations of those who advance it. What explains this difference?

The answer is that the authority that the Port Royal logicians condemn is that of superior social rank. In contrast, the authority that Locke does not condemn is that of superior learnedness and expertise, and this makes all the difference.

3. Towards a Model of the Argument in Question

We have looked at some ways in which *ad verecundiam* arguments can go wrong. We turn now to the question of what kind of argument could constitute a correct argument from authority. In previous chapters we have looked at two ways of evaluating arguments, namely using deductive and inductive logics, and it is natural to think that one of these two logics may be relevant to our current concern. For example, the Australian logician C.L. Hamblin has suggested that, when analyzing arguments from authority, we should begin with the deductively valid form of argument, "Everything X says is true, and X said that p, therefore p."[11] From this beginning, Hamblin says, we will also be able to construct weaker, though still not fallacious, forms of the argument from authority by simply weakening our first premiss.

The American philosopher Wesley Salmon disagrees with Hamblin. Salmon asserts that appeals to authority cannot be deductively valid because no authority is infallible or omniscient.[12] Since it can never be the case that "Everything X says is true" is true, this type of statement can never form a premiss in a legitimate argument from authority. Thus, in place of this premiss we will have to substitute premisses such as "Most of what X says is true" or "Almost all of what X says is true." As a result, it will always be possible for the premisses of an *ad verecundiam* argument to be true while its conclusion may be false. According to Salmon, the appeal to authority is thus best thought of as a kind of inductive argument. He suggests the form: "The vast majority of statements made by X concerning subject s are true; p is a statement made by X concerning subject s; therefore p is true."

Who is correct, Hamblin or Salmon? Given our previous discussion, it seems likely that even the most useful appeals to authority will be fallible. We have seen the various ways that such appeals can go wrong: such appeals depend on the sort of authority being consulted, on whether an opinion is being given on a subject the expert is knowledgeable about, and on how the authority's opinion squares with that of other authorities. Since it also happens that experts may disagree, it cannot be the case that every pronouncement they make will be true. Perhaps, if we find an authority who is perfectly reliable in every possible instance—an oracle or prophet—the argument from authority can be treated as a form of deductive argument, but most of the authorities we appeal to—in science, medicine, and so forth—are known to be fallible. Thus it appears that deductive logic is not the appropriate standard for evaluating arguments from authority.

What about inductive logic? As an inductively strong argument, an appeal to authority might look like this: "The vast majority (more than 90 percent) of statements made by X concerning subject s are true; p is a statement made by X concerning subject s; therefore $Pr(p) > 9/10$." Although this form of analysis may look appealing, here, too, we have a problem, and a familiar one. For suppose we have another expert, Y, who claims that not-p is true. This gives us another inductively strong argument, namely "The vast majority (more than 90 percent) of statements made by Y concerning subject *s* are true; not-*p* is a statement made by *Y* concerning subject *s*; therefore Pr(~*p*) > 9/10." Recalling the negation rule for inductive logic, we know that Pr(~*p*) = 1 − Pr(*p*). Applying this rule to the pronouncements of our authorities, we then note that if Pr(*p*) > 9/10, then Pr(~*p*) ≤ 1/10, and if Pr(~*p*) > 9/10, then Pr(*p*) ≤ 1/10. So here again we have a contradiction, for it cannot be true that the probability of *p* is both greater than 9/10 and less than or equal to 1/10. Legitimate authorities do disagree, but this hardly means that their pronouncements can have both high and low probability values. The laws of inductive logic do not allow this any more than the laws of deductive logic allow contradictions to be true. It thus appears that inductive logic does not provide an appropriate standard for understanding arguments from authority either. What shall we do?

Perhaps the reason neither deductive nor inductive logic appears to be of value in this context is that both deductive and inductive logic study only argument forms. Yet, in this case, something more than logical form may be at stake. In other words, it may be that the *ad verecundiam* is sensitive to subject matter in a way that formal deductive and inductive logics are not. If this is correct, a claim made by authority *X* may be assigned an entirely different value than a similar claim made by authority *Y*. In such cases, more than the truth value, or the probability value, of the argument's constituent propositions will be relevant. In other words, we must also consider which authority backs *p*, since what is asserted by one authority may be quite different in value from what is asserted by another, competing authority.

Before considering this point further, it is helpful to make one further preliminary distinction. This is a distinction between *de facto* and *de jure* appeals to authority. A *de facto* appeal is an appeal to factual testimony or knowledge; it is characteristic of the usual appeal to expertise. A *de jure* appeal is very different. Sometimes we refer to the titular, legislative, or structure-of-command authority invested in an individual; this authority is not conferred because of the individual's particular expertise. Rather, it comes about because of his or her position. For example, ministers and ships' captains are invested with the authority to perform marriage ceremonies, while ordinary citizens are not. In the proper circumstances, if such a duly constituted authority says, "You are now husband and wife" then, indeed, you are husband and wife; saying that it is so is all it takes to make it so. Notice that in such a situation there is at least something of the logical tightness that characterizes deductive arguments; but such *de jure* pronouncements by authorities are quite different from the *de facto* arguments from authority that we have been examining up until this point.

Many *ad verecundiam* fallacies occur as a result of a confusion between *de jure* and *de facto* authorities. Over the years, many official sources have been, by custom, invested with infallibility and finality. Religious authority, especially, has been used in this fashion to suppress heretical, disloyal, or radical opinions. In contrast, in any legitimate *de facto* appeal to authority, criteria of special competence and expertise must be met. In addition, as we saw in condition 4, hard evidence must always be available, at least in principle, and, where necessary, the putative expert must be able to cite this evidence.

> ### *De Facto* versus *De Jure* Authorities
>
> A *de facto* authority is an expert in a given field. Statements made by such authorities are true as a result of their expert knowledge. A *de jure* authority is a person who has particular abilities or knowledge as a result of his or her title or office rather than his or her particular expertise. A *de facto* authority, for example a forensic accountant who declares "You are entitled to a payment of $10,000 from your employer," may do so as a result of a detailed study of the relevant financial documents. In contrast, a *de jure* authority, for example a trial court judge who declares "You are entitled to a payment of $10,000 from your employer," may do so simply as a result of the power he has to find in your favour. One type of *ad verecundiam* fallacy results from confusing these two types of authority.

Even so, we have now eliminated elementary deductive and inductive logics as models of argument appropriate for studying the *de facto* version of the *argumentum ad verecundiam*. Where should we look next? The short answer is that we will have to find a third model or standard of argument.

4. Inconsistency

In previous chapters we have seen that classical logic does not provide much help in situations where we are confronted with false premises. It is even less helpful when our premises are inconsistent. Since we defined a valid argument as one in which it is logically impossible for the premises to be true and the conclusion false, it follows that any argument with inconsistent premises will be valid in this rather technical sense. In such an argument it will always be logically impossible for the premises to be true and the conclusion to be false. In other words, an inconsistent set of premises implies everything!

For example, consider the set of propositions {Bill has red hair, Bill does not have red hair}. This pair of propositions is inconsistent since it is not possible for both propositions to be true together. Adding more propositions to the set will not remove this inconsistency. The only way to remove it is to remove one of the propositions. This is why, when we are confronted with an inconsistency, classical deductive logic is not of much help. It can identify the inconsistency, but it does not tell us which proposition to remove or what to do next.

Nor will inductive logic be of much help. Recall that the probability of p given q is defined as the $\Pr(p \wedge q) / \Pr(q)$, but if q is inconsistent its probability is zero, and dividing by zero is simply not permitted. So, again, we are stuck.

Despite this, we need to know how best to respond when confronted with an inconsistency. As we have seen, when dealing with arguments from authority the authorities we appeal to may occasionally disagree; what they say is therefore collectively inconsistent. Moreover,

> ### Consistency and Inconsistency
> A set of propositions is *consistent* if and only if it is possible for all of the propositions contained in the set to be true together. A set of propositions is *inconsistent* if and only if it is not consistent.

in the case of a circumstantial *ad hominem,* we are confronted with an allegation of inconsistency, and we want to know how to deal with such an accusation. We therefore need a third approach to argument, one that is neither classically deductive nor classically inductive, and one that will help us understand the *ad verecundiam* and other fallacies that involve sets of premises that may be inconsistent.

However, before we look for a new approach to argument, we should first be sure that we can successfully identify inconsistent premiss sets. As we have defined it, an inconsistent set of propositions is one in which it is not possible for all of the propositions contained in the set to be jointly true. Thus the most elementary form of inconsistency is that represented by $p \land \sim p$. Recalling the truth table for negation, we see that it is in the very nature of classical negation that p and $\sim p$ cannot be true together:

p	**~p**	**p ∧ ~p**
T	F	F
F	T	F

Generally, inconsistent sets of propositions can be shown to be truth-functionally inconsistent in just this way: if you form a conjunction of all those propositions contained in the set, and if the resultant conjunction cannot be true, the original set must have been inconsistent. In other words, given a truth-functionally inconsistent set, the conjunction of its members will yield a truth table in which every row is false. In all other cases the set is truth-functionally consistent. For example, given a set of the form $\{p \lor q, \sim p, \sim q\}$, we construct a truth table for the conjunction of all three propositional variables, $[(p \lor q) \land \sim p] \land \sim q$, as follows:

p	**q**	**p ∨ q**	**~p**	**~q**	**(p ∨ q) ∧ ~p**	**[(p ∨ q) ∧ ~p] ∧ ~q**
T	T	T	F	F	F	F
T	F	T	F	T	F	F
F	T	T	T	F	T	F
F	F	F	T	T	F	F

For a conjunction to be true, each conjunct must be true; but if we scan the rows for our three conjuncts—$p \lor q$, $\sim p$, and $\sim q$—we see that in no row are all three true. Hence $[(p \lor q) \land \sim p] \land \sim q$ is false in every row. We conclude that our original set is inconsistent.

Now that we can identify inconsistency,[13] we need a way to deal with it. As we have seen, adding propositions to an inconsistent set will be of no help. Instead, we need a way to remove some of the propositions from the set. To help us in this regard, we introduce the notion of a *maximally consistent subset*[14] of an inconsistent set of propositions—that is, a subset that is consistent but that immediately becomes inconsistent if any additional propositions from the original set are added to it. For example, consider again the set $\{p \vee q, \sim p, \sim q\}$, which we know to be inconsistent; $\{p \vee q\}$ is a consistent subset, but it is not a maximally consistent subset, because we can add $\sim p$ to it and the result, $\{p \vee q, \sim p\}$, will still not be inconsistent. To check this, construct a truth table for the conjunction $(p \vee q) \wedge \sim p$ and you will see that it is consistent. But can we go any further? Suppose we add $\sim q$. This gives us the original set, which was inconsistent. So that is as far as we can go. Therefore $\{p \vee q, \sim p\}$ is a maximally consistent subset. By similar reasoning, we can see that $\{p \vee q, \sim q\}$ is a maximally consistent subset, and so is $\{\sim p, \sim q\}$. These are the only such sets.

The test for maximally consistent subsets of some original set of propositions is thus quite simple. Take each element of the original set one at a time. Test each for inconsistency. Then, for those that are consistent, keep adding other members from the original set, one at a time, until you reach an inconsistent set. The set constructed immediately before you reached an inconsistent set was a maximally consistent subset. A maximally consistent subset is one that is as large as it can possibly be without becoming inconsistent.

There is an easy way to find all of the maximally consistent subsets using truth tables. Scan each row of the truth table and list each proposition that is true in that row; this will result in a listing of all the consistent subsets. From these, those sets that are included as subsets of other subsets may then be eliminated. Those that remain are the maximally consistent subsets. For example, consider once again the truth table for the set $\{p \vee q, \sim p, \sim q\}$:

p	*q*	*p* ∨ *q*	*~p*	*~q*
T	T	T	F	F
T	F	**T**	F	**T**
F	T	**T**	**T**	F
F	F	F	**T**	**T**

Scanning the fourth row, we see that $\sim p$ and $\sim q$ are both true. Then, in the third row, we see that $p \vee q$ and $\sim p$ are both true. Next, in the second row, we see that $p \vee q$ and $\sim q$ are true. Finally, we notice that in the first row only $p \vee q$ is true. Comparing the sets $\{\sim p, \sim q\}$, $\{p \vee q, \sim p\}$, $\{p \vee q, \sim q\}$ and $\{p \vee q\}$, we then see that $\{p \vee q\}$ is already included as a subset of both $\{p \vee q, \sim p\}$ and $\{p \vee q, \sim q\}$. Thus we need not include it in our list since it is not maximal. By similar considerations, we can then be assured that the three subsets that remain form a complete listing of all the maximally consistent subsets.

Exercise 11.2

1. Determine whether each of the following sets of propositions is consistent or inconsistent:

   (a) $\{A, \sim A\}$

   (b) $\{\sim A, \sim B, A \supset B\}$

   (c) $\{A \supset B, B \supset C, \sim(A \vee B)\}$

   (d) $\{A \supset B, C \supset B, \sim B, C \wedge A\}$

   (e) $\{A \vee B, \sim(A \wedge B)\}$

   (f) $\{A \equiv (B \vee C), \sim A, \sim B, C\}$

   (g) $\{A, B, C, A \supset B, B \supset C, A \supset D, C \supset \sim D, A \wedge \sim D\}$

   (h) $\{A \supset B, B \supset A, C \equiv B\}$

   (i) $\{A \vee \sim B, B \equiv B, \sim A \supset B\}$

   (j) $\{A \vee \sim B, \sim A, C \supset B, \sim A \supset C, C \wedge \sim C\}$

2. Find all the maximally consistent subsets of each of the sets of propositions that turned out to be inconsistent in question 1 above.

5. Plausibility Screening

Suppose that an authority or group of authorities has made a number of pronouncements but that the set of propositions vouched for by these authorities is collectively inconsistent. Suppose further that we can rate the plausibility or reliability of these authorities in some comparative way. Is there a rational way to deal with such a situation? One such procedure, developed by the American philosopher Nicholas Rescher, is called *plausibility screening.*[15] In essence, Rescher's method is to scan the maximally consistent subsets and give preference to those that include the maximum number of highly plausible elements. This general process can also function in other ways. For example, for some purposes we might want to give preference to those sets that include as few low-plausibility elements as possible. It depends on whether our goal is to maximize overall plausibility or minimize overall implausibility. The two policies are not identical.

Suppose that we are given a fragment of what appears to be a thirteenth-century manuscript on logic. It has been examined by three experts on historical manuscripts on the logic of this period, Professors *X*, *Y*, and *Z*. Let us say that we can rate their respective pronouncements on a scale of one to ten as follows: *X* has a comparative plausibility value of eight, which is highly reliable; *Y* has a value of five, which is fairly reliable; and *Z* has a value of two, which is somewhat reliable. Professor *Y* ventures the opinion that the manuscript was authored by William of Sherwood, the thirteenth-century Oxford logician, or by William of Ockham, his near contemporary. Professor *X* asserts that if the document were authored by William of Sherwood then it would definitely make reference to Aristotle's doctrines on logic. But, he adds, it does not anywhere make reference to Aristotle's doctrines. Professor *Z* points out that if the document was authored by William of Ockham, then from what we know of William of Ockham, it would include references to Aristotle's doctrines, too.

We are supposing, then, that these authorities vouch for the following propositions:

Authority *X* (who has a plausibility value of 8): *A* ⊃ *B*, ~*B*
Authority *Y* (who has a plausibility value of 5): *A* ∨ *C*
Authority *Z* (who has a plausibility value of 2): *C* ⊃ *B*,

where

A = The manuscript was authored by William of Sherwood
B = The manuscript makes reference to Aristotle's doctrines on logic
C = The manuscript was authored by William of Ockham.

The set of given propositions, {*A* ⊃ *B*, ~*B*, *A* ∨ *C*, *C* ⊃ *B*}, is inconsistent, as a truth table will show, but it has four maximally consistent subsets as follows:

(1) {*A* ∨ *C*, *A* ⊃ *B*, *C* ⊃ *B* }, rejecting ~*B*
(2) {*A* ∨ *C*, *A* ⊃ *B*, ~ *B* }, rejecting *C* ⊃ *B*
(3) {*A* ∨ *C*, *C* ⊃ *B*, ~ *B* }, rejecting *A* ⊃ *B*
(4) {*A* ⊃ *B*, *C* ⊃ *B*, ~ *B* }, rejecting *A* ∨ *C*.

Notice that (1) and (3) both reject one of the highly plausible pronouncements of *X*. Therefore, given that we want to maximize plausibility, we can eliminate both (1) and (3) as preferable subsets. Looking at the remaining two subsets, we see that we have a choice between rejecting *C* ⊃ *B* (which has plausibility 2) and *A* ∨ *C* (which has plausibility 5). Again, since our policy is to maximize plausibility, we will want to reject any alternative that excludes propositions of relatively high plausibility. So the choice here is straightforward as well. We reject (4) because it excludes *A* ∨ *C*, a proposition that is more plausible than *C* ⊃ *B*, the proposition excluded by (2). All told, then, the most plausible maximally consistent subset is (2). Thus, on this model, the rational way to react to inconsistency in this instance is to accept the pronouncements of *X* and *Y* and reject the opinion of *Z*. Note that the plausibility of (2) suggests that the manuscript was authored by William of Ockham, for (2) logically implies *C*.

Unlike ordinary deductive and inductive logic, plausibility theory thus gives us a way of proceeding even when confronted with inconsistencies. In our example, we can select the most plausible subset by pruning the original, inconsistent set of data. The method of plausibility screening tells us even more, however. If we look at (2) and (4), the preferred subsets in our example, we see that the two propositions *A* ⊃ *B* and ~*B* each appear in *both* (2) and (4). In other words, no matter which of (2) or (4) we decide to accept, we are going to accept *A* ⊃ *B* and ~*B*. These two propositions therefore constitute something akin to a "common denominator." We also see that in this case the pronouncements of *X* have a certain preferred status: no matter whether we reject the opinions of *Z* by rejecting (2), or reject the opinions of *Y* by rejecting (4), we will still be accepting the opinions of *X*. Plausibility screening also tells us that (2) is not consistent with (4), as a truth table will show, and thus that we must choose between (2) and (4). As we saw, in this case it is preferable to select (2); but in choosing either (2) or (4) we will still be accepting the common subset {*A* ⊃ *B*, ~*B*}.

Generally, the method of plausibility screening that we adopt consists of several steps: First, we take the original set of pronouncements of our authorities and test them for consistency by constructing a truth table. If the set is inconsistent, we then determine all the maximally consistent subsets of this set. We then look over the alternatives and reject those that fail to include any high-plausibility propositions. If there is only one left, that will be our preferred set. If there remains more than one, then we systematically reject those sets that tend to exclude the highest plausibility propositions until only one set is left. In the event of a tie, we look to see if there is a common component among the tied sets. As well, we can try to discover whether there is a common component among any number of the maximally consistent subsets that tend to be preferable.

Should it be helpful, we could bend our example to form an illustration of a tie: suppose that Z was assigned a plausibility value of 5. Then (2) and (4) would be tied. Whichever set we rejected, we would be rejecting a proposition of value 5. Both (2) and (4) are preferable to (1) and (3), but we cannot narrow the field down to one proposition. In this context, the best we can say is that we will want to accept $\{A \supset B, \sim B\}$ because it is common to both (2) and (4).

Plausibility Screening: A Summary

Here is an example that illustrates how the method of plausibility screening works. Suppose we have the following pronouncements of three authorities, X, Y, and Z:

Authority X (who has a plausibility value of 9): $A \supset B$, $\sim C$
Authority Y (who has a plausibility value of 7): $B \supset C$, $\sim A$
Authority Z (who has a plausibility value of 2): $A \vee B$, $\sim(A \wedge B)$.

First, we construct a truth table with a column representing the truth values for each proposition in the set of propositions stated by the experts:

	A	B	C	A ⊃ B	~C	B ⊃ C	~A	A ∨ B	~(A ∧ B)
(1)	T	T	T	T	F	T	F	T	F
(2)	T	T	F	T	T	F	F	T	F
(3)	T	F	T	F	F	T	F	T	T
(4)	T	F	F	F	T	T	F	T	T
(5)	F	T	T	T	F	T	T	T	T
(6)	F	T	F	T	T	F	T	T	T
(7)	F	F	T	T	F	T	T	F	T
(8)	F	F	F	T	T	T	T	F	T

Second, we scan the truth table and highlight all combinations of true propositions, omitting only those that are proper subsets of others. Some rows, like (1), (2), (3), and (7), will have true propositions in them, but these patterns of true propositions will already be included in one or more of the other rows. For example, the true propositions in (1) form a subset of those in (5); the true propositions in (2) form a subset of those in (6); the true propositions in (3) form a subset of those in (4); and the true propositions in (7) form a subset of those in (8):

	A	*B*	*C*	*A ⊃ B*	*~C*	*B ⊃ C*	*~A*	*A ∨ B*	*~(A ∧ B)*
(1)	T	T	T	T	F	T	F	T	F
(2)	T	T	F	T	T	F	F	T	F
(3)	T	F	T	F	F	T	F	T	T
(4)	T	F	F	F	**T**	**T**	F	**T**	**T**
(5)	F	T	T	**T**	F	**T**	**T**	**T**	**T**
(6)	F	T	F	**T**	**T**	F	**T**	**T**	**T**
(7)	F	F	T	T	F	T	T	F	T
(8)	F	F	F	**T**	**T**	**T**	**T**	F	**T**

Third, we look at the truth table, one row at a time, and list those propositions that are true in each highlighted row. For example, in (8) we see that the following propositions are true: *A* ⊃ *B*, *~C*, *B* ⊃ *C*, *~A*, and *~(A ∧ B)*. Reading off the true propositions for the remaining rows that contain highlighted propositions, we find that we have a total of four maximally consistent subsets:

(4) {*~C, B ⊃ C, A ∨ B, ~(A ∧ B)*}

(5) {*A ⊃ B, B ⊃ C, ~A, A ∨ B, ~(A ∧ B)*}

(6) {*A ⊃ B, ~C, ~A, A ∨ B, ~(A ∧ B)*}

(8) {*A ⊃ B, ~C, B ⊃ C, ~A, ~(A ∧ B)*}.

Fourth, for each such maximally consistent subset, we list at the right those propositions of the original set that are not included.

(4) {*~C, B ⊃ C, A ∨ B, ~(A ∧ B)*}, rejecting *A* ⊃ *B*, *~A*

(5) {*A ⊃ B, B ⊃ C, ~A, A ∨ B, ~(A ∧ B)*}, rejecting *~C*

(6) {*A ⊃ B, ~C, ~A, A ∨ B, ~(A ∧ B)*}, rejecting *B* ⊃ *C*

(8) {*A ⊃ B, ~C, B ⊃ C, ~A, ~(A ∧ B)*}, rejecting *A ∨ B*.

Fifth, we scan the maximally consistent subsets in order to construct a preference ordering. The general rule here is that any set that rejects a highly plausible proposition should be eliminated. Clearly we can eliminate (4) because it rejects *A* ⊃ *B*, which has a value of 9. Likewise (5) must be eliminated because it rejects *~C*, which also has value 9. That leaves (6) and (8). Here the choice is also clear. Row (6) rejects *B* ⊃ *C* (which has value 7), whereas (8) rejects only *A ∨ B* (which has value 2). On the policy that plausibility is to be maximized, we therefore eliminate (6) and accept (8).

Sixth, in the event of a tie, we look to see if there is a "common denominator" subset that should be accepted even if it is necessary to reject all of the maximally consistent subsets. Looking over the maximally consistent subsets, we see that the subset {*A ⊃ B, ~C, ~A, ~(A ∧ B)*} is common to both (6) and (8). Furthermore, we see that {*~(A ∧ B)*} is common to all four maximally consistent subsets. These common components could serve as tiebreakers, although in this case this is not necessary—(8) stands out as the clear winner. Nonetheless, it is interesting to note that, despite its low individual plausibility, *~(A ∧ B)* is highly acceptable because it is "carried along" in (8) and in every other maximally consistent subset.

Finally, it is worth noting that there may exist undecidable cases. If authority *X* says *p* and authority *Y* says *~p*, and if both authorities are equally reliable and this is all the information we are given, then plausibility screening will not tell us which proposition to accept. It is simply a stalemate, and we have to wait for more information before making our decision about whether to accept or reject *p*.

Exercise 11.3

1. Given the following pronouncements of authorities *X*, *Y*, and *Z*, together with a comparative plausibility rating from 1 to 10 as given below, conduct a plausibility screening in order to determine which maximally consistent sets of propositions are the most plausible.

    (a) Authority *X* (who has a plausibility value of 6): $A \supset B$, ~*C*

    Authority *Y* (who has a plausibility value of 5): $B \supset C$, *A*

    (b) Authority *X* (who has a plausibility value of 8): $A \supset B$, *C*

    Authority *Y* (who has a plausibility value of 5): $B \supset C$, ~*D*

    Authority *Z* (who has a plausibility value of 2): $C \supset D$, *A*

    (c) Authority *X* (who has a plausibility value of 9): $A \supset$ ~*B*

    Authority *Y* (who has a plausibility value of 4): $C \supset$ ~*A*

    Authority *Z* (who has a plausibility value of 2): *C*, *A* ∧ *B*

    (d) Authority *X* (who has a plausibility value of 8): $A \equiv B$

    Authority *Y* (who has a plausibility value of 5): $A \supset$ ~*B*

    Authority *Z* (who has a plausibility value of 1): *A*, *B*

    (e) Authority *X* (who has a plausibility value of 4): $A \equiv B$

    Authority *Y* (who has a plausibility value of 6): $A \supset$ ~*B*

    Authority *Z* (who has a plausibility value of 5): *A*, *B*, *A* ∧ ~*B*

6. Plausible Argument

Up to this point, our approach to arguments from authority has been somewhat negative and circumspect. We saw how to recognize and possibly avoid five kinds of errors when appealing to authorities. We saw that arguments from authority are not best analyzed using either inductive or deductive logic, and we saw how to evaluate conflicts among authorities using the method of plausibility screening. But we still want to know what constitutes a good argument from authority.

Clearly the key notion involved is that of *plausibility*; but what is a plausible argument? How do plausible arguments relate to ordinary deductive and inductive logics? What connectives are involved? What does such an argument operate on, if not truth values or probabilities?

Plausibility theory is not as highly developed or well-entrenched as classical deductive logic. Even so, using the pioneering work of Rescher, it is possible to present a brief sketch of the essentials of the subject. To say that a proposition is *plausible* is not to say that it is true, or even that it is probably true, but only that it is rational to presume it to be true, at least provisionally. This means that it has some evidence in its favour, and that nothing has yet been discovered to show that it is false or unlikely. In other words, it may be tentatively accepted, provided it does not conflict with any other proposition that we have already accepted in our stock of commitments. Thus the plausibility of a proposition has to do not with its intrinsic truth or probability, but with how consistent it is with other propositions that we are prepared to accept. This is why, in the previous section, we adopted the policy of retaining the highly plausible propositions of a set, even if retaining them meant including some cohorts that, individually, were not individually very plausible at all.

In contrast, if your objective is to minimize the risk of error, it would be better to adopt another policy. In this case you should reject all propositions of low plausibility, even if this means rejecting some highly plausible ones as well. The reason for adopting such a policy will become more clear once we understand how plausibility operates over conjunctions. Here the rule is that, in a conjunction of propositions, the plausibility of the conjunction is equal to the plausibility of its least plausible component proposition.

In other words, if source X (who, let us say, has a value of 9 on a scale of 1 to 10) asserts p, and source Y (who, let us say, has value 2) asserts q, then the plausibility value of p & q will be rated at 2. Thus & operates something like $\land$ in deductive logic; in both functions, equal values tend to be preserved. If p and q arc both highly plausible (or true), then p & q will also be highly plausible (or true). In turn, if p and q have a low plausibility value (or are false), then p & q will likewise have a low plausibility value (or be false). In contrast, the "and" in probability theory behaves very differently. Although $\Pr(p)$ may be high and $\Pr(q)$ may be high, $\Pr(p \land q)$ may be lower. For example: if p and q are independent, and $\Pr(p) = 7/10$ and $\Pr(q) = 7/10$, then $\Pr(p \land q) = 49/100$.

In plausibility logic, negation is also altogether unlike negation in both deductive and inductive logic, for there is no way of determining the plausibility value of $\sim p$ simply from the value of p alone. This is because, given the nature of plausibility, it is possible for both p and $\sim p$ to be highly plausible, or for both to be of low plausibility. However, it remains important not to confuse low plausibility with implausibility (negative plausibility). The difference is that implausibility is a positive reason for rejecting a proposition, whereas low plausibility is a positive—but not very strong—reason for accepting it. Basically, our analogy with inductive and deductive logic breaks down when authority X (who, let us suppose, has been assigned a high value) says p, whereas authority Y (who likewise has been assigned a high value) says $\sim p$. True, they conflict; but that by itself does not determine whether we should treat p or $\sim p$ as being either plausible or implausible.

Another respect in which plausibility theory and our two logics differ is with regard to implication. In plausibility theory, the following rule obtains for implication: when a consistent set of premises entails some conclusion, then the conclusion must be at least as plausible as the least plausible premise. In deductive logic, in contrast, if a set of consistent premises entails a conclusion that is true, that need not mean that at least one premise must be true. Here are two false propositions: "If Big Ben is in Paris, then Big Ben is in England," and "Big Ben is in Paris." Together these two propositions entail the true proposition, "Big Ben is in England," yet both our original propositions are consistent with each other, and false. In inductive logic, as we saw, $\Pr(p \wedge q)$ must be less than $\Pr(p)$ and less than $\Pr(q)$, even though p and q together entail $p \wedge q$. So the implication rule for plausible inference is unique.

Now that we know a little about this model of inference, we are in a better position to understand the core logic behind the *ad verecundiam*. It is neither inductive nor deductive; rather, it is a third type of argument, with its own distinctive characteristics.

What are some of the limitations of plausible argument? Let us mention three. First, as we saw, it is often notoriously difficult to translate an expert's report into language that the layperson can understand and interpret correctly. Thus (as in deductive and inductive logic) there is a translation problem. Second, appeals to expertise are topic-sensitive, as condition 3 makes clear. But in plausibility theory, at least as it has been developed here, the propositions are treated in a subject-neutral way, just as in deductive logic. So the fallacy of *ignoratio elenchi* is as much a threat to the theory of plausible argument as it is to deductive logic. Third, we have no way of determining whether an argument is inductive or deductive by appealing to the internal mechanisms of either deductive or inductive logic. This situation has become much more difficult now that we have added a third kind of argument to the list. Clearly, some unifying theory must be introduced, perhaps using the framework of dialectic introduced in chapter 3.[16]

Summary

In this chapter we have seen that an *ad verecundiam fallacy* occurs whenever a conclusion is drawn, or invited to be drawn, on the basis of a deficient appeal to, or use of, the expert opinion of an authority. We also noted that several things can go wrong when appealing to authorities. Five factors in particular were worth noting in order to help us avoid this fallacy.

In addition, we saw that arguments from authority are not best analyzed using either inductive or deductive logic. Instead, we introduced a method of *plausibility screening*.

To say of a proposition that it is *plausible* is not to say that it is true, or even that it is probably true. Rather, it is to say only that it is rational to presume it to be true, at least provisionally. This means that it has something in its favour, and that nothing has yet come along to indicate that it is false or unlikely. In other words, it may be tentatively accepted, provided that it does not conflict with any other proposition that we have already accepted. Thus the plausibility of a proposition has to do not with its intrinsic truth or probability, but with whether it is consistent with other propositions that we are prepared to accept.

The method of plausibility screening that we adopt consists of several steps: First, we take the original set of pronouncements of our authorities and test them for consistency by constructing a truth table. If the set is inconsistent, we then determine all the maximally consistent subsets of this set. We then review the alternatives and reject those that fail to include any highly plausible propositions. If there is only one set left, that will be our preferred set. If there remains more than one, then we systematically reject those sets that tend to exclude the most plausible propositions until only one set is left. In the event of a tie, we look to see if there is a common component among the tied sets.

Weblinks

Stanford Encyclopedia of Philosophy—Informal Logic
plato.stanford.edu/entries/logic-informal/
The Nizkor Project—Appealing to Authority
www.nizkor.org/features/fallacies/appeal-to-authority.html

Notes

1. Robert L. Heilbroner tells this story in his book, *The Worldly Philosophers*, 4th ed. (New York: Simon and Schuster, 1972), 254.

2. Augustus De Morgan, *Formal Logic* (London: Taylor and Walton, 1847), 281.

3. Ibid.

4. Ibid, 282

5. Ibid., 283

6. Ibid., 284

7. Ibid, 285

8. Robert Gordon Shepherd and Erich Goode, "Scientists in the Popular Press," *New Scientist* 76 (1977): 482–484.

9. John Locke, *An Essay Concerning Human Understanding* (1690), bk. 4, ch. 17, §19.

10. Ibid.

11. C.L. Hamblin, *Fallacies* (London: Methuen, 1970), 218.

12. Wesley Salmon, *Logic* (Englewood Cliffs: Prentice-Hall, 1963), 64.

13. More properly, this is a method for identifying truth-functional inconsistency. As discussed in ch. 6, the difference between *(logical) inconsistency* and *truth-functional inconsistency* can be important. However, for current purposes we will consider only truth-functional inconsistency.

14. It is worth noting that some authors use the expression "maximal consistent subset," rather than the expression "maximally consistent subset."

15. Nicholas Rescher, *Plausible Reasoning* (Amsterdam: Van Gorcum, 1976), ch. †6.

16. Related to Rescher's work is the recently developed field of belief dynamics. This field of study allows for the systematic study of the removal, as well as the addition, of beliefs from a given belief set. For further discussion, see ch. 14.

CHAPTER 12

Economic Reasoning

"ECONOMICS," said Lord Carlyle, "is the dismal science."[1] This is a tough-sounding verdict to be sure, but many people mistake the import of Carlyle's remark. They think Carlyle meant that economic reasoning is characteristically of poor quality, or that it tends to involve too much bad logic or bad methodology or, more simply, that it is just not properly scientific. Like all other types of reasoning, economic reasoning can go wrong. Economic reasoning contains its fair share of fallacies. However, this was not the point behind Carlyle's remark. Rather, his comment was prompted by a doctrine put forward by Thomas Malthus, a nineteenth-century British economist. Malthus observed that although population growth is exponential, growth in the food supply is arithmetic. Thus Malthus predicted that exponentially growing populations would inevitably be degraded by slower-growing food supplies.

Malthus himself witnessed such degradation in England. People were starving, the consumption of drugs and alcohol was out of control, infant mortality rates were extremely high, and civil and moral corruption abounded. This was a dismal situation, if ever there were one, and so it is not surprising that Malthus was pessimistic about the possibility of widespread economic prosperity. Recalling this pessimism, the American economist, Kenneth Boulding, goes so far as to characterize two of Malthus' most serious findings as the "Dismal Theorem" and the "Utterly Dismal Theorem." According to the first, if the sole effective check on the growth of a population is misery, then the population will expand until its misery forces it to stop. According to the second, technological improvements permit populations to expand dramatically, and this provides for a commensurate increase in the number of those who will be miserable.[2] By calling economics the "dismal science," Carlyle was thus not saying that economic reasoning is incorrect, but only that its conclusions can be rather grim.

In this chapter we will not try to decide whether Malthus was correct or incorrect. Rather, given the obvious relevance of economic reasoning to personal, domestic, and international affairs, we will ask whether there are fallacies to which economic reasoning is particularly liable and, if so, how they can be avoided.

1. The Fallacies of Composition and Division

Economics can be divided into two components, microeconomics and macro-economics. *Microeconomics* studies individual markets, such as those of the auto industry or the toothpaste industry. *Macroeconomics* studies systems of markets, such as those networks of markets that make up the entire economy of a country such as Japan or of NAFTA. Roughly speaking, markets are component parts of larger economic systems. Thus microeconomics stands to macroeconomics somewhat as parts stand to wholes.

One traditional fallacy, the *fallacy of composition*, occurs when reasoning that applies to parts is confused with reasoning that applies to wholes. Economics affords some interesting and instructive illustrations of this fallacy. For example, consider the following quotation from the economist Leonard Silk:

> It is often mistakenly assumed that what is true for the parts of a system is true for the system as a whole. If you stand up at a football game, you can see better, but if everybody stands up nobody can see better.
>
> In economics, if you, as an individual, decide to save more out of your income, you will increase your wealth. But if everyone in the nation tries to save more out of income, this may reduce national wealth—by reducing, in succession, sales, the production of goods, the incomes of producers and their employees, and ultimately national saving and investment.
>
> If you as an individual are able to raise your prices, that may be a good thing for your business. But if every business [in the national economy] does the same the obvious result will be inflation, a bad thing for the nation.
>
> Balancing the budget so that outgo does not exceed income may be a sound rule for you and your family. But budget balancing does not always make sense for the national government: for the government to do so during a business slump when unemployment is rising would worsen the slump and increase unemployment.[3]

What can we conclude from these warnings? Silk's answer is to point out that when we move from micro- to macroeconomics some key concepts change. In other words, reasoning that may be valid for parts may be inadequate for the whole. To ignore this warning, whether in economics or in other branches of reasoning, is to risk committing the fallacy of composition.

It would be unfair and misleading to suggest that economists commit the fallacy of composition more often than other thinkers, but economics is one of the sciences that has two distinctive sub-branches that are related as part to whole, and so it is inherently liable to the fallacy of composition.

Of course, economic reasoning is not the only branch of reasoning that falls prey to this fallacy.[4] It crops up in other contexts as well. Here are two examples:

- Two Aspirins are effective for a headache, so the whole bottle should really do the trick.

- All the players who play for the Toronto Maple Leafs are good, so the team itself must be good as well.

Of course, not every instance of reasoning from what is true of parts to what is true of the whole involves the fallacy of composition. Here are two examples of perfectly sound reasoning:

- All the parts of the machine are made of iron, so the machine is made of iron.

- All the members of my family are in London, so my family is in London.

Sometimes it is difficult to determine, in a general way, whether reasoning from parts to wholes is correct. For example, if Sue kicks Bill's shin (and so kicks a part of Bill) she kicks Bill. This might lead us to believe that anyone who kicks a part of an object kicks that object. But what if, while he is hiking on Mount Everest, Bill kicks a stone that he sees lying on the ground. Even if we agree that the stone is a part of Mount Everest, we might disagree about whether he kicked the mountain. Such cases might undermine our earlier intuition that anyone who kicks a part of an object kicks that object. Thus, trying to determine when the fallacy of composition has occurred can be a tricky business.

Composition and Division

- The *fallacy of composition* occurs whenever reasoning that applies to parts is confused with reasoning that applies to wholes.

- The *fallacy of division* occurs whenever reasoning that applies to wholes is confused with reasoning that applies to parts.

A second fallacy related to the fallacy of composition is the *fallacy of division*. If composition is the fallacy that confuses reasoning about parts with reasoning about wholes, then division is the fallacy that confuses reasoning about wholes with reasoning about parts. Here are some examples of the fallacy of division:

- This machine is heavy, so all its parts are heavy.

- Boston has one of the most highly paid work forces in North America; consequently Bill's cousin, who lives in Boston, is one of the most highly paid persons in North America.

A more subtle example arises in connection with the following argument:

(P1) If it is more likely than not that the premisses of this argument are true (i.e., it is more likely than not that both (P1) and (P2) are true), then it is more likely than not that the conclusion (C) is true

(P2) It is more likely than not that the premisses of this argument are true (i.e., it is more likely than not that both (P1) and (P2) are true)

(C) Therefore, it is more likely than not that the conclusion (C) is true.[5]

Under one plausible interpretation, this argument is a straightforward instance of *Modus Ponens*, and hence is valid. Under a second plausible interpretation, it can be shown to contain a fallacy of division. To demonstrate, we recast the argument using elementary probability theory in two different ways as follows:

(P1') If $Pr((P1') \wedge (P2')) > 1/2$ then $Pr(C') > 1/2$

(P2') $Pr((P1') \wedge (P2')) > 1/2$

(C') Therefore, $Pr(C') > 1/2$.

In this first case we see that the argument is clearly valid; but now compare a second interpretation, as follows:

(P1") If $Pr((P1") \wedge (P2")) > 1/2$ then $Pr(C") > 1/2$

(P2") $Pr(P1") > 1/2 \wedge Pr(P2") > 1/2$

(C") Therefore, $Pr(C") > 1/2$.

Here we recognize that just because $Pr(P1") > 1/2$ and $Pr(P2") > 1/2$, it does not follow that $Pr((P1") \wedge (P2")) > 1/2$, and vice versa. (For example, in an ordinary deck of 52 playing cards, the probability of drawing a random card that is either red or a king is 28/52, and so is greater than 1/2. Similarly, the probability of drawing a random card that is either black or a queen is again 28/52, and so again this is greater than 1/2. Despite this, the probability of drawing a random card that is either red or a king *and* black or a queen is only 4/52, which is much less than 1/2.) The moral is that what is true for the whole group of premisses is not necessarily true for each premiss individually.

Once again, though, it is also possible to find examples of reasoning that go from wholes to parts that are perfectly sound:

■ This machine is made of iron, so all the parts of the machine are made of iron.

■ My family is in London, so all the members of my family are in London.

Thus, like the fallacy of composition, trying to determine when the fallacy of division has occurred is unlikely to depend on a purely mechanical process.

2. Analytical Remarks about Composition and Division

As we have noted, the fallacies of composition and division involve incorrect reasoning that goes from parts to wholes and from wholes to parts. Even so, we have also noted that not all reasoning from parts to wholes or wholes to parts is incorrect or fallacious. Can we determine, in a suitably general way, when such reasoning is fallacious?

To deal with this question, let W be a whole (or aggregate), let $P_1, ..., P_n$ be the parts of that whole (or aggregate), and let F be some property or attribute. Then we introduce the following two definitions:

- Property F is *compositionally hereditary* with regard to W whenever, if every P_i of W has property F, then so too does W. (For example, if all the parts of the machine are metal, then the machine is metal.)

- Property F is *divisionally hereditary* with regard to W whenever, if W has property F, then so too does every P_i. (For example, if this team is the Canadian Olympic Team, then all its members are Canadian.)

Perhaps the most important analytic fact about the fallacies of composition and division is this: For very many wholes or aggregates, some properties are compositionally hereditary, some are divisionally hereditary, some are both, and some are neither. Thus the following four laws governing compositional and divisional hereditary can be introduced:

- (L1): For any aggregate, W, there is some property, F, that is not compositionally hereditary.

- (L2): For any aggregate, W, there is some property, F, that is not divisionally hereditary.

- (L3): If F is compositionally hereditary with regard to W, it does not follow that F is always divisionally hereditary with regard to W.

- (L4): If F is divisionally hereditary with regard to W, it does not follow that F is always compositionally hereditary with regard to W.

It is easy to verify (L1). Suppose that we have an aggregate, A, all the parts of which are distinct from A. Then A is not compositionally hereditary with regard to the property of being distinct from A! It is also easy to verify (L3). Let F be the property of weighing more than two kilograms. Clearly this property is compositionally hereditary with respect to a machine, but it is not divisionally hereditary. That is, if all the parts of a machine weigh more than two kilograms, so does the machine, but although the machine might weigh more than two kilograms, all its parts might not. (We leave the verification of (L2) and (L4) as an exercise.)

Thus, the distinction between compositional heredity and divisional heredity is helpful in understanding the fallacies of composition and division. Still, it cannot yet be said that we have fully explained these fallacies. On the basis of our discussion so far, all we can say is that, when composition is a fallacy, it is not so solely by virtue of its elementary logical form

All the P_i of W have F

———————————————

Therefore, W has F.

Similarly, when division is a fallacy, it is not so solely as a result of its elementary logical form,

W has F

———————————————————

Therefore, all the P_i of W have F.

So we have not yet attained much generality about when composition and division are fallacies, and we have not yet said what, beyond an argument's elementary logical form, makes a composition argument or a division argument fallacious.[6] Even so, we can say this much: whether an argument in either of these two forms is fallacious will depend upon

- the precise nature of the property F;

- the precise nature of the aggregate W; and

- a suitably powerful general theory of the part–aggregate relationship.

Basically, the precise kind of property and aggregate involved in the argument makes a real difference as to whether the argument is fallacious. Knowing whether the property is compositionally hereditary or divisionally hereditary is more than a matter of elementary logical form.

Exercise 12.1

1. Which of the following arguments involve the fallacy of composition? Which involve the fallacy of division?

    (a) The all-star team this year has the best players for every position. It is sure to win its game against last year's championship team.

    (b) Technology stocks have outpaced stocks in every other sector of the economy this year, so my stock in Microsoft must have done well.

    (c) What would happen if I ran a deficit in my hardware business? I'll tell you what would happen: I'd be bankrupt. I'd have no business left! Yet the government continues to run a deficit and the national economy continues to run a huge balance-of-payments deficit. The whole country is out of business, and we're just too thick-headed to realize it!

    (d) It is quite clear that when I cut my employees' wages last year, I could afford to hire some additional people. That brought unemployment in my town down a bit. So the best thing to do for unemployment right across the country is to have all employers cut wages.

(e) Since our company wasn't profitable last year, we all have to accept a portion of the responsibility.

2. Construct an example that verifies (L2), the second of the preceding laws governing compositional and divisional hereditary.

3. Construct an example that verifies (L4), the fourth of the preceding laws governing compositional and divisional hereditary.

3. Economic Reasoning, Dialectic, and Decision Theory

It would be quite wrong to leave the impression that the most distinctive logical feature of economic reasoning is that it involves fallacies such as those of composition and division. A much more characteristic feature is its concern with decision-making in practical contexts. Silk characterizes the "problem-solving" function of economic reasoning as including the following six components:[7]

Step 1 – Define the problem

For example, when reasoning about a military campaign, is the problem to secure tactical or strategic advantage? According to some military analysts, the Dieppe Raid during the Second World War was a tactical disaster, involving terrible losses to the Canadian landing troops. Even so, many believe it was an excellent strategic victory in that it taught the Allies how best to conduct the later Normandy invasion. So, if the problem was to secure tactical advantage, then the reasoning that led to Dieppe was clearly mistaken; but, if the problem was to secure strategic advantage, this same reasoning may have been successful. Successfully determining what the problem is that you want to solve is also characteristic of good economic reasoning.

Step 2 – Identify the goals and values that you want a solution to achieve

For example, say you are a member of a trade union, and your group is worried about the corrosive effects of inflation. As the saying goes, you want to "keep ahead of inflation." In your settlement it is agreed that your wages will increase by 3 percent. Let us also suppose that the cost-of-living index stands at 4 percent. This means that, even if you are pleased that you will be getting a 3 percent raise, this is not what you wanted, and it is not what you aimed for. Your purchasing power has declined by 1 percent. Despite your 3 percent increase, you have not kept ahead of inflation.

Step 3 – List alternative courses of action

With some exceptions, considering only a single solution to a problem is usually not ideal. Suppose you believe that your weekly paycheque is about $50 short of permitting you to make ends meet. Even though you know that your industry is economically weak and uncompetitive, and that the regional economy in which your industry is set is also having difficulties, you exercise your influence as local union president and call a strike. As a result, your industry becomes even less competitive and further cutbacks are made. If your goal is to augment your income by $50 a week, almost certainly you should have considered other alternatives as well: moonlighting, upgrading your qualifications, changing jobs, and so on.

Step 4 – Weigh each alternative

It is not enough just to identity alternative courses of action; they must also be analyzed and evaluated. Comparisons need to be made and various outcomes need to be predicted. For example, if you have to choose between moonlighting and upgrading your qualifications, it is important to consider the costs as well as the benefits of each option. It is also important to compare the mid- and long-term consequences of each option, as well as those of the short term.

Step 5 – Choose the alternative that best solves your problem

Once you have the information you require and have identified your various alternatives, make your choice and act on it.

Step 6 – Check your results

If possible, after you have acted, go back and re-evaluate. Was your reasoning in steps 1 through 5 correct? Why or why not?

Guidelines for Problem-solving

1. Define the problem.
2. Identify the goals and values that you want a solution to achieve.
3. List alternative courses of action.
4. Weigh each alternative.
5. Choose the alternative that best solves your problem.
6. Check your results.

This is a helpful characterization, but can we say more about the kind of deliberate, reasoned decisions that conform to these six general precepts? Two ideas come to mind. The first is to approach decisions of this kind through a context of dialectic. That is, proceeding through these steps will require that we engage someone (often ourself!) in a kind of dialectical argument. Recall from chapter 3 that a dialectical argument is one in which, by question and answer, a participant attempts to refute a thesis. The rules of testing are carefully arranged to preserve fairness and to enhance the chances of arriving at a correct answer. Consequently, if the original thesis is refuted, then the correct answer is the negation of that thesis. If a refutation cannot be made, the original thesis has not been proved, but that thesis has attained some degree of rational support and the supporter of the thesis can continue to accept it.

Let us suppose that the original thesis is "Alternative x should be chosen." Suppose, further, that the questioner and respondent are one and the same person. This is an allowable extension of our first rule of dialectic (see chapter 3), provided that the characteristic roles of questioner and respondent are preserved and honoured.

Imagine that our dialectician, Bill, asks himself a question which, as respondent, he cannot answer. According to the original rules of dialectic, the argument must then stop, for by rule 5, the questioner is expected to help overcome the ignorance of the respondent. However, we shall also understand it to be an allowable extension of rule 5 for Bill, as respondent, to solicit independent advice about the question to which he does not know the answer, provided (a) that the information he solicits is factual and objective, (b) that it comes from an independent source with no stake in the outcome of the dialectical argument in progress, and finally (c) that, in his persona as questioner, Bill finds this method of research acceptable. "Research" is the key word here. Our extension of rule 5 permits the consultation of a factual research source, such as an encyclopedia, or a file clerk in the Hall of Records, or some other authority.

Clearly, if the original thesis is refuted, then the correct decision is not to do x. Then it is appropriate to move to the next possible alternative and to test it dialectically as well. If it, too, is refuted, Bill can move on, testing each of the alternatives in turn. In other words, we have in effect supplemented our original eight dialectical rules with the following principle: If a unique decision is desired, consider, in order, each possible decision in the range of alternatives, and test these hypotheses dialectically.

A Ninth Rule of Dialectic

If a unique decision is desired, consider, in order, each possible decision in the range of alternatives, and test these hypotheses dialectically.

We can formulate the outcome of this process as follows:

- if, in a given range of alternatives, $A_1, ..., A_n$, exactly one, A_i, is left unrefuted, then it is generally reasonable to choose A_i;

- if all alternatives are refuted, then it is generally reasonable to do nothing;

- if more than one alternative is left unrefuted, then it is important to formulate additional comparative theses; that is, we need to formulate theses of the form "Alternative A_i is more advantageous than alternative A_j under conditions C," and test these dialectically; and

- if, in the end, no comparative thesis emerges as the dialectical winner, then in general, "Do nothing" is a rational choice.

It is crucial to understand, however, that there exist important exceptions to the "Do nothing" alternative. For example, say you are required, as the buyer for a large company, to decide whether to become involved in a new product line. Doing so would take your company in quite a new direction, but not becoming involved at this time would almost certainly mean missing the opportunity to become a leader in this new market. Still, the evidence about consumer interest in this new product remains inconclusive, and now you find it difficult to make up your mind. So you reach this decision: "Do nothing!" However, this is equivalent to deciding to stay out of this new market. You are in a "forced option," as the philosopher William James called it. A forced option is one in which "doing nothing" is really "doing something." That is, your postponement of a decision is in effect equivalent to one of the decisions you wished to avoid making. In such circumstances, doing nothing may not be appropriate. It turns out that "Do nothing" is rather conservative advice; it is designed to minimize risk and to promote informed decision-making. However, in those circumstances in which doing nothing is equivalent to one of the choices you feel unprepared to make, an uninformed try is sometimes better than doing nothing whatsoever.

A second approach to explaining further the type of deliberate, reasoned decision procedure that we outlined at the beginning of this section involves what has come to be called *decision theory*. Decision theory is broad enough to encompass both *normative theories* (which involve judgments of value) and *descriptive theories* (which preclude judgments of value). It is also designed to help clarify both *individual decisions* and *group decisions*.

What is common to these various topics? Part of the answer comes from how broadly decision theory itself is construed. Let us characterize those contexts in which decisions occur as being those in which, given a particular problem and goal, the decision-maker, who may be a person or group of persons,

- is exposed to a number of alternatives;

- does not possess complete information about the current state of affairs; and

- does not possess complete information about the results and implications of each possible alternative.

Consequently, the problem for the decision-maker is to select an alternative that, relative to the available information, is *rational* and, if possible, *optimal* (i.e., the best among the available rational strategies). *Decision theory* thus attempts to provide a set of exact criteria for what is rational and optimal in such circumstances.

Normally, decision theory is taken to include *minimax theory*. The central idea of minimax theory is that estimates and choices should be made so as to minimize the maximum possible expectation of error. We will have more to say about minimax theory in the next section of this chapter. Later in the chapter we will also discuss a rather vexing problem for decision theory.

> **Decision Theory**
> Decision theory attempts to provide criteria for determining what it is rational to do under conditions of risk and uncertainty. Given that each of a decision-maker's various alternatives has associated with it an expected probability distribution of outcomes, decision theory attempts to explain which choices are optimal and which are not.

This is the problem that, despite the goals of decision theory, there appears to be no single, consistent set of principles that correspond, in a natural and intuitively satisfying way, to the general idea of rationality. In other words, we do not really know, in a theoretically respectable way, just what rationality is! Plausible definitions of key concepts actually lead to paradox. In this respect it may be helpful to recall how, in chapter 6, we saw that Tarski and others showed that from the innocent-seeming idea of a semantically closed language, contradictions also result. In both cases, how best to proceed remains an open question.

4. Expected Utility, Sure-thing, and Minimax Principles

In a historically important work, *Introduction to the Principles of Morals and Legislation*, Jeremy Bentham postulated an interesting connection between rationality and utility. "By utility," Bentham wrote,

> is meant that property in any object whereby it tends to produce benefit, advantage, pleasure, good or happiness (all this in the present case comes to the same thing), or (what comes again to the same thing) to prevent the happening of mischief, pain, evil, or unhappiness to the party whose interest is considered: if that party be the community in general, then the happiness of the community, if a particular individual, then the happiness of that individual.[8]

For Bentham, rationality consisted of maximizing utility and, from Bentham's day to the present, this idea has been a dominant theme of so-called classical economics. However, a problem for Bentham was how one might go about measuring utility. After all, pleasure and happiness are not only subjective, they are also notoriously difficult to quantify. If utility is to be identified with these kinds of subjective feelings, it too will be difficult to quantify.

This problem of formulating exact measures of utility was solved at the beginning of the twentieth century, partly through the work of the Italian economist Vilfredo Pareto and partly through the work of the eighteenth-century mathematician Daniel Bernouilli. Bernouilli had shown that, even if we are uncertain of which consequences will result from which actions, we can still assign probabilities to each of an action's various consequences. Drawing on Bernouilli's work, Pareto then showed how, using subjective preferences, we could calculate the expected utility of any given action.

Suppose that Bill must decide whether to attend a play in uncertain weather. In this context, Bill's two possible alternatives are

A_1: going to the theatre, and
A_2: not going to the theatre.

Let us also suppose that there are only two further possibilities that we need to consider, the possibility of its snowing, S, and the possibility of its not snowing, $\sim S$.

Thus, the possible consequences of Bill's decision are

C_1: going to the theatre during a snowstorm,
C_2: going to the theatre under clear skies,
C_3: staying home during a snowstorm, and
C_4: staying home under clear skies.

Imagine, further, that Bill believes it is more probable that it will not snow than that it will snow. Accordingly, he assigns the following probabilities to each of these two possibilities:

$Pr(S) = 4/10$
$Pr(\sim S) = 6/10$.

In this way, Bill gives numerical expression to the "subjective probabilities" of S and $\sim S$. For Bill, the subjective probability of its snowing or not snowing is identified with his degree of confidence that it will or will not snow. In our scenario, his degree of confidence that it will snow is expressed as the subjective probability 4/10; his degree of confidence that it will not snow is expressed as the subjective probability 6/10.

Finally, let us assume that Bill prefers C_2 to C_3, that he is indifferent between C_3 and C_4, and that he prefers C_3 and C_4 to C_1. Since it is clear that Bill's two possible alternatives present him with four possible outcomes, it follows that if he chooses A_1 he will get what he most prefers, namely C_2, or what he least prefers, namely C_1. If he selects A_2, then he is certain to achieve one of his middle preferences, either C_3 or C_4.

Obviously Bill is still not quite ready to make his decision. He must first more carefully evaluate his preferences. He can do this by assigning numerical degrees of utility to each of the four possible consequences C_1, C_2, C_3, and C_4 as follows:

$U(C_1) = -10$
$U(C_2) = 10$
$U(C_3) = 5$
$U(C_4) = 5$.

Bill now has what he needs to make his decision. With this information he can estimate the *expected* utility of each of his two possible actions, A_1 and A_2. The expected utility of A_1 we will call $E(A_1)$, and of A_2, $E(A_2)$. How does Bill compute $E(A_1)$ and $E(A_2)$?

The Principle of Expected Utility

The expected utility of an action, A, is equal to the sum of the product of the probability of each of the action's consequences, $Pr(C_n)$, with that consequence's utility, $U(C_n)$. Symbolically, we write

$$E(A) = Pr(C_1) \times U(C_1) + \ldots + Pr(C_n) \times U(C_n).$$

According to the *principle of expected utility*, that action is best that maximizes expected utility.

First, for $E(A_1)$, Bill calculates

$E(A_1) = Pr(S) \times U(C_1) + Pr(\sim S) \times U(C_2)$.

This is the product of the probability that it will snow and the utility of Bill's being caught in a snowstorm added to the product of the probability that it will not snow together with the utility of Bill's going to the theatre under clear skies. Doing the appropriate substitutions, we obtain

$E(A_1) = (4/10)(-10) + (6/10)(10) = 2$.

Second, for $E(A_2)$, Bill calculates

$E(A_2) = Pr(S) \times U(C_3) + Pr(\sim S) \times U(C_4)$.

This is the product of the probability that it will snow and the utility of Bill's remaining at home added to the product of the probability that it will not snow, again together with the utility of Bill's staying at home. Doing the appropriate substitutions, we obtain

$E(A_2) = (4/10)(5) + (6/10)(5) = 5$.

Consequently, according to the expected utilities approach, the rational thing for Bill to do is to select action A_2. Bill should stay home, for that is the way he will maximize his expected utility.

Is this a helpful way of thinking about what it means to be rational? If we look at things the way Bentham did, we will want to identify utility with pleasure. (Remember that Bentham said of benefit, advantage, good, happiness, and pleasure, that "all this ... comes to the same thing.") But what if we disagree with Bentham on this point? What if we deny that only those things that are to our advantage, or that confer benefits on us, are pleasurable?

In response to this worry, it turns out that the above method of computing expected utility can be used quite satisfactorily no matter what is meant by the word "utility." Provided that your idea of utility includes the thought that utility is something valuable, and provided that there are ways of ranking utilities (for example by identifying them with preferences), the precise interpretation we give to the term does not matter. But if this is so, will this take us out of the frying pan and into the fire? After all, if "utility" can mean just about anything that is of value, then a utility-based theory of decision will be seriously incomplete. Such a theory will tell us little about what rationality really is, especially since values often conflict with one another. Thus the maxim, "maximize your expected utility," tells us comparatively little about rationality and gives us rather incomplete advice.

Interestingly, the argument can also be made that it asks too much of us. It expects us (as it expected Bill) to provide exact numerical values corresponding to the probability of various alternatives, and exact numerical values corresponding to our outcome preferences. The plain fact is that very often a decision-maker will not have sufficient information to assign exact numerical values in this way. It follows that, in some cases at least, the principle of the maximization of expected utility will be too demanding to be of much use.

Let us therefore turn to two less demanding decision principles: the sure-thing principle and the minimax principle. Game theory and statistical decision theory are two branches of general decision theory that seek to formulate decision principles that are weaker than those of the maximization of expected utility. Such principles are said to be weaker since they do not require the decision-maker to know the exact probability or utility of each event relevant to the decision at hand.

One weaker principle is the *principle of dominance*. Imagine that our decision-maker, Bill, is faced with two possible actions, and that for each possible situation, the consequences of selecting the first action over the second are at least as desirable as those of selecting the second over the first, and sometimes better. Then the principle of dominance (sometimes also called the *sure-thing principle*) asserts that Bill should prefer the first action to the second.

What should we say about the sure-thing principle? One thing we can say is that, when applicable, the principle appears to be incontrovertible. Even so, the principle also appears to have quite limited application in situations of real-life decision-making. Recall what this principle requires: it requires that for each set of consequences, one action must dominate all other actions. To be acted upon, the principle also requires of a decision-maker that he or she recognize that this is so. But it is obvious that, relative to all sorts of real-life situations, these requirements often cannot be fulfilled.

> **The Principle of Dominance (or Sure-thing Principle)**
>
> The *principle of dominance* (or *sure-thing principle*) states that if, in all possible situations, the consequences of selecting one action over a second are at least as desirable as those of selecting the second over the first, and sometimes better, then a rational decision-maker will prefer the first action to the second.

Our second, less demanding decision principle is one that is central to game theory, namely John von Neumann's minimax principle.[9] The *minimax principle* is designed to minimize the maximum possible loss or error. Since game theory deals with situations of conflict and uncertainty, it is easy to see why following the minimax principle might be advantageous. Following such a principle will be advantageous any time we find ourselves in a situation in which we will want to minimize the risk of a large loss.

Imagine that Bill is faced with a number of alternative actions, and that he is able to determine, for each of these alternative actions, what will be the worst possible outcome. Bill must then select that action whose worst possible outcome is the most desirable. Such a decision is called the *minimax decision* since it is a decision that minimizes Bill's maximum loss.

To see how minimax decisions work, imagine yourself in a two-person, zero-sum game. A *zero-sum game* is one in which the participants are in a conflict of interest, and in which any winning strategy for one participant implies that the game will also have losers. In other words, if you win, then someone else—say, Sue—will lose. What is more, if you win, then you win to precisely the same degree that Sue loses. Thus, if the utility attaching to your win is expressed numerically as, say, 6/10, then the disutility attaching to Sue's loss must, when summed with your 6/10, yield zero.

> **The Minimax Principle**
>
> The *minimax principle* states that a rational decision-maker will prefer that action that minimizes the maximum possible loss or error.

According to von Neumann, in many two-person, zero-sum games, each player has a minimax strategy; that is, a strategy designed to minimize his maximal loss. Furthermore, if both participants are rational, the best possible strategy for each will be to select his or her minimax strategy.

In evaluating minimax strategies, it is important to notice how conservative they are. Their object is to make the best of a bad situation; they require participants to play it safe and to accept outcomes with low "payoffs" simply in order to minimize the risk of loss. There is no doubt, as we said earlier, that in certain real-life situations, the most rational course is a conservative one, and to make the best of a bad lot is exactly the right thing to do. But it is also true that, for any rational person, some situations demand high payoffs, even if they will occur only at high risk. In life-and-death situations, for example, the surgeon cannot always elect to make the best of a bad lot by letting the patient expire, comfortably medicated but without being operated upon.

Exercise 12.2

1. Use the principle of expected utility to calculate the best alternative in each of the following cases:

(a) Assume that you have to choose between two alternatives, A_1 and A_2; that alternative A_1 has consequences C_1 and C_2; that alternative A_2 has consequences C_3 and C_4; that $Pr(C_1) = Pr(C_3) = 3/10$; that $Pr(C_2) = Pr(C_4) = 7/10$; that $U(C_1) = U(C_3) = 10$; and that $U(C_2) = U(C_4) = 50$.

(b) Assume that you have to choose between two alternatives, A_1 and A_2; that alternative A_1 has consequences C_1 and C_2; that alternative A_2 has consequences C_3 and C_4; that $Pr(C_1) = 3/10$; that $Pr(C_2) = 7/10$; that $Pr(C_3) = 4/10$; that $Pr(C_4) = 6/10$; that $U(C_1) = 10$; that $U(C_2) = 100$; that $U(C_3) = 50$; and that $U(C_4) = 30$.

(c) Assume that you have to choose between three alternatives, A_1, A_2 and A_3; that alternative A_1 has consequences C_1, C_2 and C_3; that alternative A_2 has consequences C_4, C_5 and C_6; that alternative A_3 has as its sole consequence C_7; that $Pr(C_1) = Pr(C_4) = 2/10$; that $Pr(C_2) = Pr(C_5) = 7/10$; that $Pr(C_3) = Pr(C_6) = 1/10$; that $Pr(C_7) = 10/10$; that $U(C_1) = 10$; that $U(C_2) = 20$; that $U(C_3) = 30$; that $U(C_4) = 40$; that $U(C_5) = 50$; that $U(C_6) = 60$; and that $U(C_7) = 20$.

(d) Assume that you have to choose between buying stock in a technology company or buying stock in a transportation company. If you do the first, you will have a 5 percent chance of obtaining a 200-percent return and a 95 percent chance of obtaining a 9-percent return. If you do the second, you will have a sure return of 14 percent.

(e) Assume that you have to choose between doing nothing and donating an organ for an experimental medical procedure in order to try to save the life of a child. If you make the donation, there is a 50 percent chance that you will both live, and a 50 percent chance that you will both die. If you do nothing, the child will certainly die.

2. Use the sure-thing principle (or principle of dominance) to calculate the best alternative in each of the following cases:

    (a) Assume that you have to choose between two alternatives, A_1 and A_2; that alternative A_1 has consequences C_1 and C_2; that alternative A_2 has consequences C_3 and C_4; that $U(C_1) = U(C_2) = U(C_3) = 10$; and that $U(C_4) = 5$.

    (b) Assume that you have to choose between two alternatives, A_1 and A_2; that alternative A_1 has consequences C_1 and C_2; that alternative A_2 has consequences C_3 and C_4; that $U(C_1) = 150$; that $U(C_2) = 100$; that $U(C_3) = 80$; and that $U(C_4) = 90$.

    (c) Assume that you have to choose between three alternatives, A_1, A_2 and A_3; that alternative A_1 has consequences C_1, C_2 and C_3; that alternative A_2 has consequences C_4, C_5 and C_6; that alternative A_3 has as its sole consequence C_7; that $U(C_1) = 10$; that $U(C_2) = 20$; that $U(C_3) = 30$; that $U(C_4) = 40$; that $U(C_5) = 50$; that $U(C_6) = 60$; and that $U(C_7) = 20$.

    (d) Assume that you have to choose between buying a government-backed guaranteed investment certificate or investing in a new hotel complex. If you do the first, you will be guaranteed a 7 percent return per year for each of five years. If you do the second, you will get no return during the first four years, but you will be able to sell your investment for a guaranteed minimum return of 40 percent at the end of the fifth year and maybe much more.

    (e) Assume that you have to decide whether to have heart surgery in order to correct a birth defect that is restricting the ability of your heart to function normally. If you have the surgery, there is a 90 percent chance that you will die on the operating table, but a 10 percent chance you will live well into old age. If you do not have the surgery, you will not live more than a short time anyway.

3. Use the minimax principle to calculate the best alternative in each of the following cases:

    (a) Assume that you have to choose between two alternatives, A_1 and A_2; that alternative A_1 has consequences C_1 and C_2; that alternative A_2 has consequences C_3 and C_4; that $Pr(C_1) = Pr(C_3) = 4/10$; that $Pr(C_2) = Pr(C_4) = 6/10$; that $U(C_1) = U(C_3) = 1$; and that $U(C_2) = U(C_4) = 50$.

    (b) Assume that you have to choose between two alternatives, A_1 and A_2; that alternative A_1 has consequences C_1 and C_2; that alternative A_2 has consequences C_3 and C_4; that $Pr(C_1) = 2/10$; that $Pr(C_2) = 8/10$; that $Pr(C_3) = 4/10$; that $Pr(C_4) = 6/10$; that $U(C_1) = 10$; that $U(C_2) = 100$; that $U(C_3) = 80$; and that $U(C_4) = 90$.

    (c) Assume that you have to choose between three alternatives, A_1, A_2 and A_3; that alternative A_1 has consequences C_1, C_2 and C_3; that alternative A_2 has consequences C_4 and C_5; that alternative A_3 has as its sole consequence C_6; that $Pr(C_1) = Pr(C_4) = 2/10$; that $Pr(C_2) = 7/10$; that $Pr(C_3) = 1/10$; that $Pr(C_5) = 8/10$; that $Pr(C_6) = 10/10$; that $U(C_1) = 10$; that $U(C_2) = 20$; that $U(C_3) = 30$; that $U(C_4) = 40$; that $U(C_5) = 50$; and that $U(C_6) = 0$.

    (d) Assume that you are in your twenties and you have to choose between buying a government-backed guaranteed investment certificate or investing in your family business. If you do the first, you will be guaranteed a 7 percent return per year for each of five years. If you do the second, and if you and your family work hard, you will be likely to get a much larger return, but you may lose everything.

(e) Assume that you have the same choice to make as in (d), but that you are now nearing retirement age.

5. Group Decisions and the Prisoner's Dilemma

As we have seen, one leading idea behind classical economics is that of the greatest happiness for the greatest number, or the maximizing of utilities. Bentham's interest in the maximizing of utilities had to do primarily with discovering mechanisms for the distribution of economic benefits, but many thinkers have come to believe that such mechanisms are interesting even when they deliver non-economic benefits. In fact, a major concern of *welfare economics* is to investigate schemes for distributing any kind of good, whether it be an economic benefit (such as income) or a non-economic benefit (such as justice). Bentham's insight, therefore, provides the motivation for a more general problem in group decision theory: how shall we distribute benefits (of any kind) over a group so that this will result in a maximal payoff?

Given the challenge of deciding between various principles such as the principle of expected utility, the principle of dominance, and the minimax principle, we can say that individual decision theory has not yet been fully successful in formulating intuitively satisfying criteria of rationality. The same can be said for group decision theory. Interesting work in this connection has been done by Kenneth Arrow and his followers.[10] Consider a society of individuals who have the option of choosing between a number of different situations, which we will call *social states*. Suppose that each individual member of the society is able to rank these various social states according to his or her own individual preferences. Given these individual preferences, how should we arrive at a just preference-ordering for the society as a whole?

One traditional suggestion is to make such decisions on the basis of a majority vote. On this view, one social state, x, would be preferred to another social state, y, if a majority of individual citizens prefer x to y. However, it is not clear that majority decisions are always equitable. For example, consider the so-called voters' paradox.[11] Imagine that there are three alternatives being put to the vote: A_1, A_2, and A_3. For simplicity, let us also suppose that there are just three voters voting on these issues, that the first voter prefers A_1 to A_2 and A_2 to A_3, that the second voter prefers A_2 to A_3 and A_3 to A_1, and that the third voter prefers A_3 to A_1 and A_1 to A_2.

If, as seems reasonable, the vote is then taken in pairs, it turns out that there will be no unique resolution of these issues. That is, if the first vote is between A_1 and A_2, then A_1 will be selected; if the second vote is between A_1 (the winner of the first vote) and A_3, then A_3 will be selected. In contrast, if the first vote is between A_1 and A_3, then A_3 will be selected; if the second vote is between A_3 (the winner of the first vote) and A_2, then A_2 will be selected. Finally, if the first vote is between A_2 and A_3, then A_2 will be selected; if the second vote is between A_2 (the winner of the first vote) and A_1, then A_1 will be selected.

What this shows is that sometimes the outcome of a vote will depend on the (arbitrary) selection of which issues are voted on first! This is consistent with actual voting experience, in which the order of voting on, and amending, congressional or parliamentary bills can significantly influence the outcome. In general, then, majority votes are not always a rational or equitable mechanism for the fixing of social preference.

What other options have we in addition to majority vote? Pareto makes the following suggestion:

> Consider any particular position and suppose that a very small move is made [from it] ... [Then if] the well-being of all the individuals is increased, it is evident that the new position is more advantageous for each of them; *vice versa* it is less so if the well-being of all the individuals is diminished. The well-being of some may remain the same without these conclusions being affected. But if, on the other hand the small move increases the well-being of certain individuals, and diminishes that of others, it can no longer be said that it is advantageous to the community as a whole to make such a move.12

Here we meet the idea of a so-called Pareto improvement. A *Pareto improvement* on a given distribution of benefits is one in which at least some individuals do better, and every individual does *no worse* than on the initial distribution. This in turn leads to the idea of *Pareto optimality*. Consider a given distribution of benefits, *B*; and consider the set of all possible alternative distributions to *B*. If none of these other distributions makes a Pareto improvement on the initial distribution *B*, then *B* is called a *Pareto-optimal* distribution.

According to Pareto, the rational and just strategies of social decision-making are those that promote Pareto optimality. Although this sounds plausible, there are problems with this approach, too. First, all too often in real life, no alternative distributions are Pareto improvements, for each requires that at least one person would have to surrender at least some slight advantage for the advantage of the others. Second, in real-life social and economic situations, there is frequently no single best alternative strategy; that is, there is no single dominating Pareto improvement. Unfortunately, there is nothing in Pareto's theory to guide us in the preference ranking of, and the preferential choice from among, sub-optimal alternatives.

This sounds a cautionary note for logic, of course; but it is even worse for economics. In classical economics particularly, one finds a ready identification of rationality with self-interest. Thus, if it turns out that there is no way of unifying our reasoning about individual and corporate preferences, it becomes unlikely that we will be able to reach a theoretically satisfactory account of rationality. To see this in a particular, concrete case, we turn now to the *prisoner's dilemma*.[13]

Let us assume that Bill and Sue are prisoners, and that they are being held incommunicado. Each is charged with being an accomplice to a serious crime. However, a conviction will be more easily secured if at least one of Bill and Sue can be induced to confess and thereby incriminate the other. If Bill and Sue both testify against the other (that is, if there is mutual incrimination through confession), each will be jailed for ten years. However, if Bill confesses and Sue keeps silent, Sue will be convicted and she will serve twenty years while Bill goes free. Similarly, if Sue confesses and Bill keeps quiet, Bill will serve twenty years while Sue goes free. Finally, if both keep silent—that is, if neither Bill nor Sue confesses—each will be convicted on a much lesser charge, and each will serve a prison term of just one year.

What course of action should each follow? Under such circumstances, what is the rational thing to do? Here we have a two-person game, which we can represent using diagram 12.1. This type of diagram is called a "payoff matrix." The numbers in the matrix are numerical expressions of gains (or payoffs) and losses (or negative payoffs). Minus ten represents the negative payoff of ten years in prison; minus twenty represents the negative payoff of twenty years in prison; minus one represents the negative payoff of one year in prison. Zero represents the avoidance of all the negative payoffs—that is, being set free.

Bill \ Sue	Sue Confesses	Sue Does Not Confess
Bill Confesses	-10 \ -10	0 \ -20
Bill Does Not Confess	-20 \ 0	-1 \ -1

Diagram 12.1

We read the payoff matrix as follows: If Bill confesses and Sue confesses then each receives ten years. If Bill confesses and Sue keeps quiet, then Bill gets off and Sue receives twenty years. If Bill keeps quiet and Sue confesses, then Sue gets off and Bill serves twenty years. Finally, if neither talks, each gets one year.

Assuming that for both Bill and Sue the goal is to minimize their individual time in prison, what will be the rational course of action? Should they confess or keep quiet?

Perhaps surprisingly, the answer to this question is not as straightforward as it might at first seem. If neither Bill nor Sue confesses, then together they receive the shortest time in prison. However, if Sue remains silent while Bill confesses, then Bill does even better; he is let go. Of course the same thing happens, in reverse, if Bill remains silent and Sue confesses.

So perhaps both prisoners should do the safe thing; that is, perhaps they should both confess. Unfortunately, this would result in ten years for each, a much stiffer sentence than they would get had they both been trusting enough to keep silent. What is the rational thing to do?

One option is to search for a Pareto-optimal outcome. In other words, Sue should search for the decision that, no matter what decision Bill makes, will leave Sue no worse off than before. (The same will obviously be true for Bill.)

The Prisoner's Dilemma

Bill and Sue have been arrested and are being held incommunicado. Each is charged with being involved in a serious crime. However, a conviction will be more easily secured if at least one of them confesses. If they both confess, each will go to prison for ten years. If Bill confesses while Sue keeps silent, Sue will go to prison for twenty years while Bill goes free. In contrast, if Sue confesses while Bill keeps silent, Bill will go to prison for twenty years while Sue goes free. Finally, if both keep silent—that is, if neither confesses—each will be convicted on a much lesser charge, and each will serve a prison term of just one year.

Assuming that Bill and Sue's goal is to minimize their own individual time in prison, should they confess or keep quiet?

It turns out that a dilemma arises in this situation—and in others like it—since different principles, such as the principle of expected utility and the principle of dominance, give different answers to the question of what will be the rational thing to do. In other words, we appear to have equally defensible yet contradictory models of rationality. How shall we choose between them?

Now it is not hard to see that, regardless of what the other prisoner does, choosing to confess will always result in a Pareto improvement over choosing to remain silent, from the point of view of each individual prisoner. Thus, for each individual, confessing appears to produce a Pareto-optimal outcome. The trouble, of course, is that this results in both Bill and Sue going to jail for ten years and, of the four possible outcomes (no time in jail, one year in jail, ten years in jail, and twenty years in jail), this is clearly one of the worst possible outcomes. In other words, this individually dominant strategy not only fails to attain the mutually preferred outcome, it also fails to attain the outcome Bill and Sue would each prefer individually.

A second option will be for each prisoner to try to maximize his or her expected utility according to the principle of expected utility. In this case, each prisoner will do the appropriate calculation in order to discover which of the two alternative actions, confessing or not confessing, is preferable. In this case, even if the likelihood of Bill and Sue acting in concert is relatively low, say, 60 percent, we find that the preferred action is to not confess, since it is this action that produces the highest probability of a preferred outcome. The problem with this course of action is that, regardless of the outcome, each prisoner will have had to settle for "second best." That is, the outcome is not only not optimal, it is not even Pareto-optimal. Confessing would always have produced an even better outcome. Yet if so, how can it remain rational to not take advantage of this fact?

What do these arguments show? According to one author, they show "that if both players make the rational choice, ... both lose."[14] According to another, it shows that "two so-called irrational players will fare much better than two so-called rational ones."[15] Yet if it is true that the only way to obtain either a mutually, or an individually, preferred result is for there to be a breakdown of rationality, certainly this appears to be a discouraging result. Yet what is more likely? Is it more likely that rational decisions will fail to help us discover the truth of the matter in such cases as these, or is it more likely that, so far at least, our theories of what it is to be rational are still incomplete? According to much recent work in decision theory, it is the second of these two alternatives that appears to be the most plausible.[16] Thus, the moral we draw from the prisoner's dilemma is that, although we still do not have a fully correct and comprehensive theory of rationality, it is by learning to solve problems such as the prisoner's dilemma that we will make advances in this area.

Exercise 12.3

1. Calculate the expected utility for confessing and for not confessing for both Bill and Sue in the prisoner's dilemma. According to the rule of expected utility, which action is preferable?

2. Given the same situation, which action is preferable according to the principle of dominance?

3. Given the same situation, which action is preferable according to the minimax principle?

Summary

Because economics can be divided into two components—microeconomics and macroeconomics—we realized early in this chapter that economic reasoning can be susceptible to fallacies such as the *fallacy of composition* (which occurs whenever reasoning that applies to parts is confused with reasoning that applies to wholes) and the *fallacy of division* (which occurs whenever reasoning that applies to wholes is confused with reasoning that applies to parts).

Partly as a result of such considerations, we began investigating decision theory. Decision theory attempts to provide a set of exact criteria for making rational or optimal decisions under conditions of risk and uncertainty. In this context, three rules or principles seemed to be especially important. According to the *principle of expected utility*, that action is best that maximizes expected utility. According to the *principle of dominance* (or the *sure-thing principle*), if in all possible states of affairs, the consequences of selecting one action over a second are at least as desirable as those of selecting the second over the first, and sometimes better, then a rational decision-maker will prefer the first action to the second. Finally, according to the *minimax principle*, a rational decision-maker will prefer that action that minimizes the maximum possible loss or error.

The difficulty with these principles is that, although individually they may all appear quite plausible, they are jointly inconsistent. In situations such as the prisoner's dilemma, they appear to provide equally defensible yet contradictory models of rationality. Thus, until we are able to discover a more comprehensive and unified account of rationality, we will be unable to decide when it is best to use one principle rather than another. Since it is useful to classify decision theory as a type of dialectic, it follows that our theory of dialectic, too, is not yet complete. As we discover ways to improve our theory of dialectic, it is likely that we will also discover ways to improve decision theory.

Weblinks

McMaster University's History of Economic Thought

socserv2.socsci.mcmaster.ca:80/~econ/ugcm/3ll3/index.html

An Outline of the History of Game Theory

william-king.www.drexel.edu/top/class/histf.html

Stanford Encyclopedia of Philosophy—Prisoner's Dilemma

plato.stanford.edu/entries/prisoner-dilemma/

Notes

1. Quoted in Robert L. Heilbroner, *The Worldly Philosophers* (New York: Simon and Schuster, revised edition, 1972), 76.

2. See Leonard Silk, *Economics in Plain English* (New York: Simon and Schuster. 1978), 31.

3. Ibid., 83–84.

4. Physics is another such science. The laws of microphysics do not always apply to, or have counterparts in, the domain of macrophysics, and vice versa. In fact, one debate that is currently taking place in physics is whether the law of causality, which is believed to hold for macro-events, also holds for micro-events.

5. See R. Whatley, *Elements of Logic* (New York: Sheldon Press, 1826), 214–215.

6. For further discussion, see John Woods and Douglas Walton, "Composition and Division," *Studia Logica* 36 (1977), 381–406.

7. Leonard Silk, *Contemporary Economics, Principles and Issues* (New York: McGraw-Hill, revised edition, 1975), 13–14.

8. Jeremy Bentham, *Introduction to the Principles of Morals and Legislation* (London: Athlone Press, 1970), 26.

9. John von Neumann and Oskar Morgenstern, *Theory of Games and Economic Behaviour* (Princeton: Princeton University Press, 1944), 154.

10. Kenneth J. Arrow, *Social Choice and Individual Values* (New York: John Wiley, 1951).

11. This paradox was first examined by E.J. Nanson in a paper in *Transactions and Proceedings of the Royal Society of Victoria* 19 (1882).

12. Vilfredo Pareto, *Manuel d'economie politique*, translated by Alfred Bonnet (Paris: V. Girad and E. Briere, 1909), 617–618.

13. See Richmond Campbell and Lanning Sowden, *Paradoxes of Rationality and Cooperation* (Vancouver: UBC Press, 1985), and Peter A. Danielson, *Modeling Rationality, Morality and Evolution* (New York: Oxford University Press, 1998).

14. Antol Rapaport, "Escape from Paradox," *Scientific American* 217 (1967) 51.

15. R.D. Luce and H. Raiffa, *Games and Decisions* (New York: John Wiley 1957), 91.

16. For a summary of recent work in this area, see A.D. Irvine, "How Braess' Paradox Solves Newcomb's Problem," *International Studies in the Philosophy of Science* 7 (1993), no. 2, 145–164, repr. in Peter Danielson, *Modeling Rationality, Morality and Evolution* (New York: Oxford University Press, 1998), 67–91.

Legal Reasoning

OUR purpose in this chapter is to investigate several important aspects of legal reasoning that relate directly to the basic theme of this book, namely the construction and critical appraisal of arguments. In doing so, we will concentrate on several features of argument that are common to both criminal and civil law within the common law tradition.[1] Details will of course vary slightly from jurisdiction to jurisdiction. Even so, many of the most important underlying principles remain common to all jurisdictions.

1. Burden of Proof versus Standard of Proof

When there is a requirement for one party in a dispute to prove a point, we say that the *burden of proof* rests with that party. In criminal law (with only rare and controversial exceptions), the burden of proof rests entirely with the prosecution. In theory at least, this means that if a defendant believes that the prosecution has been unsuccessful in proving its case, and that this is plainly seen by all concerned, then the defendant need not even answer the charge. This is what is meant by the famous slogan, "innocent until proven guilty."

For example, consider the case of a man who has been charged with first-degree murder. To discharge its burden of proof, the prosecution must do two things. First, it must show that the defendant behaved, at the time in question, in a certain way. In this case, the prosecution must show that the defendant committed an act[2] (*actus reus*) that caused the death of the victim. Second, it must show that certain other conditions necessary for the legal definition of murder have been satisfied. These include both wilful intent and knowledge of one's actions (*mens rea*) on the part of the defendant. The prosecution will have made a successful case if, in the opinion of the jury or trier of fact, it meets its burden of proof.[3]

For its part, although the defence in theory need not respond to the prosecution's case, it will in fact respond whenever it believes it is advantageous to do so. For example, if the defence believes that the accused has an unbreakable alibi because he was in another city at the time of the crime, it may present evidence to this effect. In doing so, the defence not only argues that the prosecution's case does not discharge its required burden of proof (i.e., that the Crown has not proven its case), it also argues that no other evidence could satisfy the legal test (i.e., that the accused is innocent). However, in most criminal cases, the primary role of the defence is simply to discredit the prosecution's case more indirectly, for example by showing that witnesses for the prosecution have little credibility.

> ### Burden of Proof
>
> When there is a requirement for one party in a dispute to prove a point, we say that the *burden of proof* rests with that party. In criminal law, the burden of proof rests entirely with the prosecution. This is what is meant by the famous slogan, "innocent until proven guilty."

Among the more indirect ways of undermining a prosecution's case are these. First, the defence can admit to committing the alleged acts (for example, that his action caused the death of the victim), but deny that this behaviour meets all of the criteria required for the action to satisfy the legal definition of murder. For example, if the death of the victim were an accident, the accused could argue that he lacked the wilful intent required for murder.

Second, the defence may deny that the accused caused the death of the victim. Such a defence is not uncommon when the prosecution lacks an eyewitness account or strong forensic evidence. In such cases, the defence will attempt to show that an alternative theory of the case is also supported by the evidence. In other words, the defence will attempt to show that the prosecution's argument is, in an important sense, implausible. If the defence is successful in this regard, we say that the prosecution's case has failed to meet the required *standard of proof*.

In most jurisdictions the standard of proof in criminal matters is proof beyond a reasonable doubt. There is no exact definition of this concept, and certainly there is no way to determine whether juries honour it in all situations. However, one common misconception is that a case meets this standard only when the judge or jurors are "absolutely certain" that the accused did it. This is not what the standard requires. Rather, it requires only that (1) the prosecution's case be accepted by the jury, and that (2) had the jury not accepted it (either by rejecting it outright, or by giving sufficient credence to an alternative theory), then the jury would have acted *unreasonably*. In other words, it is not necessary that jurors be "absolutely certain" that the accused be guilty; rather, they must simply be satisfied that there is no reasonable alternative. The first of these requirements is a *psychological* property, having to do with how committed a person is to a particular belief; the second is a *logical* one, having to do with what a reasonable person would accept.

In actual practice it is often difficult for juries to keep this difference in mind. Thus, it is unsurprising that trials can be forums for argument, which are full of emotional give-and-take. If the prosecutor can arouse the jury so as to cause it to be certain that the accused committed the crime, it is highly likely that the jury will believe itself to have satisfied the requirement of finding proof beyond a reasonable doubt. After all, who among us would be willing to admit that our standards of reasoning may be less than ideal?[4]

It is interesting to observe that the level of emotion is often more subdued in civil trials than in criminal ones. This is so notwithstanding the fact that in all sorts of civil cases a loss could be devastating. One reason for this difference is because the standard of proof in civil proceedings is not "proof beyond a reasonable doubt,"

Burden of Proof versus Standard of Proof

It is one thing to know with whom the burden of proof rests, but quite another to know how much and what type of evidence is required to satisfy that burden. For example, must the evidence be absolutely conclusive? Or must it only make the case beyond a reasonable doubt? Must it merely identify the most likely of several plausible alternatives? Or must it meet some objective, or well-defined standard? To identify the *standard of proof* in an argument is, in effect, to determine how much and what type of evidence is required to satisfy the *burden of proof*.

but rather "proof on the balance of probabilities." This second standard is met when the jury, or the judge, is prepared to attach a probability of at least 51 percent to the case of either the plaintiff or the defendant.

This is a much lower standard than required in criminal law. Here too, however, this standard is often confused with an entirely different and wholly inappropriate standard. This comes about because the basic idea behind the civil standard is that the side that gets the better of the argument, no matter how slight the margin, wins. However, there are two incompatible ways in which this basic idea might be realized in practice. First, a litigant might be said to satisfy the better-case standard whenever the probability of his own case is at least slightly higher than that of his opponent's case. Second, a litigant might be said to satisfy the better-case standard whenever the probability attaching to his case and the probability attaching to his opponent's case sum to 1, and the probability attaching to the first litigant's case is the higher of the two.

Under the first of these two interpretations it would be easy to have two worthless cases presented, with one of them having a probability of, say, 0.10, and the other having a probability of, say, 0.04. If we then applied the balance-of-probabilities standard under this first interpretation, a judge or jury would be compelled to find for the side with the higher, but still disgracefully low, probability. On the other hand, under the second and correct interpretation, judges and juries are required to do two things. First, they must agree not to prejudge the case. In other words, they must acknowledge that, prior to the presentation of evidence, the probability of each side's claim is assumed to be unknown. Then, solely on the basis of the evidence presented at the trial, they must assign a conditional probability to each side's claim. In other words, letting C_1 be the claim of the plaintiff, C_2 be the claim of the defendant, and E the (total) evidence presented at the trial, they must calculate both $\Pr(C_1|E)$ and $\Pr(C_2|E)$.

If either $\Pr(C_1|E)$ or $\Pr(C_2|E)$ turns out to be 0.51 or greater, then C_1 or, as the case may be, C_2 meets the balance of probabilities standard. What is required is not just that the winning case have a higher probability than the losing case, but that the winning case be one in which the evidence raises the probability of the case from zero to more than one-half.

Being clear about this distinction between our two different ways of interpreting the civil law standard of proof helps guard against the following type of equivocation:

The case for claim C_1 is more probable [in the first sense] than the case for claim C_2

More probable cases [in the second sense] meet the standard of proof for civil cases

Therefore, the case for claim C_1 meets the standard of proof for civil cases.

Unless C_1 is not simply more probable than C_2, but also more probable than its denial, we cannot say that the appropriate standard of proof has been met.

Exercise 13.1

1. Imagine a criminal trial in which both physical and eyewitness evidence is presented. The prosecution's case is an interpretation of this evidence. If the defence has an alternative theory of the case, it will be a different and incompatible interpretation of this same evidence. Yet we know that any body of evidence will always be open to different and incompatible interpretations. Does this fact preclude the prosecution from discharging its burden of proof? Why or why not?

2. Unfortunately, Bill has been charged with writing bad cheques. The charge is fraud, a serious matter. Bill insists that it was an oversight on his part. He inadvertently drew the cheque on his chequing account when he had intended to write it on his savings account. As it happens, Bill has had three prior convictions for cheque fraud, which

the prosecution wants admitted as similar-fact evidence. Is the prosecution correct that this information is relevant? Why or why not?

3. Imagine a civil trial in which Sue is charged with breach of contract. It is a tautology, of course, that either she did or didn't do it. (In other words, either S or $\sim S$ will turn out to be true, and $Pr(S \lor \sim S) = 1$.) If so, how should we evaluate the following argument:

> $Pr(S) = 0.5$
> $Pr(\sim S) = 0.5$
> The standard of proof in civil cases is 51 percent or better
> Sue's case is a civil case
> _____
> Therefore, Sue must be acquitted.

2. Evidence and Expert Opinion

In a court of law, evidence falls into three main categories: (1) *physical evidence*, (2) *eyewitness testimony*, and (3) *expert testimony* by qualified witnesses. These items usually become evidence only when introduced by a sworn witness deemed competent by the court.

For example, consider again the case of a man accused of murder. When the charge comes to trial, the investigating police officer may testify about the physical evidence; for example, that the victim was found dead in a hotel room with an apparent gunshot wound to his chest. A forensic expert may then testify that the chest wound was caused by a .44 Magnum fired at close range, and an expert pathologist may further testify that the death was caused by that gunshot. Finally, there may be an eyewitness who testifies that Sue's friend was observed running from the crime scene shortly after the time of death, and that he was seen throwing what appeared to be a handgun into the sewer.

> **Types of Evidence**
>
> During a trial, evidence falls into three main categories: (1) *physical evidence*, (2) *eyewitness testimony*, and (3) *expert testimony* by qualified witnesses. Eyewitness testimony can be unreliable to the extent that people have faulty memories, to the extent that it is subject to leading questions by persons in authority, and to the extent that a person's memory may be inappropriately influenced by strong emotions such as terror or revulsion. Expert opinion testimony may be controversial since the decision to admit such testimony rests with a judge, someone who is a layperson in the expert's area of expertise. Also problematic are those disciplines in which experts can fall into extensive and intractable disagreement. Physical evidence is thus often thought to be the most reliable of these three main types of evidence.

We have already noticed that even under ideal conditions eyewitness testimony can be less than 100 percent reliable.[5] Memories can be faulty and eyewitness reports can be mistaken when witnesses are faced with leading or hostile questions from persons in authority. In addition, eyewitness reports often tend to be unreliable when an observation is accompanied by high levels of emotion such as fear, disgust, or horror, or when a witness is given only a short time in which to observe an unfamiliar situation.

Here we see a recurrence of several points discussed in earlier chapters. A leading or complex question (for example, "At what point did the suspect begin acting suspiciously?") carries with it a suggestion not previously volunteered by the witness. Such questions carry with them suggestions which, if untrue and if not effectively countered, may do unwarranted damage to one's position. At the same time, such suggestions are less likely to be questioned when they are made by an authority figure, such as a police officer or medical doctor. This, of course, takes us straight into the embrace of the *ad verecundiam*. In answering an officer's leading question, a witness is not likely making anything like an overt argument. However, some witnesses may tacitly reason in roughly the following way:

Leading questions nearly always are pointed questions.

Pointed questions often express the questioner's own conviction or suspicion.

When the police officer asked me the pointed question, "At what point did the suspect begin acting suspiciously?," he may well have been indicating his conviction that the suspect must have been acting suspiciously.

Police officers are not triflers. They are responsible in their actions and they know much more about these things than I do.

So, come to think of it, I guess his action could be counted as a suspicious action, and I should report this.

Courts recognize that eyewitness testimony, even when sincerely and confidently offered, is often less reliable than people sometimes think. For this reason, especially in trials concerning serious wrongdoing, a prosecutor is sometimes not considered to have met the applicable standard of proof unless he or she is able to offer corroboration for all eyewitness evidence. Corroboration can come about through a second eyewitness or through physical or forensic evidence.

It is also interesting to observe that in most systems of justice, before an expert's evidence can be heard, the judge must hear arguments from both sides as to the admissibility of this proposed evidence. When doing so the judge must consider three basic points:

First, the witness' discipline must be an expert discipline. In other words, the discipline must be based on a type of enquiry for which the concept of expertise can be objectively defined. Virtually everyone agrees that pathology, say, is an expert discipline and that creation science, say, is not. People tend to be less certain about the status of psychiatry, although at least in some areas of psychology there tends to be sufficient agreement that experts may be called.

Second, the witness must not only be a practitioner of an expert discipline, but must also be an expert in that discipline. To determine this, it is common for judges to consider indicators of expertise such as (1) the reputation of the witness among other experts and practitioners, (2) the record of peer-reviewed scientific and professional publications, including, perhaps, a leading textbook in the field, (3) the frequency with which the witness' publications are cited by other researchers in the field, (4) the reputation of the institutions he has worked for, (5) his seniority, (6) the range of his experience, and so on.

Third, it is also necessary to determine whether the witness' discipline, and his expertise in that discipline, are such as to make it reasonable to suppose that his evidence would be directly related to his discipline and would be relevant to the issue at hand.

It is also interesting to note that the person whose role it is to determine whether a would-be witness is an expert in an expert discipline is the judge, someone who is almost never himself an expert in any discipline whose expertise he must judge. In this he is guided by two powerful assumptions: (1) that a discipline's expertise is reliably fixed by the collective judgment of the scientific or scholarly community at large, and (2) that a practitioner's expertise in an expert discipline is capable of being determined by the collective judgment of that discipline.

Both of these are conservative assumptions, making it difficult to determine that a comparatively new discipline is indeed an expert discipline. In contrast, it is easier to determine whether a practitioner of a discipline is an expert in that discipline, regardless of whether the discipline itself is expert. Accordingly, in actual legal practice, it is sometimes noticeable that a judge will lean more on the guidance of the second rather than the first of these two assumptions.

> **Opinion versus Expert Opinion**
> In order for a witness' testimony to be classified as *expert opinion* (as opposed to *mere opinion*), and in order for that testimony to be admissible in court, three conditions must be satisfied: (1) the witness' discipline must be an expert discipline, (2) the witness must not only be a practitioner of an expert discipline, he or she must also be an expert in that discipline, and, (3) the testimony must be about matters covered by that discipline and must be directly relevant to the issue at hand.

One of the difficulties for people seeking to be guided by the first of these assumptions is that in many disciplines there is a high degree of disagreement, at least about some questions. Psychiatry provides a case in point. There are many contending schools of thought in psychiatry, and there is a corresponding tendency to define certain psychiatric concepts in rival ways. Psychiatric disagreement makes it possible for trial counsel to pick and choose their experts on the basis of their known theoretical leanings, leanings that increase the chances that the expert will see things in a way favourable to one viewpoint rather than another. This introduces a factor of structural bias into the practice of calling and hearing from experts. This is not to say that such witnesses are insincere, or that they see their resistance to the views of rivals as anything but scientifically well grounded, but it is a serious problem all the same.

When John Hinckley shot and seriously wounded then-U.S.-president Ronald Reagan during the early 1980s, Hinckley was charged with attempted murder. During the trial, the defence (supported by its expert witnesses) argued that Hinckley was suffering from a serious mental illness at the time of the shooting. As a result, they argued, he should not be found guilty for reasons of diminished responsibility or incapacity. The prosecution, on the other hand, had its experts testify in support of the view that Hinckley was suffering from a mere personality disorder which, though unpleasant for those having it, comes nowhere close to constituting the type of incapacity that could justify a claim of diminished responsibility. As it turns out, the jury found for the defence. Hinckley was found to be not criminally responsible on grounds of diminished responsibility and was placed indefinitely in the care of a hospital for the criminally insane; not a prison sentence, but a kind of sentence all the same.

However, not long afterwards, Hinckley's lawyers attempted to have him released from the hospital. In this they were once again opposed by a team of lawyers acting on behalf of the government. To these ends, the two teams of lawyers simply exchanged one another's opinions. The government now insisted that Hinckley was much more seriously afflicted than would be explained by a mere personality disorder, and the defence argued that he was fully competent, although somewhat neurotic—and who among us isn't just a little neurotic? Observers of Hinckley both before the trial and during his period of incarceration could discern no significant change in his psychological state. This suggests that he was mentally incompetent throughout, or modestly neurotic throughout, and that the total body of psychiatric evidence in this case was flawed.

It is not to be expected, of course, that experts from even highly unified expert disciplines will agree on all matters. Most disciplines have many open questions that research programs have yet to bring to a close. It is understood, therefore, that expert testimony is opinion testimony in two distinct senses: First, on matters on which there is a settled consensus in the discipline, this consensus may be taken as fact by the discipline, but it is taken as opinion by the court. Second, on matters in which the discipline itself is split, or in which there is an open question in the discipline, an expert's view is considered to be opinion by both the discipline and the court.

The issue of expert evidence is complex and challenging (and interesting). It is easy to see that its analysis calls into play several of the issues that we have already investigated in this book. Most obvious, perhaps, is the Lockean version of the *ad verecundiam*, arguments to the effect that it would be inappropriate (i.e., "immodest" or even "impudent") not to heed the opinions of experts. Our previous analysis of the *ad verecundiam* is relevant here at all levels. An expert's testimony is considered appropriate because he or she is an expert. A person is deemed to be an expert because he or she is judged to be so by other experts. A discipline achieves the standing of an expert discipline because it has been determined to be so by the community of scholars involved in expert disciplines, and so on.

Although there is nothing fallacious about the *ad verecundiam* as such, Locke certainly recognizes that the following argument form is not valid:

The experts agree that *p*

Therefore, *p* is the case.

Similarly, the courts also recognize that this form of argument need not be truth-preserving. As a result, they are clear that the only correct use the members of a jury can make of an expert's opinion is to weigh its plausibility and use it as they see fit. This is in line with the more modern conception of the *ad verecundiam*. Under this conception, the *ad verecundiam* is a fallacy whenever there is either something defective about the expert's "expertise," or it is expertise of a sort that is not relevant to the case at hand.

Also deeply imbedded in arguments based upon expert opinion are aspects of *ad populum* arguments (in the popularity sense). Recall that under Aristotle's definition, *endoxa* are the opinions of everyone, or of the many, or of the wise.[6] When a judge examines a discipline for expertise, and when he judges the expert credentials of a practitioner, ultimately he has, apart from his common sense, nothing to fall back upon but legal precedent and *endoxa*.

Since legal precedents always have their point of origin in legal innovations, we would be correct to say that the law on expertise is fundamentally a matter of judges relying on *endoxa*. Thus, someone is an expert in a discipline only if he is unanimously or widely believed to be an expert by practitioners of the discipline ("the wise," in Aristotle's terminology). Why is this a reliable criterion? Isn't it then the case that determinations of expertise are simply being made by way of popularity contests? It turns out that this is not so, and the reason is twofold.

First, concerning disciplines, the reason that the community of scientists believes that physics, say, is an expert discipline, is that its being an expert discipline is the best explanation for its passing the survival-of-the-fittest test. Astrology, on the other hand, enjoys no such support. The best explanation as to why so many people believe astrology to be an expert discipline is not that it is one, but rather that they are naive or uninformed. Astrology certainly does not satisfy the survival-of-the-fittest test in any epistemic sense. It has survived, of course, but not on account of its epistemic fitness. Many of its predictions succeed at a rate that is no better than chance; and of those predictions that do succeed, many are not detailed enough or accurate enough to make their success significant. The popularity of astrology, it turns out, is better explained because many people accept it as a form of entertainment—as something to lighten their day—or because they are simply uninformed, rather than as an expert discipline in any reliable epistemic sense.

Second, with respect to a judge's determination of a practitioner's expertise, the fact that within a discipline everyone, or nearly everyone, believes the witness to be an expert, including other experts, is best explained by the fact that he is indeed an expert. Here, too, the judgment about individuals is measured by the survival-of-the-fittest condition. Not only must the individual in question follow the methods of the discipline, he or she must produce results judged by the standards of that discipline to be of a kind, and on a scale, that constitutes objective, measurable success.

Exercise 13.2

1. Imagine that Bill was an eyewitness in a drive-by shooting that resulted in the death of a three-year-old girl. Bill has identified the driver in the car and has given evidence to that effect in the subsequent trial. The situation that Bill found himself in that day was as follows: (1) Bill has 20/20 vision; (2) the shooting took place at noon on a sunny day; (3) Bill was directly across the street from where the little girl was shot; (4) Bill was looking in that direction, since he wanted to photograph the little girl on her tricycle; (5) the little girl was the daughter of Bill's best friend, Tom; (6) as the shooter's car passed this point, it moved from Bill's right to left, while driving on the right-hand side of the street; (7) consequently, the driver of the car was directly in Bill's field of vision at a distance of one half the width of an ordinary residential street. You are counsel for the defence. How would you attempt to discredit Bill's eyewitness testimony?

2. In late nineteenth-century Vienna, in one of the childbirth wings of a large hospital, attending doctors would begin their days doing surgery. Following surgery they either just dried their hands or gave them a quick wash with soap and water. Then they assisted with the delivery of children. In the pediatric ward, there were many deaths attributed to "child-bed fever." Imagine that an official inquiry has been called to investigate this phenomenon. Would the chief physician of this ward qualify as an expert witness? Why or why not?

3. For many years before her death, the American astrologer Dorothy Dix was widely acknowledged to be at the top of her profession. Her opinions were directed to the whole spectrum of the human condition, and her predictions about celebrities were themselves celebrated. Her newspaper column and magazine articles were read by millions. Conceding that Mrs. Dix was an expert in her field, could she qualify as an expert witness? Why or why not?

4. In the field of economics, there are many rival schools (e.g., the neoclassical school, the school of welfare economics, and the supply-side school). In a great many instances, economists from these and other schools are called as expert witnesses before courts and government inquiries. How, given the divisions that exist in economics, can economists qualify as expert witnesses?

3. Legal Precedent and Analogical Argument

One of the great economies of legal practice is its disinclination to re-invent the wheel. On any given day, the courts are influenced by past practice and by the disposition of prior cases. When prior cases influence subsequent cases, a legal *precedent* is said to apply. During a trial the judge is the sole interpreter of the rules of procedure, the rules of evidence, and the relevant statutes and legal precedents. In a criminal trial by jury, the jury is the sole finder of fact. In a trial by a judge,[7] the judge discharges this obligation as well. Precedents arise from a judge's findings in matters of the interpretation and application of the law.

A good way to see how the concept of precedent works in practice is to consider a particular case. For example, consider a case in which a judge extends the application of a copyright and licensing agreement to include not just traditional media, but also publication on the Internet. We can assume that this would be an example of judicial innovation. Our question is, "How does an act of judicial innovation acquire the status of precedent?" In a somewhat simplified form, the answer is that unless and until the new legal ruling is overturned by a higher court, the ruling immediately falls within the rule of precedents; namely, that similar cases must be dealt with in similar ways (*stare decisis*). Thus, unless successfully challenged, the innovator's point of law must be allowed to influence the findings of future judges in cases sufficiently similar to the case in which the innovation arose. This influence may occur in either of two ways: in jurisdictions in which a lower court must pay deference, the precedent will be *binding*; in jurisdictions in which a court need not pay deference, the precedent will be merely *persuasive*.

It is instructive to contrast precedents in law with experimental findings in science. Science, too, is an innovator, discovering and producing new results and, like scientific results, legal innovations have repercussions beyond the cases in which they were first introduced. Just as a new finding in, say, biology may also have application in biochemistry, a legal innovation in a jurisdiction such as the Australian state of New South Wales may influence decisions in neighbouring states such as Victoria, or even as far away as Canada. In contrast, one point of difference between scientific and legal innovation is that a new result in science is not authoritative until confirming experiments are reproduced widely and often, and attempts at disconfirmation are also made widely and often. A legal innovation, in contrast, is a precedent on the basis of a finding in a single case, unless it is successfully overturned.

> **Legal Precedent**
> The *rule of precedent* states that similar cases must be dealt with in similar ways. In other words, the decisions on a point of law in cases that are similar to previous cases must be influenced by those cases. When earlier cases influence subsequent cases, a legal *precedent* is said to apply. This influence may occur in either of two ways: in jurisdictions in which a lower court must pay deference, the legal precedent will be *binding*; in jurisdictions in which a lower court need not pay deference, the legal precedent will be merely *persuasive*.

This concept of precedent is intimately bound up with claims of similarity, or with what is often called *analogy*. "Analogy" is a powerful word, but an ambiguous one. We must take appropriate care, therefore, to avoid confusion. Most people would interpret the statement, "Prince Philip is the First Lady of Great Britain" as an analogy. It is a statement in which the predicate "is the First Lady of Great Britain" applies to Philip only in an analogical sense. Thus it clearly has something to do with similarity. Philip resembles, or is similar to, the American First Lady in the sense that both are spouses and both fill the role of consort to the Head of State in their respective countries. However, what does an analogy like this have to do with reasoning? How can analogies help us draw reasonable or rational inferences?

To answer these questions it is worth noting something about both the *structure* and the *strength* of arguments from analogy. What structure do arguments from analogy have? As a first attempt at answering this question, we might suggest that they have the following general structure:

Case A has characteristics *a, b, c, ...*, and also has characteristic *x*.
Case B has characteristics *a, b, c, ...*

Therefore, case B also has characteristic *x*.

In other words, because there is an analogy between cases A and B, and because we know that case A has characteristic *x*, we conclude that case B will have characteristic *x* as well.

Under this analysis, it appears that analogical arguments are a type of inductive or ampliative argument. That is, although they do not provide conclusive evidence in favour of a conclusion, they may turn out to be inductively strong.

The first thing to note is that the strength of such an argument will likely depend in part on the number of similar characteristics between case A and case B. Obviously, the greater the number of similarities, the stronger the analogy and the stronger the argument. At the same time, it is also worth noting that should case A and case B also differ with regard to a number of characteristics this will serve to weaken both the analogy and the overall argument. For example, if case A and case B both share a large number of characteristics but they differ in that in A the defendant lacked the intention to commit murder but in B the defendant had this intention, this may affect the strength of the analogy. Thus we may want to modify our original argument structure to include mention of this point as follows:

Case A has characteristics *a, b, c, ...*, and also has characteristic *x*.
Case B has characteristics *a, b, c, ...*
There are no (or few) characteristics that case A has and case B lacks, or that case B has and case A lacks.

Therefore, case B also has characteristic *x*.

However, another point now arises. Every pair of cases, we know, will have differences as well as similarities, for otherwise they would be one case under two different descriptions rather than two; but, upon reflection, we see that it will not be just the *number* of similarities and differences, but the *relevancy* of these similarities and differences, that is important. Specifically when applied to legal reasoning, as opposed to the analysis of facts, we say that it is necessary to distinguish between the *ratio decidendi*, or the grounds or reasons for the decision, those factors that go to the heart of the matter, and the *obiter dicta*, or those incidental or collateral factors that are merely accidental.

For example, we recognize immediately that the defendant's intention (or lack of intention) to commit murder is relevant to the case at hand, but other factors—such as where the crime may have occurred, or whether the murderer was a man or woman, or whether the murderer wore brown socks or blue socks—will not. That is, in determining whether or not a convicted murderer should receive a particular sentence, the judge may conclude that a previous case should serve as a precedent even if the number of dissimilarities between the two cases is much greater than the number of similarities. For example, even if the murderer in the first case was male, and short, and spoke with an accent, and was estranged from his brother, and lived in the city, and was a university graduate, and enjoyed listening to Mozart, and so on, and none of these things were true of the murderer in the second case, none of these differences will turn out to be relevant. All are irrelevant. In contrast, the similarities that exist between the two cases may turn out to be comparatively small in number, but highly relevant. For example, if both murderers caused the same degree of suffering in their victims, if they both showed the same degree of remorse for their crime, and if they both had the same type of partially redeeming motive, it may turn out that the analogy between the two cases is a strong one. Thus we will want to modify the structure of our argument from analogy yet again:

> Case A has relevant characteristics *a, b, c, …*, and also has characteristic *x*.
> Case B has relevant characteristics *a, b, c, …*.
> There are no (or few) relevant characteristics that case A has and case B lacks, or that case B has and case A lacks.
>
> ---
>
> Therefore, case B also has characteristic *x*.

In other words, it is by focusing on not just the number of similarities and differences, but also on the number of *relevant* similarities and differences between the two cases, that we are able to determine the strength of an argument from analogy.

Of course, even this improvement is not enough to turn an argument from analogy into a valid argument. To do so, we would need to add a third premiss, namely that "All cases that have relevant characteristics *a, b, c, …*, also have characteristic *x*." Yet in almost all situations this proposed premiss will simply be too strong to be true. Extenuating circumstances will, in principle at least, always make it possible for further information to strengthen or weaken an analogy.

In this context we may want to consider what may be the most often-cited ethical analogy of the past half-century. The argument is due to the American philosopher Judith Jarvis Thomson:

> You wake up in the morning and find yourself back in bed with an unconscious violinist. A famous unconscious violinist. He has been found to have a fatal kidney aliment, and the Society of Music Lovers has canvassed all the available

Reasoning by Analogy

Determining whether two legal cases are similar enough for one to serve as a precedent for the other requires that we be able to reason successfully by analogy. In order to do this, we must discover those relevant respects in which the cases are similar and those relevant respects in which the cases are not. In general, arguments by analogy can be said to have the following form:

Case A has relevant characteristics *a, b, c, ...*, and also has characteristic *x*.
Case B has relevant characteristics *a, b, c, ...*

There are no (or few) relevant characteristics that case A has and case B lacks, or that case B has and case A lacks.

_____

Therefore, case B also has characteristic *x*.

records and found that you alone have the right blood type to help. They have therefore kidnapped you, and last night the violinist's circulatory system was plugged into yours, so that your kidneys can be used to extract poisons from his blood as well as your own. The director of the hospital now tells you, "Look, we're sorry the Society of Music Lovers did this to you—we would never have permitted it if we had known. But still, they did it, and the violinist now is plugged into you. To unplug you would be to kill him. But never mind, it's only for nine months. By then he will have recovered from his ailment, and can safely be unplugged from you." Is it morally incumbent on you to accede to this situation? No doubt it would be very nice if you did, a great kindness. But do you have to accede to it? What if it were not nine months but nine years? Or longer still? What if the director of the hospital says, "Tough luck, I agree, but you've now got to stay in bed, with the violinist plugged into you, for the rest of your life. Because remember this. All persons have a right to life, and violinists are persons. Granted you have a right to decide what happens in and to your body, but a person's right to life outweighs your right to decide what happens in and to your body. So you cannot ever be unplugged from him."[8]

The point of this argument is to compare this situation with that of a woman whose unwanted pregnancy is a consequence of being raped. It is argued that because the pregnant woman's case resembles this one, there is an analogy between these two cases. If you think that the argument for not forcing someone to continue to support the life of the violinist against his or her will is a good one, then, Thomson argues, you should also accept that it is wrong to force a raped woman to continue to support the life of a fetus against her will.

In general, this argument has the following structure:

The case of the violinist has several relevant characteristics, including the fact that (1) someone has been placed in a state of vital dependency upon another person, (2) realistically speaking, this other person is the only one who is able to serve this important function, (3) the period of dependency is nine months (and perhaps longer), (4) this dependency both constitutes a grievous imped-iment to the person's freedoms and is a grievous invasion of privacy, (5) had they known about these events in advance, the authorities would never have allowed them to progress as they have, and (6) these events have occurred without the consent of the people involved; and it turns out that, in this case, (7) it is wrong to force someone to continue to support the life of another per-son against his or her will.

The case of the rape victim also has the same relevant characteristics, includ-ing the fact that (1) someone has been placed in a state of vital dependency upon another person, (2) realistically speaking, this other person is the only one who is able to serve this important function, (3) the period of dependency is nine months (and perhaps longer), (4) this dependency both constitutes a grievous impediment to the person's freedoms and is a grievous invasion of pri-vacy, (5) had they known about these events in advance, the authorities would never have allowed them to progress as they have, and (6) these events have occurred without the consent of the people involved.

There are no (or few) relevant characteristics that the case of the violinist has and the case of the rape victim lacks, or that the case of the rape victim has and the case of the violinist lacks.

Therefore, we can conclude that, in the case of the rape victim, (7) it is wrong to force someone to continue to support the life of another person against his or her will.

Is this argument a good one? The answer depends upon whether or not additional rel-evant factors can be discovered that will weaken (or further strengthen) the anal-ogy. For example, in the case of the violinist, the original crime was one of kidnapping. In the case of the unwanted pregnancy, the original crime was one of rape. Is this difference relevant? If so, does it outweigh other similarities? If not, are there other fac-tors that we have not yet mentioned that do? For example, it may turn out that the kid-napping and forced stationary medical treatment of the first victim will threaten the economic self-sufficiency of that person. Will the same be true of an unwanted preg-nancy? Is this relevant? Is the fact that we know that the violinist brings great joy to many people through his music, but that we know nothing about the life of the unborn fetus, relevant? Why or why not?

Exercise 13.3

1. Consider again the violinist argument. Construct a second argument that is as similar to the violinist argument as possible, except that in the second argument the violinist is replaced with a wholly and asym-metrically dependent conjoined twin. That is, in the second argument, the first twin could not survive separation from the sec-ond, whereas the second twin could survive separation from the first. Is this argument stronger or weaker than the violinist argu-ment? Why?

2. For each of the following arguments by analogy determine whether the analogy is strong, moderate or weak:

(a) "Neither a borrower nor a lender be;
For loan oft loses both itself and friend,
And borrowing dulls the edge of husbandry.
This above all: to thine own self be true,
And it must follow, as the night the day,
Thou canst not then be false to any man."[9]

(b) "'Do you think,' said Candide, 'that men have always massacred each other, as they do today, that they have always been false, cozening, faithless, ungrateful, thieving, weak, inconstant, mean-spirited, envious, greedy, drunken, miserly, ambitious, bloody, slanderous, debauched, fanatic, hypocritical, and stupid?'

"'Do you think,' said Martin, 'that hawks have always eaten pigeons when they could find them?'

"'Of course I do,' said Candide.

"'Well,' said Martin, 'if hawks have always had the same character, why should you suppose that men have changed theirs?'"[10]

(c) "Think of the ravens: they neither sow nor reap; they have no storehouse or barn; yet God feeds them. You are worth far more than the birds! Is there a man among you who by anxious thought can add a foot to his height? If, then, you cannot do even a very little thing, why are you anxious about the rest?

"Think of the lilies: they neither spin nor weave; yet I tell you, even Solomon in all his splendour was not attired like one of these. But if that is how God clothes the grass, which is growing in the field today, and tomorrow is thrown on the stove, how much more will he clothe you!"[11]

(d) In 1889 a New York court, in the famous case of Riggs v. Palmer, had to decide whether an heir named in the will of his grandfather could inherit under that will, even though he had murdered his grandfather to do so. The court began its reasoning with this admission: "It is quite true that statutes regulating the making, proof and effect of wills, and the devolution of property, if literally construed, and if their force and effect can in no way and under no circumstances be controlled or modified, give this property to the murderer." But the court continued to note that "all laws as well as all contracts may be controlled in their operation and effect by general, fundamental maxims of the common law. No one shall be permitted to profit by his own fraud, or to take advantage of his own wrong, or to found any claim upon his own iniquity, or to acquire property by his own crime." The murderer did not receive his inheritance.[12]

(e) "That the aggressor, who puts himself into the state of war with another, and unjustly invades another man's right, can, by such an unjust war, never come to have a right over the conquered, will be easily agreed by all men, who will not think that robbers and pirates have a right of empire over whomsoever they have force enough to master, or that men are bound by promises which unlawful force extorts from them. Should a robber break into my house, and with a dagger at my throat, make me seal deed to convey my estate to him, would this give him any title? Just such a title by his sword has an unjust conqueror who forces me into submission."[13]

4. Legal Facts and Legal Justification

In criminal cases, we have noticed, juries are finders of *fact*, while judges are finders of *legal fact*. What is the difference between facts and legal facts?

In its verdict, a jury is required to come to a determination of what actually happened in the case in question, and whether what actually happened satisfies those criteria that would make the action illegal. These are the facts of the matter about which juries make decisions. In addition, the legal system is required to discover these facts as expediently as possible.

During this process, the judge routinely guides the jury by interpreting the meaning and applicability of legal criteria and rules. In many jurisdictions, juries are bound by a judge's ruling and are not free to provide their own legal interpretations, no matter how keenly and confidently felt.[14] For their part, judges are not free to press their views about what actually happened. This is true even though they play an indispensable role in explaining and analyzing the relevant legal rules and precedents. However, once the jury's decision has been made and a court takes notice of it, this decision becomes a legal fact. The hope, of course, is that this legal fact will then correspond to the actual fact of the matter, the fact in the world or in objective reality.

Legal facts, for the most part, are those facts recorded in legal decisions, and in interpretations and explanations of the legal rules and statutes that are given to the jury. Both are important. Legal interpretations especially can be both influential and controversial. However, the most important and dramatic legal fact in a particular case is the jury's own verdict. If the verdict is "not guilty," then it becomes a legal fact that the accused is indeed not guilty, and there is then a legal requirement that he be acquitted of the charge brought against him and freed from whatever restrictions have been placed upon his liberty. If the verdict is "guilty," then it is a legal fact that the accused is indeed guilty, and there is then a legal requirement that the appropriate sanction be applied. Some such sanctions are dire, especially in jurisdictions permitting execution, but even imprisonment can be awful and, though a fine is often considered the lesser penalty, a large fine can cause financial ruin. The legal facts constituted by verdicts are therefore more or less momentous. Their importance is considerable and enduring. Of course, they are not facts; that is, real facts, but they run proxy for real facts and are intended to coincide with them to the highest degree possible. This is not to overlook a jury's intimate involvement with the legal facts imposed by a judge's instructions; but the "biggest" legal fact with which a jury comes into contact is the legal fact constituted by its own verdict.

Of course, a legal fact as constituted by a jury's verdict does not imply a real fact, a fact in the world. In other words, should it be made, the argument

It is a legal fact that *p*

———————————————

Therefore, *p*

would be invalid. It commits the Aristotelian fallacy of

> **Facts versus Legal Facts**
> In order for knowledge to advance during a dispute, there must be a significant amount of premissory stability between the various parties. Legal facts constitute the required premissory stability in a court of law. *Legal facts* may originate in a judge's interpretations and explanations of the relevant legal rules and statutes. They may also originate in the verdicts of previous juries that serve as precedents for the case under consideration.

secundum quid. In Aristotle's usage, *secundum quid* is the mistake of omitting a qualification. In our present example, it is the mistake of interpreting the above argument as if it were the following:

It is a fact that *p*

Therefore, *p*

which of course is valid. However, in giving it this interpretation we omitted the qualification "legal," and we overlooked the important point that legal facts stand to facts as city maps stand to cities, or as artificial silk stands to silk.

A real fact cannot be dislodged or displaced by a higher court or by another jury at a second trial. The fact that the chemical formula for water is H_2O (if indeed it is a fact) is impervious to legal findings to the contrary. In contrast, everyone knows that a legal finding can be mistaken and that, unfortunately, there are occasionally miscarriages of justice. These are cases in which a legal fact of guilt, say, obtains even though the real fact is to the contrary.

It is hardly surprising that we are occasionally drawn to the *secundum quid* fallacy with regard to legal facts. In reasoning about such facts, it is convenient to drop the adjective "real," but this is not the only source of the fallacy. Its main source is that legal facts trigger precisely the actions and sanctions that would be required to be triggered were they real facts. In capital punishment jurisdictions, for example, a verdict of guilty in a first-degree murder case constitutes the legal fact of guilt. This in turn triggers a series of actions leading to eventual execution. State-administered homicide is so dire, so consequential, that it is small wonder that people occasionally find it difficult to distinguish between facts and legal facts, and so commit the *secundum quid* fallacy.

In saying that the state treats a legal fact as if it were a real fact, there is no necessity to pretend that this is an undesirable thing to do. For if a system of justice works properly—that is, justly—there is in general good reason, or at least sufficient reason, to identify the two.

Verdicts, after all, are produced by trials, and trials are modes of enquiry pledged to the discovery of truth. Witnesses are sworn to tell the truth; jurors are examined and, when necessary, are excluded for bias; contending counsel relentlessly criticize each other's cases (giving rise to repeated exposure to the survival-of-the-fittest condition); and juries are obligated to reach their conclusions solely on the basis of the evidence presented to the court. What is more, a guilty verdict (in criminal cases) is held to such a high standard of proof (proof beyond a reasonable doubt) that it is reasonable to suppose that, in general, a verdict produced by a trial will be correct. In other words, the argument

It is a legal fact that *p*

Therefore, *p*

though not valid, is in general a plausible or inductively strong argument, one in which the conclusion is a plausible consequence of the premiss. Most students of the law are satisfied that in the systems of justice we have been considering in this chapter, the requirement of very high plausibility is indeed met much more often than not. Of course, strictly speaking, it is not met by this argument, plausible though its conclusion is given its premiss. Rather, the required high plausibility is obtained by regarding this argument as an enthymeme, the missing premisses of which are given by the detailed structure of the legal process itself.

Summary

When there is a requirement for one party in a dispute to prove a point, we say that the *burden of proof* rests with that party. In criminal law, the burden of proof rests entirely with the prosecution. This is what is meant by the famous slogan, "innocent until proven guilty." In contrast, to identify the *standard of proof* is, in effect, to determine how much and what type of evidence will be required to satisfy the burden of proof.

Criminal law and civil law have different standards of proof. In criminal law a verdict to convict meets the required standard of proof whenever the evidence indicates that no reasonable doubt can be maintained. In civil law the standard of proof is slightly lower. It is not "proof beyond a reasonable doubt," but rather "proof on the balance of probabilities."

During a trial, the law concerns itself with three types of evidence: (1) *physical evidence*, (2) *eyewitness testimony*, and (3) *expert opinion* testimony. Eyewitness testimony can be unreliable because of the fallible way in which perception and memory function. It can also be unreliable to the extent that it is subject to leading questions by persons in authority and to the extent that the recounting of events may be influenced by strong emotions such as terror or revulsion. Expert opinion testimony may occasionally be problematic since the decision to admit it rests with someone who is a layperson in the expert's area of expertise. Also problematic are those disciplines in which experts can fall into extensive and intractable disagreement. The modern *ad verecundiam* fallacy is especially relevant in this context.

Determining whether two legal cases are similar enough for one to serve as a precedent for the other requires that we be able to reason successfully by analogy. Thus a good deal of legal argumentation involves the drawing of analogies. In order to reason successfully by analogy, we must discover those relevant respects in which two cases are similar and those relevant respects in which the cases are dissimilar.

Finally, it is worth noting the distinction between facts (or real-world facts) and legal facts. Legal proceedings result in legal facts, which may not correspond to real facts. A legal system is a system of justice to the extent that its procedures make it unlikely that the legal facts it produces fail to be real facts as well.

Weblinks

Jurist Canada
jurist.law.utoronto.ca/

Supreme Court of Canada

www.scc-csc.gc.ca/services.htm

The Internet Encyclopedia of Philosophy—Philosophy of Law

www.utm.edu/research/iep/l/law-phil.htm

Notes

1. In contrast, little is said in this chapter that is specifically relevant to the French civil law (or code) tradition. Unlike the common law tradition that characterizes the legal systems of the United Kingdom, most Commonwealth countries, and most parts of the United States, the civil law tradition prevails throughout many countries in continental Europe, Africa, and South America. In Canada the two traditions coexist, with the civil law tradition prominent in the province of Quebec, and the common law tradition prominent in the remainder of the country. Among the main differences between the civil and common law traditions are that (1) the civil law tradition does not normally involve the use of juries, (2) the civil law tradition is inquistorial rather than adversarial, (3) the civil law tradition does not use the concept of precedent arising from binding court decisions at higher levels, and (4) the civil law tradition does not rely upon unenacted law in the way that the common law tradition does.

2. In some jurisdictions, the omission as well as the commission of certain acts may serve as the *actus reus* in a court of law.

3. For some criminal offences in some jurisdictions, defendants can elect to be tried by judge and jury, or by judge alone. Again, this difference is not important for current purposes.

4. As Descartes reminds us, "Good sense is the most fairly distributed thing in the world, for everyone thinks himself so well supplied with it that even those who are hardest to satisfy in every other way do not usually desire more of it than they already have." (See René Descartes, "Discourse on the Method of Rightly Directing One's Reason and of Seeking Truth in the Sciences," *Philosophical Writings* (Don Mills: Ontario: Nelson's University Paperbacks, 1954), 7.

5. See ch. 2.

6. See ch. 2.

7. Most of the time, in most jurisdictions, civil trials are trials by judge alone.

8. Quoted from Judith Jarvis Thomson, "A Defense of Abortion," *Philosophy and Public Affairs* 1 (1971), 48–49.

9. William Shakespeare, *Hamlet*, Act I, Scene III, 75–80.

10. Voltaire, *Candide*, ch. 21.

11. *Luke* 12, 27–28.

12. Ronald Dworkin, *Taking Rights Seriously* (Cambridge, Mass.: Harvard University Press, 1978), 23; citation: 115 N.Y. 506, 22 N.E. 188 (1889).

13. John Locke, *Of Civil Government*, ch. 16, §176.

14. In contrast to Canadian law, many American juries are allowed to disregard a judge's instructions on the law if they think that it would be unjust not to do so.

CHAPTER 14

Artificial Intelligence

THE STUDY of *artificial intelligence* (or *AI*) is the study of reasoning and other cognitive processes in non-naturally occurring systems or agents. In large measure, it is the study of how computers can be used to model many of the most complex and important aspects of human thought.

Areas in which advances in artificial intelligence have been made include natural language processing, speech recognition, natural and artificial language translation, machine learning, computer vision, and many types of search and retrieval. In addition, a large number of more specialized problem-solving skills have been developed in what are called *expert* or *knowledge-based systems*. Expert or knowledge-based systems allow computers to function at or near the level of a human expert in many specialized domains or areas of application. These areas of application include investment analysis, product-demand forecasting, medical diagnosis, transportation scheduling, industrial quality control, chemical analysis, risk assessment, and estate and insurance planning. Typically, work in AI can involve many disciplines, including computer science, philosophy, psychology, linguistics, robotics, and the neurosciences.

It may or may not turn out that the best or most efficient way to design an intelligent system is to mimic the reasoning processes that occur naturally in human beings. Even deciding what these processes are is not a simple task. As a result, most researchers measure success and failure in terms of operational outcomes rather than specific architectural ideals. Even so, there will inevitably be clear connections and analogies between AI and theories of human rationality, regardless of the degree of design similarity. In this chapter we examine some of the connections and analogies, as well as some of the differences and disanalogies, between natural and artificial intelligence.

1. Artificial Intelligence, Logic, and Computability

Most types of AI involve both a knowledge base and an inference engine. The *knowledge base* includes either expert or common-sense knowledge that is relevant to a given area or domain of reasoning. It may include detailed factual knowledge about a specific topic or topics, common-sense information of use in a variety of contexts, or a more general set of heuristics, or "rules of thumb," relevant to a particular domain.

The *inference engine* provides a mechanism for generating new knowledge or other types of output. It uses incoming data specific to a given problem together with information drawn from the knowledge base to produce these outputs. Typically, the incoming data are obtained directly from the user.

An inference engine normally consists of either a rule-based or a connectionist-based software program. In the case of a *rule-based program* (also called a *classical computationalist program*), most rules take the form of a series of nested "If ... then ___" statements. These rules allow the program to proceed to a well-defined output when given any particular set of inputs.

According to classical computationalism, computer intelligence is based upon a central processing unit that operates on information given in some recognizable symbolic language. This information is processed serially in such a way that even the most complex tasks are broken down into series of more and more simple tasks, which eventually end in combinations of binary on-off switches not dissimilar to the types of logical connectives found in truth-functional logic.

In the case of *connectionist-based programs*, the required software is developed using a set of interconnected mathematical processing elements or nodes. Using these nodes, the system is able to process information associated with any particular case. It learns from past cases by adjusting the weights (or probabilities) associated with each node. As a result, connectionist systems are often able to recognize patterns or draw analogies even when input data are noisy or ambiguous. On this model, because cognition is distributed across a network of interconnected nodes, there is no central processing unit and individual linguistic symbols are not as important as in classical computationalist programs.

Although connectionist architectures are closer in structure to what we know about the neurological arrangement of the human brain, both types of inference

AI Systems

The study of *artificial intelligence* (or *AI*) is the study of reasoning and other cognitive processes in non-naturally occurring systems or agents. In large measure, it is the study of how computers can be used to model many of the more complex and important aspects of human thought. In addition, a large number of *expert* or *knowledge-based systems* that involve problem-solving skills have been developed. Expert or knowledge-based systems allow computers to function at or near the level of a human expert in specialized domains or areas of application.

Most types of AI, including expert systems, require both a knowledge base and an inference engine. Each *knowledge base* includes either expert or common-sense knowledge that is relevant to a given domain of reasoning. Each *inference engine* provides a mechanism for generating new knowledge or other types of output. The two main types of inference engine are *rule-based* and *connectionist-based* software programs.

engine have outperformed human reasoners in some aspects of problem-solving and underperformed human reasoners in others.

What both types of architecture have in common is the idea that an intelligent agent is primarily an information-processing system. For given input, using its knowledge base together with its inference engine, the system produces a reasonable output. Regardless of whether the inference engine is understood to be primarily rule-based or primarily connectionist-based, it is the output that is judged to be either reasonable or not.

However, in the case of classic computationalism, the connections between artificial intelligence and traditional theories of logic are especially strong. On the one hand, such theories provide a familiar and easily understood method of knowledge representation, since well-understood syntactic formulas may be used to stand proxy for meaningful semantic units.

On the other hand, these same theories provide well-tested and highly successful methods of inferring new knowledge. Once information is represented and stored in logical formulas, this information is easy to manipulate using either classical or nonclassical logics. Thus, it is not accidental that one of the first systems of artificial intelligence to be developed was used to prove theorems in formal logic.

Systems of formal logic such as system P also have the advantage that they are both complete and sound. A logical system is *complete* if and only if all of the valid formulas expressible in the system are theorems of the system.[1] In other words, it is complete provided that using it we can prove *all* of the formulas that need to be proved. In contrast, a logical system is *sound* if and only if all theorems of the system are valid.[2] In other words, it is sound provided that, using it, we can prove *only* those formulas that should be proved. If system P is both sound and complete, this means that its theorems coincide exactly with the set of valid formulas expressible in that system. The system proves neither too few nor too many theorems.

Finding a logic that is complete—a logic that proves all the valid formulas—is not difficult. For example, a system of classical logic such as system P, if augmented by an axiom of the form $p \wedge {\sim} p$, would always be complete. In this logic, since everything follows from a contradiction, every well-formed formula will turn out to be a theorem,[3] and if every well-formed formula turns out to be a theorem, then obviously all of the valid formulas will be theorems as well. Of course, since this logic is not sound it will be of very little practical use.

Similarly, finding a logic that is sound—a logic that proves only valid formulas—is again not a difficult task. For example, a system of logic that proves only formulas of the form $p \supset p$ will be sound. In this logic, since all propositions of the form $p \supset p$ are tautologies, then obviously only valid formulas will be theorems. Once again, though, since this logic is not complete, it, too, will be of very little practical use.

In contrast, a system such as P that is both sound and complete is more difficult to find. However, once formalized, it will have all of the advantages and none of the disadvantages of the above two systems.

In this context it is also important to note that system P is also *decidable*. This means that for any arbitrary well-formed formula there exists an algorithm (an effective, finite, mechanical decision procedure) for determining whether or not it is truth-functionally valid. In other words, the property of being truth-functionally valid is *computable* in system *P*. Not only are all and only the valid formulas theorems of this system, there also exists an effective, finite, mechanical method for discovering whether an arbitrary formula is provable as a theorem.

Soundness, Completeness, and Decidability

A logical system is *complete* provided that all the valid formulas expressible in the system are theorems of the system. In contrast, a logical system is *sound* provided that all theorems of the system are valid. In other words, a system that is both sound and complete is one in which all and only the valid formulas are provable.

In addition, a logical system is *decidable* provided that, for any arbitrary well-formed formula, there exists an algorithm (an effective, finite, mechanical decision procedure) for determining whether or not it is valid.

Classical propositional logic turns out to be complete, sound, and decidable. In contrast, classical predicate logic is complete and sound, but not decidable.

These properties are clearly desirable for any system of artificial intelligence. For example, compare the two methods we have developed for proving a formula valid in system *P*. Given an argument from premises *p* and *q* to conclusion *r*, we construct the formula $(p \wedge q) \supset r$. If we use our truth-table method correctly, we are guaranteed that in a finite number of steps, using a purely mechanical procedure, we will be able to discover whether this formula is a tautology. In contrast, if we use our system of natural deduction, we know that, if we discover a proof of this formula, then it will in fact be a tautology. However, if, after working at the problem for several days, we have not yet come up with a proof, this tells us very little. It may be that the reason we have not discovered a proof is that the formula is not in fact a tautology. Alternatively, it may be that the reason we have not discovered a proof is just that we are not smart enough to do so. How are we to know the difference?

Using truth tables we are able to decide—in a finite number of steps, using a purely mechanical procedure—whether an arbitrary formula is or is not truth-functionally valid. This means that if we design a computer program to carry out this task we are guaranteed to obtain the correct solution. Our computer will be able to obtain this solution for any arbitrary formula, and it will not depend on factors such as creative insight or plain good luck.

Thus, it turns out that classical propositional logic is sound, complete, and decidable. In contrast, although classical predicate logic was proved to be complete in 1930 by the Austrian logician Kurt Gödel, and although it was also known to be sound, the American logician Alonzo Church and the English mathematician Alan Turing both proved that there is no effective decision procedure for determining whether an arbitrary well-formed formula of predicate logic is a theorem. Surprisingly, what this means is that even if logics that are more complex than propositional logic turn out to be sound and complete, there is no guarantee that, in a finite number of steps, a computer will mechanically be able to prove whether or not an arbitrary formula is a theorem.

Flashback on...
Kurt Gödel (1906–1978)

KURT Gödel is widely regarded as the most important logician of the twentieth century. By the time he was thirty, Gödel had proved several important results, any one of which would have given him a position of importance in the history of logic. Together they guaranteed his unique stature. These results included his proofs of the completeness of predicate logic in 1930 and his proof of the incompleteness of arithmetic in 1931. They also included results in computation theory and his groundbreaking work in set theory. Today, Gödel is also remembered for his imaginative, nonstandard models of general relativity theory and for his strong championing of Platonism in the philosophy of mathematics.

Gödel was born in what is now Brno in the Czech Republic and was educated at the University of Vienna, where he obtained his Ph.D. in 1930. In 1938 he moved to Princeton and in 1940 became a member of the Institute of Advanced Studies at Princeton University.

Gödel's publications, together with a series of informative commentaries, can be found in his *Collected Works* (1986, 1990, 1995).

Exercise 14.1

1. State whether each of the following is an effective, finite, mechanical decision procedure:

   (a) Using truth tables to determine whether or not a well-formed formula in system *P* is truth-functionally valid.

   (b) Using a coin flip to determine whether or not a well-formed formula in system *P* is truth-functionally valid.

   (c) Using an encyclopedia to determine whether or not a well-formed formula in system *P* is truth-functionally valid.

   (d) Using Venn diagrams to determine whether or not a syllogism in term logic is formally valid.

   (e) Using a natural deduction proof to determine whether or not a well-formed formula in predicate logic is formally valid.

2. Expert Systems

As we said at the beginning of this chapter, one main type of AI involves so-called *expert* or *knowledge-based systems*. Expert systems are used to solve real-life problems that would normally require a specialized human expert. The best such systems allow computers to function at or near the level of a human expert.

Although expert systems have been developed for a broad range of specialized domains, each such system usually has a very narrow range of application. Thus a software program that has been developed to help assess the risk associated with particular markets on the stock exchange will be of no use for purposes of medical diagnosis, and vice versa.

Because expert knowledge often involves both detailed factual knowledge and more general heuristic knowledge—for example knowledge in the form of "rules of thumb" or summaries of conventional wisdom—both of these types of knowledge need to be represented in an expert system. In so-called *case-based reasoning*, these two categories of information often coincide.

Expert Systems

Expert or *knowledge-based* systems are one type of artificial intelligence. They are used to solve real-life problems in specific, well-defined domains. In an expert system the *knowledge base* includes a large amount of detailed factual knowledge as well as topic-specific heuristic knowledge that has been collected from experts or specialists in the relevant field. The best such systems allow computers to function at or near the level of human experts.

Case-based reasoning is built on the assumption that human beings often use analogical reasoning to solve complex problems, especially in areas such as legal analysis and medical diagnosis. This type of reasoning can be especially effective when general similarities between cases are recognized but when detailed information about a particular case is incomplete. Case-based reasoning requires that there be both a set of basic cases and a method for determining degrees of similarity between cases, as well as a method for efficiently identifying and retrieving those cases that meet the required degree of similarity.

Regardless of the type of system, expert systems typically have both advantages and disadvantages when compared to human experts. For example, they are often more consistent and more efficient. Because they inevitably give identical outputs when fed identical inputs, expert systems guarantee that similar situations will be handled in similar ways. Also, although they can be expensive to build, they also tend to be inexpensive to operate. Expert systems are easily reproducible in a way that human experts are not. Transactions are also more easily documented and records more easily stored.

Despite these advantages, expert systems are also often limited in the type of inputs that they can use. Most such systems require symbolic inputs and do not yet have available to them the broad range of sensory and other experiences that are available to human beings. In addition, almost all expert systems lack common-sense knowledge, and they are limited in the degree of creativity that they bring to new or unusual situations. System degradation is a case in point, since most expert systems are not good at recognizing when no answer exists, or when a given problem falls outside their area of expertise.

For example, consider a case in which the engine on Bill's boat fails to work and we want to discover why. We know that there are several possible problems: the engine may not be receiving fuel, there may be a problem with the spark plugs, the battery may be dead, or there may be a problem with the starter. If Bill has access to an expert system that has been designed to provide diagnoses in situations such as this, the resulting exchange may be something like the following:

System: Is there fuel in the tank?
Bill: Yes.
System: Do the lights come on?
Bill: No.
System: Does the engine turn over?

Bill: No.
System: There is a problem with the battery.

Underlying this exchange will be a set of rules (or commands) such as this:

1. R_1 = Is there fuel in the tank?
2. R_2 = Do the lights come on?
3. R_3 = Does the engine turn over?
4. $R_4 = R_5 = R_6 = R_7 = R_8 = R_9 = R_{10} = \phi$
5. PRINT (R_1)
6. IF (Yes)
   THEN (R_4 = There is fuel in the tank)
7. PRINT (R_2)
8. IF (Yes)
   THEN (R_5 = The lights come on)
9. PRINT (R_3)
10. IF (Yes)
    THEN (R_6 = The engine turns over)
11. IF NOT (R_4 = There is fuel in the tank)
    THEN (R_7 = There is a problem with the fuel) AND
    PRINT (R_7) AND STOP
12. IF NOT (R_7 = There is a problem with the fuel)
    AND NOT (R_5 = The lights come on)
    THEN (R_8 = There is a problem with the battery) AND
    PRINT (R_8) AND STOP
13. IF NOT (R_8 = There is a problem with the battery)
    AND NOT (R_6 = The engine turns over)
    THEN (R_9 = There is a problem with the starter) AND
    PRINT (R_9) AND STOP
14. IF NOT (R_9 = There is a problem with the starter)
    THEN (R_{10} = There is a problem with the spark plugs) AND
    PRINT (R_{10}) AND STOP.

The first thing that the system does is prepare its registers (or storage units, R_1 through R_{10}) to ensure that it is ready to answer a new query. It then collects all the relevant data that it can obtain from Bill and stores these data in registers R_4 through R_6. In this case, it will ask whether there is fuel in the tank, whether the lights come on, and whether the engine turns over when Bill tries to start it. For example, if Bill replies "Yes" to the question "Is there fuel in the tank?" then "There is fuel in the tank" is stored in register R_4. If he replies "No," or gives some other answer, or gives no answer at all, then R_4 remains empty. The system then proceeds through the above commands, until it is able to return with a positive diagnosis. For example, if there is no fuel in the tank, the system saves "There is a problem with the fuel" in R_7 and reports this information to Bill before stopping. If there is not a problem with the fuel but the lights do not come on, then "There is a problem with the battery" is stored in register R_8 and this is again reported to Bill before the system shuts down.

Of course given the simplicity of this system, there are numerous ways in which the system may fail. For example, it may turn out the there is fuel in the tank, but that it is not reaching the engine; or it may turn out that there is more than one problem, and until the first of these is fixed, the second (and third?) will not be diagnosed.

Even so, it is easy to see how a system such as this might be developed and then augmented. By learning more about how human experts diagnose engine problems, and more about how users interact with such systems, more "If ... then ___" rules could be added to the system to produce a more reliable interface together with a more reliable diagnostic.

Exercise 14.2

1.   Design an expert system that will determine whether or not arbitrary wffs in system *P* are truth-functionally valid.

3. Theories of Belief Revision

In an expert system the inference engine provides a means of generating new knowledge. It uses incoming data specific to the assigned problem together with information in its knowledge base to generate this new knowledge.

If the inference engine is based on classical propositional or predicate logic, the resulting outputs will be monotonic. In other words, the addition of new information will never require the elimination of a previously established conclusion. New information can only supplement, and never overturn, a previously accepted conclusion. In such systems, knowledge is cumulative.

However, in many real-life situations rational agents are required to do more than simply add new beliefs to their belief sets. Sometimes circumstances force us to revise or abandon beliefs that we once thought were true.

In order to help model these more complex types of epistemic change, philosophers and computer scientists have begun to develop theories of belief revision that do more than involve theories of ordinary logical consequence.

For example, imagine that Bill and Sue have just returned from a holiday to Morocco.[4] While they were there, Bill gave Sue a necklace as a memento of their trip. At the time, Bill believed that the necklace was made of gold. He had bought it, as well as a ring for himself, at a jewellery shop in Casablanca at what he thought was a good price. The jeweller had claimed that both items were made of 24-carat gold, but just to be safe, Bill had taken the ring and the necklace to a second jeweller next door. The second jeweller confirmed that both items were made of genuine gold and that the price was a fair one. However, after they returned home, Bill noticed that the sulfuric acid that he was using to repair his boat stained his ring. He remembered his high school chemistry teacher telling him that the only acid that affects gold in this way is aqua regia, so he also tested Sue's necklace and discovered that it, too, was stained by the acid. As a result, Bill was faced with a dilemma: either he had to accept an inconsistency (namely that the jewellery both was and was not gold) or he had to revise his beliefs. He could not deny that the jewellery was stained. He briefly wondered whether, by accident, he had bought aqua regia instead of sulfuric acid, but he soon gave up this idea. So, because he had greater confidence in what he had been taught in high school than in what the two jewellers had told him, Bill had to conclude that the jewellery was not made of gold after all. He also came to believe not just that the jewellers in Casablanca had been mistaken, but also that they had been lying, and that they were likely working in collusion with each other.

Theories of Belief Revision

Theories of belief revision study ways in which sets of beliefs change or develop. Most such theories are based on the assumption that for any belief set, S, and any proposition, p, set S may (1) accept, (2) reject, or (3) be indeterminate with regard to p. Changes to S may then take any of the following three forms: (1) *expansions*, in which beliefs that formerly have been indeterminate become either accepted or rejected; (2) *contractions*, in which beliefs that formerly have been either accepted or rejected become indeterminate; and (3) *revisions*, in which beliefs that formerly have been accepted become rejected and beliefs that formerly have been rejected become accepted.

The Swedish philosopher Peter Gärdenfors tells this story as an everyday example of a *belief revision*, a change in belief brought about by some piece of information (the stained ring) that contradicts a previously accepted belief. In order to avoid the contradiction, Bill finds that he has to change or revise some of his beliefs. Before his discovery, Bill was convinced that the jewellery he had bought was made of gold. Afterwards, he has not only changed his belief about this, he has also changed (some of) his beliefs about the two jewellers in Morocco, and perhaps some other beliefs as well.

Belief revision is thus different from both *belief expansion* and *belief contraction*. If Bill learns some new fact, for example that there has recently been an earthquake in Morocco, then this new information is consistent with his previous beliefs. As a result, there is no need to revise any of his previous beliefs and he simply adds this new belief, together with its consequences, to his old belief set.

At the same time, we can also imagine cases in which Bill contracts his belief set, again without there being any need to revise his previous beliefs. For example, before he heard about the earthquake, Bill may have been convinced that the two jewellers would continue to dupe unsuspecting tourists; but because of the earthquake he is now not so sure. He does not know whether the earthquake affected them, or whether they are even still in business. So, being a careful reasoner, he simply deletes this proposition, and its consequences, from his belief set.

In this context, it is worth noting that, just like inferences in general, revisions, expansions, and contractions may or may not be rational. If Bill, for example, gives up his belief that Sue is left-handed as a consequence of his learning that his ring is not made of gold, it would be difficult to consider this a rational revision. Similarly, if he avoids his original inconsistency by denying that the ring is stained, or by claiming that the widely accepted chemical theory of gold is wrong, or by telling himself that he had discovered a new form of gold, we would at least want to hear some further arguments before thinking that this was a rational thing to do.

In order to begin to formalize these basic ideas, belief revision theorists assume that the belief set, K, of a rational agent can be represented by a collection of propositions, p. For simplicity, we assume that K is consistent and that it contains all of its own logical consequences. (In other words, if propositions p, q, ... are accepted in belief set K, and if r is entailed by p, q, ..., then r will be accepted in K as well.) For any proposition, p, one of the following three cases then obtains:

- *Acceptance.* In this case p is accepted as a member of belief set, K. In other words, $p \in K$ and $\sim p \notin K$.

- *Rejection.* In this case p is rejected as a member of belief set, K. In other words, $p \notin K$ and $\sim p \in K$.

- *Agnosticism.* In this case p is indeterminate (i.e., neither accepted nor rejected) as a member of belief set, K. In other words, $p \notin K$ and $\sim p \notin K$.

Epistemic changes will then take any of the following three forms:

- *Expansions.* In an expansion, beliefs that formerly have been indeterminate become either accepted or rejected. For example, assuming that p is currently neither accepted nor rejected, belief set K is expanded, either by concluding that p is now to be accepted (together with its consequences) or by concluding that p is now to be rejected (together with its consequences).

- *Contractions.* In a contraction, beliefs that formerly have been accepted or rejected become indeterminate. For example, assuming that p is currently either accepted or rejected, belief set K is contracted by concluding that p is now to be indeterminate (together with its consequences).

- *Revisions.* In a revision, beliefs that formerly have been accepted become rejected and beliefs that formerly have been rejected become accepted. For example, assuming that p is currently accepted, the belief set K is revised by concluding that p is now to be rejected (together with its consequences). Alternatively, assuming that p is currently rejected, the belief set K is revised by concluding that p is now to be accepted (together with its consequences).

It is the job of the belief revision theorist to develop axioms that precisely describe rational expansions, contractions, and revisions. Among the various axiom sets that have been developed, one of the best known is due to Gärdenfors. Assuming once again that K is a consistent set of propositions closed under logical consequence, Gärdenfors' axioms for K_p^+, the expansion of K by p, are as follows:

(K+1) K_p^+ is a belief set

(K+2) $p \in K_p^+$

(K+3) $K \subseteq K_p^+$

(K+4) If $p \in K$, then $K_p^+ = K$

(K+5) If $K \subseteq H$, then $K_p^+ \subseteq H_p^+$

(K+6) K_p^+ is the smallest belief set that satisfies (K+1) through (K+5).

According to these axioms, $^+$ is a function that goes from pairs of belief sets and propositions to (new) belief sets (axiom 1); the new proposition, p, is a member of the expanded belief set (axiom 2); an expanded belief set retains all of the propositions found in the original belief set (axiom 3); adding a belief that is already contained in a belief set results in no change (axiom 4); and belief set expansion is monotonic (axiom 5). It also follows that if $\sim p \in K$, then $K_p^+ = K_\perp$, where $K_\perp$ represents the inconsistent belief set. Since in classical logic all propositions follow from a contradiction, $(K_\perp)_p^+ = K_\perp$, for all p.

Similarly, letting K_p^- represent the contraction of K by p, Gärdenfors' axioms governing contractions are as follows:

(K-1) K_p^- is a belief set

(K-2) $K_p^- \subseteq K$

(K-3) If $p \notin K$, then $K_p^- = K$

(K-4) If p is not a logical truth, then $p \notin K_p^-$

(K-5) If $p \in K$, then $K \subseteq (K_p^-)_p^+$

(K-6) If $p \equiv q$, then $K_p^- = K_q^-$

(K-7) $K_p^- \cap K_q^- \subseteq K_{p \wedge q}^-$

(K-8) If $p \notin K_{p \wedge q}^-$ then $K_{p \wedge q}^- \subseteq K_p^-$.

Again, it is assumed that $^-$ is a function that goes from pairs of belief sets and propositions to (new) belief sets (axiom 1). It also turns out that the contracted belief set will contain nothing not found in the original belief set (axiom 2); that when p is not in the original belief set, a contraction results in no change (axiom 3); that p is not a member of the contracted belief set unless it is a logical truth (axiom 4); that all propositions in K are recovered after first contracting and then expanding with respect to the same proposition (axiom 5); that logically equivalent propositions lead to identical contractions (axiom 6); and that iterated contractions function in much the same way as simple contractions (axioms 7 and 8)

Finally, letting K_p^* represent the revision of K with respect to p, we have the following axioms governing revisions:

(K*1) K_p^* is a belief set

(K*2) $p \in K_p^*$

(K*3) $K_p^* \subseteq K_p^+$

(K*4) If $\sim p \notin K$, then $K_p^+ \subseteq K_p^*$

(K*5) $K_p^* = K_\perp$ iff $\sim p$ is a logical truth

(K*6) If $p \equiv q$, then $K_p^* = K_q^*$

(K*7) $K_{p \wedge q}^* \subseteq (K_p^*)_q^!$

(K*8) If $\sim q \notin K_p^*$ then $(K_p^*)_q^+ \subseteq K_{p \wedge q}^*$.

Once again, * is assumed to be a function that goes from pairs of belief sets and propositions to (new) belief sets (axiom 1). It also turns out that p is a member of the revised belief set (axiom 2); that expansion is a special case of revision (axioms 3 and 4); that K_p^* is consistent unless p is a logical falsehood (axiom 5); that logically equivalent propositions lead to identical revisions (axiom 6); and that iterated revisions function in much the same way as simple revisions (axioms 7 and 8).

Exercise 14.3

1. Prove each of the following:

    (a) $K_p^- \subseteq K_p^+$

    (b) $(K_p^-)_p^+ \subseteq K_p^+$

    (c) $(K_p^*)_p^+ = K_p^*$

    (d) $K_{p \wedge \sim p}^* = K_\perp$

    (e) If $q \in K_p^+$ then $(K_p^+)_q^+ = K_p^+$

4. Can Machines Think?

With the advent of the information revolution we have become accustomed to having computers carry out a wide range of remarkable tasks. Even so, can machines honestly be said to have the ability to reason? Although we know that they are able to manipulate bits of electronic material in complex and systematic ways, can they actually be said to have knowledge? Can they experience doubts and other propositional attitudes? Will they eventually have the same wide range of mental imagery and feelings that people do? In short, is it possible for computers to think?

Many people believe that the answer to all of these questions is yes. Many others believe that the answer is no. However, before we try to decide this issue, it is important to decide what it means to say that someone, or something, is thinking.

One of the first people to address this issue was the British mathematician Alan Turing. According to Turing, something can be said to be thinking whenever it is impossible to distinguish its actions from those of someone else whom we already know to be thinking.[5] Thus the inability to distinguish, say, a computer's responses to a series of questions from those of a human would count as a positive solution to what has become known as the *Turing test* for artificial intelligence.

One of the most famous versions of the Turing test occurred in 1997. In the spring of that year, the world chess champion, Gary Kasparov, played the only multi-game match in professional competition against a single opponent that, as champion, he has ever lost. His opponent was the IBM supercomputer Deep Blue.

The match serves as a good example of a Turing test since, should you or I, or even a chess grandmaster, be presented with a printout that recorded the various moves of these games, it would be impossible to know in advance which moves belonged to Kasparov and which to Deep Blue. As a result, Deep Blue can clearly be said to have passed the Turing test when it comes to playing chess. Does this mean that Deep Blue is capable of human thought?

> **The Turing Test**
>
> According to the *Turing test* for artificial intelligence, something can be said to be thinking whenever it is impossible to distinguish its actions from those of someone else whom we already know to be thinking. Thus the inability to distinguish, say, a computer's responses to a series of questions from those of a human would count as a positive solution to the Turing test.

Flashback on…
Alan Turing (1912–1954)

ALAN Mathison Turing was a British mathematician especially noted for his contributions to the development of modern high-speed computers. During the Second World War, Turing was involved in Allied code-breaking efforts at Bletchley in England. He was also instrumental in the development of the decoder that broke the famous German coding machine, Enigma. After the war, Turing made important contributions to the development of both modern computer technology and programming theory.

Turing's life ended unhappily after he was arrested in 1952. After being convicted under the antiquated British Obscenity Act and having to choose between prison or mandatory psychoanalysis and hormone treatments designed to "cure" his homosexuality, Turing apparently committed suicide in 1954. His publications include the articles "On Computable Numbers, with an Application to the *Entscheidungsproblem*" (1936–37), and "Computing Machinery and Intelligence" (1950).

Since even the number of forty-move chess games is over 25×10^{115}, both Kasparov and Deep Blue obviously had to rely upon more than brute combinatorial power. Even so, many people believe that, unlike Kasparov, Deep Blue failed to act intentionally. They also believe that other factors—such as the ability to be aware of one's own actions, or the ability to understand the meanings of contentful symbols—are more important for defining intelligence than is the mere manipulation of data.

Among the most famous advocates of this view is the American philosopher John Searle. According to Searle, intelligence requires more than human-like behaviour. To see why this is so, we consider Searle's famous Chinese room thought experiment.[6]

We begin by selecting a language that we do not understand. Since Searle neither speaks nor writes Chinese, he selects Chinese. For anyone who understands Chinese, another language will work equally well. Now suppose you are placed in a room that contains many baskets full of Chinese symbols. In the room there is also a rule book that is written in a language that you do understand (say, English). The rule book tells you how to identify Chinese symbols entirely by their shapes. It also tells you what procedures to follow when presented with any particular sequence of Chinese symbols.

Now, imagine that there are people outside the room who understand Chinese and who pass sequences of symbols to you through a slot in the door. In response you then manipulate these symbols according to the rules in the rule book and hand back other sequences of symbols that you find in the baskets, again through the slot in the door.

For convenience, we may decide to call the rule book a "computer program," the people who wrote it "programmers," the containers full of symbols a "database," the sequences of symbols that are handed to you through the door "questions," and the sequences of symbols that you hand back "answers."

Now, says Searle, suppose that the rule book is written in such a way that your answers to the questions you receive are indistinguishable from those of a native speaker of Chinese. For example, the people outside the room might pass you some symbols that, unknown to you, mean "Is 26 a prime number?" After working through the rules, you might then pass back another sequence of symbols that, again unknown to you, means, "No, 26 is not a prime number." If so, and if you continue to do this for several days, or months, or years, you will clearly have passed the Turing test for understanding Chinese. Even so, you will remain totally ignorant of what any of these symbols mean. Like a computer you will successfully manipulate the symbols, but without a mechanism for learning what these symbols mean, neither you nor the computer may properly be said to understand Chinese. Neither you nor the computer may properly be said to be thinking.

Thus, the point of Searle's thought experiment is roughly this: if you do not understand Chinese solely on the basis of running a computer program, then neither will a digital computer, despite its speed and sophistication. Computers merely manipulate formal symbols according to series of commands. In contrast, genuine reasoning (or knowledge, or understanding) requires more than the mere manipulation of symbols. It also requires that we be aware of the meanings of these symbols. As a result, says Searle, computers cannot properly be said to be thinking.

If Searle is right, when Deep Blue plays chess it merely manipulates symbols according to a set of predetermined rules. Thus, Deep Blue cannot properly be said to understand what it is doing. As Searle himself puts it, the Chinese room thought experiment demonstrates that a computer program "is not constitutive of thinking because the program is purely a matter of formal symbol manipulation—and we know independently that symbol manipulations by themselves are not sufficient to guarantee the presence of meanings."[7]

Where does this leave us? Is Searle correct?

At this point it is helpful to introduce a distinction between what is often called strong and weak AI. *Weak AI* is the view that suitably programmed computers can at most simulate human cognition. On this view, despite their successes, AI systems can never actually exhibit many of the most important aspects of human intelligence. *Strong AI*, in contrast, is the view that suitably programmed machines are capable of doing more than merely simulating human cognition. Advocates of strong AI believe that, when suitably programmed, computers are capable of actually exhibiting some types of cognitive mental states.

Weak AI is unproblematic in a way that strong AI is not. Since a machine that merely simulates human cognition need not actually exhibit cognitive mental states, many advances in AI can be explained purely in terms of weak AI. In contrast, the claims of strong AI are much more controversial. If correct, strong AI entails that computers really do have cognitive mental states. According to strong AI, when Deep Blue plays chess, it really is thinking. Deep Blue may not have a particularly broad range of cognitive abilities but, at least in this one area, it is capable of genuine thought.

Advocates of weak AI typically advance the claim that the Turing test is insufficient for distinguishing between intelligence and the mere simulation of intelligence. They accept Searle's claim that there is more to human cognition than mere behaviour, no matter how indistinguishable from human action this behaviour might be. For the advocate of weak AI, simulation is not duplication. Thus, just as a computer model of tomorrow's weather is not itself real weather, a model of human thought is not itself real thought.

In contrast, advocates of strong AI are often more willing to accept the Turing test as a suitable test of intelligence. For example, when we test for intelligence in humans, all we have access to is observations about their behaviour. Even if Searle is correct, the advocate of strong AI might say, the only way we can determine whether someone understands the meaning of a symbol is through how he or she uses the symbol, for example through his or her answers to questions involving that symbol. In short, the only way we can determine whether someone understands the meaning of a symbol is through his or her behaviour. Yet if this is true with regard to humans, why change the test when it comes to machines?

> **Weak versus Strong AI**
>
> *Weak AI* is the view that when suitably programmed computers can at most simulate human cognition. If weak AI is correct, then, despite their successes, AI systems can never exhibit many of the most important aspects of human intelligence. In contrast, *strong AI* is the view that suitably programmed machines are capable of doing more than merely simulating human cognition. If strong AI is correct, then, suitably programmed, computers are capable of actually exhibiting many types of cognitive mental states.

Summary

In this chapter we have examined some of the connections and analogies, as well as some of the differences and disanalogies, between natural and artificial intelligence.

Because systems of *artificial intelligence* (or *AI*) have been designed to model some of the most complex aspects of human thought, it is not surprising that there are similarities. However, it is difficult to know whether these similarities are sufficient to conclude that AI systems duplicate human intelligence in any robust sense, or whether they merely simulate human intelligence in the same way that a model of the weather simulates real weather without itself being real. According to the *Turing test*, once a machine exhibits behaviour that is indistinguishable from an intelligent agent, the machine must also be said to have intelligence. According to an argument based on the *Chinese room thought experiment*, mere behaviour is not enough.

Most AI systems are composed of both a *knowledge base* and an *inference engine.* The *knowledge base* includes either expert or common-sense knowledge that is relevant to a given domain of reasoning. The *inference engine* provides a mechanism for generating new knowledge or other types of output. The two main types of inference engine are *rule-based* and *connectionist-based* software programs.

Some of the most successful AI systems that have been developed are called *expert* or *knowledge-based* systems. Expert or knowledge-based systems are used to solve real-life problems in specific, well-defined domains. In an expert system the *knowledge base* includes a large amount of detailed factual knowledge as well as a large amount of topic-specific heuristic knowledge that has been collected from experts or specialists in the relevant field. The best such systems allow computers to function at or near of the level of human experts.

In an expert system the inference engine provides a means of generating new knowledge. However, in many real-life situations rational agents are required to do more than simply add new beliefs to their belief sets. In order to help model these more complex types of epistemic change, philosophers and computer scientists have begun to develop theories of *belief revision*. In such theories, beliefs that formerly have been indeterminate become either accepted or rejected; beliefs that formerly have been either accepted or rejected become indeterminate; and beliefs that formerly have been accepted become rejected and beliefs that formerly have been rejected become accepted.

Weblinks

Episteme Links—Philosophy of Mind, Cognitive Science and Artificial Intelligence
www.epistemelinks.com/Topi/MindTopi.htm

MIT Encyclopedia of Cognitive Science
mitpress.mit.edu/errors/mitecs-please-subscribe.tcl?url=/MITECS/

Online Computing Dictionary
www.instantweb.com/~foldoc/

Stanford Encyclopedia of Philosophy—The Church–Turing Thesis
plato.stanford.edu/entries/church-turing/

Stanford Encyclopedia of Philosophy—Turing Machine
plato.stanford.edu/entries/turing-machine/

The Turing Test Page
cogsci.ucsd.edu/~asaygin/tt/ttest.html

The Internet Encyclopedia of Philosophy—Chinese Room Argument
www.utm.edu/research/iep/c/chineser.htm

Notes

1. This definition of completeness is due to Kurt Gödel. Experts will recognize that it is not equivalent to the definition of completeness given by E.L. Post. According to Post, a logistic system is complete whenever, for any well-formed formula, either that formula is a theorem of the system or, if added to the system as an axiom, the resulting system would become inconsistent. In Post's sense, classical propositional logic is complete, but classical predicate logic is not. In Gödel's sense, both are complete.

2. Of course, this definition is different from the definition of soundness given in ch. 4. For one thing, the definition in ch. 4 applies to arguments, while this definition applies to entire logical systems.

3. For example, see question 2 in exercise 6.2 in ch. 6 and the argument given in §2 of ch. 15.

4. This example is a slightly modified version of an example given by Peter Gärdenfors in his *Knowledge in Flux* (Cambridge, Mass.: MIT Press, 1988), 1–3.

5. See Alan Turing, "Computing Machinery and Intelligence," *Mind* 59 (1950), 433–460.

6. See John Searle, "Minds, Brains and Programs," *Behavioral and Brain Sciences* 3 (1980), 417–458, and "Is the Brain's Mind a Computer Program?," *Scientific American* 262 (January 1990), 26–31.

7. John Searle, "Is the Brain's Mind a Computer Program?," *Scientific American* 262 (January 1990), 27f.

CHAPTER 15

Issues in Argument Theory and the Philosophy of Logic

WE BEGAN this book by distinguishing between *argument theory* (or *critical reasoning*), which studies arguments in the broad (or social) sense, and *logic*, which studies arguments in the narrow (or purely propositional) sense. We then spent several chapters studying both of these subdisciplines before turning to examples of reasoning in areas such as economics, law, and artificial intelligence. It is now time to review some of what we have learned and to discuss several fundamental issues concerning the nature of reasoning and logic more generally.

1. Choosing the Right Logic

A good argument in the narrow sense has true premisses[1] and a strong or valid consequence relation. If an argument's consequence relation is inductively strong and its premisses are true, then it is likely that its conclusion will be true as well. If an argument's consequence relation is valid and its premisses are true, then it is not just likely, but necessary, that its conclusion will be true too. In either case, we have good reason to believe that we will not unwittingly accept a false conclusion.

However, as we have also seen, there is more to good arguments in the broad sense than just a strong or valid consequence relation and true premisses. Arguments in the broad sense attempt to advance knowledge. They purport to offer good reasons in favour of their conclusions. As a result, they must satisfy several criteria in addition to having true premisses and a strong or valid consequence relation.

Good arguments must not commit the fallacy of *petitio principii*. For example, when John Locke tries to prove that everything has a cause, merely by pointing out that "man knows, by an intuitive certainty" that "bare nothing" can never cause anything,[2] we are left wondering how this claim differs in any significant way from his conclusion. As we saw in chapter 10, even if an argument such as this, whose conclusion merely repeats the information contained in one of its premisses, is sound, it will not advance knowledge. To put this point another way, the conclusions of such arguments do not *follow* from their premisses in any interesting sense.

At the same time, as we saw in chapter 6, a good argument must also have premisses that are relevant to the topic at hand. In other words, a good argument must not commit the fallacy of *ignoratio elenchi*. Just as with arguments that beg the question, an argument with irrelevant or contradictory premisses will also not advance the cause of knowledge. As before, even if such an argument is valid or sound, it will not have a conclusion that *follows* from its premisses. Thus, in answer to the question we set for ourselves early in chapter 4, we now see that although validity can serve as an approximate guide to entailment, the two notions do not coincide completely.

Related to this, it is also worth noting that in many real-life contexts even arguments whose premisses entail their conclusions need not be good ones. For example, consider an argument that has as its premisses all the axioms of Euclidean geometry, and as its conclusion the Pythagorean theorem. For the sake of argument, let us suppose both that the Pythagorean theorem is entailed by these axioms and that these axioms are true. Even so, for most of us, this still will not constitute a good argument. Until we discover, or are presented with, all of the (psychologically necessary) steps that show why the conclusion follows from the premisses, these premisses will hardly serve as convincing reasons for accepting the Pythagorean theorem. Thus, as we saw in chapter 3, any good argument will be sensitive to its dialectical context: its premisses must be acceptable to the parties involved and the argument must progress in a way that aids the advancement of knowledge.

In other words, in order to advance knowledge an argument will need to have premisses that are not only true and relevant, but also acceptable. It will also need a strong or valid consequence relation. It must be non–question-begging and it must be sensitive to its particular dialectical context.

Seen in this way, the various logics and theories of argument that we have studied may all be understood as hypotheses about what makes good arguments good and bad arguments bad. However, having advanced these various hypotheses, we

---

Evaluating Arguments

A good argument advances knowledge. In order to do so, it must have *premisses* that are

- true,
- relevant, and
- acceptable.

It must also have a *consequence relation* that is

- strong or
- valid.

Finally, the *argument* itself must be

- non–question-begging and
- sensitive to its particular dialectical context.

now need to evaluate them, and doing so requires that we understand how logical knowledge advances.

Of course, it is easy to see that even the advancement of logical knowledge requires the use of logic. For example, consider the following short dialogue from the ancient Greek philosopher Epictetus:

> When one of his audience said, "Convince me that logic is useful," he said, "Would you have me demonstrate it?"
>
> "Yes."
>
> "Well, then, must I not use a demonstrative argument?"
>
> And when the other agreed, he said, "How then shall you know if I impose upon you?" And when the man had no answer, he said, "You see how you yourself admit that logic is necessary, if without it you are not even able to learn this much—whether it is necessary or not."[3]

In other words, logic is necessary even for deciding whether or not we should use logic! In slogan form, only logic can defeat logic.

As a result of this insight, for many centuries the justification of logic has been assumed to be a purely *a priori*, or logical, matter. It has been believed that because logical truths are necessary, the right logic could be discovered using reason alone. But as we saw when we discussed the arguments of both David Hume and Sextus Empiricus, it is at this point that we need to raise the issue of possible circularity.

If inductive reasoning could be justified deductively, Hume reminds us, then it would not be inductive. On the other hand, trying to justify inductive reasoning inductively is bound to be circular. Such a justification assumes the very point at issue; namely, that inductive reasoning is, at least on occasion, reliable.

In contrast, if we think that we should abandon inductive reasoning in favour of deductive reasoning, the same problem of circularity reappears in different form. If Sextus is right in suggesting that all valid arguments are reliable only because they assume the very propositions that they are trying to prove, then all deductive reasoning will be question-begging. In other words, either we will have to abandon deductive reasoning or else conclude that deductive logic is nothing more than the art of saying the same thing in different words.

To see why circularity is such a difficult problem, recall that an argument or inference is inductively strong if, assuming that its premises are true, it is likely (but not necessary) that its conclusion will be true as well. Induction by simple enumeration, for example, can be used to obtain support for general claims such as the proposition that all S are P:

(P1) S_1 is P
(P2) S_2 is P
...
(Pn) S_n is P

(C) All S are P.

Evaluating Logics and Theories of Reasoning

In this book we have introduced several logics and theories of reasoning, including sample systems of classical propositional logic, relevance logic, modal logic, epistemic logic, deontic logic, many-valued logic, term logic, predicate logic, inductive logic, probability theory, decision theory, and so on. Not all of these logics or theories of reasoning are compatible with one another, and deciding which is correct, or which best describes rational inference, is not a simple matter. Over the centuries many people have argued that because logical truths are necessary, we should be able to discover the right logic using reason alone. This seems unlikely. Using reason alone to decide how best to reason raises the question of circularity. It is more likely that logic, like any other branch of scientific or scholarly inquiry, will best be tested using a broad range of practical and theoretical criteria.

In this type of argument, the greater the value of n, the more probable the conclusion. But if so, it appears that we may use induction by simple enumeration to justify the general claim that "All applications of induction by simple enumeration are reliable."[4] In other words, by using induction by simple enumeration we will be able to show that induction by simple enumeration is itself a reliable form of argument. We do so as follows:

(P1) Application 1 of induction by simple enumeration is reliable
(P2) Application 2 of induction by simple enumeration is reliable
...
(Pn) Application n of induction by simple enumeration is reliable

(C) All applications of induction by simple enumeration are reliable.

In other words, seeing that many previous applications of induction by simple enumeration have been reliable (for example, in arguing that all emeralds are green, or that all ravens are black, or that all objects within a particular gravitational field fall with a particular rate of acceleration, etc.), we can conclude that all applications of induction by simple enumeration are reliable.

However, it turns out that induction by simple enumeration is not the only type of reasoning that is self-justifying in this way. For example, consider a new form of argument, which we shall call *induction by anti-enumeration*. We say that an argument is an instance of induction by anti-enumeration if it has the following form:

(P1) S_1 is not P
(P2) S_2 is not P
...
(Pn) S_n is not P

(C) All S are P.

Now obviously induction by anti-enumeration is a terrible form of argument! For example, after observing a large number of black ravens, none of us would be willing to accept the following instance of induction by anti-enumeration as a good argument:

(P1) Raven number 1 is not red
(P2) Raven number 2 is not red

...

(Pn) Raven number *n* is not red

(C) All ravens are red.

Even for large values of *n* (*especially* for large values of *n*!) no one would ever think that this was a good argument! For one thing, using this rule, the same evidence (the observation of *n* black ravens) would also have us conclude that all ravens are pink, that all ravens are yellow, that all ravens are white, and so on.

However, despite its lack of reliability (in fact, *because* of its lack of reliability!) induction by anti-enumeration is self-justifying in exactly the same way that induction by simple enumeration is self-justifying. That is, using induction by anti-enumeration allows us to prove the reliability of induction by anti-enumeration. We do so as follows:

(P1) Application 1 of induction by anti-enumeration is not reliable
(P2) Application 2 of induction by anti-enumeration is not reliable

...

(Pn) Application *n* of induction by anti-enumeration is not reliable

(C) All applications of induction by anti-enumeration are reliable.

Of course, the result of this "proof" is not that induction by anti-enumeration is reliable. Rather, it is that if we think that the self-justification of induction by simple enumeration is a sufficient reason for accepting that induction by simple enumeration is reliable, then we will also have to think that induction by anti-enumeration is reliable, and this is something that none of us should be willing to do.

2. Paraconsistent Logics

Even though the justification of logic by reason alone is open to the charge of circularity, and even though inappropriate logical rules (such as induction by anti-enumeration) are self-justifying just as are other logical rules, perhaps we should not give up quite yet. It may still be reason that lets us decide which logics are reliable and which are not. After all, as we defined them in chapter 6, logical truths such as the law of excluded middle ($p \lor \sim p$), and the law of non-contradiction $\sim(p \land \sim p)$, are true regardless of how the world might happen to be. Yet, if they are necessarily true, or true in all possible worlds, then it appears to follow that it will be reason, rather than experience, that helps us discover such laws. For example, it is reason that tells us that induction by anti-enumeration cannot be reliable since it leads to the inconsistent conclusion that all ravens are red, and pink, and white, and so on. Perhaps by eliminating all contradictions we will eventually be able to distinguish good logics from bad.

Unfortunately, it turns out that, just as we can develop self-justifying inductive logics that accept principles such as induction by anti-enumeration, we can also develop self-justifying deductive logics that accept contradictions. Not only are such logics competitors to classical deductive logic, in many real-life situations they are even more useful than traditional logics.

For example, imagine that you have been asked to develop the computer software to accompany a large database at the Department of Motor Vehicles. In addition to storing and retrieving information, this software will be required to make a number of basic inferences. For example, since the computer will be required to mail out renewal notices the month before each driver's birthday and then mail out receipts once payments have been received, the software you develop will be used to manipulate information about drivers and their vehicles. In other words, using information stored in the database (such as "Bill's date of birth is July 14"), together with other propositions (such as "The month immediately prior to July is June"), your software will have to draw simple conclusions (such as "Bill's renewal notice is to be mailed on June 14"), and then have the computer act accordingly.

Now, what will happen if you base your software on a system of classical logic such as system P? Everything should work just fine. By using system P's rules of natural deduction your software will draw all of the required inferences. However, what if somewhere in the database we have mistakenly stored a contradiction? For example, what will happen if at one place Bill's date of birth has been recorded as July 14, but somewhere else it has mistakenly been recorded as July 4? Given this contradiction, your computer software will not only conclude that Bill needs to be mailed a renewal notice on June 14; it will also conclude that he needs to be mailed a renewal notice on June 4.

In addition, because of the following simple argument,

1.	$p \wedge \sim p$	Premiss
2.	p	1 Simp
3.	$p \vee q$	2 Add
4.	$\sim p$	1 Simp
5.	q	3, 4 DS

we know that everything follows from a contradiction. Thus, not only will your computer software conclude that it should begin sending out daily renewal notices to Bill, it will do this for every other driver as well! In order to avoid this type of inferential explosion, we need to develop a so-called *paraconsistent logic*, a logic that tolerates, but does not exploit, contradictions.

What does it mean for a logic to tolerate but not exploit contradictions? One explanation is that such a logic prohibits inferential explosion despite the fact that it accepts some contradictions as true. In other words, the logic will be both consistent and inconsistent, but in difference senses. It will be consistent in the sense that

Paraconsistent Logics

A *paraconsistent logic* is a logic that is inconsistent in the sense that it contains contradictions, but consistent in the sense that not every well-formed formula is a theorem. Equivalently, in a paraconsistent logic some, but not all, propositions are true; some, but not all, propositions are false; and some, but not all, propositions are both true and false. Paraconsistent logics tolerate, but do not encourage, inconsistencies.

not every well-formed formula will be a theorem, but inconsistent in the sense that it accepts at least some contradictions (propositions that assert both a proposition and its denial) as true.

What reason could we have for thinking that some propositions are both true and false? As we saw in chapter 7, one way of interpreting the third value in Łukasiewicz's three-valued logic is to let I stand for "indeterminate," or "neither true nor false." Initially, this looked like a promising way to resolve paradoxes such as the problem of future contingents and the liar paradox, but the paradox of the strengthened liar led to new difficulties.

The paraconsistent logician takes these difficulties seriously. If we have a sound argument that concludes that "This proposition is not true" is true, and another sound argument that concludes that this same proposition is false, then the paraconsistent logician concludes that Aristotle must have been wrong: some propositions must be both true *and* false! In other words, many paraconsistent logicians deny *bivalence*, the doctrine that every proposition has exactly one of the two truth values (truth and falsehood), and they accept *dialetheism*, the doctrine that there exist some propositions that are both true and false. An equivalent way of saying this is that they believe that there exist true contradictions, true propositions of the form $p \land \sim p$.

Of course, this solution to the liar paradox and related difficulties comes at a tremendous cost. What could it mean to say that a proposition is both true *and* false? As we normally understand the term, a proposition is true when it accurately describes an actual state of affairs in the world; and since any given proposition will either accurately describe the world or it will not, truth and falsehood are normally thought to be not only objective but also mutually exclusive.

We normally say that a proposition is *objective* if its truth value is independent of the knowledge, beliefs, expectations, and other attitudes of the person asserting it. In contrast, a proposition is *subjective* if its truth value depends on that particular person's knowledge, beliefs, expectations, and so on. For example, propositions such as "Bill is pleasant to be around" and "The weather is uncomfortable at this time of year" are subjective, since their truth values depend upon the preferences of the person asserting them. In contrast, propositions such as "Bill is in Vancouver this week" or "It rains a lot at this time of year" are both objective. Both are true or false independently of the subjective attitudes of the person asserting them.

Propositions such as "Sue finds Bill pleasant to be around" and "Sue thinks that Mill's *On Liberty* is the greatest book ever written" represent a special case. In one sense they may seem to be subjective since they depend upon Sue's particular beliefs and preferences. On the other hand, according to our definition, they are objective. It is either a fact that Sue finds Bill pleasant to be around or it is not, and it is either a fact that she thinks that Mill's *On Liberty* is the greatest book ever written or she does not. In other words, the truth of these claims can be determined independently of the beliefs, attitudes, expectations, and feelings of the speaker asserting them and, as such, we say that they are objective.

Another way of saying this is that although propositional attitudes such as belief, fear, expectation, desire, and so on are relative, truth is not. Although beliefs, for example, vary from person to person and over time, truths do not. If it is true that Archimedes perished during the capture of Syracuse, then this is true regardless of what any person might believe.[5] Similarly, if it is false that Buzz Aldrin was the first man to set foot on the surface of the moon, then no amount of false belief will change this fact. Yet if this is so, how can propositions ever be both true and false together? The objectivity of truth values seems to provide some (modest) evidence against the idea that some propositions are both true and false.

Even so, many advocates of paraconsistency are willing to accept the objectivity of truth values, pointing out that a proposition can be both true and false in the same objective way that a proposition can be true or false *simpliciter*. Criticizing dialetheism thus turns out to be not an easy task. After all, finding a contradiction—something that in most other contexts would constitute a satisfactory *reductio ad absurdum*—cannot be viewed as a criticism of dialetheism without begging the question. Proving within a paraconsistent logic that dialetheia both exist and fail to exist, or even that something might both be and not be a dialetheia, will be of very little consequence. Far from being disturbed, the paraconsistent logician takes such contradictions as confirmatory instances of his theory! However, as Graham Priest, the Australian advocate of dialetheism, puts it, it is also important to recognize that contradictions such as these should not be "multiplied beyond necessity."[6]

In this context, not multiplying contradictions "beyond necessity" is no empty adage. Should contradictions be allowed to spread unchecked within the theory, they would soon commit us to believing everything, just as in classical logic, thus eliminating any practical advantage that paraconsistent theories might have.

What would such a logic look like? Letting T stand for "true," F stand for "false," and B stand for "both true and false," the connectives for one such logic may be defined as follows:

Conjunction

	$p \land q$	T	B	F
			q	
p	T	T	B	F
	B	B	B	F
	F	F	F	F

Disjunction

	$p \lor q$	T	B	F
			q	
p	T	T	T	T
	B	T	B	B
	F	T	B	F

Negation

p	~*p*
T	F
B	B
F	T

Conditional

	$p \supset q$	T	B	F
			q	
p	T	T	B	F
	B	T	B	B
	F	T	T	T

Biconditional

	$p \equiv q$	T	B	F
			q	
p	T	T	B	F
	B	B	B	B
	F	F	B	T

Thus we see that the paraconsistent logician is able to reason with propositions that are both true and false in much the same way that the three-valued logician reasons with propositions that are neither true nor false.

Having defined our connectives in this way, we can now revisit our proof that in classical logic everything follows from a contradiction. As we see from the following truth table, propositions of the form $(p \wedge \sim p) \supset q$ are tautologies when looked at from the perspective of classical logic:

	p	*q*	*~p*	*(p ∧ ~p)*	*(p ∧ ~p) ⊃ q*
(1)	T	T	F	F	T
(2)	T	F	F	F	T
(3)	F	T	T	F	T
(4)	F	F	T	F	T

However, using our paraconsistent logic, we obtain the following quite different truth table:

	p	*q*	*~p*	*(p ∧ ~p)*	*(p ∧ ~p) ⊃ q*
(1)	T	T	F	F	T
(2)	T	B	F	F	T
(3)	T	F	F	F	T
(4)	B	T	B	B	T
(5)	B	B	B	B	B
(6)	B	F	B	B	B
(7)	F	T	T	F	T
(8)	F	B	T	F	T
(9)	F	F	T	F	T

As we can see, in one sense $(p \wedge \sim p) \supset q$ is still a tautology, but in another sense it is not. Since B means "both true and false," we see that $(p \wedge \sim p) \supset q$ is always true, but it is also sometimes false. We thus introduce the following three new definitions. We say that an *impure tautology* is a proposition that is always true, but also sometimes false, as a result of its truth-functional form. In contrast, a proposition that is always false, but also sometimes true, as a result of its truth-functional form or that is the negation of an impure tautology, is an *impure contradiction*. Finally, a proposition that is sometimes only true, sometimes only false, and sometimes (but not always) both true and false as a result of its truth-functional form is an *impure contingency*.

Propositions of the form $(p \wedge \sim p) \supset q$ thus turn out to be impure, rather than pure, tautologies. Recalling that an argument or inference is valid if and only if it is not possible for the premises to be (jointly) true and, at the same time, the conclusion to be false, we see that the argument from $p \wedge \sim p$ to q is no longer valid. In other words, validity requires not just that the conclusion be true whenever the premisses are true; it also requires that the conclusion never be false whenever the premisses are true. In other words, as we said at the outset, a paraconsistent logic tolerates but does not encourage the existence of contradictions.

Impure Tautologies, Contradictions, and Contingencies

In a paraconsistent logic, propositions may be true, false, or both true and false. In paraconsistent logics we define impure tautologies, impure contradictions, and impure contingencies as follows:

- A proposition that is always true, but also sometimes false, as a result of its truth-functional form is an *impure tautology*.
- A proposition that is always false, but also sometimes true, as a result of its truth-functional form is an *impure contradiction*.
- A proposition that is sometimes only true, sometimes only false, and sometimes but not always both true and false as a result of its truth-functional form is an *impure contingency*.

The paraconsistent logician now points out that there are many cases in which useful theories contain inconsistencies. Our story about a computer database that contains inconsistent information will not be unique. Many real-life scientific theories have been inconsistent. For example, old quantum theory is widely recognized to have harboured contradictions, and on some interpretations the infinitesimal calculus also turns out to be inconsistent. Now, if classical logic rules the day, these theories should become unworkable; but if one looks at the actual history of scientific theories we see that they are typically not disabled by inconsistencies such as these. This is some evidence that, at least on occasion, rational people use some type of paraconsistent logic. In other words, whatever logic we work with must allow us to tolerate at least some contradictions.

Consider again the case of the liar paradox. Let us abbreviate "This proposition is false" by A and assign it the value B. It then follows that the negation of this proposition, $\sim A$, is also both true and false. Thus the proposition $(A \wedge \sim A) \supset C$ will have either the value T or B depending upon the value assigned to C. In other words, given our definition of validity, we can conclude that $A \wedge \sim A$ does not validly entail arbitrary C, since sometimes $(A \wedge \sim A) \supset C$ will be false.

Alternatively, consider again the case of an inconsistent database. Let us abbreviate "Bill's date of birth is July 14" by B and assign it the value T. Since we have also accepted "Bill's date of birth is July 4" as true, and since we know that July 4 is not the same date as July 14, it follows that the negation of B, $\sim B$, will also be true. Thus the proposition $B \wedge \sim B$ will be true (as well as false), and the proposition $(B \wedge \sim B) \supset C$ will be either T or B depending upon the value assigned to C. In other words, once again the argument from $B \wedge \sim B$ to C will not be valid.

Returning to our original proof that everything follows from a contradiction, we see that it is the inference from lines 3 and 4 to line 5 that need not be accepted as valid.

If lines 3 and 4 are going to imply line 5 by Disjunctive Syllogism, then the ~*p* in line 4 must contradict the *p* contained in line 3. But this is not the case. The reason is that both *p* and ~*p* have the same truth value; namely, the paradoxical value *B*. By this reasoning, disjunctive syllogism is not a valid rule; it fails for paradoxically valued sentences.

Returning finally to the issue of selecting the right logic, we see that merely asserting the importance of consistency takes us very little distance towards deciding how best to reason. Not only are paraconsistent logics self-justifying, they are also more useful than classical logics in many real-life contexts. Thus, like any other branch of scientific inquiry, logical theories will have to be tested and justified by a broad range of practical and theoretical criteria, rather than by any particular, privileged set of logical desiderata.

Exercise 15.1

1. Determine whether the following propositions are objective or subjective:

   (a) Sue is the kindest person I know.

   (b) No one loves Bill more than Sue.

   (c) Whistler and Aspen are the two largest ski resorts in North America.

   (d) Whistler and Aspen are the two best ski resorts in North America.

   (e) Homosexuality is wrong.

2. Where *P* is true, *Q* is false, and *R* is true and false, determine the truth values of each of the following propositions:

   (a) *Q* ∧ ~*R*

   (b) *R* ∧ ~*R*

   (c) *R* ∨ (*Q* ∨ *P*)

   (d) (*P* ∨ (*Q* ∨ *P*)) ∨ (*R* ∧ ~*P*)

   (e) ~(*P* ∨ *Q*) ∧ ~(~*Q* ∨ ~*R*)

   (f) *P* ⊃ (*Q* ⊃ ~*R*)

   (g) (*P* ⊃ *R*) ⊃ (~*P* ⊃ ~*R*)

   (h) ((*P* ⊃ *R*) ⊃ *P*) ⊃ *Q*

   (i) (*P* ≡ *R*) ≡ (*P* ∧ ~*Q*)

   (j) ((*P* ∧ *Q*) ⊃ *R*) ≡ (*P* ⊃ (*Q* ⊃ *R*))

3. Which of the following propositions are impure tautologies, which are impure contradictions, and which are impure contingencies:

   (a) *P* ∧ ~*P*

   (b) *P* ∨ ~*P*

   (c) ~(*P* ∧ ~*P*)

   (d) ~(*P* ⊃ *P*)

   (e) *P* ⊃ ~ ~*P*

   (f) *P* ≡ ~ ~*P*

   (g) [(*P* ⊃ *Q*) ∧ (~*P* ∨ ~*Q*)] ⊃ ~*P*

   (h) [(*P* ≡ *Q*) ∧ ~*Q*] ⊃ ~*P*

   (i) ~(*P* ⊃ ~*P*)

   (j) (*P* ⊃ *P*) ≡ (*Q* ⊃ *Q*)

3. The Enlightenment Ideal

Reasoning well is crucial for the advancement of knowledge. Knowledge, in turn, gives us power over our world. It gives us the power to fight disease, to improve our working conditions, to avoid the many miseries of war, and to understand other cultures. It is this connection between careful reasoning and improved human well being that is characteristic of periods of enlightenment. In the famous words of the eighteenth-century thinker Paul-Henri Holbach, "Man is unhappy because he is ignorant of nature."[7]

Being the type of fallible creature that we are, psychological conviction need not always indicate justified belief. Thus, as we noted in chapter 1, it is important to distinguish reasons from feelings, and evidence from intuition. In Hume's words, "A wise man, therefore, proportions his belief to the evidence."[8]

Among the various sources of evidence that we all have at our disposal, some are more fundamental than others. *Empiricists* argue that experience is the primary source of knowledge. On this view, all knowledge ultimately comes through our senses. At bottom, even the most abstract knowledge is traceable back to our observation of, and our interaction with, the world. In contrast, *rationalists* argue that it is reason, rather than experience, that is the primary source of knowledge. On this view, all knowledge is ultimately justified through reason, since it is reason that allows us to distinguish veridical experiences and intuitions from their less reliable counterparts.[9]

Even so, deciding how best to reason, and learning how best to avoid the fallacies, can be a tricky matter for both the empiricist and rationalist alike. When the ancient Greeks began discussing these matters more than two thousand years ago, they saw that the methods of rational inquiry, or *logos*, could be a powerful tool for the advancement of knowledge. They also saw that mistakes in reasoning could be dangerous.

The first fruits of *logos* centred on developments in theoretical physics and astrophysics in the sixth century BCE, but before long these same methods of rational inquiry were directed to other issues as well, and it was these early stirrings that eventually led to what today we call the natural and social sciences. Concurrently, the methods of *logos* were called into service in a self-critical way, for the purpose of criticizing *logos* itself. Thus were born the main subdisciplines of Western philosophy: logic, metaphysics, epistemology, and ethics.

However, barely two hundred years following its introduction, the study of *logos* entered a period of crisis. The Sophists[10] began teaching that every viewpoint could be defended equally well, and a series of logical and metaphysical paradoxes—including the liar paradox—were discovered.[11] *Logos* had lost control of the distinction between arguments that *looked* good and arguments that *were* good. In short, the methods of *logos* had been visited by a virus and much of the intellectual history of Greek antiquity can be seen as an attempt to subdue this virus.

It would be a mistake to underestimate how bad a problem this was. Some of the most damaging of the paradoxical metaphysicians, such as Heraclitus and Parmenides, and some of the most notorious of the Sophists, such as Gorgias and Protagoras, were greatly admired and respected (and believed!) by some of the brightest of their contemporaries and successors.[12] In contrast, philosophical moderates saw the problem for what it was. Logos needed to be reined in and disciplined.

It was at this point that Aristotle entered the picture. Aristotle recognized that procedures for distinguishing between good and bad arguments needed to be developed. To this end he began his study of logic. Logic would keep the methods of *logos* honest.

Today we not only have Aristotle's theory of rational inference, we have many other theories as well. Choosing between them is thus not a simple task. What are we to do?

Sources of Knowledge

Among the various sources of evidence that we all have at our disposal, experience and reason are often thought to be the most fundamental. For example, *empiricists* argue that the primary source of knowledge is experience. On this view, all knowledge ultimately comes through our senses. At bottom, even the most abstract knowledge originates in our observation of, and our interaction with, the world. In contrast, *rationalists* argue that it is reason, rather than experience, that is the primary source of knowledge. On this view, all knowledge is ultimately justified through reason, since it is reason that allows us to distinguish veridical experiences and intuitions from their less reliable counterparts. In contrast to both empiricists and rationalists, *coherentists* argue that there is no single, privileged source of knowledge. On this view, advances in knowledge rely upon a wide range of practical and theoretical criteria, including both reason and experience.

One solution is to reject both empiricism and rationalism and to continue, instead, to rely upon a wide range of practical and theoretical criteria. This does not mean abandoning either observation or reason. Instead, it means accepting that neither is more fundamental than the other. Advocates of this view are often called *coherentists*.

Consider, for example, the common use of coherentism with regard to ethical belief.[13] We all begin, rightly or wrongly, with a haphazard collection of ethical beliefs: for example, lying is immoral, kindness is a virtue, and it is wrong to torture innocent creatures simply for fun. Coming upon hard cases, we look to our previous storehouse of beliefs in the hope that we will find guidance. In doing so, we may begin looking for some unifying principles, noticing, perhaps, that most of our current ethical beliefs are consistent with the maximization of human well being, or of happiness, or of justice. After discovering such principles, we will not only apply them to our troublesome hard cases, but we will also modify some members of our initial belief set in order to bring them more fully into line with these newly discovered principles. For example, in order to help maximize the coherence of our overall belief set, we may modify our original belief that lying is immoral, accepting in its place the belief that lying is immoral unless it aids in the promotion of some greater good. Spreading misinformation to the enemy in wartime, for example, may now be considered to be a moral, rather than an immoral act. Such developments, in turn, may cause us once again to modify our newly discovered general principles. In this way we will continue to try to maximize coherence, stopping only when we reach some satisfactory degree of reflective equilibrium.

Much the same thing happens in other branches of knowledge as well. For example, consider the process of developing and testing a simple scientific hypothesis such as "Water boils at 212 degrees Fahrenheit."[14] As before, we begin with a haphazard collection of beliefs, this time about various containers of boiling water. Noticing, perhaps, that most of our observations cluster around 212 degrees, we use induction by simple enumeration to conclude that water always boils at 212 degrees Fahrenheit. At this point we may even modify some of our original beliefs in order to make them consistent with this newly accepted generalization. Where before we believed that the fifth container of water we tested boiled at 211 degrees, we now revise this belief to help maximize the coherence of our overall belief set, concluding instead that it really did boil at 212 degrees, but that we mistakenly thought it was 211 degrees as a result of careless measuring. However, as we continue to notice that other containers of water boil at 211, 210, and even 215 degrees, we may eventually develop a more refined hypothesis. Noticing that these nonstandard measurements all occur either when we have placed lids on our containers or when we are camping in the mountains, we soon conclude that our original hypothesis was mistaken, accepting instead the proposition "Water at standard pressure boils at 212 degrees." This change in belief may then again cause us to modify some of our previously accepted beliefs, and so on. As before, we will continue to try to maximize the over-all coherence of our belief set, stopping only when we reach some satisfactory degree of reflective equilibrium. Thus, even apparently straightforward observational knowledge such as "Water at standard pressure boils at 212 degrees" is justified through a combination of observation and careful reasoning.

In logic we have seen this same strategy at work. After developing the hypothesis early in chapter 4 that an argument's premises will entail its conclusion if and only if the argument is valid, we continued to gather evidence that helped us modify this hypothesis until we reached the account of good arguments offered in section 1 of this chapter. Thus, just as with any other branch of scientific or scholarly inquiry, logical theories will be tested using a broad range of practical and theoretical criteria. This requires a large amount of hard work, but it is this hard work that distinguishes genuine advances in knowledge from the commonplace process of simply accepting or doubting whatever propositions come to mind. As the mathematician Henri Poincaré reminds us, "To doubt everything or to believe everything are two equally convenient solutions; both dispense with the necessity of reflection."[15]

Exercise 15.2

1. Determine whether your knowledge of each of the following comes primarily from reason, experience, authority, or some combination of these three:

   (a) The words on this page are black.

   (b) The words on this page are black or it's not the case that the words on this page are black.

   (c) Socrates died by drinking hemlock.

   (d) Some rainwater is wet.

   (e) All rainwater is wet.

   (f) $E = mc^2$.

   (g) Ghosts do not exist.

   (h) $2 + 2 = 4$.

   (i) There are an infinite number of twin primes.

   (j) Murder is wrong.

Summary

Our goal in this book has been to learn what it means to reason well. To this end we have begun the study of both *logic* and, more broadly, the *theory of argument*. We have also introduced several sample systems of logic, including classical propositional logic, relevance logic, modal logic, epistemic logic, deontic logic, many-valued logic, term logic, predicate logic, and inductive logic, and several sample theories of reasoning including decision theory, probability theory, and Aristotle's theory of dialectic.

We have also studied many of the most famous and seductive of the fallacies and learned that many types of arguments, including *ad baculum*, *ad hominem*, *ad populum*, *ad misericordiam*, *ad ignorantiam*, *ad verecundiam*, and *ignoratio elenchi* arguments, may be either reliable or fallacious depending upon a variety of logical and contextual factors. We have pointed out that good arguments must have premises that are true, relevant, and acceptable. They must have consequence relations that are strong or valid. They must be non–question-begging, and they must be sensitive to their particular dialectical contexts.

Above all, we have noted that good arguments advance the cause of knowledge, and it is by this standard that all arguments are ultimately to be judged.

Weblinks

Stanford Encyclopedia of Philosophy—Paraconsistent Logic

plato.stanford.edu/entries/logic-paraconsistent/

Notes

1. At this point alert readers may recall that two of the forms of valid argument introduced in chapter 6 do not appear to require true premises. In the rule of Conditional Proof (CP) the assumptions may or may not turn out to be true, and in the rule of Indirect Proof (IP) the assumptions are always, in fact, false! However, it is important to remember that these are *assumptions* and not *premises*. Unlike premises, assumptions need not be accepted as truths. Put another way, the real premises in these arguments appear as sub-arguments to the right of each scope line. For example, in an argument from Indirect Proof the real premisses are a proposition of the form $p \supset (q \wedge \sim q)$ together with an implicitly accepted proposition of the form $\sim(q \wedge \sim q)$. It is from these two (true) premisses that we conclude $\sim p$. Similarly, in the case of Conditional Proof, the real premiss is a proposition of the form $p \supset q$, and it is from this (true) premiss that we conclude another proposition that is also of the form $p \supset q$.

2. John Locke, *An Essay Concerning Human Understanding* (London: Dent, 1977), bk. 4, ch. 10, §3. (Italics removed.)

3. Epictetus, *The Discourses and Manual*, 2 vols, (Oxford: Clarendon, 1916), bk. II, ch. 25.

4. In this context it is helpful to note that "reliable" does not mean infallible.

5. Of course it is important to distinguish between the assertion "Archimedes perished during the capture of Syracuse" stated in 323 BCE prior to the capture of Syracuse, and the assertion "Archimedes perished during the capture of Syracuse" stated in 321 BCE one year

following the capture of Syracuse. Despite their similarity in form, these two assertions represent two distinct propositions, one of which is false and one of which is true. The branch of logic that studies the differences between propositions such as these is called *tense logic* or *temporal logic*.

6. Graham Priest, *In Contradiction* (Dordrecht: Martinus Nijhoff Publishers, 1987), 90.

7. Paul-Henri Holbach, *Système de la Nature* (Paris: Fayard, 1990), 11.

8. David Hume, *Enquiries Concerning the Human Understanding and Concerning the Principles of Morals*, 2nd ed. (Oxford: Clarendon, 1902), 110 (§10, "Of Miracles," pt. 1, 87).

9. Of course, much of our knowledge is also justified via authority but, as we saw in ch. 11, this knowledge must ultimately find its ground in some other source.

10. The Sophist Gorgias, for example, is purported to have developed a proof to the effect that (1) nothing exists; (2) even if something did exist, no one could ever know it; and (3) even if someone could know it, no one could ever communicate this knowledge.

11. Heraclitus constructed a purported proof that the world was absolutely inconsistent (that is, that each proposition about the world was both true and false); Parmenides had a purported proof that everything is identical to everything (that is, that there is no difference or multiplicity in the world); and Zeno, his pupil, is famous for purporting to prove, among other things, that motion is impossible.

12. Protagoras was an extreme relativist, not just about matters of taste and moral judgment, but about *everything*.

13. This type of reasoning is also sometimes referred to as *inference to the best explanation* or as *reasoning based upon wide reflective equilibrium*.

14. We use the Fahrenheit rather than the Celsius scale in order to emphasize that this is a synthetic, rather than an analytic, claim. See "Is Water Really Wet?" in ch. 2 for further discussion on this point.

15. Henri Poincaré, *Science and Hypothesis* (New York: Dover, 1952), xxv.

Selected Readings

Chapter 1: The Quarrel

Logic and Argument Theory

Bocheński, I.M., *A History of Formal Logic*, 2nd edn, Notre Dame, Indiana: University of Notre Dame, 1961

Kneale, William, and Martha Kneale, *The Development of Logic*, Oxford: Clarendon Press, 1962

Van Eemeren, Frans H., et al., *Fundamentals of Argumentation: A Handbook of Historical Backgrounds and Contemporary Developments*, Mahwah, New Jersey: Lawrence Erlbaum Associates

Fallacies

Hamblin, C.L., *Fallacies*, London: Methuen, 1970

Hansen, Hans V., and Robert C. Pinto, *Fallacies: Classical and Contemporary Readings*, University Park, Pennsylvania: Pennsylvania State University Press, 1995

Walton, Douglas N., *A Pragmatic Theory of Fallacy*, Tuscaloosa, Alabama: University of Alabama 1995

Woods, John, *The Death of Argument: Fallacies and Other Distractions*, Newport Beach, Virginia: Vale Press, 2000

Woods, John, and Douglas N. Walton, *Fallacies: Selected Papers 1972–1982*, Berlin and New York: de Gruyter, 1989

Ad Baculum Arguments

Van de Vate, Dwight, "The Appeal to Force," *Philosophy and Rhetoric*, 8 (1975), 4–60

Woods, John, and Douglas N. Walton, "*Ad Baculum*," *Grazer Philosophische Studien* 2 (1976), 133–140

Ad Hominem Arguments

Barth, E.M., and J.L. Martens, "*Argumentum Ad Hominem*: From Chaos to Formal Dialectic," *Logique et Analyse* 77–78 (1977), 76–96

Johnstone, Henry W., "Philosophy and the *Argumentum Ad Hominem*," *Journal of Philosophy* 49 (1952), 489–498

Walton, Douglas N., *Ad Hominem Arguments*, Tuscaloosa, Alabama: University of Alabama Press, 1998

Woods, John, and Douglas N. Walton, "*Ad Hominem*," *The Philosophical Forum* 8 (1977), 1–20

Chapter 2: The Debate

Debate

Bauer, Otto F., *Fundamentals of Debate: Theory and Practice*, Glenview, Illinois: Scott Foresman, 1966

Borovoy, A. Alan. *When Freedoms Collide*, Toronto: Lester and Orpen Dennys, 1988

Irvine, A.D., "Let Truth and Falsehood Grapple," *University of Toronto Quarterly*, vol. 67 (1998), no. 2, 549–566

Perelman, Chaim, and L. Olbrechts-Tyteca, *The New Rhetoric*, Notre Dame, Indiana: University of Notre Dame Press, 1969

Mill, John Stuart, *On Liberty*, New York: Norton 1975

Ad Populum Arguments

Walton, Douglas N., *Appeal to Popular Opinion*, University Park, Pennsylvania: Pennsylvania State University Press, 1999

Walton, Douglas N., "Why is the *Ad Populum* a Fallacy?," *Philosophy and Rhetoric*, 13, 1980, 264–278

Ad Misericordiam Arguments

Walton, Douglas N., *Appeal to Pity*, Albany, New York: State University of New York Press, 1997

Chapter 3: Dialectic

Dialectic

Hamblin, C.L., "Mathematical Modes of Dialogue," *Theoria* 37 (1971), 130–155

Mackenzie, J.D., "How to Stop Talking to Tortoises," *Notre Dame Journal of Formal Logic* 20 (1979), 70–717

Rescher, Nicholas, *Dialectics*, Albany, New York: State University of New York Press, 1977

Walton, Douglas N., *The New Dialectic: Conversational Contexts of Argument*, Toronto: University of Toronto Press, 1998

Walton, Douglas N., and Erik C.W. Krabbe, *Commitment in Dialogue*, Albany, New York: State University of New York Press

Appeals to Ignorance

Walton, Douglas N., *Arguments from Ignorance*, University Park, Pennsylvania: Pennsylvania State University Press, 1996

Woods, John, and Douglas N. Walton, "The Fallacy of Ad Ignorantiam," *Dialectica* 32 (l974), 87–99

Logic of Questions

Aqvist, Lennart, *A New Approach to the Logical Theory of Interrogatives*, Uppsala: Filosofiska Studier, 1965

Belnap, Nuel D., and Thomas B. Steel, *The Logic of Questions and Answers*, New Haven: Yale University Press, 1976

Harrah, David, *Communication: A Logical Model*, Cambridge, Massachusetts: MIT Press, 1963

Chapter 4: Deductive Logic

Propositional Logic

Bergmann, Merrie, James Moor, and Jack Nelson, *The Logic Book*, 3rd edn, New York: McGraw-Hill, 1998

Quine, W.V., *Methods of Logic*, 3rd edn, New York: Holt, Rinehart and Winston, 1972

Tidman, Paul, and Howard Kahane, *Logic and Philosophy*, 8th edn, Belmont, California: Wadsworth, 1999

Woods, John, *Proof and Truth*, Toronto: Peter Martin Associates, 1974

Fallacies of Relevance

Hamblin, C.L., *Fallacies*, London: Methuen, 1970

Hansen, Hans V., and Robert C. Pinto, *Fallacies: Classical and Contemporary Readings*, University Park, Pennsylvania: Pennsylvania State University Press, 1995

Chapter 5: Formal and Informal Logic

Informal Logic

Engel, S. Morris, *With Good Reason*, 5th edn, New York: St Martin's Press, 1994

Johnson, Ralph H., and J. Anthony Blair, *Logical Self Defense*, Toronto: McGraw-Hill Ryerson, 1977

Logical Form

Sainsbury, Mark, *Logical Forms*, Oxford: Blackwell, 1991

Equivocation

Kirwan, Christopher, "Aristotle and the So-called Fallacy of Equivocation," *Philosophical Quarterly* 29 (1979), 3–46

Woods, John, and Douglas N. Walton, "Equivocation and Practical Logic," *Ratio* 21 (1979), 31 43

Paradox of the Liar

Barwise, Jon, and John Etchemendy, *The Liar*, New York: Oxford University Press, 1987

Irvine, A.D., "Gaps, Gluts, and Paradox," Bruce Hunter and Philip Hanson (eds), *Return of the* A priori, *Canadian Journal of Philosophy*, Supplementary vol. 18 (1993), 273–299

Martin, R.L., *Recent Essays on Truth and the Liar Paradox*, Oxford: Clarendon, 1984

Sainsbury, Mark, *Paradoxes*, Cambridge: Cambridge University Press, 1988

Smullyan, Raymond M., *What Is the Name of This Book?*, Englewood Cliffs, New Jersey: Prentice Hall, 1978

Chapter 6: Formal Deductive Systems

Formal Systems

Church, A., *Introduction to Mathematical Logic*, Vol. 1, Princeton: Princeton University Press, 1956

DeLong, Howard, *A Profile of Mathematical Logic*, Reading, Massachusetts: Addison-Wesley, 1970

Pollock, John L., *Technical Methods in Philosophy*, Boulder, Colorado: Westview, 1990

Chapter 7: Extending Deductive Logic I

Relevance Logic

Anderson, Alan R. and Belnap, Nuel D., *Entailment*, 2 vols, Princeton: Princeton University Press, 1975, 1990

Epstein, Richard L., "Relatedness and Implication," *Philosophical Studies* 36 (1979), 137–173

Read, Stephen, *Relevant Logic*, New York: Blackwell, 1988

Walton, Douglas N., "Philosophical Basis of Relatedness Logic," *Philosophical Studies* 36 (1979), 11–136

Modal Logic

Bradley, Raymond, and Norman Swartz, *Possible Worlds*, Cambridge, Massachusetts: Hackett, 1979

Chellas, Brian, *Modal Logic*, Cambridge: Cambridge University Press, 1980

Hughes, G.E., and M.J. Cresswell, *An Introduction to Modal Logic*, London: Methuen, 1968

Loux, M.J., *The Possible and the Actual*, Ithaca, New York: Cornell University Press, 1979

Epistemic Logic

Schlesinger, G.N. *The Range of Epistemic Logic*, Aberdeen: Aberdeen University Press, 1985

Deontic Logic

Rescher, Nicholas, *The Logic of Commands*, London: Routledge and Kegan Paul, 1966

Multi-valued Logic

Rescher, Nicholas, *Many-Valued Logic*, New York: McGraw-Hill, 1969

Chapter 8: Extending Deductive Logic II

Aristotle's Logic

Bocheński, I.M., *Ancient Formal Logic*, Amsterdam: North Holland, 1951

Łukasiewicz, Jan, *Aristotle's Syllogistic*, 2nd edn., Oxford University Press, 1957

McKeon, Richard, *The Basic Works of Aristotle*, New York: Random House, 1941

Predicate Logic

Barwise, J. and Etchemendy, J., *The Language of First-Order Logic, including Tarski's World*, Stanford: Center for the Study of Language and Information, 1991

Church, A., *Introduction to Mathematical Logic*, Vol. 1, Princeton: Princeton University Press, 1956

DeLong, Howard, *A Profile of Mathematical Logic*, Reading, Massachusetts: Addison-Wesley, 1970

Layman, C. Stephen, *The Power of Logic*, Mountain View, California: Mayfield, 1999

Nolt, John, *Logics*, Belmont, California: Wadsworth, 1997

Quine, W.V., *Methods of Logic*, 3rd edn, New York: Holt, Rinehart and Winston, 1972

Chapter 9: Inductive Logic

Inductive Logic

Baird, Davis, *Inductive Logic*, Englewood Cliffs, New Jersey: Prentice Hall, 1992

Giere, Ronald H., *Understanding Scientific Reasoning*, 4th edn, Fort Worth: Harcourt Brace 1997

Gillies, Donald, *Philosophy of Science in the Twentieth Century*, Oxford: Blackwell, 1993

Jeffrey, R.C., *Studies in Inductive Logic and Probability*, 2 vols, Berkeley: University of California Press, 1980

Salmon, Wesley C., *The Foundations of Scientific Inference*, Pittsburgh: University of Pittsburgh Press, 1966

Probability Theory

Kolmogorov, A.N., *Foundations of the Theory of Probability*, New York: Chelsea, 1950

Kyburg, Henry E., *Probability and Inductive Logic*, London: Collier Macmillan, 1970

Resnick, Michael, *Choices*, Minneapolis: University of Minnesota Press, 1982

Skyrms, Brian, *Choice and Chance*, Belmont, California: Dickenson, 1966

Hasty Generalization

Campbell, Stephen K., *Flaws and Fallacies in Statistical Thinking*, Englewood Cliffs, New Jersey: Prentice Hall, 1974

Post Hoc, Ergo Propter Hoc

Woods, John, and Douglas N. Walton, "*Post Hoc, Ergo Propter Hoc*," *Review of Metaphysics* 30 (1977), 569–593

Chapter 10: Arguing in a Circle

Arguing in a Circle

Barker, John A., "The Fallacy of Begging the Question," *Dialogue* 15 (1976), 241–255

Johnson, Oliver, "Begging the Question," *Dialogue* 6 (1967), 13–150

Mackenzie, J.D., "Question-Begging in Non-Cumulative Systems," *Journal of Philosophical Logic* 8 (1978), 117–133

Sanford, David H., "Begging the Question," *Analysis* 32 (1972), 197–199

Walton, Douglas N., *Begging the Question*, New York: Greenwood Press, 1991

Woods, John, and Douglas N. Walton, "Arresting Circles in Formal Dialogues," *Journal of Philosophical Logic* 7 (1978), 7–90

Woods, John, and Douglas N. Walton, "*Petitio* and Relevant Many-Premissed Arguments," *Logique et Analyse* 20 (1977), 97–110

Woods, John, and Douglas N. Walton, "*Petitio Principii*," *Synthese* 31 (1975), 107–127

Chapter 11: Arguments from Authority

Arguments from Authority

Coleman, Edwin, "There Is no Fallacy of Arguing from Authority," *Informal Logic* 17 (1995), 365–383

Walton, Douglas N., *Appeal to Expert Opinion*, University Park, Pennsylvania: Pennsylvania State University Press, 1997

Woods, John, and Douglas N. Walton, "*Argumentum Ad Verecundiam*," *Philosophy and Rhetoric* 7 (1974), 135–153

Plausibility Screening

Rescher, Nicholas, *Plausible Reasoning*, Amsterdam: Van Gorcum, 1976

Chapter 12: Economic Reasoning

Composition and Division

Woods, John, and Douglas N. Walton, "Composition and Division," *Studia Logica* 36 (1977), 381–406

Economic Reasoning

Menges, Gunter, *Economic Decision Making: Basic Concepts and Models*, London: Longman, 1974

Silk, Leonard, *Contemporary Economies: Principles and Issues*, 2nd edn, New York: McGraw-Hill, 1975

Decision Theory

Arrow, Kenneth J., *Social Choice and Individual Values*, 2nd edn, New York: Wiley, 1964

Jeffrey, Richard C., *The Logic of Decision*, 2nd edn, Chicago: University of Chicago Press, 1983

Williams, J.D., *The Complete Strategist*, New York: McGraw-Hill, 1966

Prisoner's Dilemma and Related Paradoxes

Campbell, R., and Sowden, L., *Paradoxes of Rationality and Cooperation*, Vancouver: University of British Columbia Press, 1985

Danielson, Peter A., *Modeling Rationality, Morality and Evolution*, New York: Oxford University Press, 1998

Irvine, A.D., "How Braess' Paradox Solves Newcomb's Problem," *International Studies in the Philosophy of Science*, vol. 7 (1993), 145–164

Chapter 13: Legal Reasoning

Legal Reasoning

Feinberg, Joel, and Hyman Gross, *Philosophy of Law*, 5th edn, Belmont, California: Wadsworth, 1995

Golding, Martin P., *Philosophy of Law*, Englewood Cliffs, New Jersey: Prentice Hall, 1975

Levi, Edward H., *An Introduction to Legal Reasoning*, Chicago: University of Chicago Press, 1949

Rodes, Robert E., and Howard Pospesel, *Premises and Conclusions*, Upper Saddle River, New Jersey: Prentice Hall, 1997

Chapter 14: Artificial Intelligence

Logic and Artificial Intelligence

Barwise, J. and Etchemendy, J., *The Language of First-Order Logic, including Tarski's World*, Stanford: Center for the Study of Language and Information, 1991

Poole, David L., Alan Mackworth, and Randy Goebel, *Computational Intelligence: A Logical Approach*, New York: Oxford University Press, 1998

Portoraro, Frederic, and Robert Tully, *Logic with Symlog*, Englewood Cliffs, New Jersey: Prentice Hall, 1992

Rich, Elaine, and Kevin Knight, *Artificial Intelligence*, 2nd edn, New York: McGraw-Hill, 1991

Expert Systems

Joseph Giarratano and Gary Riley, *Expert Systems, Principles and Programming*, Boston: PWS Publishing Co., 1994

Belief Dynamics

Gärdenfors, Peter, *Knowledge in Flux*, Cambridge, Massachusetts: MIT Press, 1988

Computability

Boolos, George S., and Richard C. Jeffrey, *Computability and Logic*, 3rd edn, Cambridge: Cambridge University Press, 1989

Irvine, A.D., "Philosophy of Logic," in S.G. Shanker, *Philosophy of Science, Logic and Mathematics in the 20th Century* (Volume IX of *The Routledge History of Philosophy*), London: Routledge, 1996, 9–49

Can Machines Think?

Churchland, Paul M., and Patricia Smith Churchland, "Could a Machine Think?," *Scientific American* 262 (January 1990), 32–37.

Dreyfus, Hubert L., *What Computers Can't Do*, New York: Harper and Row, 1972

Haugeland, John, *Mind Design*, Cambridge, Massachusetts: MIT Press, 1980

Searle, John R., "Is the Brain's Mind a Computer Program?," *Scientific American* 262 (January 1990), 26–31

Searle, John R., "Minds, Brains and Programs," *Behavioral and Brain Sciences* 3 (1980), 417–458

Turing, Alan M., "Computing Machinery and Intelligence," *Mind* 59 (1950), 433–460

Chapter 15: Issues in Argument Theory and the Philosophy of Logic

Philosophy of Logic

Engel, Pascal, *The Norm of Truth*, Toronto: University of Toronto Press, 1991

Haack, Susan, *Deviant Logic, Fuzzy Logic*, Chicago: University of Chicago Press, 1996

Haack, Susan, *Philosophy of Logics*, Cambridge: Cambridge University Press, 1978

Putnam, Hilary, *Philosophy of Logic*, New York: Harper and Row, 1971

Quine, W.V. *Philosophy of Logic*, 2nd edn, Cambridge, Massachusetts: Harvard University Press, 1986

Rescher, N. *Topics in Philosophical Logic*, Dordrecht: Reidel, 1968

Paraconsistent Logic

Irvine, A.D., "Gaps, Gluts, and Paradox," Bruce Hunter and Philip Hanson (eds), *Return of the A priori*, *Canadian Journal of Philosophy*, Supplementary vol. 18 (1993), 273–299

Priest, Graham, *In Contradiction*, Dordrecht: Martinus Nijhoff, 1987

Priest, Graham, "The Logic of Paradox," *Journal of Philosophical Logic* 8 (1979), 219–241

Priest, Graham, R. Routley, and J. Norman, *Paraconsistent Logic*, Munich: Philosophia Verlag, 1989

Subject Index

Name Index